Conflict Transformation and Peacebuilding

This book seeks to examine the causes of escalation and de-escalation in intrastate conflicts.

Specifically, the volume seeks to map the processes and dynamics that lead groups challenging existing power structures to engage in violent struggle; the processes and dynamics that contribute to the de-escalation of violent struggle and the participation of challengers in peaceful political activities; and the processes and dynamics that sustain and nurture this transformation. By integrating the latest ideas with richly presented case studies, this volume fills a gap in our understanding of the forces that lead to moderation and constructive engagement in the context of violent, intrastate conflicts.

This volume will be of great interest to students of conflict management, peace studies, conflict resolution, ethnic conflict and security studies in general.

Bruce W. Dayton is Associate Director of the Moynihan Institute of Global Affairs at the Maxwell School of Syracuse University. He also serves as Executive Director of the International Society of Political Psychology.

Louis Kriesberg is Professor Emeritus of Sociology, Maxwell Professor Emeritus of Social Conflict Studies, and founding director of the Program on the Analysis and Resolution of Conflicts (1986–1994), all at Syracuse University.

Security and conflict management

Series editors:

Fen Osler Hampson
Carleton University, Canada

Chester Crocker
Georgetown University, Washington DC

Pamela Aall
United States Institute of Peace, Washington DC

This series will publish the best work in the field of security studies and conflict management. In particular, it will promote leading-edge work that straddles the divides between conflict management and security studies, between academics and practitioners, and between disciplines.

Conflict Transformation and Peacebuilding

Moving from violence to sustainable peace

Edited by Bruce W. Dayton and Louis Kriesberg

LONDON AND NEW YORK

First published 2009
by Routledge
2 Park Square, Milton Park, Abingdon, Oxon OX14 4RN

Simultaneously published in the USA and Canada
by Routledge
270 Madison Ave, New York, NY 10016

Routledge is an imprint of the Taylor & Francis Group, an informa business

© 2009 Selection and editorial matter, Bruce W. Dayton and Louis
Kriesberg; individual chapters, the contributors

Typeset in Baskerville by
Wearset Ltd, Boldon, Tyne and Wear

British Library Cataloguing in Publication Data
A catalogue record for this book is available from the British Library

Library of Congress Cataloging-in-Publication Data
   Conflict transformation and peacebuilding : moving from violence to
sustainable peace / edited by Bruce W. Dayton and Louis Kriesberg.
      p. cm.
   1. Political violence. 2. Political violence–Case studies. 3. Peace-building.
4. Conflict management. 5. Social conflict. 6. Mediation. I. Dayton,
Bruce W. II. Kriesberg, Louis.
   JC328.6.C656 2009
   303.6'9–dc22   2008039093

ISBN10: 0-415-48084-1 (hbk)
ISBN10: 0-415-48085-X (pbk)
ISBN10: 0-203-88104-4 (ebk)

ISBN13: 978-0-415-48084-0 (hbk)
ISBN13: 978-0-415-48085-7 (pbk)
ISBN13: 978-0-203-88104-0 (ebk)

Contents

Contributors

Michael Allison received his PhD from Florida State University in 2006 and is currently Assistant Professor of Political Science at the University of Scranton in Pennsylvania. Dr Allison's research has focused on the transition of armed groups to political parties in Central America.

Elham Atashi is Assistant Professor of peace studies at Goucher College. Her broad research area is sources of violence in protracted conflicts. She focuses on peace processes, post-conflict peace building, transitional justice and other processes of reconciliation. Dr. Atashi also works extensively as a practitioner conducting dialogue processes in Northern Ireland and the Middle East and as a consultant in various programs focusing on gender, rule of law and youth empowerment in the Middle East, the Balkans, Cyprus, South and Central Asia.

Andrea Bartoli is the Founder of the Center for International Conflict Resolution (CICR) at Columbia University where he is a Senior Research Scholar. He is the Drucie French Cumbie Chair of Conflict Analysis and Resolution at George Mason University Institute for Conflict Analysis and Resolution (ICAR). He has been actively involved in conflict resolution and preventive diplomacy since the early 1980s as a member of the Community of St. Egidio (which he joined in 1970 and of which he is the representative in the USA and to the UN), focusing on Mozambique, Algeria, Burundi, Kosovo and the Democratic Republic of the Congo (DRC). More recently he coordinated CICR conflict resolution initiatives in Colombia, East Timor, Myanmar (Burma) and Iraq.

Aldo Civico is the Director of the Columbia University Center for International Conflict Resolution (CICR) in New York City. His research interests are mainly related to democracy, state, sovereignty, political violence, human rights, conflict, refugees, resistance, and civil society.

Bruce W. Dayton is the Associate Director of the Moynihan Institute of Global Affairs at the Maxwell School of Syracuse University. He also serves as Executive Director of the International Society of Political

Psychology. Dr. Dayton's research and teaching at the Maxwell School focuses on the impact of third-party interventions on conflict transformation; leadership decision making in times of crisis; and forecasting the emergence, escalation, and de-escalation of political crises.

Gavan Duffy is Associate Professor of Political Science at the Maxwell School of Syracuse University, where he conducts research and teaches courses in political conflict and research methods. He has published essays on conflicts in Northern Ireland, Bosnia, and Vietnam. He has also published the results of conflict simulations conducted in a massively concurrent computational environment.

Adir Gal has an MA in International Relations from the London School of Economics where he wrote his thesis on private security companies. He worked as researcher and assistant to the Director of the Conflict Resolution program at the Interdisiplinary Center, Herzliys. He is currently working in the private sector.

Catherine Gerard serves as Associate Director of Executive Education Programs and Co-director of the Program on Analysis and Conflict Resolution at Syracuse University's Maxwell School of Citizenship and Public Affairs. In that role, she manages the Master of Arts in Public Administration degree program, serves as graduate course professor for the Department of Public Administration, and designs and delivers executive education programs for domestic and international customers.

Leone Gianturco is an economic and financial expert at the Ministry of the Economy and Finance (Italy), International Relations Directorate, Treasury Department. He has conducted economic research and project evaluation in both Africa and Europe. Gianturco received his PhD in Development Economics at the Department of Economic and Social Science, University "Federico II," Naples.

Galia Golan is the Jay and Leoni Darwin Professor of Russian and East European Studies and the Chairperson of the Lafer Center for Women's Studies at the Hebrew University of Jerusalem. She is the founder of the Herezeg Program on Sex Differences in Society (Israel's first program in gender studies) and one of the founders and a member of the Board of Directors of the Jerusalem Link – An Israeli–Palestinian Women's Joint Venture for Peace. Professor Golan is the author of eight books on Soviet foreign policy and on Eastern Europe, including a book on the Soviet Union and the PLO and a book on Gorbachev's attitude toward terrorism. In addition, she has published a number of articles on women and politics in Israel and on the Middle East peace process.

Juan Gutierrez founded the Peace Research Center "Gernika Gogoratuz" in Gernika, Spain, and was its director until 2002. He has worked with John Paul Lederach and Dr Christopher Mitchell conducting informal mediation among top level policymakers trying to contribute to peaceful transformation of the Basque conflict. Dr Gutierrez has been awarded the German Cross of Merit (1999) as well as the Gernika Prize for Peace and Reconciliation (2005) and has acted as European, and world, coordinator of the UN's International Week of Science and Peace. After the terror attacks on Madrid's rail network in 2004 he has participated in the creation of the International Network for Peace, linking people in over 20 countries affected by Political Violence.

Margaret G. Hermann is Gerald B. and Daphna Cramer Professor of Global Affairs and Director of the Moynihan Institute of Global Affairs at the Maxwell School. Her research focuses on political leadership, foreign policy decision making, and the comparative study of foreign policy. She is currently involved in exploring the effects of different types of leaders and decision processes on the management of crises that cross borders and boundaries as well as in a large interview study of the governance challenges facing the leaders of transnational non-governmental organizations. Her books include *The Psychological Examination of Political Leaders; Describing Foreign Policy Behavior* and *Political Psychology: Issues and Problems.* Among her journal articles are "Presidents, Advisers, and Foreign Policy," "Leadership Styles of Prime Ministers" and "The US Use of Military Intervention to Promote Democracy: Evaluating the Record."

Louis Kriesberg is Professor Emeritus of Sociology and Maxwell Professor Emeritus of Social Conflict Studies at Syracuse University. He was the founding director of the Program on the Analysis and Resolution of Conflicts (1986–1994) and continues as an associate of the program. In addition to over 130 book chapters and articles, his published books include: *Constructive Conflicts: From Escalation to Resolution, Social Processes in International Relations; Intractable Conflicts and Their Transformation; Timing the De-escalation of International Conflicts* and *International Conflict Resolution: The US–USSR and Middle East Cases.* He lectures and consults regarding Middle East issues, conflict resolution, peace studies, and national security.

Tom Lodge is Professor of Peace and Conflict Studies at the University of Limerick in Ireland. He has held posts at the University of York, the Social Science Research Council in New York, and the Electoral Institute of Southern Africa. He is the author of several books on South African politics, most recently, in 2006, *Nelson Mandela: A Critical Life.*

Terrence Lyons is Associate Professor of Conflict Resolution at the Institute for Conflict Analysis and Resolution, George Mason University. His research has focused on the relationships between protracted civil wars and processes of political development and sustainable peace, with a particular focus on Africa and on policy issues. Among his publications are: *Demilitarizing Politics: Elections on the Uncertain Road to Peace* and *Voting for Peace: Postconflict Elections in Liberia*.

Gearoid Millar is Research Assistant at the Program for the Analysis and Resolution of Conflict at the Maxwell School and is a PhD student in the multidisciplinary Social Science program researching post-conflict reconciliation processes in West Africa. Gearoid has a Masters degree in International Peace and Conflict Resolution.

Camilla Orjuela is currently a researcher with Göteborg University's School of Global Studies. Her research has focused on ethnic conflicts and the role of civil society in conflict resolution, primarily in Sri Lanka.

Thania Paffenholz is Lecturer for Peace, Conflict and Development at the Graduate Institute of International Relations and Development (IHEID) in Geneva. Her main fields of research are: conflict analysis and peacebuilding, conflict-development nexus and the role of development actors in peacebuilding; critical analysis of the aid system's role in peacebuilding/conflict; international peacemaking strategies; role of civil society in peacebuilding; evaluation in peacebuilding. Her regional focus is Africa and Asia. Thania Paffenholz has edited and authored various articles and books on peacebuilding as well as on the role of development in conflict and peacebuilding. Her more recent book publications include *Peacebuilding: A Field Guide* and *Aid for Peace: A Guide to Planning and Evaluation for Conflict Zones*.

Nigel Parsons is currently Lecturer and Political Programs Director at Massey University in New Zealand. Dr. Parsons' research focuses heavily on the politics of the Arab World and has published articles on Israel, Sudan, Egypt, and the Palestinian situation.

Kenneth P. Serbin, Professor of History at the University of San Diego, is the immediate past president of the Brazilian Studies Association (2008–2010). His research focuses on the history of the Catholic Church and social and reproductive issues and the relationship between religion and democracy in Brazil. His publications include *Secret Dialogues: Church–State Relations, Torture, and Social Justice in Authoritarian Brazil* and *Needs of the Heart: A Social and Cultural History of Brazil's Clergy and Seminaries* both of which were awarded the Book Prize of the Brazil Section of the Latin American Studies Association. Serbin's current project is "From Revolutionaries to Rulers: How Brazil's Leftist Insurgents Went from Kidnapping the American Ambassador to Guiding a Democratic and Capitalist Giant." His many articles have appeared in the *Hispanic American Historical Review*, the *Journal of Latin American Studies, Latin American Politics and Society*, the *Christian Century, National Catholic Reporter, In These Times, Folha de S. Paulo, O Estado de S. Paulo, Valor* and other publications. Serbin teaches courses on Latin America, world history, and religion.

Bradford Vivian is Dean's Scholar and Assistant Professor in the College of Visual and Performing Arts at Syracuse University. His research specialties include the study of rhetoric and subjectivity, cultural politics, and public memory. He is the author of *Being Made Strange: Rhetoric beyond Representation*. His work has appeared in the *Quarterly Journal of Speech, Philosophy and Rhetoric, Rhetoric and Public Affairs*, the *Western Journal of Communication*, and the *Journal of Speculative Philosophy*. He is the recipient of an NEH Summer Stipend and the B. Aubrey Fisher Award.

1 Introduction[1]

Bruce W. Dayton and Louis Kriesberg

This book focuses on challenging organizations that rely in significant measure on violent means of struggle in intrastate conflicts. Our goal is to better understand how these organizations shift away from violent forms of struggle, engage in politics, and then continue in non-violent relations with their former adversary. Such changes have become more common since the end of the 1980s, with violent conflicts more frequently ending through negotiations or by petering out than through the defeat of one side by the other (Human Security 2008). At the same time, a closer look at the data shows that those intrastate conflicts that ended through negotiation or by petering out had a higher probability of reemerging within five years than those conflicts that ended in victories. Non-violent forms of conflict termination may be on the increase, but nearly 40 percent of peace agreements fail within five years (Harbom *et al.* 2006). What explains these trends? What contributes to the movement of antagonists away from using violent methods of struggle? How are some processes of political engagement sustained while others are not? Each of the chapters in this book offers some clues to help answer these questions by providing new insights about the conditions and context that nurture and sustain constructive forms of conflict transformation.

This book proceeds from three premises. First, we do not assume that governments occupy a morally privileged position. Some challenged groups may be oppressively dominant and maintain their dominance by recourse to violence or the threat of violence, while others are varyingly responsive to the needs and concerns of their citizenry. Second, although the focus of this book is on the transformation of challenging organizations away from reliance on violent struggle, these transformations always occur in the context of a relationship whereby the actions of each side impacts the perception and choices of the other. As such, we see the actions of both challenger groups and the government that they oppose as shaped by changes occurring within and between them. Finally, we regard social conflicts to be an inevitable and essential aspect of social interaction that allows social groups to change and flourish, to challenge norms and values that they judge to be harmful, and to address the distribution of power at the heart of political processes. Yet the form that social conflict takes does not have to be violent. Groups in conflict can choose to wage their struggle through a variety of non-violent means including forming social movements, entering the political arena, withdrawing cooperation, and enlisting the help of intermediaries. The question, therefore, is not how to avoid conflicts, but rather how to wage conflicts in ways that are constructive rather than destructive (Kriesberg 2007).

Contextual backdrop

Three interesting developments in the frequency, deadliness and duration of intrastate violence are particularly relevant for this volume. First, there has been a world-wide decline in armed violence over the last 15 years. Analysis of data from the Uppsala Conflict Data Program (UCDP), for instance, shows that between the early 1990s and 2006 the number of internal armed conflicts decreased from over 50 to fewer than 30, armed conflicts being defined as having at least 25 battle-related deaths per calendar year in one conflict dyad (Uppsala Conflict Data Program 2008). This decrease mirrors an overall decline in other types of violent conflict, including interstate armed conflicts and conflicts between non-state entities (Human Security 2008). A similar study conducted by the Center for International Development and Conflict Management (CIDCM), which used over 1,000 battle deaths to define violent conflicts, also shows a decline in interstate wars since the end of the 1980s, and a marked decline in societal wars after a spike in their incidence at the beginning of the 1990s (Marshall and Gurr 2005).

Second, these decreases in the incidence of armed conflicts may well be celebrated, but they do not signify global peace and harmony. Using a longer time frame, the incidence of armed conflicts defined by 25 or over battle deaths per year or by over 1,000 battle deaths rose steadily starting in 1946, until the declines began around 2000. The levels of violence found in 2006 may be impressive by 1990 standards, but are still equal to those found in the mid-1950s; with the occurrence of armed conflict in 2006 roughly twice what it was in 1946 (Harbom *et al.* 2006). The difference is not so great if the large increase in the number of independent countries that occurred during this period is taken into account, which raises the number of countries within which and among which violent conflicts can occur (Gleditsch 2008).

Finally, new outbreaks of conflicts often are the result of a recurrence of a conflict that was once thought to have ended. Uppsala's Conflict Data Program in collaboration with the International Peace Research Institute (PRIO) has published a database describing peace agreements between 1989 and 2005, which includes data on the success or failure of those agreements over periods of one and five years (Harbom *et al.* 2006). Analyses of these data reveal that between 1989 and 2005, 40 percent of the conflicts ending in peace agreements had seen a return to violence within five years. These data further show that conflicts ending with "full peace agreements" (the whole incompatibility is settled) were far more likely to hold than those ending in "partial agreements" (agreements where only a portion of the incompatibility is settled) and partial agreements more likely to hold than "peace process agreements" (agreements where the parties agree to initiate a process to settle the incompatibility). In addition, agreements that included particular provisions were much more likely to be sustained than those without those provisions. Agreements including provisions for elections, for example, failed 38 percent of the time, while those without failed 45 percent of the time. Only 12 percent of peace agreements that included provisions for local government, short of autonomy, failed within five years, while 49 percent of those without such provisions failed in the same time frame.

Data about trends in violent conflict provide an interesting backdrop to the study of peacebuilding following intrastate conflict. Such data do not, however, fully explain why intrastate adversaries engage in violent forms of conflict to begin with, why violent opposition movements sometimes choose to terminate their activities peacefully, and why some processes of political engagement succeed while others fail. We know, for instance, that between 1989 and 2005 more violent intrastate conflicts ended without a formal peace agreement than did with a peace agreement (Human Security 2006). We also know, as outlined above, that close to 40 percent of all conflicts observed between 1946 and 2005 returned to violence at some point after termination was achieved (Harbom *et al.* 2006). We do not know, however, the reasons that protagonists in these cases chose to end the violent phase of their struggle or why peace processes were successfully sustained in some cases, but not in others.

This book seeks explanations for such transformations by using case studies, supported by theories about the causes of conflict escalation and de-escalation, to uncover the processes and dynamics that lead protagonists to turn either toward or away from non-violent means of opposition. Included in the volume are two types of chapters. First, we include a set of thematic chapters that identify critical factors that facilitate, nurture, and sustain the movement of opposition groups from violence to peace, among them: political leadership, globalization processes, intermediaries, the representation of "the enemy" in public speech acts, the impact of the "street," and the de-militarization of politics during interim post-conflict periods. Second, we include a set of cases where protagonists have changed their strategies away from reliance on violent means and toward other modes of contestation, even for a brief period.

Each chapter is a product of several months of interaction among contributing authors, including a workshop on the transformation of organizations using violence held at the Maxwell School of Syracuse University and a subsequent roundtable discussion at the 2008 International Studies

Association annual meeting. Despite our work together, the authors in this book are by no means unified in their assessment of the most important factors that contribute to intrastate conflict de-escalation. Some contributors stress the importance of material dynamics to conflict transformation processes, while others focus on social-psychological dynamics or leadership style. Yet cross-cutting themes and commonalities can be seen across the chapters. The first of these relates to changes to the structural or material conditions that underlie conflict dynamics. Several cases and thematic chapters show how improving the economic conditions of communities, expanding the educational and employment opportunities available to individuals, and liberalizing access to political power within formal political structures, make it less likely that opposition movements will pursue their aims through violence. Other chapters and cases show how, those communities facing high levels of structural violence, lacking economic or educational opportunities, and facing institutionalized disparities in access to power often suffer from the emigration of skilled workers, a deepening of the conflict cycle, and an increase in militancy on the part of the population.

Second, this book speaks to the general importance of transforming the cognitive and emotional dynamics that sustain intergroup violence. Violent conflicts occur, in part, because of social-psychological processes related to dehumanization, stereotyping, and the application of negative attributions to the motivation of one's adversary and positive attributions to the motivations of one's own side. These social-psychological dynamics can be exacerbated by lack of contact over time or through the leaders' use of inflammatory references to past grievances and loses. Evidence in this volume suggest that re-humanizing one's enemy and/or creating a superordinant identity among conflicting parties can help to create conditions where peacemaking is possible. By extension, the absence of contact across groups only serves to concretize negative stereotyping and dehumanization and makes more likely the use of violence to achieve political objectives.

Third, changes to the internal politics within one or both sides appear to frequently shift opposition movements toward or away from violent tactics. All challenging organizations, as well as the governments they challenge, experience significant levels of internal heterogeneity and fractionalization. These internal political dynamics play an important role in determining their strategic choices for contestation with adversaries. The results of these dynamics, which include the splitting of the movement into different factions, expected or unexpected leadership transitions, or changes in the way that decisions are made within the group, have a great effect on their reliance on, resort to, or renunciation of violence. Several of the cases presented in this volume illustrate, for instance, how the splintering of opposition organizations may weaken them while also complicating negotiations. Other cases show how changes in group leadership become a critical factor in either advancing peace processes or undercutting them.

Fourth, this volume suggests that the actions of external parties often have a powerful impact on the trajectory of conflicts. The parties in intrastate conflicts frequently depend upon the resources of external actors to sustain their activities. This external support is not, however, endless. Diaspora communities, which often provide substantial material support for opposition movements, may shift in their attitudes toward armed struggle and begin to pressure those that they are supporting to engage in peace processes. Similarly, opposition movements or governments may gain or lose the support of those states that are acting as their patrons. This was true, for instance, in Guatemala where long-standing US support for the hard-line policies of the government gave way to new policies as the strategic interests of the US shifted in the 1990s. Such shifts are most evident after the end of the Cold War in 1989 and the dissolution of the Soviet Union in 1991. After this global transformation, support for proxy wars dropped sharply as the US and the Soviet Union disengaged from several conflicts.

Finally, evidence from this book suggests that constructive engagement often occurs because of the changing prospects of military defeat or of military victory. In some cases the opposition movements shift away from violence and embrace processes of political incorporation because of defeat or near defeat. In other cases the application of violence by the opposition group had the effect of bringing state actors to the negotiation table. That violence is sometimes an effective tool for conducting and managing a conflict may be an uncomfortable reality for practitioners of peacebuilding and constructive conflict transformation. Yet this conclusion points to one of the most important questions raised by this volume: when can some kinds of violence be constructive?

Of course, ending intrastate conflicts is only the first half of what is most often a long and difficult process of achieving a sustainable peace. This volume also suggests that fragile peace agreements easily relapse back to violence if they are not accompanied by post-conflict social integration, economic development, committed leadership, and the demilitarization of politics. Sustainable peacebuilding, in other words, requires transformation across multiple fronts including changed attitudes and perceptions, changed behaviors, and changes to the structural inequalities that provide uneven benefits within political systems.

Overview of chapters

The first eight chapters in this book examine the dynamics and processes that account for constructive engagement in intrastate conflicts. These thematic chapters begin with Kriesberg and Millar's analysis of the primary adversaries in a conflict and the strategies they adopt as they escalate and de-escalate their struggle against each other. Kriesberg and Millar examine the relevant internal features of each side in the conflict and also the way each adversary's actions affect the opponent's choices of methods of struggle in the course of the conflict.

In the second thematic chapter, Margaret G. Hermann and Catherine Gerard examine how learning about leadership can help us gain access to knowledge about the processes occurring within the groups and organizations of interest to us in this volume.

Elham Atashi then argues that current models, practices and analyses of peacebuilding tend to focus on changes at the leadership level and neglect what happens to people in the streets. Consequently, she notes, post-conflict societies can be plagued by an "uneven peace;" that is, a situation in which the benefits of the peace process are not shared by all. Uneven peace agreements, in turn, reduce the likelihood of achieving a sustainable peace as marginalized groups at the local level continue to fight on, even in the context of a negotiated settlement.

The next three chapters examine different processes that are instrumental in the enduring transformation of violent conflicts. Bruce Dayton examines how parties that are not primary adversaries may or may not intervene to help transform large-scale violent conflicts. Dayton provides a theoretical framework for intermediary activities in violent intrastate conflict, considers the conditions and contexts that lead armed groups to engage with intermediaries, and concludes with observations about the prospects and limits of intermediary activities in transforming organizations that use violence.

Bradford Vivian's chapter addresses two closely related questions: In what forms do public appeals to collective memory foster peace and political reconciliation? And by what principles can we recognize their more destructive varieties, which perpetuate conflict and hostility? Vivian's chapter adopts a rhetorical approach to the subject of collective memory; analyzing how particularly influential speakers persuade target audiences to act upon those visions of the past (either violent or peaceful) that they construct in their public discourse. He argues that transforming collective perceptions of the past – and consequently of the present and future – can establish vital preconditions for motivating antagonists to participate in conflict resolution.

Next, Terrence Lyons cautions against an overemphasis on elections as the most important event in achieving sustainable peace. Lyons uses numerous case examples to demonstrate that democratization processes must be accompanied by broader efforts to demilitarize politics in post-conflict societies and that to be successful, such demilitarization processes need to begin during transitional periods from violence to peace.

The final two thematic chapters focus on the societal and the global contexts. Gavan Duffy argues that intrastate political conflicts concern groups' perceptions of their own security. Accordingly, Duffy examines recent efforts to apply the security dilemma analysis, borrowed from neorealist international relations scholarship, to intrastate conflicts. He argues that such analyses have limited usefulness because they lack generality and also because they consider only the threats that groups perceive and not their perceived opportunities. Analysis based on political opportunity structures is described and illustrated by reference to several conflicts. Duffy discusses the implications of the political opportunity framework for conflict transformation and indicates pathways to peaceable conflict outcomes that are inconceivable from within the security dilemma framework.

In the last thematic chapter, Galia Golan and Adir Gal examine the global context and how it contributes to conflict transformation or obstructs it. This chapter provides an examination of the many ways that globalization contributes to the constructive transformations of violent intrastate conflicts and the moderation of violent opposition groups. Among the variables considered are the media, diaspora communities, non-governmental organizations (NGOs), and the transnational private sector; each of which have expanded their capacity to impact intrastate conflicts because of globalization dynamics. The authors caution, however, that globalization entails many developments that may produce negative effects as well as positive ones.

The final eight chapters in this book are case studies. Not all the case studies examined are "success" stories. Even the most constructive conflict transformations have some limitations and exhibit regressive episodes. On the other hand, even the conflicts that have failed to be enduringly transformed do include some interludes without violence. Furthermore, some factions or subgroups within one or more of each side may have withdrawn support for employing violent methods, and adopted non-violent means of struggle.

The eight case studies in this book differ in the extent to which adversaries relying heavily on violence change and engage in non-violent political processes. As the diverse cases illuminate, such transformations sometimes come about as result of victories and of defeats. Interestingly, attributions or claims of success or of failures are often ambiguous and disputed.

The cases vary in other significant ways. One is the content of the issue of contention and the goals the adversaries formulate. In many cases the adversaries struggle for dominance or at least a strong voice in a shared political system, differing in the magnitude of the change they seek. The struggle may be related to the way the adversaries define themselves, by class-based ideological differences, by ethnic or other communal identities, or by organizational or gang claims for political power for themselves. In varying ways this is true for Brazil, Mozambique, Guatemala, South Africa, and Nepal. In other cases, the adversaries struggle about separating from each other and forming independent entities, as in Spain, Sri Lanka, and Palestine–Israel. This difference is also related to variation between conflicts waged in the context of the ideologically-oriented Cold War and in the context of post-Cold-War era.

Finally, the cases vary in the degree and nature of the violence used by each side in a conflict. The repression in Guatemala by the government was particularly vicious and bloody. The fighting in Sri Lanka was and is deadly, due to government and challengers' actions. Beliefs about the effectiveness and the virtue of violence, of killing and dying for the cause affect the recourse to violence. For example in the 1960s and 1970s, some elements of the revolutionary left believed that violence could be used to create a revolutionary situation (Fanon 1966; Debray 1967). This was influential for groups in the Basque Country, Brazil, and the Middle East. That glorification of violence contributed to the use of terror, which was counterproductive. The recent celebration of the use of violence, of martyrdom and even of suicidal violence in terror attacks, is prone to the same counterproductive consequences of the earlier period (Fontan 2008). On the other hand, the growing adoption of non-violent strategies of resistance can assist in making effective and sustainable conflict transformations (Sharp 2005).

The case of Mozambique examined by Andre Bartoli, Aldo Civico and Leone Gianturco exemplifies outcomes in which the primary adversaries do reach a negotiated settlement, after a stalemate in which neither side was able to overcome the other. The Mozambique case exemplifies how a peace processes can utilize local traditions and culture in combination with external assistance to achieve peace, a new shared identity, and a sustainable political system.

In South Africa, as analyzed by Tom Lodge, the Afrikaner government and the whites generally accepted equality in political rights for all South Africans, as insisted upon by the African National Congress (ANC) leadership and by the blacks. This outcome was not violently imposed; indeed violence was recognized by large numbers of people on all sides as likely to ultimately fail and have shared destructive consequences. Lodge discusses the many developments that converged to provide the reassurances needed for a mutually acceptable sequence and shows how the ANC's own transformation into a mass party helped it to curb the expectations of its followers.

Thania Paffenholz examines the conflict in Nepal where, after ten years of People's War and two years of political maneuvering, the Communist Party of Nepal (CPN) achieved their main political demands and the reintegration of the CPN into political life began. Paffenholz suggests that the CPN's history as a political actor in Nepal helped to facilitate their re-entering the political arena in 2006. She also notes that the consistency of their strategic plan, as well as the high-level of flexibility and pragmatism within the movement, significantly contributed to their transition from revolutionary movement to political actor.

Kenneth Serbin examines a low-intensity conflict between revolutionary guerrillas and an authoritarian regime and specifically how Ação Libertadora Nacional (ALN, or National Liberating Action), the largest guerrilla group to resist the Brazilian military regime (1964–1985), made the transition from violence to participation in democratic politics. Although the ALN was militarily defeated, many of its members entered the political mainstream during Brazil's transition to democracy and occupied high governmental posts. The study examines variables such as the restoration of civilian rule and elections, but also the individual and collective efforts of a generation of revolutionaries struggling to overcome the authoritarian legacies and violence of both the right and the left.

The case of the Guatemalan National Revolutionary Unit (URNG), as discussed by Michael Allison, is interesting in that the revolutionary challengers were so defeated, that they have been unable to be an effective political force after turning to electoral politics. Guatemala's civil war was both the longest and bloodiest of the Central American conflicts with an estimated 200,000 Guatemalans killed or "disappeared" between 1960 and 1996. For almost 15 years, the URNG struggled against a government that launched a genocidal campaign against the URNG and both its actual and its potential base. After ten years of negotiations, the URNG and the government of Alvaro Arzú of the National Advancement Party (PAN) brought an end to the war through the signing of the Firm and Lasting Agreement in December 1996 in Guatemala City. Since the conclusion to the country's civil war and the transformation of the URNG into a political party, it has remained a marginal player in Guatemalan politics.

Juan Gutierrez examines how the Basque people have gained much autonomy and Euskadi 'ta Askatasuna (ETA) has become small and isolated, yet persists in some acts of violence. He provides an overview of the rise of the ETA and discusses the factors that help to explain why the Basque nationalist conflict has been waged violently, why processes of political accommodation have moved forward, and why those processes have been only partially successful.

In the next chapter, by Nigel Parsons, Palestinian oscillation between armed struggle and diplomacy is examined up to and through the Oslo process, wherein the state of Israel incorporated the PLO into restructured governance arrangements for the indigenous population of the Occupied Palestinian Territories. Parsons places armed struggle in the context of a dispossessed refugee people reconstituted through violence and sees the perpetuation of armed struggle as a function of the PLO's long-term inability to translate diplomatic success into political gain. He attributes the temporary de-escalation of the conflict via Oslo to institutional imperatives on the part of the PLO, socio-structural change to Palestinian society, and shifts in the international order. Ultimately Parsons sees the failure of a sustainable peace process to be a consequence of incorporation without accommodation.

In the last chapter, Camilla Orjuela analyzes how tentative agreements also have proven unsustainable in Sri Lanka. Orjuela focuses on how the leadership of the Liberation Tigers of Tamil Eelam (LTTE), and Vellupilai

Prabhakaran in particular, has found the transition from fighter to peace-maker highly difficult. After reviewing the escalation of violence and eventual attempts at peacemaking in 2002, Orjuela then turns to the main dynamics that impact attempts at peacemaking.

Conclusion

The chapters in this book compel us to reflect on the complexities of resorting to violence in societal conflicts. Many workers in the fields of conflict resolution and peace studies tend to argue against the use of violence and give relatively little attention to different kinds and degrees of violence. Other analysts as well as those engaged in large scale conflicts generally take violence and the threats of violence for granted as an inherent part of major societal conflicts, sometimes with regret and sometimes with exhilaration. Given the evidence in this volume and elsewhere, a third perspective deserves consideration. In this perspective, extreme violence is recognized as having many unanticipated and negative consequences for the parties in a conflict. Those consequences, however, can be mitigated by greatly limiting its usage and combining it with a broad array of other methods of struggle.

All the primary adversaries in the cases examined here used some kinds of violence in various degrees and contexts. Using violence often failed to yield the desired goals, prolonged the fight, and hampered recovering from the conflict. Sometimes, however, it seems to have contributed to achieving some of the objectives that at least one party in the conflict desired. That still leaves open the possibility that alternative non-violent strategies or more limited violence, in scope or duration, would have been even more effective.

Certainly, the reliance on violence and its possible effectiveness depend, like any approach, on the goals being sought. Extreme goals, denigrating the enemy and its members' needs, tend to be associated with extreme methods of conducting a conflict and are more often unattainable than more modest goals. This suggests that adopting goals and methods that do not threaten the survival, identity, or dignity of the opposing side will tend to increase prospects for constructive engagement. Evidence for this can be noted in many of the chapters.

The contributions in this book identify many of the great variety of kinds of violent and non-violent ways to wage fights: what they are, how they are implemented and what their effects are. Violence includes deadly attacks on noncombatants intended to terrorize a population, drive people away and de-stabilize a government. The attacks may be implemented by non-governmental underground or above ground organizations, and also by governments or units within governments. It also includes massive governmental repression in which persons who may be or may become opponents are disappeared, villages are emptied, demonstrators are shot down, and people are closely monitored. It includes narrowly targeted and exe-cuted violence, conducted by police and legally circumscribed judicial procedures, which are widely believed to be legitimate. Finally, violence can also be considered to be structural, in the sense that some people under existing institutional arrangements suffer conditions below a basic standard of living while other people do not (Galtung 1969).

Vast arrays of non-violent and non-coercive ways are used by people to resist aggression and oppression and to increase equality, security and freedom. They include persuasive rhetorical efforts based on shared values and beliefs and persuasive demonstrations of cooperative possibilities and benefits. They include many forms of non-violent but coercive campaigns of resistance and of non-cooperation. A wide variety of persons and groups within and beyond the opposing sides affect the transformation of a violent conflict. Leaders play crucial roles at each stage of a conflict's esca-lation and de-escalation. However, rank and file members of each side generally are needed to sustain a struggle and to reach and maintain a mutually acceptable agreement (Wanis-St. John and Kew 2008). In addi-tion, groups that are not members of any organization directly engaged as partisans in a fight also contribute to conflict transformation by helping to limit destructive methods of struggle and by helping sustain an accommo-dation that is reached.

The transformation of a violent conflict requires engaging in many dif-ferent strategies in a sequence of changing combinations of complemen-tary strategies. No single strategy is good for all participants throughout the course of a conflict's transformation. What set of strategies among which actors will prove effective in transforming a violent conflict depends upon a wide range of conditions and perceptions of those conditions among relevant players. We trust that this book assists the great variety of persons affected by a violent conflict, whether as partisans, intermediaries or onlookers, to better understand the conflict and its consequences and to act more effectively to transform the conflict. We believe that the variety of cases and ways of contending examined in this book will expand the repertoire of responses that persons affected by a violent conflict can make. We also trust that this book will prompt more reflection and research about the circumstances and policies that tend to prevent the eruption of violent conflicts, to contain and limit their escalation, to more quickly end them and to help sustain and improve constructive relations among former antagonists.

Note

1 We wish to acknowledge the important editorial assistance throughout the project made by Gearoid Millar. Gearoid helped in literature searches, assisted in reviewing chapter drafts and managed the website related to the project. We also wish to thank the Moynihan Institute of Global Affairs and the Program on

the Analysis and Resolution of Conflicts for their generous financial support for this project. Finally, we'd like to thank Catherine Gerard and Galia Golan for their conceptual guidance throughout the project.

References

Debray, R. (1967). *Revolution in the Revolution?* New York, Grove Press.

Fanon, F. (1966). *The Wretched of the Earth.* New York, Grove Press.

Fontan, V. (2008). *Voices from Post-Saddam Iraq: Living with Terrorism, Insurgency and New Forms of Tyranny.* Westport, CT, Praeger.

Galtung, J. (1969). "Violence, Peace, and Peace Research." *Journal of Peace Research* 3 (3): 168.

Gleditsch, N. P. (2008). "The Liberal Moment Fifteen Years On." *International Studies Quarterly* (4).

Harbom, L., Högbladh, S. and Wallensteen, P. (2006). "Armed Conflict and Peace Agreements." *Journal of Peace Research* 43 (5): 617–613.

Human Security Report Project (2008). *Human Security Brief 2007.* Vancouver, Canada, Simon Fraser University.

Kriesberg, L. (2007). *Constructive Conflicts.* Lanham: Rowman & Littlefield.

Marshall, M. G. and Gurr, T. R. (2005). *Peace and Conflict 2005.* College Park, MD, Center for International Development and Conflict Management, University of Maryland.

Sharp, G. (2005). *Waging Nonviolent Struggle: 20th Century Practice and 21st Century Potential.* Boston, Porter Sargent.

Uppsala Conflict Data Program (2008). UCDP Database, Uppsala University. Online, available at: www.ucdp.uu.se/database.

Wanis-St. John, A. and Kew, D. (2008). "Civil Society and Peace Negotiations: Confronting Exclusion." *International Negotiation* 13: 11–36.

2 Protagonist strategies that help end violence

Louis Kriesberg and Gearoid Millar

This chapter examines the choices that particular organizations make as they contend against each other. We examine the various goals adversaries set, the strategies they adopt to progress toward them, and how and why such choices are made. Because the choice of objectives and the means to attain them impact each other, both are discussed. The focus throughout is on non-violent strategic choices.

Conflict circumstances

Resource asymmetry is evident in most conflicts and profoundly affects the equity of their resolution (Mitchell 1995). Asymmetry is often discussed as the relative capacity to exercise coercion, particularly violence, and although this is important in many struggles, it is never all important. Noncoercive capacities also can be decisive, such as the commitment to a struggle, as evident in the Vietnam War. Conflicting partisans have access to and actualize different resources as group capacities, which then impact each side's choice of strategies. Adversary groups therefore differ in their capacities to use both noncoercive and coercive inducements to affect each other's conduct.

The resources available to a party in any particular conflict environment are social, economic and demographic. Social resources may include relationships with allies and external powers, strong leadership, cohesive identity, or perceived legitimacy. Such resources affect the conflict when actualized as organizational capacities, but may be used either for violent or non-violent strategies. Strong leadership, for example, may influence the capacity to conduct long and costly military operations, such was the leadership of George Washington, but it may also be required, as in the case of Mohandas Gandhi or Martin Luther King, for a campaign of non-violence.

Likewise, economic resources can be utilized to purchase weapons, hire mercenaries, train troops, or to build defensive or offensive infrastructure. Alternatively they can be used to import supplies during a boycott, support striking workers, hold anti-war rallies, or build monuments to peace.

Finally, demographic resources can be actualized to struggle for various ends. The character of a population, whether large or small, well or badly educated, homogenous or heterogeneous, young or old, is influential; but it does not dictate a particular strategy of conflict. A large, young population may be turned to peaceful protest just as it is to violent rioting.

Most conflict resources persist over time, but some change significantly and quickly. Thus, states that regard as criminals the leaders of a challenging organization may kill or imprison them, depriving that organization of a critical resource. In 1992, for example, the Peruvian government captured Abimel Guzmán, the primary leader of the Shining Path (Sendero Luminosa), greatly diminishing the capacities of that organization (Thomas and Casebeer 2004: 49). In 1999, the Turkish government imprisoned Abdullah Öcalan, leader of the Kurdistan Workers Party (PKK), which contributed to modifying their conflict (Radu 2001).

Similarly, many partisans throughout the world suddenly lost important external support when the Cold War ended, staunching the flow of arms and money from the US and the Soviet Union. What might previously have been considered long term resources in these environments were suddenly eliminated, and affected parties were forced to change strategies or even goals.

Significantly, perceptions of relative resources and the anticipation of future changes can also have large effects on a party's goals and strategies. White South Africans, anticipating becoming a smaller proportion of the population, had reason to move toward an accommodation sooner rather than later. Similarly, many Jewish Israelis, foreseeing a growing Palestinian population, favored a territorial separation that could preserve a predominantly Jewish Israel.

It is therefore insufficient to view power differences only in terms of relative coercive capabilities and the ability to exercise them (negative sanctions). Power is also based on non-coercive inducements (Boulding 1989). One set of such inducements result from a capacity to promise benefits to reward desired conduct (positive sanctions). Noncoercive inducements can also be based on persuasive arguments derived from shared norms and values or on shared identities based on ideology or religion. In actuality, power is exercised in various combinations of these inducements, depending in part upon organizational capacities and characteristics.

Organizational characteristics

Four qualities characterizing contending organizations are particularly relevant for the matters analyzed in this volume. They are: structure, ideology, relations with other organizations, and attachment to violence. The internal and external factors affecting these features will be discussed, taking into account the effect of resource availability and decisions regarding their actualization.

Structural features

The distinction between state and non-state entities is often based on their structural differences, but this can be exaggerated. States are often regarded as having clear boundaries, clearly defined members (citizens), and clearly recognized decision-making procedures, yet they vary in these regards. Conversely, while non-state entities may tend to have fewer of such attributes, many have them to a significant degree.

Both differ in the extent to which rank-and-file members follow the directions of their official leaders, the degree to which particular groups of supporters influence or direct the official leaders, and the degree to which rivals can mobilize and direct people they regard as their constituents. Both state and non-state actors may sometimes incorporate armed groups, functioning somewhat autonomously, and leaders of both tend to make broad claims about who they represent and can control. For example, government officials, who may or may not have been acting independently of their official leaders, have been known to operate in cooperation with armed militia groups in South Africa, Colombia, and Guatemala. Such failures of command structures within state hierarchies are similar to splits within non-state armed groups such as Hamas.

The internal structure of the adversaries may also vary greatly over time as the circumstances of the conflict change. Thus, the increase in international governmental and non-governmental organizations increasingly affects the structure of contending parties through the provision or restriction of resources that influence their strategies. For example, the Organization for Security and Co-operation in Europe (OSCE) contributed to the largely peaceful transitions and transformations among and within the countries in Eastern Europe and the former Soviet republics (McMahon 2007; Möller 2007). Similarly, expanding transnational linkages can strengthen some groups in particular countries, affecting the structure of societal and organizational political processes and relative influence. Expanding diaspora communities, which sustain relations in their former homelands, may provide economic and social resources that further influence the group's structural characteristics there, as discussed by Galia Golan and Adir Gal in their chapter in this volume.

Ideologies

The diverse groups in each adversary camp often have some sense of shared identity. Members of each group try to define both themselves and the other. They may define themselves exclusively and believe they have certain rights relative to other persons within or outside their own camp.

These identities may not be precisely formulated and articulated, or be contradictory and shifting as circumstances change. Yet some aspects of these identities can become dominant within an ideology and drive the choice of violent strategies.

Some ideologies are highly institutionalized, incorporated in legislation and with special agencies dedicated to their maintenance. This is the case, for example, in states that are constituted to embody or to serve a particular religion, ethnicity, or political ideology. They also may be vigorously challenged by minority groups who object to the subordinate treatment they suffer. Alternatively, secular democratic governments may be challenged by organizations to establish a state that gives priority to an exclusive religious, ethnic, or political ideology. Such matters are prone to conflicts that are waged violently, such as in Afghanistan during the 1980s, but can also be waged peacefully, such as the Hizbut Tahrir movement for a global Caliphate, active in over 40 countries (Cornell 2002).

Additionally, changes in major ideologies, norms, and belief systems can significantly impact the ideologies of local organizations. The breakup of the Soviet Union not only ended Soviet material assistance to Marxist governments and revolutionary movements, it also reduced the adherence to Marxist ideologies and the concern among others about their threat. Conflicts became more frequently couched in ethnic and religious terms. In this way different ideological characteristics became salient, as one ideological resource was replaced by another.

Relations with other organizations

As highlighted above, each organization in a conflict is affected by its interaction with other organizations in the conflict environment, including its primary adversaries, organizations allied with the adversaries, and non-engaged third parties. Furthermore, each side usually consists of a coalition of organizations, each with internal factions and sub-groups. It is useful to keep this complexity in mind, even if a particular subunit is the primary one in the choice and employment of strategies.

The autonomy or dependency, for example, of a particular conflict unit in relation to supporting, allying, and ruling organizations affects its leader's options. An adversary may be highly dependent upon an outside government for material support and adhere to the goals and interests of that outside government in order to maintain its assistance. This was evident during the Cold War for the organizations relying greatly on American or Soviet support. Global economic and technological developments have greatly contributed to increasing inter-dependence and transnational linkages. For example, the increasing scope of international trade and investment, combined with increased capital mobility, enhances governmental interdependence, while also increasing vulnerability to policies of major corporate actors and particular IGOs, such as the International Monetary Fund (IMF).

Attachment to violence

For this book project the capability and readiness to use violent methods by various contending groups must receive special attention. Factions and groups who prepare for and carry out violent actions are significant components of most major conflict organizations. The army, police, and other armed units may be highly influential components of larger organizations. In many societies membership in such armed groups is attractive because alternative ways of earning a living are few. These factors both increase the chances of escalation and hamper the de-escalation and settlement of conflict.

In addition, various beliefs serve to sustain an attachment to violence. There is often little popular knowledge or faith in alternative means of struggle and the enemy is often regarded as "only understanding force." Indeed, channels for non-violent pressure, influence, and persuasive efforts are often closed by the opposing party or competing internal factions, cutting off potential alternative choices.

Outside actors and influences also sometimes contribute to local reliance upon violent methods. For example, during the 1960s some leaders and interpreters of wars of national liberation and revolutionary change influentially argued that violence could help establish conditions needed for a successful revolution (Fanon 1966; Debray 1967). Recourse to violence was romanticized and those ready to commit violent deeds celebrated. This glorification of violence was a resource for partisan actors, but one that could only be actualized in strategies utilizing violence, thus it restricted strategic options. Such influences contributed to the adoption of violent strategies by the Palestine Liberation Organization, as discussed by Nigel Parsons in this volume.

Currently, some strands of Islamic religious beliefs are used to legitimate such violence against civilians deemed enemies of Islam. Terrorist attacks with transnational support have some novel features, but terrorism has a long history, and is an important means of struggle at particular times. Strategies within the Liberation Tigers of Tamil Eelam (LTTE) in Sri Lanka are prominent examples, as discussed in the chapter by Camilla Orjuela in this volume.

Interestingly, however, in recent years, non-violent methods of struggle also have gained adherents through their successful application in the Philippines, Poland, the Ukraine and many other countries and through external actors' encouragement of non-violent methods and provision of training and counseling. For example, El Servicio de Paz y Justicia (SERPAJ), a non-violent human rights organization, resisted military dictatorships in many Latin American countries, in the 1970s and 1980s

(Pagnucco and McCarthy 1992; Pagnucco 1997). Gene Sharp's analyses of, and his prescriptions for, non-violent action have also been translated into many languages and organizations in many countries consider adopting those strategies (Sharp 1973).

Each of the four partisan characteristics we highlight here is a function of available resources and decisions regarding their actualization. In each case the characteristic's development is influenced not only by group leadership decisions, but by the impact of external third parties, allies, internal divisions, and the contending party. Having analyzed both conflict circumstances and organizational characteristics, we now turn to protagonists' strategic choices.

Strategies of protagonists

Partisan strategies differ in many ways: by time frames and in the combination of inducements used; by who is undertaking them and toward whom they are directed; and by the stage of the conflict in which they are undertaken. This discussion is organized in terms of the latter, the major conflict stages in which strategies are employed: (*a*) escalation; (*b*) de-escalation and settlement; and (*c*) post-violence recovery. We stress the de-escalation and settlement stage but highlight those strategies at each stage that may best allow for a later transition to non-violent struggle. For each stage we examine partisan strategies directed internally, toward various members of the protagonists' own side, and externally, toward members of the opposing side.

This discussion is not limited to carefully considered strategies, consciously selected after comparing many alternatives. Actions may be taken with little reflection, being regarded as the only possible choice under the circumstances. In such cases we sometimes note alternatives that were not considered or were rejected by the protagonists. We infer a strategy and its objectives from the sequence of actions undertaken by contending groups and by the reasons that they give for their conduct. Admittedly, the reasons may be misleading, as the actors seek to justify their goals and how they strive to achieve them, and do so in ways that they think will win them support from other people. Further complicating matters, goals and strategies are often re-formulated, after the fact in order to justify past actions or to claim success.

This chapter is focused on strategies, both proactive and reactive, employed by each side, and intended, presumably, to affect the conduct of the other. However, it should be recognized that actions directed toward the adversary may be chosen for their effects on the perpetrator's own side. Thus they may be intended to reassure constituents that "something is being done," or to satisfy the desire to "get even." Alternatively, they may provide benefits to some members of the acting group, ranging from looted goods, control of resources, or constituents' rewards such as increased regard. Such considerations should not be ignored, since they frequently affect the choice of strategy and also the targeted adversary's responses. Furthermore, such considerations often account for the selection of strategies ill-suited to influence the external opponent.

Additionally, strategies that may be effective at one stage may be ineffective or even counterproductive at the next and the transitions between stages are fraught with difficulties. Some of the goals and strategies of the Palestine Liberation Organization (PLO) illustrate this. The PLO leadership had great difficulties in building an independent Palestinian organization after 1948, and these difficulties increased after the 1967 war. Rashid Khalidi observes of the PLO that "the deviousness and subterfuge that were indispensable for a weak PLO in dealing with the predatory mores of the states that dominated Arab politics were much less well adapted to ... other arenas" (Khalidi 2006: 174). Most notably, he observes, such strategies were ill-suited to dealing with the Western powers and were a major contributing factor in the failure of the PLO to develop the infrastructure for a Palestinian state.

Finally, it is also important to recognize that strategies directed internally, at the various constituent elements and individual members of the organization, shape what strategy choices are available for waging the external conflict. The strategic choices of protagonists, therefore, are not only directed in two directions, internally and externally, and vary depending on the conflict stage, but are also temporally and causally related, with the external conflict strategy chosen by each protagonist being reliant on previous internally directed capacity building strategies.

Escalation

The strategies adopted by an organization as it begins to escalate a conflict have great import for the violent or non-violent trajectory of the conflict. Conflict escalation is often regarded as necessarily involving the use of violence, but it is important to consider the many non-violent ways partisans can increase a conflict's scope and intensity. We note the choice of policies that are conducive to non-violent escalations as well as violent ones.

Directed internally

Escalation generally requires the devotion of increased resources to the struggle. This usually necessitates greater mobilization of people. One strategy to achieve this is to arouse emotions of fear and hatred, forming a negative identity for the enemy relative to the group's own members. By depicting the enemy as subhuman or evil, leaders justify extreme methods of struggle. Such a strategy, however, tends to make de-escalation, settlement and recovery very difficult because the creation of polar identities limits future strategic options.

A contrary policy would be for leaders to stress differences within the opposing side. Constituents may be assured that not everyone in the adversary camp is an enemy, that many share important values and concerns with them. This has the effect of isolating the enemy within the opposing side, providing the opportunity later to revert to peaceful, or at least non-violent, relations with the bulk of the adversary's population.

Unfortunately, one internally directed strategy is to attack internal factions that are considered rivals; dissenters are threatened, intimidated and killed. This may be the result of seeking greater power, ideological purity, or unity about goals and means. For such reasons the LTTE leadership has suppressed rival Tamil groups in Sri Lanka and in the diaspora, as discussed by Orjuela in this volume. As a result, consideration of alternative strategies hardly occurs and Tamils are relatively isolated. Other options then might be available to the group if additional resources were available; alternative leadership, knowledge, identity; have been denied them because of the internally directed strategy of factional elimination.

Since conflicts are interlocked, acts of violence may occur on many fronts at the same time. Wars of national liberation and civil wars often incorporate fights among clans, tribes, and families. Leaders of one sub-group may exploit the larger conflict to defeat a rival. As the number of parties increases and their interrelationships become more knotted and entangled, the odds of the two main parties clearly communicating their readiness to de-escalate become less favorable.

In many cases, however, some factions and elements within the adversarial camps have interests, values, or beliefs that tend to constrain violent escalation or to foster non-violent goals and strategies. This occurs when business, religious, educational, and other leaders cooperate with similar people in the opposing camp. Such connections potentially limit escalation in order to protect those relationships.

Directed at the external adversary

Many contending groups initially escalate their conflict through non-violent means such as petitions or demonstrations. However, if they believe that these efforts have been ignored or forcibly repressed, some resort to violent means. This has been true in South Africa, Sri Lanka, Northern Ireland, and elsewhere. Alternatively, a government's response recognizing that the challengers feel aggrieved and offering some concessions may avert violent escalations. This was the case in Belgium, Malaysia, and Canada, where protests did not escalate into destructive, protracted violence.

An obstacle to such accommodating responses is that challengers are often protesting policies the government deems to be appropriate or even essential. In such situations government officials are limited in how responsive they can be. Furthermore, they may believe that any concession is a sign of weakness inviting greater demands, or feel constrained by the expectations of their constituents. Consequently, they resort to violent suppression.

In many conflicts, this dynamic results in each side claiming that it is the aggrieved party, threatened by the other side. Both sides claim to be acting defensively and become locked into violent reciprocating escalation, with both internally and externally directed strategies of confrontation channeling the party's options ever more narrowly in the direction of greater violence.

The dynamics of violent conflict escalation can be a trap for both sides. A challenging group may use violence to provoke government overreactions, which serve to isolate government leaders (Debray 1967). This seems to have occurred in Cuba in the 1950s when Fidel Castro's small group of revolutionaries conducted attacks against the government. In response, Fulgencio Batista, the self-appointed president, undertook increasingly harsh and indiscriminate countermeasures, antagonizing many segments of the population. The government became isolated and fell in January 1959. Che Guevara considered this strategy to be an effective way to foment revolution and he and many others attempted to follow the strategy in several countries. These efforts failed when countermeasures were limited, and sometimes handled as police, rather than military, matters. In these situations the government proved effective by not responding too aggressively against challenging parties. Overreaction is a severe risk in responding to challenges, often proving to be counterproductive (Mueller 2006). As discussed below, relying on violence can entrap the initiating challengers.

The goals set by the opposing sides greatly affect the likelihood of destructive escalations. Some group goals threaten the existence of the opposing side but more often groups seek changes, not elimination. In many cases the opposing groups contend over the control of particular territories or of other valued resources, such as in the case of ETA, as discussed by Juan Gutierrez in this volume.

These varying goals provide an important context for choosing the means of struggle, and their effects on the opponent. The goals and strategies adopted by the ANC in its conflict with the South African government illustrate their importance in reaching a non-violent and negotiated settlement, as discussed by Tom Lodge in this book. Nelson Mandela and other ANC leaders consistently proclaimed the non-racist character of their party and the South African society they sought. They reassured the whites of South African that they were viewed as another people enjoying equal protection under the law in the new rainbow nation.

In addition, early decisions regarding organizational goals fostered the possibility of non-violent conflict and de-escalation in the future. At the beginning of the struggle the ANC relied on non-violent methods, in the tradition of Mohandas Gandhi as a young lawyer in South Africa. The decision to use violence, but also the kind of violence chosen, had implications for turning away from it at a later time. This was recognized, for example, in the explicit decision by ANC leaders to eschew terrorism in order to negotiate later (Mandela 1994).

Using particular violent methods requires specific human capabilities and non-human materials. The development of such resources then creates a vested interest in continuing to rely on those methods. Members and leaders gain status and other rewards as fighters. Yielding benefits in a peaceful accommodation with the adversary may not be attractive. In addition, committing violent acts binds fighters to their organizations, and armed fighters and their leaders develop skills for combat and may lack the skills needed for alternative means of making a living. Because the skills needed for non-violent governance are not developed, if a peaceful accommodation is reached, implementation is difficult.

When the fighters are only one wing of a broader entity some difficulties in transitioning into non-violent relations with an opponent may be alleviated. Organizations with open, democratic structures are more likely than authoritarian organizations to avoid such limitations and to make the transformation from relying on violence to struggling non-violently (Wanis-St. John and Kew 2006; Pace and Kew 2008; Kew forthcoming). The social resources provided by such structures provide for the development of non-violent capacities that can then be utilized in later conflict stages.

Finally, we discuss escalating actions taken at the grass roots and mid-elite levels within adversary camps. Forming connections between particular groups or persons who are members of opposing sides not only adds resources but weakens the solidarity of the opposition. This was true in the US during the civil rights movement where blacks and whites together formed CORE. Similarly, religious organizations and trade unions have often provided channels for mobilizing people across ethnic or class lines in escalating struggles for improved conditions for particular groups (Rose 2000).

In short, carefully controlled strategies may escalate conflicts in ways that set the stage for de-escalation and sustainable mutual accommodations. As analyzed in Lodge's chapter, this was the case as opposition against apartheid surged across the black townships of South Africa in 1985. Nationally the United Democratic Front (UDF) undertook low-key acts of defiance, such as rent boycotts, labor strikes, and school stayaways. The blacks of Port Elizabeth launched an economic boycott of the city's white-owned businesses. The country was becoming ungovernable under apartheid. Such acts escalated the conflict between whites and blacks, between the ANC and the National Party, but it also developed the capacity for non-violent conflict and set the stage for later de-escalation and settlement.

A comparison of the first and second Palestinian intifadas is also illuminating (Hammami and Tamara 2001). During the first intifada, beginning in 1987, the Palestinians engaged in various forms of non-violent resistance including boycotts of Israeli goods, as discussed in the chapter by Nigel Parsons in this volume. Lethal weapons were eschewed and the image of stone-throwing youths pursued by heavily armed Israeli soldiers won widespread sympathy for Palestinians. The second intifada, which erupted in 2000, was conducted by armed Palestinian militias and security forces, with relatively little popular engagement. The Israeli military suppression of the armed struggle was widely seen as justified. The chosen strategies of the first intifada contributed to the Israeli belief that a negotiated two-state resolution was desirable, whereas those of the second convinced many Israelis that negotiation was not feasible (Kriesberg 2002).

De-escalation and settlement

The stage of primary interest in this volume is that of de-escalation and settlement. Even the most intractable violent conflicts eventually become tractable or otherwise terminated. Often militias and other armed groups abandon violence because they are defeated, and they submit to the other side, suffer separation, or even disappear as an organized entity. However, we are particularly interested here in the transformation of conflicts and the adoption of non-violent means of contention.

Internally directed

Because persistent conflicts generate strong feelings of fear and hatred, as well as a strengthened commitment to winning in order to justify accrued losses, compromising with the enemy is very difficult. Leaders at all levels must prepare their constituents to accept some unpleasant realities. Preparing for a settlement, and therefore broadening strategic options can help ensure successful implementation of later accommodations. The ANC was thoughtful in this regard, encouraging higher ranking persons to become educated in ways relevant to governance, thus ensuring that they added a resource necessary for the capacity to govern, and developed new strategic options. Interestingly, some of the ANC leaders carried out such studies while imprisoned on Robben Island.

Reaching a sustained accommodation is often obstructed by factionalism and spoilers on each side of a conflict, including governments. The partisans in any large-scale conflict consist of varyingly autonomous subgroups and coalition partners, some of which may not accept the de-escalation movement. They may take covert or overt actions that undermine the reaching and implementing of any joint agreement. For example, when the negotiations for ending apartheid were underway a third force, some elements within the South African security agency, supported black South African groups that attacked the ANC. How contending groups on a de-escalating course handle challenges to that process is critical. If they are able to demonstrate increased commitment, they may be able to prevent the breakdown of the de-escalation movement. In South Africa, winning a general referendum helped isolate and marginalize the would-be spoilers (Kydd and Walter 2002).

Subversion is another complication that must be dealt with handily. Leaders of the de-escalating adversaries may make concessions to some members or factions of their constituencies and coalition partners in order to keep their support. The concessions may however be viewed by the opposition as evidence of unwillingness or inability to take the necessary steps to reach a mutually acceptable accommodation. This was evident in the Israeli–PLO peace process of the 1990s during which Jewish settlements were expanded in the occupied territories and episodes of terrorist attacks by Palestinians recurred. Strategies that take these matters into account can contribute to maintaining de-escalating momentum. It may be helpful to make such considerations explicit.

And finally, just as they can promote non-violent strategies of escalation, grass roots and mid-level leaders sometimes campaign to pressure their own official leaders to de-escalate. Finding their interests harmed by the diversion of resources to a destructive escalation, they pressure their own leaders to end the fight. This has played a role in the transformation of many international conflicts, including the US–Soviet Cold War (Suri 2003). Peace Now is a good example in Israel.

Directed externally

At some point particular members of one or more sides employ strategies directed at the adversary that promote a joint de-escalation (Evangelista 1999). These strategies range from tentative signals and probes to bold unilateral de-escalating gestures. The adoption of one or another strategy arises from the convergence of several sets of conditions. A positive response to a unilateral de-escalatory action, so that joint moves are made, requires the convergence of even more developments. This may require the shared perception of a hurting stalemate and a feasible better option.

Several developments within and between adversaries, as well as external to them, affect the belief that better options than painful stalemate are possible. Formerly impossible options become credible when one side can demonstrate the existence of its internal differences or can act on the recognition of differences within the other side. One strategy is for at least one side to initiate gestures that convey that it desires de-escalation and it can be trusted to deliver what it is promising (Mitchell 2000; Kriesberg 2007). Once de-escalation has been initiated additional strategies are useful in consolidating the early progress. Tools such as confidence-building measures (CBMs) proved successful during the Cold War.

Calling upon and utilizing external actors can also help undertake and consolidate de-escalation steps. One adversary may attract allies and so increase its resources relative to its opponent. This may enhance coercive strength, but it may also provide increased moral suasion for its side, a powerful social resource that opens up new strategic options. Undoubtedly, the ANC's success in winning widespread condemnation of apartheid undermined the conviction of many white South Africans that apartheid was morally defensible, thus promoting alternate strategies. Outside parties may also be drawn into a conflict as mediators, as guarantors of agreements and as providers of joint benefits for the antagonists, as discussed by Bruce Dayton in his chapter in this volume.

De-escalating initiatives are sometimes undertaken by grass roots and mid-level leaders from the opposing camps. When the violence in Northern Ireland was high in 1976, Máiread Corrigan Maguire and Betty Williams organized weekly peace marches and demonstrations. Very quickly over half a million people throughout Northern Ireland, as well as in England and the Republic of Ireland, came out on marches. The women co-founded the Community of the Peace People to continue their peace-making initiatives and were later awarded the Nobel Peace Prize. Such strategies break down bi-polar conceptions of group identities and promote the choice of non-violent strategies.

Academics and various NGOs can initiate and facilitate meetings, workshops, and exercises in dialogue which accomplish similar outcomes. For example, in December 1984 an Afrikaner sociologist, Hendrik W. van der Merwe, organized a series of meetings between ANC officials and Afrikaner newspaper editors (Van der Merwe 1989; Van der Merwe 2000) which contributed to the recognition that the different peoples in South Africa were all South Africans, thus promoting de-escalation.

An additional strategy practiced by some NGO and grass roots organizations is the establishment of "Zones of Peace." This has been accomplished in both the Philippines and in Colombia (Hancock and Mitchell 2007). Such zones enable people in a particular locality to opt out of the fighting, demonstrating that security can be achieved without complying with the demands of any armed party.

Post-settlement and recovery

Establishing secure and equitable relations between former enemies and avoiding a recurrence of violence has become a matter of high concern since the 1980s. Increased recognition is being given to the value of positive peace (Paris 2004; Mac Ginty 2006). Many analyses of peacebuilding focus on external intervention, but the partisans themselves bear the greatest burden in building a stable and just peace.

Directed internally

One method of consolidating peacebuilding is for leaders of formerly con-tending groups to secure access to education, employment, and social welfare for their followers. Such assurances of well-being help ensure that not only the leadership but their constituents commit to a non-violent future. Additionally, competence in governance is necessary for transfor-mation to endure. Moving from reliance on violence to active governance is very difficult and some organizations simply fail to make the transition. The PLO is one such example.

Another strategy is for the leaders of each group to undo the damage caused by the creation of polar identities. Just as leaders painted the other as evil or subhuman, it is also possible for them to reaffirm the similarities and shared humanness of the antagonists (Boudreau and Polkinghorn 2008). Religious and civic leaders have important roles to play in this process and at times actively engage their constituencies in this redefini-tion of the self and the other. Closely related to this is the need for leaders to promote the acceptance of what cannot be changed. Leaders can help their constituents accept unpleasant realities, since some compromises usually have to be made. Of course, the more sober the group's initial goals, the easier this process will be.

Directed externally

Reaching out to former enemies and demonstrating at least minimal respect for them are fundamental elements of many strategies to estab-lish enduring peace. This is often expressed in policies and laws ensur-ing basic human rights for all. One common strategy in post-violence environments is the creation of Human Rights Commissions, Commis-sions of Inquiry, War Crimes Tribunals, and other official bodies tasked with ensuring the rule of law. Additionally, resources are very often pro-vided for the restructuring and retraining of military and police forces in order to ensure their purging of rogue factional elements or war crimi-nals. These policies often contribute to building confidence between the former antagonists.

Other strategies are geared toward the construction of a shared identity by creating common symbols such as new anthems, flags, and monuments. Such symbols can blend elements from old symbols of the formerly con-tending groups, signifying their unity and shared future (Ross 2007).

Reconciliation is receiving growing attention and is an important aspect of post-violence recovery. But reconciliation is not a single condition that does or does not exist; rather, it is multidimensional and varies over time for different members of the previously antagonistic sides (Kriesberg 1999). Considerable attention has been given to the establishment of various forms of truth commissions in order to foster reconciliation, most notably the Truth and Reconciliation Commission of South Africa. They are thought to contribute to managing resentments between members of the formerly antagonistic sides.

Grass roots and local level accommodations are also important, since it is at the grass roots level that relationships are built and communities are restored after violence (Pouligny *et al.* 2007). A stable peace is fostered by small acts between individuals, such as friendships or marriages across lines of division. Groups that foster mutual understanding may be established in neighborhoods and cities, such as dialogue circles, neighborhood redevelopment schemes and economic cooperatives.

Finally, for agreed-upon settlements to endure, it is important to build institutions, both to handle conflicts, and to deliver mutual gains (Paris 2004). Such institutions can help ensure an equitable distribution of resources among the parties. The failure to adopt such a strategy risks a return to violence in the future by those who feel newly aggrieved by the post-conflict disposition of resources, as discussed in the chapters by Elham Atashi and by Gavan Duffy in this volume.

Conclusion

Adversaries in a violent conflict can use a wide variety of strategies to transform their struggle and continue to engage each other without relying on the threat or commission of violence. The process of transformation, however, is usually very lengthy and requires different strategies at various conflict stages. Important strategies are directed both internally and externally, but sometimes inconsistently in regard to advancing conflict transformation.

The strategies are joined together in complex, sometimes contradictory, sometimes complementary ways, and often constituting campaigns that change over time with externally directed strategies being reliant on prior internally directed and capacity creating strategic decisions. Adding to the complexity, different persons and groups within each adversary camp enact particular strategies, consistent with or contrary to the primary campaign.

Some general patterns regarding the choices and the consequences of different strategies and their combinations were suggested. Certainly much more research is needed to verify, correct, amplify and specify them. However, since every conflict has unique features, no body of theory and research can prescribe the precise set of strategies that will maximize the diverse set of goals which members of one or another side in a conflict seek to advance. Recognition of many possible alternative strategies and likely responses to them nevertheless can improve the chances of avoiding destructive conflict escalations. Thinking ahead about possible responses and subsequent counter-responses to a chosen strategy is a sound principle for policy making.

Finally, we wish to acknowledge that people rarely regard the resort to violence as the worst possible means of struggle. People often assert that there are some goals for which it is worth both dying and killing to advance. In retrospect, however, after periods of extreme violence, many people come to believe they were mistaken. These considerations are important, but they go beyond this chapter's parameters.

References

Boudreau, T. E. and B. Polkinghorn (2008). "Changing an Enemy into a Friend: A Model for Reframing Narratives in Protracted Social Conflict through Identity Affirmation," in R. Fleishman, R. O'Leary and C. Gerard (eds.) *Pushing the Boundaries: New Frontiers in Conflict Resolution and Collaboration.* Bingley, UK, Emerald Press.

Boulding, K. E. (1989). *Three Faces of Power.* Newbury Park, Sage.

Cornell, S. E. and R. A. Spector (2002). "Central Asia: More than Islamic Extremists." *Washington Quarterly* 25 (1): 193–206.

Debray, R. (1967). *Revolution in the Revolution?* New York, Grove Press.

Evangelista, M. (1999). *Unarmed Forces: The Transnational Movement to End the Cold War.* Ithaca and London, Cornell University Press.

Fanon, F. (1966). *The Wretched of the Earth.* New York, Grove Press.

Hammami, R. and S. Tamara. (2001). "The Second Uprising: End or New Beginning?" *Journal of Palestine Studies* 30 (2) (118): 5–25.

Hancock, L. E. and C. Mitchell, (eds.) (2007). *Zones of Peace.* Bloomfield, CT, Kumarian.

Kew, D. (Forthcoming). *Classrooms for Democracy: Civil Society, Conflict Resolution, and Building Democracy in Nigeria.* Syracuse, Syracuse University Press.

Khalidi, R. (2006). *The Iron Cage: The Story of the Palestinian Struggle for Statehood.* Boston, Beacon Press.

Kriesberg, L. (1999). "Paths to Varieties of Inter-Communal Reconciliation," in H. W. Jeong (ed.) *Conflict Resolution: Dynamics, Process and Structure.* Fitchburg, MD, Dartmouth, 105–129.

Kriesberg, L. (2002). "The Relevance of Reconciliation Actions in the Breakdown of Israeli–Palestinian Negotiations, 2000." *Peace & Change* 27 (4): 546–571.

Kriesberg, L. (2007). *Constructive Conflicts: From Escalation to Resolution,* 3rd edn., Lanham, MD, Rowman & Littlefield.

Kydd, A. and B. F. Walter. (2002). "Sabotaging the Peace: The Politics of Extremist Violence." *International Organization* 56 (2): 263–296.

Mac Ginty, R. (2006). *No War, No Peace: The Rejuvenation of Stalled Peace Process and Peace Accords.* New York, Palgrave Macmillan.

McMahon, P. C. (2007). *Ethnic Cooperation and Transnational Networks in Eastern Europe.* Syracuse, Syracuse University Press.

Mandela, N. (1994). *Long Walk to Freedom.* Boston, Little, Brown.

Merwe, H. W. van der (1989). *Pursuing Justice and Peace in South Africa.* London and New York, Routledge.

Merwe, H. W. van der (2000). *Peacemaking in South Africa: A Life in Conflict Resolution.* Cape Town, Tafelberg.

Mitchell, C. R. (1995). Asymmetry and Strategies of Regional Conflict Reduction. in I. W. Zartman and V. A. Kremenyuk (eds.) *Cooperative Security: Reducing Third World Wars.* Syracuse, NY, Syracuse University Press: 25–57.

Mitchell, C. R. (2000). *Gestures of Conciliation: Factors Contributing to Successful Olive Branches.* New York, St. Martin's Press.

Möller, F. (2007). *Thinking Peaceful Change: Baltic Security Policies and Security Community Building.* Syracuse, Syracuse University Press.

Mueller, J. E. (2006). *Overblown: How Politicians and the Terrorism Industry Inflate National Security Threats, and Why we Believe Them.* New York, Free Press.

Pace, M. and D. Kew. (2008). "Catalysts of Change Applying New Forms of Practice to the Context of Nigeria's Democratic Development," in R. Fleishman, R. O'Leary and C. Gerard (eds.) *Pushing Boundaries: New Frontiers in Conflict Resolution and Collaboration.* Bingley, UK, Emerald Press.

Pagnucco, R. (1997). "The Transnational Strategies of the Service for Peace and Justice in Latin America," in J. Smith, C. Chatfield and R. Pagnucco (eds.) *Transnational Social Movements and Global Politics.* Syracuse, Syracuse University Press: 123–138.

Pagnucco, R. and J. D. McCarthy (1992). "Advocating Nonviolent Direct Action in Latin America: The Antecedents and Emergence of SERPAJ," in B. Misztal and A. Shupe (eds.) *Religion and Politics in Comparative Perspective.* Westport, CN, Praeger: 125–147.

Paris, R. (2004). *At War's End: Building Peace After Civil Conflict.* Cambridge, UK, Cambridge University Press.

Pouligny, B., S. Chesterman and A. Schnabel, (eds.) (2007). *After Mass Crime: Rebuilding States and Communities.* Tokyo, United Nations University Press.

Radu, M. (2001). "The Rise and Fall of the PKK," *Orbis* 45 (1): 47-63.

Rose, F. (2000). *Coalitions across the Class Divide: Lessons from the Labor, Peace, and Environmental Movements.* Ithaca, NY, Cornell University Press.

Ross, M. H. (2007). *Cultural Contestation in Ethnic Conflict.* Cambridge, UK, Cambridge University Press.

Sharp, G. (1973). *The Politics of Nonviolent* Action. Boston, Porter Sargent.

Suri, J. (2003). *Power and Protest: Global Revolution and the Rise of Detente.* Cambridge, MA and London, Harvard University Press.

Thomas, T. S. and W. D. Casebeer (2004). *Violent Systems: Defeating Terrorists, Insurgents, and Other Non-State Adversaries.* USAF Academy, CO, USAF Institute for National Security Studies: 1-108.

Wanis-St. John, A. and D. Kew (2006). "The Missing Link? Civil Society and Peace Negotiations: Contributions to Sustained Peace," *Annual Convention of the International Studies Association.* San Diego, CA.

3   The contributions of leadership to the movement from violence to incorporation[1]

Margaret G. Hermann and Catherine Gerard

Although we often mention who the leaders are when describing particular terrorist groups, independence movements, paramilitaries, militias, and protest groups, little effort has gone into exploring why leadership might matter in understanding the decisions such entities make regarding the use of violence and moves toward cooperation. It is the intention of this chapter to push beyond merely acknowledging who is in charge. We propose to examine how learning about leadership can help us gain access to knowledge about the processes occurring within the groups and organizations of interest to us in this volume.

What is leadership?

Several pundits have likened leadership to standing on a moving sidewalk with fire at either end while trying to juggle a number of problems with people pushing and shoving their positions at you from each side. At issue in leadership is remaining standing and continuing to move toward a set of goals while at the same time developing and maintaining a consensus among those involved. Or, as some have argued (e.g. Wriggins 1969; Kotter and Lawrence 1974; Hermann 1986; Hermann and Kegley 1995), leadership involves persuasion in the service of setting an agenda, building networks (coalitions), and accomplishing things. Thus defined, leadership is more than leaders; it is composed of a set of ingredients, each of which is important to understanding what is happening at any point in time.

Indeed, we do not have leaders without some sort of followers, constituents, or supporters. Even someone who appears to have complete control such as Kim Jung Il, the head of the government in North Korea, is responsive to certain others who keep him in power and in his position – in Kim Jung Il's case, the military. One of the dilemmas currently facing the people in Iraq is that different constituencies have chosen different leaders and there is no consensus among these various stakeholders on who is the "leader of the Iraqi government." In Afghanistan, the US and some constituencies are supporting one leader while other constituencies are being pushed and pulled by potential leaders to engage in violence in an attempt to seize authority and assert leadership.

The relationship between the leader and his/her constituents is also important to leadership. Consider how the low approval rating of a leader such as George Bush affects what he can and cannot do, the scrutiny of his policies, his latitude in negotiating with other leaders, and his influence on the 2008 presidential campaign. Contrast this example with the continuous positive relationship between Vladimir Putin and the Russian people and between Nasrallah and members of Hezbollah. Putin represents economic and political stability to the Russian people and they continue to elect him to positions of authority; Nasrallah, in the eyes of the participants in his movement, is viewed as working for improvement in their quality of life and increased political power for the Shia in Lebanon. The desires and expectations of a leader's constituents are important determinants of this relationship, as are the leader's skills in moving an agenda forward, building coalitions, and accomplishing things of relevance to his/her constituents.

Leaders and constituents work together in a particular context. In effect, the nature of the context can facilitate or hinder a leader being selected or the development of the relationship between the leader and those led. Research tells us that constituents select different types of leaders in times of crisis than in times of peace, in democracies versus more authoritarian political systems, in times of plenty as opposed to periods of recession, to lead revolutionary movements versus institutionalize change, and when developing a vision is critical in contrast to when maintaining stability is the name of the game (for an overview of this literature, see Nixon 1982; Hargrove 1989; Hermann 2003). Consider how difficult it is for many leaders to move from being continuously in the opposition to a position of authority – for example, Arafat as the leader of the PLO and as the head of the Palestinian Lands. Two oft-used illustrations of the effects of context are those of Charles de Gaulle and Winston Churchill who were elected during periods of crisis and war and then not elected as their countries moved into more peaceful times. Both of these people were hard-driving, take charge individuals whose relationships with their constituents were more likely to meet expectations when a crisis was at hand because they were decisive and forceful than when these same constituents wanted their own views listened to and taken into account. Interestingly, there is a 0.56 correlation between a leadership style that indicates responsiveness to constituents and the situation and the organization of the political system or movement (Hermann *et al.* 2001). As Quincy Wright (1942: 847–848) observed in his famous study of war, democracies "tend to give leadership to personalities of a conciliatory type" while autocracies tend to select more "aggressive types of personalities." The more democratic the system or movement, the more responsive the leader to what is happening around them – both to their constituents and to the context. As one moves to more hierarchical and authoritarian systems, leaders are less responsive generally.

In effect, this approach to leadership has led to the development of something called the contingency theory of leadership (e.g. Fiedler *et al.* 1976; Fiedler and Garcia 1987; Winter 1987; Bass 1990; Hermann 2003). This theory emphasizes the importance of the "match" between what the leader is like, what relevant constituencies want, what the setting calls for, and the nature of the relationship between leader and led to understanding successful leadership. For leaders as diverse as American presidents and African revolutionaries, we have found that leader appeal, too, appears to depend on the nature of this match. Who can become a political leader is shaped by the match between candidate, constituents, and context (Hermann 1987, 2003; Winter 1987). If the match is good, all move in concert and much can be done in accomplishing specific goals. Consider Mahatma Gandhi and the movement to gain independence for India, Nelson Mandela and his work within the African National Congress against apartheid in South Africa, and Pol Pot and his radical reforms in Cambodia. But what if the match is not so good – say the expectations of the constituents change, the leader becomes less responsive to relevant constituents, or the context changes. In our examples, Gandhi had difficulty with his quest once the focus of attention changed from independence for India from Britain and became a battle between religious groups regarding the nature of the new country; Pol Pot became so caught up in his reform that he engaged in genocide in his own country, eliminating the very people he needed to build the society he desired. This contingency or match theory of leadership suggests that we can better understand what is possible and when change is likely by keeping in mind that leadership involves not only leaders but also who they are working to lead, their relationship with these supporters, and the nature of the context in which the leadership is taking place.

Leadership style as a surrogate indicator

One way that those studying leadership have tried to take into account these various aspects of the phenomenon is by exploring leadership style; that is, the way the leader interacts with constituents and those around them. Leadership style goes a long way to helping us determine how leaders will structure decision making, from whom they will seek advice, the kinds of contexts they are likely to prefer, and the processes they will usually follow in working toward goals (e.g. Preston 2001; Kowert 2002; Mitchell 2005; Kille 2006). Historians, journalists, political scientists, and politicians themselves generally use three terms to describe leadership style. They refer to leaders as being ideologues (crusaders, highly principled, advocates), strategists, or pragmatists. Each is viewed as a unique way of approaching politics and leadership. The ideologue has a set of goals, an ideology, a cause, or a problem to be solved that focuses the agenda – movement on this agenda is of paramount importance to such leaders who, in turn, believe their constituents share their priorities. Persons who are more strategic have a set of goals, a cause, or a problem of particular interest, but how they go about working on these issues is dependent on what is possible in the particular situation. In other words, their goals are set but the means to achieving such goals vary with the context and what constituents will support – political timing is critical. For the pragmatist, goals are determined by what constituents want and expect in a particular context. The agenda is adaptable to the expectations of constituents and the situation. In effect, each of these leadership styles, although involving all the ingredients of leadership, tend to emphasize one ingredient over the others. The ideologue focuses attention on the leader whose beliefs and desires are driving the agenda for the entity. The strategic leader is focused on the relationship between themselves and their constituents in a context, while pragmatists are the agents of their constituents and responsive to their needs in a particular situation.

In what follows, we will consider the implications of these leadership styles as they have been reinforced through research (e.g. Hermann 1977, 1980, 1987, 2005; Hermann and Hermann 1989; Stewart *et al.* 1989; Hermann and Hagan 1998; Kaarbo and Hermann 1998; Hermann *et al.* 2001; Preston and Hermann 2003). In ascertaining leadership style, we have used an assessment-at-a-distance method developed by the first author and available now in a software package called Profiler Plus (see www.socialscienceauthomation.com). The technique is described in detail in Hermann (2005, 2008).

Ideologues – leaders with an agenda

Research suggests that leaders who come to their positions with an agenda (a cause, a definite goal, a problem to solve, an ideology) are intent on expanding their power and influence as well as the number of converts to that agenda to get where they want to go. They are interested in maintaining both formal and informal control over the focus of their group, organization, or government and, as a result, generally challenge the constraints in their environment, selectively perceive and use that information which furthers their agenda, and choose to work with others who support that same agenda. Indeed, these leaders select "implementers" as advisers and lieutenants, people who are committed to furthering the agenda and to spinning, selling, and persuading others of that agenda.

These leaders tend to come to power in authoritarian political systems, in strong one-party systems, and in democracies where the "winner takes all" as well as in hierarchically organized revolutionary groups and terrorist organizations. They are likely to repress or ignore opposition depending on its strength (that is, its salience, size, degree of influence, commitment to its position) and are willing to engage in the diversionary use of force should the opposition appear to be gaining the upper hand. If there is a match between what the broader population wants and the agenda of these leaders, activity and movement on the agenda is likely to be rapid and difficult to interrupt. But should the broader population not be as focused on the particular agenda or be changing its mind across time, there is often an increase in clashes between the leadership and this broader population which, at the extremes, can lead to violence and even civil war.

If such leaders view the world as a threatening place, their decisions are prone to reflect this "paranoia." They are likely to confront those whom they consider the "enemy" or as perpetrating the threat and to commit resources as well as engage in unilateral actions against such groups, organizations, and governments. They will mobilize their resources (and those of any allies) to contain such a threat particularly if it means less movement on their agenda.

Consider as examples two leaders of independence movements in Africa, Nkrumah of Ghana and Houphouet-Boigny of the Ivory Coast. Their profiles suggest that they were ideologues with very different views of the path to development. Nkrumah believed that by pitting the superpowers – the US and Soviet Union at the time – against one another, he and his country would become the beneficiary and be able to leap forward exponentially. Houphouet-Boigny argued that development would only come slowly and by working with the former colonial powers not against them. Indeed, once their countries were independent, these two leaders engaged in what has been called the "West African wager" betting on which of these paths would be more successful in a ten-year period of time.

Strategic leaders

As already noted, these leaders come to their positions with a set of goals but are willing to be flexible in the means they use to reach those goals – they are strategic, that is, interested in pursuing what is feasible in a particular context. They believe that having a well-tuned sense of political timing is important to moving forward on one's goals as well as to maintaining one's position in power. At issue is maintaining the group, organization, or government's maneuverability and flexibility in order to take advantage of opportunities and to avoid threats. Critical to such a view of leadership is maintaining control over information and having ways of gathering information from across a variety of perspectives. These leaders challenge political constraints but do so informally in a manipulative and machiavellian manner; they are best when they can interact face-to-face behind closed doors with those to be influenced. Advisors are sought who represent important constituencies, giving these leaders access to diverse points of view and information as well as entry points for engaging in influence.

Such leaders tend to come to power in organizations that are in transition and where expectations, values, and norms are in flux. They are also often found in arenas that are ethnically, religiously, or culturally diverse. These leaders try to co-opt any opposition, working to assume as their own the ideas of important constituencies or to bring the leadership of such constituencies into their advisory group. If an opposition cannot be co-opted, they will work to highlight the differences between themselves and "these others" in an attempt to educate the lay public on why their position (stand, idea) is to be preferred in this particular instance. Only when their persuasive skills are exhausted and the opposition continues to resist will such leaders engage in repression or violence against an opposition.

To the outside observer, strategic leaders at times appear to have no sense of purpose as they move to get what they want by the most feasible means available at the moment; their actions seem "irrational" until one takes into account their goals, charts the views of their important constituencies on that issue or policy, and considers what is feasible in the particular setting. In the policy arena, these leaders are likely to engage in "tit for tat" behavior until they can decide what is feasible in the interaction with outside parties to facilitate moving toward their goals. Indeed, these leaders will seek to meet face-to-face with those leading these other organizations to gain more specific information about what is happening as well as to play a role in framing and shaping any future agenda. This behavior is most characteristic of strategic leaders when they view the world as affording more opportunities than threats. When they perceive that threats dominate, these leaders will first respond with a relatively low risk option to see if the situation can be brought under control without the use of force. If not, they will match the force levels of those doing the threatening.

An example of a strategic leader of an "independence" movement currently in the news is Moqtada al Sadr, cleric and head of the Mahdi Army in Iraq. He is one of the persons working to shape the nature of the government of Iraq and intent on seeing that his constituents, the residents of Sadr City in Baghdad, see improvement in the quality of their lives. As a strategic leader he has shown flexibility in getting people from his group elected and working within the ruling circle when such behavior is opportune, using violence when such actions seem warranted, and re-shaping his Mahdi Army when rogue elements appear to be diverting the group from its cause. All the time the emphasis is on staying influential or, at the least, a force that has to be reckoned with if Iraq is to move forward.

Pragmatic leaders

Pragmatic leaders are driven by the situation in which they find themselves. They have come to power through being able to represent the wishes of a broad set of constituents and excel at the art of compromise and consensus building. They are diplomats and mediators at heart. They respect the constraints under which they have to operate, seeking change within the political system or organization in which they find themselves. In effect, they are agents of the constituencies that selected them, working on the needs and wants – the agenda – of these people. Dealing with problems around which a consensus or compromise cannot be reached is often postponed. These leaders are avid listeners and generally seek advice from a wide array of individuals. Advisors are viewed as an integral part of the decision-making process; their advice is sought and they share in accountability for the decision.

These leaders are usually found in democratic systems, particularly those with multiple parties where there are generally coalition governments as well as in networks and organizations that are decentralized with a lateral or non-hierarchical structure. They generally try to bargain with oppositions, working on how to bring them on board and on devising a way that the various points of view can be accommodated to achieve a compromise. Thus, they may engage in bargaining even as an opposition is becoming stronger and be caught off guard when such an opposition seeks to take power, often losing out in such power struggles. These leaders believe in debate and dialogue and in the fact that consensus and compromise bring with them a sense that while none has gotten what they wanted, none has lost everything either. Something has been achieved and there is some down time before the issue becomes a problem again.

In the policy arena, these leaders are interested in engaging in collaborative ventures that will maximize their benefits while limiting their costs in the current situation and international environment. Should these leaders perceive themselves in a context full of threats, they will seek support from friends as well as work for some amelioration of the situation within international organizations.

Arafat as leader of the Palestinian Liberation Organization (PLO) is an example of a pragmatic leader. Comprised of many different groups, the PLO was ripe for this kind of leader; indeed, perhaps only a pragmatic leader could have kept the various pieces of the organization together and moving forward. These types of leaders may, at times, appear highly indecisive as they work to build some form of consensus or compromise between warring factions. And they may at other times seem pushed more by one group within the organization over another as that group asserts its goals more forcefully and garners the attention of the leader. Learning what is going on within the various pieces of the organization becomes important to ascertaining whether compromise and action are possible and how united the organization is likely to be at any point in time.

Some data and their implications

Leaders of African independence movements

In developing profiles of the leaders of 11 independence movements in Africa from the 1960s onward and then following their rise to power in the nations that were established following independence, it is possible to draw some implications for understanding the effects of leadership on the movement from violence to political incorporation (see Hermann 1987; Hermann *et al.* 2001). Among these leaders were Kaunda (Zambia), Kenyatta (Kenya), Mugabe (Zimbabwe), Nkrumah (Ghana), and Nyerere (Tanzania). The profiles were based on the examination of around 7,000 words for each leader taken from interviews with the press across their tenure as leaders of independence movements and then of their countries. The materials were all verbatim. Interviews were examined because they contain the most spontaneous public materials available on this type of public figure, lessening the effects of "ghost-written" and planned communications. In the interview setting, the leader is usually the author of his or her comments and has little time in which to plan a response. Comparisons of scores from speeches and interviews have shown scores using interview responses to be more predictive of leadership style than material from speeches (Schafer 2000; Hermann 2008).

Each of the three leadership styles described above was exemplified in the group of 11 leaders. Indeed, during the fight for independence, 36 percent of the leaders were ideologues, 36 percent were strategists, and 28 percent were pragmatists. During the consolidation of power period after their countries achieved independence, 27 percent were ideologues, 27 percent were strategists, and 46 percent were pragmatists. In effect, over half (54 percent) of the leaders' styles changed as they moved from leading an independence movement to putting together a country; those that changed tended to move from being ideologues and strategists to becoming more pragmatic – moving from challenging constraints to trying to work within the constraints that they were establishing for the government. The other 46 percent retained the same leadership style they had adopted when pushing for independence. Mugabe of Zimbabwe was the only leader to move from being pragmatic during the push for independence to becoming more strategic when he was consolidating his power after independence was won. The data suggest a move on the part of the leaders to focus on building relationships with a broader set of constituents – including those not necessarily in their independence movement – and on the context as they focused on becoming politically incorporated into a legitimate government, whereas the focus during the fight for independence was on a particular agenda and a set of constituents who believed in that same agenda. Nevertheless, just under half of the leaders carried on the style that brought them through the fight for independence into building a country with little concern for the change in the context from one of tearing down institutions to one of developing and maintaining them.

An examination of the behavior of these leaders during the struggle for independence indicates that those with an ideologue approach to leadership were more likely to engage in violence than those who were more strategic and pragmatic ($r=0.60$; $p<0.05$), particularly if they viewed the world as being full of threats as opposed to opportunities ($r=0.50$; $p<0.10$). Indeed, these leaders were more likely to engage in fairly continual civil strife in the form of guerrilla raids, indiscriminant killings, riots, strikes, and civil warfare. But perhaps as a consequence of their violent push for freedom from colonialism, leaders with an ideologue leadership style were more likely to achieve independence in a shorter period of time than those with a strategic or pragmatic style ($r=0.52$; $p<0.05$). Leaders who were more strategic in their approach to leadership were more likely than the others to spend time in detention or under arrest on the way to achieving independence for their countries ($r=0.57$: $p<0.05$) and to take longer to see that independence achieved ($r=0.47$; $p<0.10$), while leaders with a pragmatic leadership style were the least likely to spend time under arrest or in detention ($r=0.46$; $p<0.10$). The data suggest that even though having a agenda and pushing for it helped leaders achieve independence in a quicker time frame, they could do so only by engaging in violence; while those leaders who were concerned about what the context would allow (the strategic leaders) or ensuring that their constituencies' needs were being met in the process (the pragmatic leaders) took longer to see independence, they were less likely to use violence as the way to achieve their goals. This finding was most characteristic of the leaders with strategic and pragmatic styles who were optimistic about what was possible, viewing the world around them as affording more opportunities than threats – the world and politics were not anarchic, cooperation was not only possible but made for good policy.

The leaders with an agenda – the ideologues – spent less time in consolidating their power and forging a one-party state once independence was achieved than leaders with a strategic or pragmatic focus ($r=0.42$; $p<0.10$) but they did so with the greatest number of coup attempts and successful coups ($r=0.46$; $p<0.10$). By taking more time and focusing on the process of leadership, that is, considering how to co-opt or accommodate the broadest range of constituents and what the particular context made feasible at any point in time, the leaders with strategic and pragmatic leadership styles were able to avoid coup attempts as well as to serve their countries for a longer period of time ($r=0.60$; $p<0.05$). Indeed, succession – that is, having those leaders who fought for and achieved independence as well as established the first governments in their countries consider leaving office for another generation – became a significant problem for the states with strategic and pragmatic leaders for whom political timing and the building of networks and coalitions was second nature. One of these leaders, Mugabe, continues to hold on to power after 28 years and several unsuccessful attempts to elect another leader even as the quality of life in his country deteriorates.

Two case studies

Moving forward in time, let us examine the leadership styles of two persons who have been observed by some to lead terrorist organizations and by others to be patriots and "freedom fighters" – al Sadr of Iraq and Nasrallah of Lebanon. Both lead movements that have engaged in violence and both head organizations that are attempting to become politically incorporated into their respective political systems. As we noted earlier in this chapter, Moqtada al Sadr is a Shia cleric and leader of the Mahdi Army which serves the Sadr City area of Baghdad. He has been called at various times "the most dangerous man in Iraq" by the US media (Bartholet 2006) but has also seen 30 of his "people" become elected as part of the Iraqi parliament. Moreover, he has led two uprisings as well as had an arrest warrant out for him. Nasrallah currently leads the Hezbollah organization in Lebanon which primarily represents the growing Shia population in that country and is supposedly financed and armed by the government of Iran with the collusion of Syria. Nasrallah's movement has engaged in periodic skirmishes as well as war with Israel (summer of 2006). It has also worked to gain influence within the Lebanese political system and provided social services for the residents in southern Lebanon.

Using the Profiler Plus software program mentioned above and around 10,000 words for each leader taken from interviews with the press, appearances on talk shows, sermons at Friday prayers, and speeches to rallies (only when more spontaneous material was not available), we have analyzed the materials for the following set of characteristics. Is the leader more likely to: (*a*) challenge or respect constraints; (*b*) be responsive to a wide range of perspectives or fairly closed to outside information; (*c*) focus on the problem or the process; and (*d*) view the political world as more full of threats or opportunities (see, e.g. Winter *et al.* 1991; Hermann and Preston 1998; Kaarbo and Hermann 1998; Hermann *et al.* 2001; Hermann 2005). Scores on the characteristics represent the percentage of time that a leader exhibits a trait when he or she could have done so. To ascertain whether or not al Sadr's and Nasrallah's scores were high or low, we have compared their scores to the average scores of 23 terrorist leaders (including Osama bin Laden and al Zawahiri) as well as 44 leaders of Middle Eastern countries during the last 25 years. Scores were considered high if they were one or more standard deviations above the means of the terrorist or Middle Eastern leaders and low if one or more standard deviations below these means.

Both al Sadr and Nasrallah exhibited a strategic leadership style when compared to either the terrorist leaders or the Middle Eastern national leaders. That is, they challenge constraints but do so in a way that allows them to be open to the nature of the context and what is feasible at any point in time. They are incremental in their approach to their goals, sensitive to political timing and what their relevant constituents want or need. Al Sadr's and Nasrallah's scores, however, indicate that each challenges constraints in a different way. Whereas Nasrallah is more likely to challenge constraints directly – be direct in stating what his goals and interests are, al Sadr challenges constraints more indirectly – more informally and behind the scenes. Al Sadr appears more machiavellian in his approach to influence, though still challenging any constraints imposed on him. Both complement their strategic leadership styles with a preference for worrying about the survival, maintenance, and cohesion of their movements over a problem-solving focus. But they differ in their orientation to politics. Al Sadr views politics as a zero-sum game; conflict, competition, and confrontation are inherent in politics. What is important is dealing with any threats and coming out ahead. Nasrallah sees politics as being conflict-prone but if one is vigilant, the conflicts can be managed; indeed, politics often affords one opportunities that can be taken advantage of in moving toward one's goals.

Since we have selected these two leaders' styles to examine more closely because they have engaged in both violence and attempts at political incorporation, what happens when we explore their leadership in periods when violence was the "name of the game" and contrast it with times when they have sought out political engagement in a non-violent manner? The Profiler Plus software allows us to divide up the materials for each leader into these two types of time periods and to compare the leaders' scores with one another. For al Sadr, 2003–2004 represent years in which his Mahdi Army was engaged in skirmishes against the US military as well as Sunni insurgents – indeed, there was a warrant out for his arrest during this time period. In 2005–2006, there was a move both on the part of al Sadr, other Shia clerics and politicians, and the US military to bring him into the political process. We have compared materials from these two time periods. Materials for Nasrallah during the war with Israel in the summer of 2006 were compared with materials surrounding Hezbollah's push to become part of the Lebanese government's leadership.

Al Sadr's scores, when compared to those of the norming groups, indicate a pragmatic leadership style during the 2003–2004 period when he perceived violence as "the name of the game." He was working within the constraints he viewed were affecting his followers in Sadr City on the ground and what he viewed the US military and Sunni insurgents were trying to do to his movement. He was responding to the pushes and pulls of the environment and working on preserving his leadership. He was constantly seeking information from the environment in order to know what to do next – his focus continuously on how to deal with the needs of the poor who resided in Sadr City whom he considered his responsibility as well as the maintenance of the militia that he viewed as critical to providing security for those he served. During this time he considered politics as conflict-prone but manageable; the important thing was to take advantage of opportunities that the situation made available.

As he moved to engage in the political process in 2005–2006, al Sadr's scores suggest that his leadership style became more strategic. He began to challenge the constraints in his environment instead of trying to work within them. But his challenge was indirect, behind the scenes; learning where the levers of power were, he worked informally to advance his agenda and to test out potential moves. Still very open to information from the environment, he began to work all sides of an issue broadening the constituencies that he viewed as important. Even more than before, al Sadr focused on the process and political timing. He pursued "a dual strategy – rebuilding his militia even as he capitalized on his control of key ministries, like Health and Transportation, to provide services to the poor and jobs to his followers" (Bartholet 2006: 33). By this time, however, he had begun to see politics more as a zero-sum game in which there were winners and losers and the role of the leader was to deal with threats and come out on top.

Nasrallah's scores, when compared to the scores of the norming groups, indicate our third leadership style when he is engaged in the political process. He is a leader with an agenda that he is pushing – our ideologue leadership style – when working for what he perceives as the important role that Hezbollah can, and indeed should, play in the Lebanese political system. He challenges the powers that be directly and tends to seek out only that information from the environment that can be used to persuade them of his cause. His focus throughout is on the survival of Hezbollah and the important work that he views this organization is doing on behalf of the growing Shia population in Lebanon that are among the country's poorer peoples. Although Nasrallah views politics as conflict-prone, his focus is on taking advantage of the opportunities that he perceives are ever present to advancing his goals.

The Nasrallah we see in his scores during the war with Israel in the summer of 2006 is the strategic leader. Although still challenging constraints in his environment directly, he is very open to contextual information, seeking out data and reports on what is going on from as wide a set of sources as is possible. His moves are incremental as he tests what is feasible before taking any action. Although his focus is still on process and the survival of his organization, Nasrallah has become somewhat more problem-oriented. His focus moves between process and problem depending on the situation. Moreover, his orientation to politics also becomes context-specific; when conflict arises, one deals with it on a case-by-case basis rather than by some rule-bound orthodoxy.

In the cases of both al Sadr and Nasrallah, how they exercised leadership differed during periods of violence and periods where they were engaged in the political process. To understand what is happening as movements twist and turn between violence and political engagement, these two case studies suggest it may be critically important to learn how their leaders are operating. The two case studies indicate the presence of all three leadership styles. They also suggest that the strategic leadership style may facilitate use of the other two types since it falls midway between the leader with an agenda – the ideologue – and the pragmatist. The direction of movement from the strategic leadership style is hinted at in the way in which the strategic leader naturally challenges constraints. Strategic leaders like Nasrallah who tend to challenge constraints directly are more likely to choose an ideologue – or advocate – style of leadership when they move away from being more strategic, whereas strategic leaders like al Sadr who challenge constraints indirectly or more informally and behind the scenes appear more likely to become pragmatic when they change.

Conclusion

We have tried to make the case that leaders can matter as grass roots groups and organizations make decisions to engage in violence or to become incorporated into the political process. And we have stressed that leadership is more than just one person, the leader, but involves considerations of the needs of constituents, relationships with those constituents, and the impact of context. Leadership style has been used here as a proxy for these ingredients of leadership. The data that we have provided on the leaders of African independence movements and two more current leaders who want to see their organizations count in the political systems developing in their countries indicate some of the ramifications that leadership style can have. And the data show that leadership styles can change with the context – some leaders being more adept at responding to changing conditions than others. The content analysis tool that we have used to learn more about leaders – Profiler Plus and its leadership trait analysis – provides a mechanism for others interested in studying particular groups and movements to use to understand the effects of leadership style. It facilitates us putting leaders and leadership into the mix of factors that are considered relevant to answering the question regarding when groups will move from violence to political engagement.

Note

1   The authors would like to thank Azamat Sakiev for his assistance with the analyses reported in this chapter as well as participants in the conference that launched this volume for their perceptive insights and suggestions.

References

Bartholet, J. (2006) Sword of the Shia. *Newsweek*, 4: 26–36.

Bass, B.M. (1990) *Bass & Stogdill's Handbook of Leadership.* New York: Free Press.

Fiedler, F.E. and Garcia, J.E. (1987) *New Approaches to Leadership, Cognitive Resources and Organizational Performance.* New York: Wiley.

Fiedler, F.E., Chemers, M.M. and Mahar, L. (1976) *Improving Leadership Effectiveness: The Leader Match Concept.* New York: Wiley.

Hargrove, E.C. (1989) Two Conceptions of Institutional Leadership. In *Leadership and Politics: New Perspectives in Political Science*, edited by B.D. Jones. Lawrence: University Press of Kansas.

Hermann, M.G. ed. (1977) *A Psychological Examination of Political Leaders.* New York: Free Press.

Hermann, M.G. (1980) Explaining Foreign Policy Behavior Using Personal Characteristics of Political Leaders. *International Studies Quarterly*, 24: 7–46.

Hermann, M.G. (1986) The Ingredients of Leadership. In *Political Psychology: Contemporary Problems and Issues*, edited by M.G. Hermann. San Francisco: Jossey-Bass.

Hermann, M.G. (1987) Assessing the Foreign Policy Orientations of Sub-Saharan African Leaders. In *Role Theory and Foreign Policy Analysis*, edited by S.G. Walker. Durham, NC: Duke University Press.

Hermann, M.G. (2003) Validity and Limitations of Generational Change. In *The Next Generation of World Leaders*, edited by the Strategic Assessment Group. Washington, DC: Central Intelligence Agency.

Hermann, M.G. (2005) Assessing Leadership Style: A Trait Analysis. In *The Psychological Assessment of Political Leaders*, edited by J.D. Post. Ann Arbor: University of Michigan Press.

Hermann, M.G. (2008) Using Content Analysis to Study Public Figures. In *Qualitative Analysis in International Relations*, edited by A. Klotz and D. Prakash. New York: Palgrave.

Hermann, M.G. and Hagan, J.D. (1998) International Decision Making: Leadership Matters. *Foreign Policy*, 110 (Spring).

Hermann, M.G. and Hermann, C.F. (1989) Who Makes Foreign Policy and How: An Empirical Inquiry. *International Studies Quarterly*, 33: 361–387.

Hermann, M.G. and Kegley, C.W. (1995) Rethinking Democracy and International Peace: Perspectives from Political Psychology. *International Studies Quarterly*, 39: 511–533.

Hermann, M.G. and Preston, T. (1998) Presidents, Leadership Style, and the Advisory Process. In *Domestic Sources of American Foreign Policy*, edited by J. McCormick and E.R. Wittkopf. New York: Rowman & Littlefield.

Hermann, M.G., Preston, T., Korany, B. and Shaw, T.M. (2001) Who Leads Matters: The Effects of Powerful Individuals. *International Studies Review*, 3 (2): 83–131.

Kaarbo, J. and Hermann, M.G. (1998) Leadership Styles of Prime Ministers: How Individual Differences Affect the Foreign Policymaking Process. *Leadership Quarterly*, 9: 243–263.

Kille, K.J. (2006) *From Manager to Visionary: The Secretary-General of the United Nations.* New York: Palgrave Macmillan.

Kotter, J.P. and Lawrence, P.R. (1974) *Mayors in Action: Five Approaches to Urban Governance.* New York: Wiley.

Kowert, P.A. (2002) *Groupthink or Deadlock*. Albany: State University of New York Press.

Mitchell, D. (2005) *Making Foreign Policy: Presidential Management of the Decision-Making Process*. Burlington, VT: Ashgate.

Nixon, R.M. (1982) *Leaders*. New York: Richard Warner Books.

Preston, T. (2001) *The President and His Inner Circle: Leadership Style and the Advisory Process in Foreign Affairs*. New York: Columbia University Press.

Preston, T. and Hermann, M.G. (2003) Presidential Leadership Style and the Foreign Policy Advisory Process. In *The Domestic Sources of American Foreign Policy*, edited by E.R. Wittkopf and J. McCormick. New York: Rowman & Littlefield.

Schafer, M. (2000) Issues in Assessing Psychological Characteristics at a Distance. *Political Psychology*, 21 (special issue).

Stewart, P.D., Hermann, M.G. and Hermann, C.F. (1989) Modeling the 1970 Soviet Decision to Support Egypt. *American Political Science Review*, 83: 35–59.

Winter, D.G. (1987) Leader Appeal, Leader Performance, and the Motive Profiles of Leaders and Followers: A Study of American Presidents and Elections. *Journal of Personality and Social Psychology*, 52: 196–202.

Winter, D.G., Hermann, M.G., Weintraub, W. and Walker, S.G. (1991) The Personalities of Bush and Gorbachev Measured at a Distance: Procedures, Portraits, and Policy. *Political Psychology*, 12: 215–243.

Wriggins, W.H. (1969) *The Ruler's Imperative: Strategies for Political Survival in Asia and Africa*. New York: Columbia University Press.

Wright, Q. (1942) *A Study of War*. Chicago: University of Chicago Press.

4 Challenges to conflict transformation from the streets

Elham Atashi

Introduction

The transition of violence to peace often begins when different factions enter into negotiations and start what is commonly known as a peace process. Among the challenges to implementing a political agreement and fulfilling the promises made during formal peace processes is gaining public support on the ground. The literature on post-conflict transformation emphasizes that the sustainability of peace agreements requires top-down and bottom-up approaches or, in other words, involvement from the entire society (Miall *et al.* 1999). Some scholars acknowledge that peace-building approaches must target the populations that typically experience the violence and trauma associated with war (Lederach 1997). For instance, Saunders (2001) argues that peace agreements will not produce peace until they focus on transforming relationships among citizens on the ground or a "public peace process." However, little is known about effective strategies to enhance the support of the people on the ground or the factors that may lead them to withdraw their support for peace processes and renew violence.

Following a peace agreement, the path to the transformation of a war-shattered society often begins with the implementation of various peace-building measures. This chapter is focused on the post-agreement period and whether such measures deter or provide new conditions for violence. I explore the challenges from the ground and the gap between the national and local contexts. First, a peace agreement may lead to transformation of conflict at a national level, but local level problems, such as inequality, divisions, mistrust, economic deprivation, fear and violence, may persist. In other words, transformation measures may not transfer to localities. Local problems in these areas can lead to new splinter groups ready to take up the cause of those marginalized by the peace process. Second, despite the acknowledgment that a peace process needs support from "the ground," the term as commonly used is fraught with conceptual ambiguity. The same is true for "people on the ground," where there is little reflection about the persons to whom this label refers. Who are the people on the ground? In post-conflict societies, can all civilians be considered as a uniform category?

People on the ground

The term "on the ground" suggests ordinary people or civilians who live with the realities of a violent conflict. The civilian category distinguishes them from militant, state and armed forces, but does not differentiate among the context-specific experiences of people on the ground. Literature in the field of conflict transformation would suggest dealing with a "residual" group of people – not "leaders," "influentials," "elites" or "Track I." Because this is a residual category, in past research if not demographically, there is no accepted collective term to refer to civilians. Lederach (1997) has described them with the term "grass roots." A colloquial expression in the Arab world refers to them collectively as "the street people." Other scholars have referred to them as "the people" or the "local population." An older Marxist tradition refers to them as "the masses." None of these is a perfect term, and all come with some conceptual or ideological baggage. Referring to this complex and non-homogenous group as "residents of conflict zones" may be a more appropriate term, yet it does not distinguish them based on their demographic experiences of conflict.

Various publications point to the significance of "the streets" and civilian experiences of conflict, based on the demographic division method of separating areas into those that have experienced high or low levels of violence (Boal 1978; Murray 1982; Poole 1983; Shirlow and McGovern 1997; Smyth and Fay 2000). Although these studies do not deal with challenges in conflict transformation from particular demographic zones, they do examine the significance of space and specific social and political conditions. These studies observe that the level of violence in a society may be context-specific, limited to certain cities, locations or neighborhoods. Cairns and Wilson (1991) argue that in addition to the meaning and impact on people of their experiences of violence, there is a need to take account of the characteristics of people's environment, including the levels of overt violence that will vary by location. For example, political violence in Northern Ireland has mainly touched upon the lives of working class communities living in certain areas from which most of the recruits, as well as victims of paramilitary groups, are also drawn (Coulter 1999). In their examination of sectarian violence in India, Mehta and Chatterji (2007) argue that the pattern of communal violence is isolated to certain areas within particular neighborhoods. They point out that historically the narrative of violence and the impact, experience and perceptions of victimhood are unique to residents living in specific zones – often the slums. This creates boundaries and separates these residents from the local level.

The merit of my argument lies in widening the role of demographic space and violence and their effects on residents, based on different social environments. If a conflict is to be transformed on the ground, distinction among civilians based on experiences of conflict seems pertinent. Residents who have experienced the highest level of socio-economic deprivation, violence, civil unrest and uprisings in the time period of the violent conflict may be considered as being "directly" affected. In other words, the communities that are living in the "direct zones" of conflict consider that they bore the brunt of the devastation caused by the high level of violence there. The other cluster is "indirect zones" of conflict, which are areas where residents are not directly impacted by high levels of economic deprivation, violence, uprisings and political movements, but are nevertheless affected indirectly by the impact of conflict on their lives. In Northern Ireland, for example, Belfast and Derry–Londonderry had the highest death rate of any area throughout the conflict. However, not all communities within Belfast were equally affected on both sides. The number of deaths is concentrated in particular areas scattered within Belfast, which I consider "direct zones." Considerable variation exists between areas, in terms of socio-economic deprivation and the level of psychological trauma, based on both death rates of residents and death rates for those killed within specific areas (Smyth 2000). Since conflict and violence affect the people on the ground asymmetrically, this will play a role in the development of appropriate measures to address context-specific needs to transform society from war to a sustainable peace.

Peace benefits

The term "peace dividend" has often been defined as various incentives in the prospects of peace as opposed to war. Several studies have explored the role of economic and social peace benefits based on external aid and the potential to bring about positive results in different stages of a conflict (Seliktar 1998; Vayrynen 1997). In the negotiation stage, different set of peace benefits are often used as incentives to create stakeholders among the different factions that may be opposed to ending violence (Sriram and Wermester 2003). For example, Doyle (1997) suggests that third parties can enhance consent among parties to end violence by offering peace benefits in the form of diplomatic and economic measures. Zaher (2003) considers peace benefits as a strategy to reduce the likelihood of future "spoilers." She argues that the structure of benefits can lock parties in the cycle of commitment to peace, since going back to war would not only mean factoring in the costs of war, but also the loss of peace benefits. Stedman's (1997) study on spoilers defines them as an obstacle to a peaceful settlement by actors directly involved in a conflict. He argues that if spoilers succeed in the post-agreement period, violence can escalate to a higher stage with more casualties than during the actual conflict. This was seen in the Angola and the Rwanda peace processes. The link between achieving peace benefits and creating stakeholders is extended to other spoilers.

Darby (2001), for example, considers former militants as a type of spoiler and adds that not only should they be included in the negotiation process, but they should also be provided with peace incentives to integrate into normal society.

What about people on the ground? Can they be considered as spoilers if they withdraw their support for a peace agreement? People on the ground derive their power from their ability to disrupt the peace process negatively by withdrawing their support or by influencing the peace process positively through their continuing support. The power to disrupt or support the peace process gives ordinary people an atypical power, which is often ignored in discourse of the post-agreement period. If peace incentives can play a role in winning over factions at the negotiation table, can they do the same on the ground? Understanding expectations on the ground can assure that peace benefits are created at the political, as well as the ground level. For example, Bartoli *et al.* in Chapter 10 of this volume discuss that people in Mozambique felt a direct ownership of the peace process as transformation strategies had an impact in the streets.

Peace benefits can help people on the ground to perceive that their minimal expectations are fulfilled to a satisfactory level, offering a sense of normalcy and improvement in life, at least when compared to conditions prior to the agreement (Atashi 2005). In considering themselves as stakeholders, people on the ground would feel a sense of individual and collective responsibility to support the agreement, because stability in the agreement would translate into continuous benefits.

Rothchild (2003) warns that failure to invest in the peace process by creating peace benefits in the form of minimal opportunities after the war may lead to an increase in public frustration and a possible weakening of support. However, creating opportunities on the ground may not benefit all communities. In terms of the immediate objectives in a post-conflict society, I am arguing that boosting support by creating peace benefits in direct zones should have a priority. This requires a shift in understanding and implementing peacebuilding measures that often address the ground level as a uniform category. The proposed approach is not very different to the acknowledgment by policy makers that, in planning and developing a response to conflict situations, a context-specific, rather than a universal blueprint, is more likely to bring about a successful outcome.

Impact from the streets

Gurr (1970) argues that a group's route to violence begins with dissatisfaction and frustration with present conditions and the belief that it is entitled to more rights or resources than it presently possesses. The eruption of violence may be sudden or gradual, as discussed by Kriesberg (2007). Violence in the post-agreement period can be fueled by dissatisfaction with tangible improvements in particular demographic zones. Over time, the residents in these zones may give vent to their rage against the political actors and institutions they find responsible for the deteriorating circumstances. Despite initial support for an agreement on the ground, lack of improvements in certain zones may lead to decreasing public support. For example, in the May 1998 referendum, the people of Northern Ireland voted in favor of a peace agreement by a 71 percent majority, providing it with a substantial mandate. Since then, support for the agreement has faltered as the raised expectations of improvements in quality of life have not been met, particularly in communities worst affected by the violence (Smyth 2004).

Although the perception of deprivation among groups and the mobilization of political action have been topics of extensive research, the impact on undermining the sustainability of a peace process has remained marginal. In the post-agreement stage, dissatisfaction with lack of improvements on the ground may provoke different reactions. Decreasing public support, for example, may lead to the victory of hard-liners in elections, civil disobedience, unrest, rebellion or, at worst, violence. All of this could potentially undermine the stability of the peace process. In other words, people on the ground choose different strategies to demonstrate their frustration with lack of improvements and violence may be a component of the strategies they choose. Many factors influence this choice, as discussed by Kriesberg and Millar in Chapter 2 of this volume. For example, available resources play a role on the decision by groups to use violent or non-violent strategies to achieve their objectives. Given that post-conflict societies face an alarmingly high risk of reversion to violence, identifying areas where levels of violence and socio-economic deprivation had been the highest during the conflict and creating stakeholders in these areas in return for public support can be considered as a preventative approach.

Transforming the streets

In what way can transformation strategies adapt a context-specific agenda to incorporate the high-impact areas referred to here as direct zones? A violent conflict can lead to considerable decline in the ability of a war-torn country to function. Often the first step involves elections leading to a governance structure. However, restoring political institutions has to be balanced with addressing people's expectations on the ground. Paris (2004) argues that the preference for rapid democratic and economic liberalization policies make it difficult to provide the inhabitants of war-shattered states with tangible improvements. Macro policies may not address people's expectations for tangible improvements. For example, after the elections and the establishment of the new government in Afghanistan, many Afghans supported the newly elected government and democratization efforts by President Karzai. For the majority of Afghan people, the promise of a democratic system had brought expectations of improvements in the quality of life. Rahmani (2006) points out a sharp increase in levels of insecurity and violence in Afghan areas where the government has lost its support and credibility in the streets. This has strengthened the power of warlords who control and provide stability in most of the provinces.

Peace agreements are often followed by democratic elections, as seen in Northern Ireland, Mozambique, South Africa and El Salvador. Terrence Lyons argues in this volume that elections after violent conflicts are considered a crucial step in moving a society from war to peace. Elections also provide people on the ground with an opportunity to select the new transitional government. A group's victory in post-agreement elections can be one way of fulfilling the promises to people on the ground in the hopes for continual support. For example, many analysts consider El Salvador's transition to peace as a success. The 1992 peace agreement was followed by elections leading to the demobilization and transformation of the FMLN into a political party. But political victory aside, they had made promises to implement social and economic programs to benefit people on the ground. Through its election victory, the FMLN had been able to reduce some of the socio-economic grievances that had led to its taking up arms. In other words, elections were the means rather than an end to bring about tangible improvements on the ground.

Mani (2002) argues that political power and the holding of post-conflict elections do not necessarily lead to economic equality for certain sectors of society that had traditionally been excluded. Furthermore, electoral power and political equality may not be a priority for all people in society. This suggests that following a peace agreement, exploring people's expectations from a peace process can be useful.

Expectations on the ground

If on-the-ground expectations are influenced by experiences of a conflict, in what way can transformation strategies be specific in direct and indirect zones? Evidently, strategies such as dealing with socio-economic, security, violence and reconciliation dynamics need to differ according to the priorities of residents in each zone. I examine each of these dynamics.

Socio-economics

An interesting pattern among respondents in an extensive study of "in the street" expectations of the Good Friday Agreement in Northern Ireland (Atashi 2005) revealed that residents in indirect and direct zones had very different expectations. In indirect zones, most residents considered issues such as political and economic stability as important priorities in their expectations from the peace process. In contrast, for the Protestant and Catholic communities located in direct zones, employment opportunity contributing to a better life was among the most expected results of the peace process (Atashi 2005).

This pattern is significant in two ways. First, it demonstrates that despite sectarian divisions, the majority of residents in direct zones were experiencing the *same* problems. *Both* communities had expected that employment opportunity contributing to a better life would be a result of the peace process. I use the term opportunity, because clearly it was not just the availability of more money, but also the total absence of socio-economic opportunity and the apathy of residents in these areas that required improvement. Second, many in direct zones felt dissatisfied with improvements in their communities. They experienced very little difference in their lives despite elections and macro political changes brought about as the result of the peace agreement. Residents of direct zones, which had demographically been affected the most throughout "the conflict," were the people who were left behind by "the peace." "Peace benefits" that are distributed unevenly can add a layer to divisions between the "gots" and the "leftouts" in an already divided society.

A similar pattern can be observed in the post-Oslo period. The lives of Palestinians living in refugee camps had not changed, while certain demographic areas in Gaza and the West Bank had benefited from the peace process. These included Jericho, Bethlehem, and Ramallah, where the head offices of PLO were located. In the areas some businesses had prospered, freedom of movement was eased, and employment opportunities had increased. Those who benefited were the new but influential "economic class" that had emerged under Oslo with privileged access to economic gains in the private sector. Hammami and Tamari (2001) give the example of Palestinian owners of the Jericho casino, along with other new businesses, such as hotels and resorts, advertising and telecommunications companies, and major contracting firms that had benefited from the post-Oslo agreement. This was due, in part, to donor investments in infrastructure. Those living in the refugee camps in the Gaza Strip and the West Bank continued to depend on international aid agencies for their most basic human needs, such as food, water, education and health. The refugee camps had suffered continued socio-economic deprivation and violence throughout the conflict. Refugees had the minimal expectation of secure and well-paid employment resulting from the Oslo Agreement, as well as the perception of equality in seeking opportunities. Many began to ask: "Why should we support a process that does not make a difference to our lives?" (Atashi 2005). As Nigel Parsons notes in this volume, this also discredited Arafat's legitimacy and strengthened other groups such as Hamas. The declining role of the Palestinian Authority in providing social services in Palestinian areas that continued to be marginalized, despite a peace agreement, created a vacuum. Hamas was able to expand its support on the ground by addressing the minimal expectations of residents in socio-economically deprived areas (direct zones) by building schools and health clinics. The lack of peace benefits in these areas points toward structural explanations connected with persistent violence, social exclusion and inadequacy in transformation strategies. This is a dangerous pattern. If the benefits of peace do not materialize in these zones, residents may begin to direct their frustration with the lack of improvement directly by opposing a process that has further marginalized them.

Violence

In the post-conflict period, the pattern of violence may change from outgroup to in-group, from high- or low-intensity political violence to various forms of crime. Given that violence in the post-agreement period often occurs in the same areas where violence had persisted throughout conflict, direct zones are placed in a particularly vulnerable position. The absence of legitimate state police and security in these communities often provides a vacuum for the emergence of alternative, non-state security forces. The same threat that gives power to militias, paramilitaries, gangs and criminals during conflict helps to sustain violence after an agreement. The threat of punishment secures respect and continuity in the power of such forces.

As argued by Juan Gutierrez in this volume, the violence affecting the Basque Country and Spain has different forms, happens in different areas at different levels, and is exerted by different institutions and groups. Gutierrez notes that the pattern of violence in the Basque conflict has continually changed and is performed by various groups loyal to ETA, with the addition of low-intensity organized "street violence." A peace agreement may include provisions by third parties to monitor the rules of the ceasefire. This is often translated as sectarian or political violence against members of the other community. But agreements do not include provisions for dealing with crime and local low-intensity violent activities. Other forms of violence may exist, though the groups responsible for such activities may not be in violation of a peace agreement. This poses a challenge in dealing with these types of violence. As Bruce Dayton argues in this volume, third-party intermediaries play various roles, among them ending political violence and monitoring a ceasefire. However, they may have less incentive to intervene in local violence, as peace agreements do not generally make provisions for the changing patterns of violence.

In Northern Ireland, for example, punishment attacks are often carried out against "in-group" members rather than members of the "other" community. Therefore their impact and level of significance has not been given the same attention as attacks committed against members of "other" group. Neil Jarman, in his assessment of the patterns of violence in Northern Ireland since the peace agreement, argues that "the combined figures for beatings and shootings are running at significantly higher levels than before the ceasefire agreement" (Jarman 2004: 423). Violence committed against the members of other community is considered "sectarian" and therefore has the potential to spill over to the political level and impact the peace process. In contrast, violence committed toward "in-group" members, such as punishment beatings, lawlessness, kidnapping, criminal activities and attacks, are considered local problems, a local nuisance or as the normal pattern of violence in direct zones. Despite a peace agreement, paramilitary and other militarized groups in direct zones often maintain control by changing their strategies from political violence to organized crime. In Colombia, despite the Ralito I Accord and promises of demilitar-ization, the far-right paramilitary group, AUC, continues to maintain control of numerous city neighborhoods (International Crisis Group 2004). Since they are termed local crime issues, they fall outside of issues that a peace agreement could deal with and are regarded by the political leaders as insignificant because they are not political or "sectarian" in nature and have less impact on the political process.

The change in the pattern of violence could be associated with the com-petition for power, suspension of political institutions, lack of order, and the question of whom should be trusted to take care of security issues in direct zones in the absence of legitimate state forces and policing. Alterna-tive security forces and paramilitary's position of power in direct zones also meant that feuds over control and direction between rival organizations became common, particularly after the peace agreement. Michael Poole (2004) argues that in Northern Ireland, despite the ceasefires and the peace agreement, paramilitary activities persist because of a complex rela-tionship between paramilitaries and political leaders. On the one hand, political leaders publicly denounce paramilitary violence while they also use paramilitaries to exercise their political influence in communities. Fear from criminal and paramilitary groups adds to the increasing acuity among people on the ground that the state remains incapable and ineffec-tive to exercise power and authority in direct zones.

Security

In conflicts in which the police are considered repressive and dominated by one ethnic group, measures to ensure security for everyone may be part of the peace agreement. Even when the agreement contains provisions for extensive police reform, lack of trust based on previous experiences with the police force may hinder implementation efforts. When the police or the military is distrusted or unable to protect its citizens, the citizens are likely to go elsewhere, looking for guarantors for their safety. A simplistic approach would point out the violent and destructive nature of parami-tary activities. However, a closer analysis reveals a complex pattern brought about by the demand for security from certain sectors of society. In North-ern Ireland, the paramilitary organizations on both sides provide much more than a speedy, if violent solution to antisocial behavior and local crime. They can also provide a sense of safety, protectedness and psychological security. The perception is that there is someone to call on if you have problems and need a solution. Often in a post-agreement stage, levels of insecurity within communities can increase as a result of uncertainty, an ineffective police force and lack of order. Given public insecurities, paramilitary organizations tend to expand their roles, as residents turn to non-state groups to address their grievances, therefore increasing reliance in paramilitary groups. For example, the leaders of the paramilitary group in Colombia, the AUC, consider themselves as heroes for protecting civilians in certain zones (Arnson 2005). Many landowners relied on AUC for security as they were frustrated by the government's inability to provide them with protection against the left-wing FARC.

In the post-agreement period, paramilitary members and combatants adjust to the new political environment by constraining and reshaping their previous activities within the boundaries of the agreement, carefully going around rigid definitions of the ceasefire rules. In Northern Ireland, despite the peace agreement and periods of decreased violence by paramilitary organizations, residents in direct zones continue to live in fear of paramilitaries (Atashi 2005). Ceasefires do not always lead to a significant decrease in violence associated with paramilitary organizations in direct zones.

The South African and the Irish peace process have both faced challenges in drawing members of various criminal gangs and paramilitary organizations into the state security forces. In South Africa, the post-Apartheid government provided a fertile ground for criminal violence. One way to address this would be to enlist paramilitary members into the security forces of the state. In South Africa, following the peace agreement, a general observation can be made that while some former members of paramilitary organizations have joined the police forces, many have not been drawn into the discipline of the state and society. Criminal gangs are reported to have become an integral dynamic of the urban social structures of the poorest sections of the South African black population, unaffected by peace (Toit 2001). In rural areas, some villages were reported to have resorted to lawless actions of self-protection on their own, having completely abandoned the hope of state authorities being able to secure their safety. As is the case with Iraq, private armies have appeared in many residential areas, providing protection to communities, particularly in rural areas. In Guatemala, following the peace agreement, criminal violence has increased and the death rate has reached the same level as during the war (Allison in this volume). In El Salvador, despite the transformation of FMLN into a political party, many organized gangs operate in certain areas in cities and the countryside, becoming the chief source of public insecurity. The peace agreement addressed public security specifically but neglected to deal with crime. Despite the success of demobilization, many former combatants remained unemployed. The continuity of violence in certain areas has seriously affected the state's capacity to respond to the rise in organized crime (Costa 2001).

In the post-agreement stage, many paramilitary organizations in direct zones find the use of violence less appealing on ideological grounds. The quest for maintaining traditional power and continuation of an active role in communities leads some paramilitary organizations to turn to other means of control and power. In the absence of a unified collective ideology, acts of violence become privatized (for personal power, money through illegal commercial trades and advantage) and individualized (power feuds). In an effort to increase personal gains, the criminal and violent activities of paramilitary organizations can often destabilize the peace process.

Lessons from other cases demonstrate that the sustainability of violence can be addressed by dealing with security in direct zones. In Sierra Leone, the Lome Peace Agreement was followed by a brief period of violence leading to elections in 2002. Since then, the absence of political strife and a remarkable decrease in criminal violence has contributed to the sustainability of the peace agreement. This has been attributed to the disarmament, demobilization and reintegration (DDR) program to disarm and rehabilitate more than 70,000 combatants who took part in the country's brutal war (World Bank Brief 2002). The successful example of Sierra Leone can be used to draw important lessons in measures contributing to security on the ground.

The relationship between lack of employment opportunities and membership in non-state security forces that exist in direct zones needs to be explored further. Given the high level of unemployment in direct zones, criminal groups may be seen by local youth as an alternative means to gain income. Creating peace benefits, by providing education and job opportunities among the youth, can be considered as a counter-strategy to recruitment by paramilitaries (Collier 2007). In the case of Sierra Leone, transformation strategies in direct zones have focused on the reintegration of former combatants. More effort is needed to prevent recruitment in the first place by locating the demographic areas where such patterns subsist.

Reconciliation

Various studies in conflict transformation regard reconciliation and restoring relations between people on the ground as an important component in preventing future violence (Montville 1993; Mani 2002; Rothstein 1999; Lederach 1997). While reconciliation may be an essential part of the post-conflict transition, one of the challenges is the assumption that in the aftermath of a conflict, people on the ground are all equally interested in dealing with the past. Mendeloff (2004), for example, argues that truth seeking and dealing with the past without taking into account the specific social conditions may threaten post-conflict stability and lead to reemergence of violence. In the post-conflict period, dealing with the past – considered as necessary on a national level particularly among international third parties, political leaders and the elites – might not be a priority for everyone. Shaw (2005) argues that in Sierra Leone, people in urban and rural locations were divided on supporting a truth commission. In several communities people would not participate in such a process. Shaw cautions that such a process must have support, not only among the international community, but also among ordinary people on the ground. Often, such measures may be considered as a luxury to people in the front lines of conflict who often seem to be much less interested in a truth commission than they are in safety, having enough to eat, jobs, housing, health, education and future prospects for their children.

Furthermore, in post-conflict societies, truth about uncovering the past and breaking the silence, as vital as they may be, do not necessarily lead to healing while certain segments of the society continue to suffer from violence, inequality, social and economic deprivation. Brounéus (2008), for example, argues that in Rwanda, the women who testified in the community-style reconciliation courts, known as Gacaca, have experienced marginalization and isolation by their community during and after the process. The literature on reconciliation suggests that the victim's testimony will lead to healing and conciliatory effects (Lederach 2001). However, Brounéus questions whether these goals can be achieved without consideration of the post-conflict social environment, which also plays a role in healing. In the post-testimony period, far from the experience of healing, the majority of the women felt a great sense of fear and insecurity because they have been continually threatened and harassed within their communities. Indeed, the suffering of past and the memories of the past victims can only be considered *in the past* if there are no further victims *in the present*. The purpose of a reconciliation process in any society coping with a violent past should *not* be to erase all the memories of past suffering, but to prevent further suffering. If the peace process cannot guarantee that there will be no further "victims" and "suffering," there cannot be an atmosphere of forward and future thinking leading to reconciliation. Views and perceptions leading to expectations in dealing with the past vary across different zones of conflict.

Communities recall the suffering, fear and misery of having lived in a violent conflict differently, based on their experiences of the past. In indirect zones, suffering associated with pre-agreement times may be considered a thing of the past associated with the context of conflict. In the meantime, there is a demographic continuity; those who suffered the most often continue to suffer in the post-agreement period.

If safety is a key component of healing and reconciliation, then the post-agreement state may not lead to this environment in direct zones. The necessary element for the transformation from victimhood and suffering to healing is the perception of security and safety. Healing must at some level depend on the group or individual's recovery environment. In order to heal, the group must begin to feel safe from the possibility of any further unjustified aggression, i.e. safe from the past happening again. Healing cannot begin without establishing an integrative view of safety that includes physical, as well as psychological dynamics. A peace agreement and its established political and economic structures can lead to a decrease in perceptions of suffering on a national level, but local grievances in direct zones may remain unresolved. Once safety and security in these communities is dealt with, victims can begin the process of healing. This would suggest that healing and dealing with the past are intertwined with feelings of safety and cannot be isolated without addressing the components necessary to achieve reconciliation.

Conclusion

The approach outlined in this chapter can be a way to enhance the involvement of the general public in the transformation of violence to peace by exploring the complex structure of the post-agreement period as perceived by people on the ground.

I make a few suggestions in response to the challenges discussed in this chapter. First, by examining expectations, political leaders can determine the focus of security, social and economic development strategies in the transformation of a conflict on the ground. Following a peace agreement, the new government should assess the situation on the ground by locating direct and indirect zones. Areas where violence and deprivation had been consistent throughout the conflict should be considered a priority. This strategy should direct tangible resources that will create opportunities among the people who have been impacted the most by conflict and create structures that can distribute them evenly. Given that providing benefits leads to perceptions of improvements, violence from anti-agreement and various spoiler groups is less likely to gain popular support. It would also provide ground-level assurance that political leaders are active and involved in addressing local concerns. Hence, "the streets" would have a greater incentive to support the transformation to peace.

Addressing practical challenges such as: (*a*) employment and job security; (*b*) investment in housing, education and health; (*c*) safety and security; and (*d*) fair allocation and realistic distribution of funds as assessed by the needs of communities will go a long way in keeping the streets engaged, rather than marginalized by transformation strategies. Tangible improvements will reinforce trust in the transitional political structure enforced by the peace agreement. It will also signal the state's credibility in addressing the minimal expectations of residents in direct zones and prevent the ability of spoiler groups to fill that vacuum. Finally, in the transition from war to peace, transformation strategies need to take a more comprehensive approach in defining security. It should include dealing with crime in direct zones and preventative measures. The demand for disarmament should be followed by monitoring the availability of small arms, particularly in areas with a history of paramilitary activity. Third parties cannot remain benign to the changing patterns of violence in the post-conflict period. They can play a role in more broadly redefining violence in the post-conflict period.

The implementers in the post-agreement period need to recognize that the effects of creating peace benefits that alleviate the level of hardship in direct zones can be a productive strategy in gaining positive support. Building a stronger bridge and narrowing the gap between academic research and practical approaches can deliver what conflict transformation strategies set out to do: to make a positive difference in people's lives.

References

Arnson, C. J. (eds.) (2005) The Peace Process in Colombia with the Autodefensas Unidas de Colombia – AUC, Woodrow Wilson Report on the Americas, No 13.

Atashi, E. (2005) The Peace Process in the Street, unpublished thesis, Institute for Conflict Analysis and Resolution, George Mason University.

Boal, F. (1978) Territoriality on the Shankill–Falls Divide, Belfast, *Irish Geography*, no. 6: 30–50.

Brounéus, K. (2008) Truth-Telling as Talking Cure? Insecurity and Retraumatization in the Rwandan Gacaca Courts, Security Dialogue, vol. 39, no. 1, 55–76.

Cairns, E. and Wilson, R. (1991) Psychological Coping and Political Violence: Northern Ireland, in Y. Alexander and A. O'Day (eds.) *The Irish Terrorism Experience*, Worcester: Billing and Sons Ltd.

Collier, P. (2007) Post-Conflict Recovery: How Should Policies be Distinctive? Centre for the Study of African of Economics, Oxford University. Online, available at: http://users.ox.ac.uk/~econpco/research/pdfs/PostConflict-Recovery.pdf accessed 16 May 2008.

Costa, G. (2001) Demilitarizing Public Security Lessons from El Salvador, in E. Margarita and S. Studemeister (eds.) *El Salvador Implementation of the Peace Accords*, Washington, DC: United States Institute of Peace Press.

Coulter, C. (1999) Absence of Class Politics in Northern Ireland, in P. Shirlow and P. Stewart (eds.) *Northern Ireland Between Peace and War*, London: Conference of Socialist Economics.

Darby, J. (2001) *The Effects of Violence on Peace Processes*, Washington, DC: United States Institute of Peace Press.

Doyle, M. W. (1997) *Ways of War and Peace: Realism, Liberalism, and Socialism*, New York: Norton.

Gurr, T. R. (1970) *Why Men Rebel*, Princeton, NJ: Princeton University Press.

Hammami, R. and Tamari, S. (2001) The Second Uprising: End or New Beginning?, *Journal of Palestine Studies*, 30 (2), 5–25.

International Crisis Group (2004) Demobilizing the Paramilitaries in Colombia, an Achievable goal? *ICG Latin America Report*, no. 8.

Jarman, N. (2004) Demography, Development and Disorder: Changing Patterns of Interface Areas Report, Belfast: Institute for Conflict Research.

Kriesberg, L. (2007) *Constructive Conflicts: From Escalation to Resolution*, 3rd edn., Lanham, MD: Rowman & Littlefield.

Lederach, J. P. (1997) *Building Peace Sustainable Reconciliation in Divided Societies*, Washington, DC: United States Institute of Peace Press.

Lederach, J. P. (2001) Civil Society and Reconciliation, in C. A. Crocker, F. O. Hampson and P. Aall (eds.) *Turbulent Peace: The Challenges of Managing International Conflict*, Washington, DC: United States Institute of Peace Press.

Mani, R. (2002) *Beyond Retribution, Seeking Justice in the Shadows of War*, Cambridge: Polity Press.

Mehta, D. and Chatterji, R. (2007) *Living With Violence: An Anthropology of Events and Everyday Life*, London: Routledge.

Mendeloff, D. (2004) Truth Seeking, Truth Telling, and Post-Conflict Peacebuilding: Curbing the Enthusiasm?, *International Studies Review*, vol. 6, 355–380.

Miall, H., Ramsbotham, R. and Woodhouse, T. (1999) *Contemporary Conflict Resolution: The Prevention, Management and Transformation of Deadly Conflicts*, Cambridge: Polity Press.

Montville, J. (1993) The Healing Function in Political Conflict Resolution, in D. Sandole and H. W. van der Merwe, (eds.) *Conflict Resolution Theory and Practice: Integration and Application*, Manchester and New York: Manchester University Press.

Murray, R. (1982) Political violence in Northern Ireland 1969–1977, in F. W. Boal and J. N. H. Douglas (eds.) *Integration and Division: Geographical Perspectives on the Northern Ireland Problem*, London: Academic Press.

Paris, R. (2004) *At War's End: Building Peace After Civil Conflict*, Cambridge: Cambridge University Press.

Poole, M. (1983) The Demography of Violence, in J. Darby (ed.) *Northern Ireland, The Background to the Conflict*, Belfast: Appletree Press.

Poole, M. (2004) Has it Made any Difference? The Geographical Impact of the 1994 Ceasefire in Northern Ireland, *Journal of Terrorism and Political Violence*, vol. 16, no. 3, autumn, 401–419.

Rahmani, W. (2006) Domestic Factors Driving the Taliban Insurgency, *Journal of Terrorism Monitor*, vol. 4, issue 13, 29 June.

Rothchild, D. (2003) Third Party Incentives, in C. L. Sirim and K. Wermester (eds.), *From Promise to Practice: Strengthening UN Capacities for the Prevention of Violent Conflicts*, Boulder, CO: Lynne Rienner.

Rothstein, R. (ed.) (1999) *After the Peace, Resistance and Reconciliation*, Boulder, CO: Lynne Rienner.

Saunders, H. (2001) *A Public Peace Process: Sustained Dialogue to Transform Racial and Ethnic Conflicts*, New York: Palgrave Macmillan.

Seliktar, O. (1998) The Economy of Israel and the Peace Process, in I. Peleg (ed.), *The Middle East Peace Process: Interdisciplinary Perspectives*, Albany, NY: SUNY Press.

Shaw, R. (2005) *Rethinking Truth and Reconciliation Commissions: Lessons from Sierra Leone*, Washington, DC: United States Institute for Peace Press.

Shirlow, P. and McGovern, M. (1997) *Who are the people? Unionism, Protestantism and Loyalism in Northern Ireland*, London: Pluto Press.

Smyth, M. (2004) The Process of Demilitarization and the Reversibility of the Peace Process in Northern Ireland, *Terrorism and Political Violence*, vol.16, no. 3, autumn, 544–566.

Smyth, M. and Fay, M. T. (2000) *Personal Accounts from Northern Ireland's Troubles: Public Conflict, Private Loss*, London: Pluto Press.

Sriram, C. L. and Wermester, K. (2003) *From Promise to Practice: Strengthening UN Capacities for the Prevention*, Boulder, CO: Lynne Rienner.

Stedman, S. (1997) Spoiler Problems in Peace Processes, *International Security Journal*, 22 (2), Fall, 5–53.

Toit, P. du (2001) *South Africa's Brittle Peace: The Problem of Post Settlement Violence*, New York: Palgrave.

Vayrynen, R. (1997) Economic Incentives and the Bosnian Peace Process, in D. Cortright (ed.) *The Price of Peace*, Lanham: Rowman & Littlefield.

World Bank Brief (2002) Sierra Leone: Disarmament, Demobilization and Reintegration (DDR), *WBB Africa Region*, no. 81, October 2002.

Zaher, M. J. (2003) Reframing the Spoiler Debate in Peace Processes, in J. Darby and R. Mac Ginty, (eds.) *Contemporary Peacemaking: Conflict, Violence and Peace Processes*, Hampshire: Palgrave MacMillan.

5 Useful but insufficient

Intermediaries in peacebuilding

Bruce W. Dayton

It is tempting to believe that intermediaries are the deciding factor between violence and peace when it comes to intrastate conflicts. Indeed, the literature in conflict resolution and peacebuilding provides a number of dramatic anecdotal stories of intrastate conflicts that were transformed due to the skillful actions of an international mediator, the determination of a committed non-governmental organization (NGO), or the forceful intervention of an international organization. The case studies contained within this book tell a different story. Taken collectively, these cases show that intermediaries do play a critical role in peacebuilding by providing a forum in which adversaries can interact, pressuring stakeholders through coercion or inducements, helping to identify options for settlement, or strengthening democratic institutions once a settlement takes hold. However, the ability of intermediaries to drive peacemaking processes when the parties to the conflict are committed to violent forms of contention is limited. Intermediaries, in other words, are a useful and sometimes necessary component of intrastate peacebuilding, but rarely a sufficient one.

This chapter examines the varied roles played by intermediaries in intrastate conflicts and considers the conditions and contexts that lead armed groups to engage with them. It begins by defining what an intermediary is and then goes on to discuss the different functions that intermediaries perform to help de-escalate violent conflicts. The chapter concludes with a set of observations about the prospects and limits of intermediary activities when it comes to intrastate peacebuilding.

Intermediaries in interstate conflicts

Intermediaries are generally regarded as parties who intervene in disputes for the purpose of influencing or facilitating a settlement, but who do not take sides in the conflict (Princen 1992). They may include judges, arbitrators, government officials, representatives of non-governmental organizations (NGOs), or even private citizens (Burgess 2004). The scope of intermediary work is a matter of some dispute. While some definitions emphasize the intermediary's role as a conduit for information exchange and problem solving alone, it is generally accepted that intermediary activities at the international and intrastate levels may also include coercive measures, such as the application of military force to halt violence.

For the purposes of this chapter I define intermediaries as actors that intervene in conflict situations with the intent to help the conflicting actors transform their conflict from a negative to a more positive state. By including the qualifier that intermediaries must be engaged in positive forms of conflict transformation, I consciously omit from this chapter those intermediary activities that are done primarily in order to advance power, defeat an enemy, or protect parochial political interests. So, for instance, US support of the Contras during the Nicaraguan Civil War or the Soviet intervention in Afghanistan in 1978 would lie outside of the scope of this chapter given that those interventions were conducted to advance strategic interests of one side, rather than to advance a mutually acceptable peace.

Roles, functions, and types of intermediaries

The role and impacts of intermediaries is widely studied in the field of conflict management, particularly in a domestic context where intermediaries have been shown to play a central role in resolving labor-management disputes, public policy controversies, community disputes, and interpersonal conflicts of all kinds (Moore 1996). Significant but less attention has been paid to the role of intermediaries in international conflict prevention and resolution, with the work that has been done focusing mainly on official (state) interventions via peacekeeping missions, shuttle diplomacy, and other forms of state-to-state negotiation during times of violence (Kissinger 1994; Princen 1992; Holbrooke 1999). Still less attention has been devoted to the role of intermediaries in violent intrastate conflicts, where one of the parties is a non-state actor (Hume 1994; Regan 2002).

The power of intermediaries comes from the fact that in high-intensity conflict situations the parties to the conflict often lack an ability to de-escalate the conflict themselves. Sometimes this is because the conflict is militarized such that the infrastructure for communication between each side is non-existent. Other times, the parties lack a sufficient degree of trust and thus find it difficult to communicate without the assistance of an outsider. Still other times, de-escalation cannot occur because the partisans become trapped in a "negative sum" relationship, or simply lack the resources needed to carry out, monitor, and/or sustain any agreements that they achieve. Intermediaries can help to overcome each of these barriers to peace by assuming a number of different roles: from information providers, to meeting conveners, to guarantors of those agreements that are made.

The wide variation in intermediary activities across different contexts has resulted in a number of typologies of intermediary characteristics, roles, and activities (Crocker 2001; Kriesberg 2007). This chapter argues that there are six distinct functions that intermediaries perform when addressing violent intrastate conflicts: using coercion to halt violence; mediating agreements; transforming relationships between communities in conflict; addressing the structural sources of the conflict; providing consultation and/or conflict resolution training services; and providing early warning and post-conflict monitoring services.

Using coercion to halt violence

Ending overt forms of hostility through coercive means is one of the most visible functions of intermediaries. During intrastate conflicts the parties involved often reach a situation of military stalemate where neither side can achieve victory, where the loss of life continues daily, and where a lack of communication or negotiation between the partisans locks them into a continuing cycle of violence. In such cases intermediaries may be called in to separate the warring sides and/or to provide a buffer zone between them. Intervention in order to halt overt violence may not directly lead to conflict resolution or negotiation, but it does provide a cooling off period where diplomatic activity can emerge, where refugees can be evacuated and cared for, and where the cycle of daily violence is broken.

The work of United Nations (UN) peacekeepers is perhaps the best known example of this kind of intermediary activity. Although UN peacekeeping was originally conceptualized as a way that the international community could intervene in interstate conflicts, recent years have seen an expansion of "second generation" peacekeeping activity to include intervention in intrastate conflicts, such civil wars or conflicts between various factions in "failed states" (Jeong 2002). The role of peacekeepers extends from keeping the conflicting parties from fighting by physically separating them, to policing conflict zones and authoritatively enforcing ceasefires, to providing political and administrative services as part of "complex peacekeeping operations." Recent peacekeeping missions to intrastate conflicts have included, for instance, those in Haiti, Liberia, Somalia, Burundi, Sierra Leone, and East Timor.

Stopping violence can also be achieved through means other than intervening with a formal peacekeeping intervention. At times intermediaries may empower the weaker side in the conflict by providing them with arms, technical or logistical expertise, or direct military assistance. In Kosovo in the late 1990s, for instance, NATO led an intervention campaign that included bombing Serbian infrastructure in an attempt to raise the costs to Yugoslav authorities of conducting their campaign of violence against ethnic Albanians in Kosovo. Ending violence may also be pursued by imposing economic sanctions on aggressors so that they are encouraged to engage in negotiation, mediation, or other forms of conflict resolution activities. Such was the case in South Africa where efforts by Bishop

Desmond Tutu, among others, resulted in a transnational boycott against South African goods and services as well as moratoriums on investments in South African businesses (see Thomas Lodge this volume, Chapter 11).

Mediating agreements

A second function of conflict resolution intermediaries is to work with the parties in conflict as a mediator. Mediation, in this sense, can be defined as "interventions by credible and competent intermediaries who assist the parties in working toward a negotiated settlement on substantive issues through persuasion, the control of information, the suggestion of alternatives, and, in some cases, the application of leverage" (Fisher and Keashly 1991: 30). Similarly, mediation can be seen as,

> An accommodative process of conflict management whereby parties in a conflict seek the assistance of, or accept an offer of help from, an individual, a state or organization to settle their conflict or resolve their problem without resorting to physical force or invoking the authority of the law.
>
> (Bercovitch *et al.* 1991: 8)

Mediators can assist in the conflict settlement process in several ways. They can convene face to face meetings, moderate discussions, bring technical expertise to the table, develop new options for settlement, represent groups that are not present in the negotiation, and add resources that make negotiated agreements more appealing and/or realistic to each side (Bercovitch and Rubin 1994; Kriesberg 2007). For instance, US President Bill Clintons' efforts to mediate a peace agreement between Israeli Prime Minister Ehud Barak and Palestinian Authority President Yasser Arafat, which included the successful Wye River Memorandum in 1998 and the unsuccessful Camp David Summit in 2003, included a mix of these elements.

Mediation is a voluntary process. Mediators do not coerce the partisans toward any particular solution; rather, they provide a forum in which grievances can be aired, conflict narratives told, and the underlying interests of the parties explored so that a mutually accommodative solution can be found. Advocates of mediation often stress that one of its biggest strengths is its participatory nature and the fact that while the mediator may suggest options for settlement, the parties to the conflict maintain substantial control over the decision making process and outcome.

Often mediators active in intrastate conflicts are representatives of states or international organizations. Richard Holbrook, for instance, was acting in his capacity as the US Assistant Secretary of State when he brought together leaders of Serbia, Croatia and Bosnia in Dayton Ohio in 1995. The resulting Dayton Peace Agreement on Bosnia-Herzegovina committed the signatories to a ceasefire and set forth a series of agreements on governance, territory, minority rights, and international oversight. Similarly, representatives of the United Nations often assume a mediator role in intrastate conflicts, as was the case with the work of Alvero de Soto in El Salvador in the early 1990s, and the work of Ibrahim Gambari in Angola in the early 2000s and Myanmar in 2007.

Private individuals and ex-government officials with significant international status may also assume the role of mediator in intrastate conflicts, as with Jimmy Carter's work in Haiti in 1994 and Nelson Mandela's mediation efforts in Burundi. While private actors may not have the ability to commit the kinds of resources to conflict de-escalation that their public counterparts do, influential private actors do have the capacity to bring international media attention and access to public officials "to the table." Finally, NGOs have taken a leadership role as mediators of intrastate conflicts in several instances, including the work of the Community of Sant'Egidio to end the civil war in Mozambique (see Bartoli *et al.* this volume, Chapter 10) and the work of the Norwegian Institute for Applied Social Science to achieve the Oslo Accords between the Palestinian Authority and the State of Israel in 1993.

Transforming relationships between communities in conflict

While formal mediation involves working with official representatives of the conflicting parties to negotiate agreements concerning substantive matters, intermediaries may also initiate activities focused on improving the relationships among influential elites or members of the grass roots on both sides of the conflict. The primary goal of these relationship-building activities is to improve communication, trust, and understanding across the conflict divide so that any formal agreements that eventually do take hold are sustained by elite sentiment and/or popular grass roots support. Perhaps most celebrated of this type of this third type of intermediary activity is "track two" or citizens' diplomacy (Davies and Kaufman 2002; Montville 2006). Citizens' diplomacy has emerged in recent years as a complement, as well as alternative, to traditional state-based diplomatic initiatives, particularly in conflict zones where intractable conflicts have proven resistant to official peacemaking efforts. Generally defined as interventions in which representatives from communities in conflict are brought together informally by an unofficial third party to consider the roots of the conflict and means for its transformation (Davies and Kaufman 2002), citizens' diplomacy provides a venue for off-the-record and sustained contact between representatives of adversary groups, even when official negotiations are not possible. This form of facilitated communication can take place across different kinds of groups: from officials acting in an unofficial capacity, to teachers, to business groups, to journalists to religious leaders.

Citizens' diplomacy is often based on social-psychological approaches to intergroup relations. Contact theory, in particular, argues that as members of distinct identity groups with equal status interact their pre-conceived notion of the other is challenged, commonalities across groups are revealed, and dehumanization is overcome. Today, contact brought about through intermediaries engaged in citizens' diplomacy is claimed to reduce inter-group bias, improve relations and pave the way for official negotiations to take place (Fisher 2005). Citizens'/track two diplomacy has been widely used in protracted conflict zones from Northern Ireland, to Cyprus, to Sri Lanka, to Kashmir, to East Timor, to Tajikistan, and beyond (Fisher 2005; Saunders 2005).

Addressing the structural sources of the conflict

Some intermediaries focus their work on changing the institutions that may be at the root of violent intrastate conflicts. This type of intermediary work has been labeled "structural" as opposed to "direct" because of its focus on the indirect "root causes" of conflict including: un-integrated social systems, weak democratic institutions, high-levels of economic inequality, and a lack of educational opportunities (Wallensteen and Möller 2002). In conflict ridden societies, these kinds of structural inequal-ities can exacerbate the tensions between partisans and undermine the sustainability of any peace agreements that are achieved. It is believed that by strengthening core societal political and economic institutions, conflict-prone societies will become more resilient to any violence that does occur as social networks, faith in government institutions, participatory forms of government, and economic self-interest work together to limit conflicts from escalating to the point of violence (Uvin 2002). Moreover, strong democratic and economic institutions might limit the ability of leaders to manipulate public sentiment toward acts of future violence.

Structural transformation work done by intermediaries is highly varied and includes such activities as: improving educational and vocational train-ing opportunities for ex-combatants; building democratic institutions, such as election commissions and voting stations; establishing legal institu-tions that are capable of enforcing human rights norms; and improving basic infrastructure, such as access to safe water, electricity, and medical care, such that human security is enhanced for all (Galtung *et al.* 2002). For instance, in Sierra Leone the World Bank's International Develop-ment Association (IDA) has funded vocational training for ex-combatants as part of its Community Reintegration and Rehabilitation Project. The Carter Center provides election monitoring in fragile democracies such as Ethiopia, Nepal, and Nigeria. In the realm of microfinance, CARE, Mercy Corps, and World Vision, have partnered with intergovernmental organi-zations to provide microfinance assistance in Bosnia-Herzegovina (Ohanyan 2002).

So-called complex peacekeeping operations belong in this category of intermediary activity as well, adding to the traditional military role of peacekeepers a number of non-military responsibilities such as election monitoring, building public administration infrastructure, and protecting human rights (Jeong 2002; Mingst and Karns 2007). Indeed, peacekeeping authorities have gone so far as to serve as transitional authorities in several recent post-conflict settings, including Kosovo and East Timor where UN bodies have assumed temporary responsibility for virtually all aspects of governance from judicial affairs, to the regulation of the media, to the certification of individuals running for public office (Paris 2004). Even state military entities have formed units dedicated to addressing the structural dimensions of conflict, such as the US Army's Civil Affairs Brigades.

Providing consultation and conflict resolution training

Fifth, as the field of peacebuilding and conflict resolution has grown, so too has the number of consultants and trainers in the field. Training in conflict management is now offered throughout the world, and many leadership groups in conflict zones regularly consult with conflict resolution specialists in order to consider alternatives to violence. Consulting and training of this sort is carried out by individuals as well as by organizations, both public and private. Transcend, the Berghof Research Center for Constructive Conflict Management, and Search for Common Ground, for instance, are three well-known international conflict management organizations with a wide variety of projects designed to train and educate leaders and citizens in conflict management methods and skills. Additionally, academic settings, such as the Fletcher School at Tufts University, George Mason University's Institute for Conflict Analysis and Resolution, the Center for International Conflict Resolution at Columbia University, the United Nations University for Peace, INCORE, Syracuse University's Program on the Analysis and Resolution of Conflicts, the International Peace Research Institute (PRIO), and others have applied research and training units dedicated to translating theories about conflict escalation and de-escalation into practice. Many of the individuals working within these institutions provide individual consultation services to leaders as peacebuilding initiatives are mobilized. Others have set up fellowships, workshops, or educational programs for various stakeholders residing in conflict zones.

Providing early warning and post-conflict monitoring services

The sixth and final type of intermediary function is monitoring conflict escalation and de-escalation processes and/or monitoring whether or not partisan groups are living up to the peace agreements they have signed. Intermediaries engaged in conflict monitoring are able to provide all sides, as well as the international community, with information about the course of the conflict. This type of intervention is essential for keeping the public eye on the conflict of concern, reassuring the parties and maintaining pressure on the partisans to moderate their behavior or to live up to any agreements which have been signed. A good example is the International Crisis Group, founded in response to the failures of the international community to adequately anticipate and respond to crises in conflicts in Somalia, Rwanda, and Bosnia. Through their Crisis Watch database, conflict zones throughout the world, and substantial media division, ICG acts as the eyes and ears of the international community as it monitors conflict emergence and escalation.

State versus non-state intermediaries

The discussion above illustrates that diverse individuals and organizations can and do perform intermediary functions in intrastate conflicts. This collection of actors can be further divided according to whether they are acting on behalf of a state, an international organization, or a non-governmental entity. Membership in each of these groups brings with it certain advantages and disadvantages.

Official state intermediaries most often work on "track one" level mediations. These actors maintain exclusive legal authority to commit public resources, the capacity to deploy them, and the legal standing to represent their citizens via official peacemaking efforts, war, or other kinds of security-related interventions. States play an important role in post-conflict reconstruction activities as well; devoting resources to rebuilding political and economic institutions, funding the work of civil society organizations, and guaranteeing the loans necessary for post-conflict economic liberalization. States actors remain the primary players in intrastate interventions precisely because of the authority they hold and the resources they are able to mobilize. These powers often make state actors more appealing agents of conflict management to protagonists than are non-state actors.

At the same time, the transformation of the international system from one based largely on the activities of state actors to one where intergovernmental organizations and non-governmental organizations play a significant role in governance, has opened up new avenues for IGOs and non-state actors in the realm of conflict resolution and peacebuilding (Mathews 1997). Non-state intermediaries include the hundreds of NGOs active in peace and conflict work, whether as formal transnational NGOs or as part of a network of civil society organizations that coalesces around particular issue areas at distinct periods of time (Clark 2003). Non-state intermediaries differ from state intermediaries in several important ways. Representatives of NGOs lack the capacity to oversee formal agreements or commit economic or military resources necessary for achieving piece, but they are often seen as having a better ability than do states to connect to the needs of the grass roots, to see early signs of emerging conflicts, and to more flexibility respond to quickly changing conditions on the ground (Goodhand 2006).

The scope of intermediary activities in intrastate conflict

Over the past 20 years few violent intrastate conflicts have erupted in which intermediaries did not have some hand in managing. Uppsala University's conflict management database, for instance, reveals that out of the 122 violent intrastate conflicts that occurred between 1989 and 2006, 100 of them involved third party interventions of some type, with 55 of these cases ending in a negotiated agreement (Human Security Brief 2007). This trend toward third party involvement in intrastate conflict appears to be accelerating. For instance, of the 61 UN peacekeeping operations initiated between 1948 and 2007, 43 of these missions took place since 1990.

The role of NGOs in peacebuilding is likely to be accelerating at an even faster rate, but is more difficult to measure. While state actors tend to play highly visible roles as mediators, shuttle-diplomats, and peacekeepers, NGOs often work "out of the spotlight" on grass roots projects such as people-to-people dialogues, skills-building projects, and other less-celebrated ventures. In 1996, *The International Guide to NGO Activities in Conflict Prevention and Resolution*, produced by the Carter Center, listed 83 NGOs active in conflict prevention and resolution work at the global level, not all of which engage in conflict zones as intermediaries. In 2007, the US-based organization Charity Navigator listed 136 not-for-profit organizations working in the international peace and security sector. Finally, in 2007, the Berghof Research Center for Constructive Conflict Management listed 350 NGO affiliates that are engaged in peacebuilding work across every region of the globe. These numbers are likely dwarfed by the actual extent of conflict management organization involvement in some form of intermediary activity simply because such actors are rarely in the public eye.

When do opposition movements engagement with intermediaries?

Not all partisans seek out the help of intermediaries during the course of interstate conflicts. Why, then, do the parties that are engaged in violent intrastate conflict sometimes choose to engage with intermediaries but other times do not? The cases in this volume suggest that the turn toward engagement with intermediaries tends to occur during a stage of the conflict known as a ripe moment (Zartman 2000). The notion of a ripe moment is premised on the belief that conflicts are never static, but move through several stages of evolution as they mature. The classic bell-shaped diagram of the lifecycle of conflicts developed by Pruitt *et al.* (1994), for instance, posits that conflicts move through seven stages of evolution:

latent conflict, emergence, escalation, stalemate, de-escalation, dispute settlement, and post-conflict peacebuilding. The intensity of the conflict is low during the latent period, then gradually builds to the point of stalemate, then just as gradually dissipates through the post-conflict peace-building stage. At each stage, a different set of social-psychological, military, and material dynamics are at play, each of which will make the work of intermediaries more or less difficult.

The ripe moment notion suggests that conflicts are fluid social processes that may be more amenable to third party interventions at certain stages of their evolution than at other stages. Bercovitch (1984), for example, argues that mediation is only successful when: the conflict has lasted a long period of time, the conflicting parties have reached an impasse, the parties involved decide that they no longer want to shoulder the costs of escalation, and both parties are ready to engage with each other. In other words, the turn toward peaceful engagement will occur only when the parties recognize that their interests are not being served by the application of violence and that the current costs of waging the conflict violently outweigh the perceived "loses" associated with mediation, compromise, and negotiation. Zartman calls this stage of psychological transition a "hurting stalemate" and sees it as a transformation point where new possibilities for de-escalation suddenly appear. It is these moments where intermediaries may have their biggest impact.

The point here is that peace cannot be forced by an external intermediary, but intermediaries can make the best of those brief windows of opportunity when the adversaries have reached some kind of threshold or "tipping point" that makes peacebuilding work possible. Each of the case studies contained within this book would appear to support this claim. In commenting on the role of intermediaries in the Mozambique conflict for instance, Bartoli *et al.* (this volume, Chapter 10) comment that:

> Third-parties were, by character or by choice, weak; they did not have the capacity (or the will) to forcefully influence either party or the process. This "weakness" led to the paradoxical result that the parties had to be committed to the process and to one another because they were not forced into it. The final test of the transformation rested in their capacity to develop direct partnerships.

Similarly, the case of South Africa, which is often held up as a success story in constructive conflict transformation, illustrates that international sanctions were not the decisive factor in moving the ANC and the De Klerk government toward peaceful resolution of their conflict. Rather, as Lodge (this volume, Chapter 11) suggests, a confluence of factors came together to make peace possible, foremost among them being a pragmatic recognition on the part of the ANC and its leader Nelson Mandela that there could be no military solution to the South African conflict. The limits of intermediary work can also be seen in the case of the PLO as well (Parsons this volume, Chapter 16). Parsons reminds the reader that the massive effort of intermediaries to end hostilities between Israelis and Palestinians not only failed, but may even have been counterproductive. In the Guatemala case Allison (this volume, Chapter 13) notes that intermediaries did not appear on the scene until long after the bloody civil war began to ebb because of the decimation of the URNG by government forces. Allison goes on to note that intermediaries in Guatemala played an important but limited role, largely confined to facilitating peace negotiations after the parties had already committed themselves to a path of negotiation. Finally, from Orjuela's chapter (this volume, Chapter 17) on the LTTE in Sri Lanka it is clear that impediments to peacebuilding have overwhelmed the ability of intermediaries, in particular the government of Norway, to sustain the little momentum toward sustainable peace that began to build in the beginning of the 2000s. These impediments included a mistrust of the peace process, power asymmetry between the sides, and leadership that could not make the transition from violent opposition movement to peace partner.

Conclusion

Intermediaries are important players in most attempts to constructively manage violent intrastate conflicts, particularly during ripe moments. Yet the power of intermediaries is tempered by the fact that both sides of a conflict must be ready to engage before intermediary pressures, inducements, or assistance is likely to push them toward dramatic de-escalation. Intermediaries function most successfully after the parties to the conflict have already made the decision to engage because of a ripe moment, a change in leadership, a change in the structural conditions that support the conflict, the erosion of support from a key external ally, or because one or both sides start to believe that they cannot achieve their interests through violence alone.

Finally, it is important to remember that there is nothing inherently positive about intermediary activity. Indeed, a lack of research on outcomes resulting from intermediary work leaves open the possibility that sometimes such interventions may have no impact whatsoever, or even be counterproductive. Fortunately researchers are now looking more closely at the conditions and contexts that facilitate or inhibit the success of intermediaries in helping to manage violent conflict. The good news is that the institutionalization of conflict research centers and the expanding scope of research on conflict and conflict transformation will yield more evidence about the impact of these important actors in the years to come.

References

Bercovitch, J. (1984) *Social Conflicts and Third Parties: Strategies of Conflict Resolution*, Boulder: Westview Press.

Bercovitch, J. (ed.) (1996) *Resolving International Conflicts: The Theory and Practice of Mediation*, Boulder: Lynne Rienner.

Bercovitch, J. and Rubin, J. (eds.) (1994) *Mediation in International Relations: Multiple Approaches to Conflict Management*, reprint edn., New York: Palgrave Macmillan.

Bercovitch, J., Agnoson, J. T. and Wille, D. (1991) "Some Contextual Issues and Empirical Trends in the Study of Successful Mediation in International Relations," *Journal of Peace Research*, 28: 7–17.

Burgess, H. (2004) "Intermediaries," in Burgess, G. and Burgess, H. (eds.) *Beyond Intractability*, Conflict Research Consortium, University of Colorado, Boulder.

Clark, J. (2003) *Worlds Apart: Civil Society and the Battle for Ethical Globalization*, Bloomfield: Kumarian Press.

Crocker, C. (2001) "Intervention: Toward Best Practices and a Holistic View," in Aall, P., Hampson, F. O. and Crocker, C. (eds.) *Turbulent Peace: The Challenges of Managing International Conflict*, Washington, DC: United States Institute of Peace Press.

Davies, J. and Kaufman, E. (2002) *Second Track/Citizens' Diplomacy*, Lanham: Rowman & Littlefield.

Fisher, R. (2005) *Paving the Way: Contributions of Interactive Conflict Resolution to Peacemaking*, Oxford: Lexington Books.

Fisher, R. and Keashly, L. (1991) "The Potential Complementarily of Mediation and Consultation within a Contingency Model of Third Party Intervention," Journal of Peace Research, 28 (1): 29–42.

Galtung, J., Jacobsen, C. and Brand-Jacobsen, I. (2002) *Searching for Peace: The Road to Transcend*, London: Pluto Press.

Goodhand, J. (2006) *Aiding Peace: The Role of NGOs in Armed Conflict*, Boulder: Lynne Rienner.

Holbrooke, R. (1999) *To End War*, New York: Modern Library.

Human Security Brief (2007) Human Security Center, University of British Columbia, Canada. Online, available at: www.humansecuritybrief.info/2007/index.html.

Hume, C. (1994) *Ending Mozambique's War: The Role of Mediation and Good Offices*, Washington, DC: United States Institute of Peace Press.

Jeong, H. W. (2002) "Peacekeeping Strategies for Peacebuilding: Multi-Functional Roles," in Jeong, H. W. (ed.) *Approaches to Peacebuilding*, New York: Palgrave.

Kissinger, H. (1994) *Diplomacy*, New York: Simon and Schuster.

Kriesberg, L. (2007) *Constructive Conflicts*, Lanham: Rowman & Littlefield.

Mathews, J. (1997) "Powershift," *Foreign Affairs*, 97: 50–66.

Melvern, L. (2004) *Conspiracy to Murder: The Rwandan Genocide*, New York: Verso.

Mingst, K. and Karns, M. (2007) "The United Nations and Conflict Management: Relevant or Irrelevant?" in Crocker, C., Hampson, F. O. and Aall, P. *Leashing the Dogs of War*, Washington, DC: United States Institute of Peace Press, 497–520.

Montville, J. (2006) Track Two Diplomacy: The Work of Healing History, *Whitehead Journal of Diplomacy and International Relations*, Summer/Fall 2006, 15–25.

Moore, C. W. (1996) *The Mediation Process: Practical Strategies for Resolving Conflict*, San Francisco: Jossey-Bass.

Ohanyan, A. (2002) "Post Conflict Global Governance: The Case of Microfinance Enterprise Networks in Bosnia and Herzegovina," *International Studies Perspective*, 3: 396–414.

Paris, R. (2004) *At War's End: Building Peace after Civil Conflict*, Cambridge: Cambridge University Press.

Princen, Thomas. (1992) *Intermediaries in International Conflict*, Princeton: Princeton University Press.

Pruitt, D., Rubin, J. and Kim, S. (1994) "Stalemate and De-escalation," in Pruitt, D. and Rubin, J. (eds.) *Social Conflict: Escalation, Stalemate, and Settlement,* 2nd edn., New York: McGraw Hill College Division.

Regan, P. (2002) "Third Party Interventions and the Duration of Intrastate Conflicts," *Journal of Conflict Resolution*, 46 (1): 55–73.

Saunders, H. (2005) *Politics is about Relationship: A Blueprint for the Citizens' Century*, New York: Palgrave.

Uvin, P. (2002) "The Development/Peacebuilding Nexus: A Typology and History of Changing Paradigms," *Journal of Peacebuilding and Development*, 1 (1): 5–24.

Wallensteen, P. and Möller, F. (2002) *Conflict Prevention: Methodology for Knowing the Unknown*, Uppsala Peace Research Papers no. 7, Department of Peace and Conflict Research Uppsala University, Sweden.

Zartman, W. (2000) "Ripeness: The Hurting Stalemate and Beyond," in Stern, P. and Druckman, D. (eds.) *International Conflict Resolution after the Cold War*, Washington, DC: National Academy Press, 225–250.

6 Rhetorical arts of praise and blame in political transformation

Bradford Vivian

Sectarian violence in Iraq following its occupation by US-led forces illustrates vividly how divisive collective memories among ethnic, political, or religious groups can subvert intrastate conflict resolution. The case of Iraq exemplifies this premise in two crucial aspects. First, militant Sunni or Shiia agents fomented discord in post-Saddam Iraq by reviving memories of centuries-old sectarian controversies or perceived offenses previously censored under the Baathist regime. Collective memories in such cases have bases in the historical past, however selectively – and often distortedly – they have been revised in contemporary group recollection. Second, armed factions also appealed to supporters by merely appropriating traditional religious or ethnic symbolism. Doing so conveys the impression of a fervently remembered past, albeit one invented in the present to justify continued hostilities. In both contexts, inflammatory invocations of memory – whether real or imagined, historically-based or superficially fabricated – provide dangerously potent inducements for supporting programs of armed violence and political instability (Hashim 2006: 99–120; Rogers 2006: 65–74).

Collective remembrance of violence and repression, when judiciously cultivated, can offer a basis for productive political relations. The oft-cited case of the South African Truth and Reconciliation Commission suggests how formal testimony regarding state-sponsored atrocities (an act of official collective memory) can enlist victims of authoritarian abuse as agents of transitional justice (see Asmal 1997; Boraine 2001; Chapman and Van der Merwe 2008; Christie 2000; Edelstein 2002; Meredith 1999; Nuttall and Coetzee 1998; Wilson 2001). But collective remembrance in the aforementioned Iraqi context represents, contrary to much conventional wisdom, the very source of ongoing aggression (albeit in new forms) that prevents political reconciliation and the development of democratic institutions. One may observe the symbolic uses and destructive consequences of collective memory in conflicts other than those of post-Saddam Iraq. Incendiary appeals to collective memory have long characterized militant rhetoric on both sides of the Israeli–Palestinian conflict (McKnight 2004; Penslar 2005; Rotberg 2006; Swedenburg 1995). A number of commentators recognize that recollections of historical injustice and atrocity can incite formerly victimized peoples' desires for violent revenge against their victimizers (Margalit 2002; Olick 2003; Wiesel 1977). Expressions of collective memory suggest potentially useful resources for ending violence in order to promote peace and democracy; yet those resources are inherently capricious, equally capable of inspiring anti-democratic violence, and so must be delicately managed (see also this volume, Chapter 1).

This chapter addresses two related research questions: In what forms do appeals to collective memory foster peace and political reconciliation? And by what principles can we recognize their more destructive varieties, which perpetuate armed conflict? The chapter uses a rhetorical methodology to address these questions. The premise that collective memory is communicative, discursive, or rhetorical in nature appears throughout interdisciplinary literature on the subject (Bodnar 1992; Halbwachs 1992; Young 1993). This notion reflects the metaphorical character of "collective memory": collectivities do not literally remember events in the linear, uniform way that individuals apparently do; rather, complex processes of collective narration, dialogue, and debate – the ways in which communities tell stories, converse, and argue about the past – produce frames of historical understanding that social, ethnic, or religious groups commonly accept as shared recollections (Zelizer 1995). "Memory" is a handy metaphor for the verbal and symbolic work that communities maintain in order to adapt existing perceptions of the past to their changing needs and interests in the present (Bodnar 1992). Every putative "memory" essentially functions as an implicit or explicit argument about what should be remembered, who should remember it, and why. This chapter scrutinizes especially instructive linguistic or symbolic appeals to collective memory in order to identify heuristics useful for distinguishing invocations of the past that may assist conflict resolution from those that exacerbate it.

The aim of this inquiry is to suggest principles for intervening in conflicts where the rhetoric of collective memory, in all its linguistic and symbolic variety, motivates opposed groups to view one another as lacking a common past, and thus lacking bases for articulating common and future-oriented needs, goals, and priorities. Such intervention would endeavor to create forms of public expression by which opposed communities might relinquish one way of talking about the past – as a justification for sustaining cycles of violence and retribution – and learn to speak of it as a source of commonality (and ideally reconciliation) in the present. The present study accordingly extends Jeffrey Alexander's insights regarding the role of social performances in fostering productive communal relations. One may view rhetorical appeals to popular memory voiced by influential figures as social performances in which, Alexander writes, "audiences identify with actors, and cultural scripts achieve verisimilitude" (2004: 527) as guides for collective decision-making. In the process, new modes of public dialogue about the past may help to interrupt debilitating cycles of what Robert Rothstein calls a "conflict syndrome," or "a set of attitudes, assumptions, and beliefs that become embedded over decades of bitter conflict and are difficult to unlearn even if some kind of peace agreement – or exploratory truce – has been signed" (2006: 1).

This chapter does not argue that adjusting the rhetoric of collective memory provides a guaranteed or comprehensive method for resolving intrastate conflict. But it does argue that transforming collective perceptions of the past – and consequently of the present and future – can establish vital preconditions for motivating antagonists to participate in conflict resolution. Such transformation encourages armed factions to recognize mutual incentives for overcoming seemingly intractable historical divisions or injustices in order to pursue inclusive frameworks for peaceful and productive relations.

The following analysis employs an especially apt key concept to examine the rhetoric of collective memory. Epideictic speech in classical rhetorical theory designated ceremonial performances designed to ritually remind audiences of common civic origins, values, and priorities (Aristotle 2007: I.3.3). The exercise of publicly reaffirming traditional values, identities, and codes of conduct often requires that one remind audiences of the communal origins that first inspired such articles of collective belonging and rehearse listeners in historical narratives that explain how the community has subsequently upheld those values, identities, and codes. Epideictic is therefore an especially apt heuristic with which to investigate how appeals to collective memory can assist in shaping collective opinions, attitudes, and behaviors in support of some form of sociopolitical order.

The concept of epideictic rhetoric not only holds explanatory force for traditional rituals of ceremonial praise or blame but also yields vital insights, in modernized and expanded form, into political uses and abuses of collective memory across a variety of armed conflicts. To that end, the following analysis begins by translating classical theories of epideictic rhetoric, and their natural emphasis on public rituals of praise and blame, into modern geopolitical terms. Amending the concept of epideictic as such provides a framework for then distinguishing between politically constructive and destructive appeals to collectively memory according to their propensity for either perpetuating or mitigating conflict.

Redefining epideictic address

The simplest definition of epideictic rhetoric is a speech of praise (*epainos*) or blame (*psogos*) in which orators ritualistically recommend (or praise) traditional values, identities, and codes of conduct while discouraging undesirable (or blameworthy) norms and behaviors (Herrick 2005: 81). Epideictic addresses customarily evince a strong commemorative dimension (Herrick 2005: 81). In classical literature, the genre of epideictic was distinguished from judicial argument and political address (Aristotle 2007:

I.3.2–6). Early teachers of rhetoric observed that ceremonial speeches on civic holidays, commemorations, memorials, or dedications required different conventions of public speech than strictly political or legal addresses in order for listeners to deem them persuasive and agreeable (Aristotle 2007: I.9.1–41).

Academic distinctions between ceremonial speech and political or legal discourse unfortunately imply that public expressions of communal origins, identity, and values lack political or legal significance. Gerard Hauser, however, argues to the contrary:

> Epideictic encouraged the constitutive activity propaedeutic to action: reflection on public norms for proper political conduct.... [E]pideictic constructs accounts of nobility worthy of *mimesis* [insofar as] its narrative character sets the conditions for a viable public sphere in which a people may engage in politics.
>
> (Hauser 1999: 17–18)

In the classical vein, epideictic rhetoric publicized "accounts of nobility worthy of *mimesis*" (or imitation); it sought to instill in listeners a common reverence for past leaders or heroes and thereby encourage audiences to imitate such fabled exemplars of "nobility" in public conduct. Epideictic rhetoric, so defined, has profound political and legal effect. Chaïm Perelman and Lucie Olbrechts-Tyteca maintain that epideictic speech is vital to political processes insofar as its rituals of praise and blame enshrine collective values upon which future actions are justified (1971: 48). Ritual praise of inspirational figures and episodes from the shared or imagined past thereby substantially informs the vocabulary of citizenship used in a community's daily political and legal affairs (see also Chase 1961; Hauser 1999; Loraux 1986).

This account of classical epideictic, however, tells only half the story. It describes an ideal, not actual, rhetorical form and function. The past as publicly remembered through epideictic rituals of praise and blame may not conform to, or might even wildly contradict, some groups' collective recollections. Authoritative appeals to collective memory are not a priori agreeable to all members of a community. Publicly praising certain ideals of communal conduct, moreover, doesn't necessarily provide sufficient or widely agreeable motivations for peaceful participation in political or legal institutions. To cite Hauser (1999), "people may" decide to "engage in politics" by imitating historical exemplars praised in public addresses; but they may not. Indeed, many public rituals of praise and blame (traditional or contemporary) may intentionally or unintentionally produce collective responses that undermine peaceful political and legal decision-making.

Appeals to collective memory as incentives for coordinated action in the present may fail as often as they succeed in resolving conflict because their characteristic discourses of praise logically imply divisive grounds for blame. Consider Pericles' Funeral Oration (430 BCE) and Abraham Lincoln's Gettysburg Address (1863), supposedly timeless benchmarks of epideictic speech to which other attempts should aspire (Lincoln 1989; Pericles 1979). Both are remembered nostalgically as ceremonial performances that united the populace by activating its supposedly shared sense of communal origin and political destiny. Yet Pericles and Lincoln gave their respective addresses amidst the carnage of war in order to solidify support for continued military – or nonpolitical – action. Pericles and Lincoln alike praised one version of the communal past, present, and future – and one version of the civic identity and norms of conduct it celebrated – in order to justify further aggression against their own civic kin. The appeal of epideictic rhetoric in its most publicly visible and consequential forms, despite roseate perceptions to the contrary, is often ardently nationalistic (if not xenophobic or militaristic). In praising the community's historical origins, traditional beliefs, and standards of conduct, one implicitly argues that its members should not debase themselves by imitating the objectionable norms or customs of other groups. Such appeals can provide potent incitements to violence when authorities express them as moral lessons conveyed by the collectively remembered past.

Recognizing the alternately constructive and destructive political effects of epideictic rhetoric allows one to expand the category beyond classical masterpieces of oratory to include consequential rhetorical rituals of praise or blame throughout the modern world. In standard academic definitions, "epideictic" may only be an artificially specialized, originally Eurocentric term for generally observable patterns of praise and blame used to establish group solidarity by furnishing common explanations of a people's historical past and the lessons (whether peaceful or violent) it betokens for the group's present and future. In sum, collective memories may provide compelling group motivations for acting in particular ways in the present – in order to seek either peaceful redress or violent revenge for previous abuses of power, for instance. But those memories, and the motivations they engender, circulate and gain the status of conventional wisdom to a significant degree through the public speech of a community's most widely accepted spokespersons (including elected leaders, public servants, intellectuals, religious authorities, military heroes, and communal advocates (see also Chapters 2 and 6 in this volume)). Such rhetoric conventionally encourages audiences to recognize the meaning of the collective past as a ground of present-day judgment concerning its relations with others – as a mode of epideictic praise and blame.

One may observe communal spokespersons invoking collective memory in order to consolidate support for violent or peaceful agendas in a variety of modern intrastate conflicts. The following analysis contributes to literature on conflict resolution by evaluating specific but broadly applicable patterns of public praise and blame for their tendencies to either mitigate or exacerbate armed violence. For policy-makers, such an analysis may be useful in determining: (a) how public spokespersons can shape group perceptions of the past to justify conflict in the present; (b) how particular forms of historical narration and vocabularies of praise or blame evince especial rhetorical potency in doing so; and (c) how the public expression of different historical narratives and novel vocabularies of praise and blame might redefine inflammatory invocations of collective memory into positive justifications for armed groups to entertain political reconciliation. In sum, productive rituals of praise and blame, or public appeals to communal memory so conceived, can be an ameliorative factor in ending violence and helping to create conditions for political reconciliation.

The key, however, is to determine what forms of praise and blame facilitate dialogue in which armed groups can recognize themselves as mutually invested in upholding particular values or codes of conduct and, by implication, how to counteract rhetoric that invokes communal memory as a way of justifying continued division and violence. The remaining sections of this chapter offer a series of contrasts between particularly significant examples of politically destructive and constructive epideictic rhetoric. On this basis, the sections to follow do not present guaranteed prescriptions for achieving such results but instead identify especially vivid and representative instances of more generally observable forms of praise and blame in the rhetoric of collective remembrance. Such generally observable forms may be used as templates to assist the practical work of conflict resolution where violent contestation of the past motivates armed hostilities in the present.

Politically destructive arts of praise and blame

Praising an ideal past

A notable rhetorical technique for justifying armed violence is to advocate the forcible restoration of a previous sociopolitical order. The symbolic mission of restoring an era during which one's group was ostensibly unburdened by the oppression or indignity it has suffered more recently can provide an appealing warrant for both overthrowing the present order and disenfranchising groups that supposedly benefit from it. Al-Qaeda's public relations materials elaborately illustrate such rhetorical techniques. The organization's self-produced media content consistently features invocations of a medieval caliphate as the motivating ideal for their jihad. "Al Qaeda's leadership, its membership and some of its associate groups," Rohan Gunaratna writes, "genuinely believe that they have created a new Islamic Universal Order" (2002: 92). Al-Qaeda propaganda implies that its mission is to reconstruct, within contemporary Arab states, Muslim theocracies in which its version of Islam dictates government policies rather than being marginalized or suppressed by present-day political regimes.

Some commentators counter that Al-Qaeda's religious symbolism – the public dress of its leaders, Osama bin Laden's recitations of the Koran, and so forth – represent merely superficial displays of Muslim piety. The organization's leaders indeed parade religious symbolism in elaborate sociopolitical performances. This fact, however, only underscores the rhetorical appeal, to susceptible audiences, of public praise for a distant and idealized past. The religious trappings and overtones of Al-Qaeda's communications may be rhetorical window dressing, but they reframe complex and prolonged conflicts in a theological vernacular potentially understood by millions. Osama bin Laden's "Declaration of War against the Americans" illustrates his appeal to disaffected Arabs when he adopts the persona of a persecuted Islamic prophet:

> We – myself and my group – have suffered some of these injustices ourselves; we have been prevented from addressing the Muslims. We have been pursued in Pakistan, the Sudan and Afghanistan – hence this long absence on my part. But, by the Grace of Allah, a safe base is now available in the high Hindu Kush mountains in Khrasan.
>
> (quoted in Gunaratna 2002: 90)

Repressive Arab governments and imperialist Western armies have "pursued" and inflicted "injustices" on bin Laden and his followers; but "Allah" protects Al-Qaeda and its leader. Reframing contemporary geopolitical hostilities in putatively pre-modern theological language and argumentation produces a series of rhetorical effects advantageous to groups such as Al-Qaeda.

It reinterprets present intrastate conflicts, for example, according to simple logical dichotomies and thus provides conveniently stark alternatives according to which predisposed audiences can understand those conflicts' supposedly deeper historical and religious significance. Consider bin Laden's proclamations in a particularly famous video tape:

> These events have split the world into two camps: the camp of the believers and the camp of the infidels. It is the duty of every Muslim to make sure that his religion prevails. The winds of faith and the winds of change are blowing against the infidels who occupy the land of the prophet Mohammed, may peace and God's blessing be upon him.
>
> (quoted in Tuman 2003: 139)

Modern political and economic developments threaten to extinguish the righteous community of believers; those believers must therefore take action against such threats. "They" are the offending "infidels"; "we" are the true "believers." Couched in religious terminology, such dichotomies remove discussions over the sources of present-day conflicts and possible alternatives for remedying them from procedural debate and negotiation.

Modern political institutions are, by this logic, the source of the group's woes; actions should be dictated by incontrovertible moral precepts, to which all must assent, and not by the arbitrary outcome of deliberative processes.

In this light, the superficiality of Al-Qaeda's religious displays creates an especially potent rhetoric, if not reality, with which to justify the substitution of violence for politics, of past for present. The potency of such rhetoric is especially palpable when bin Laden cites the Koran as a divine, incontrovertible justification for Al-Qaeda's jihad, thus rooting his modern-day crusade in early Islamic history:

> Praise be to God, who revealed the Book, controls the clouds, defeats factionalism, and says in His Book: "But when the forbidden months are past, then fight and slay the pagans wherever ye find them, seize them, beleaguer them, and lie in wait for them in every stratagem (of war).

> (quoted in Gunaratna 2002: 88)

Religious piety in such cases may be mere verbal costuming; the piously remembered caliphate may be a mirage. The costume and caliphate nonetheless facilitate a potentially potent performance of praise and blame designed to recruit supporters bitterly disenchanted with state power to programs of armed violence against it.

Blame and dehumanization

Still other rhetorical appeals containing public praise of an idealized past reveal how the rhetoric of collective memory can inspire patterns of dehumanization that perpetuate armed conflict. Former Serbian President Slobodan Milosevic's now-infamous speech on 28 June 1989 at Gazimestan commemorating the 600-year anniversary of the Battle of Kosovo (1389) exemplifies how detailed collective remembrance can inflame rather than pacify religious, political, and ethnic hatreds between groups with long and thickly intertwined histories (Judah 2000). In his speech, Milosevic appeals for Serbian unity, invoking the collective memory of Serbian disunity and defeat on the Field of Kosovo, the very site of his address, six centuries prior. "In the memory of the Serbian people," he declares, "this disunity was decisive in causing the loss of the battle and in bringing about the fate which Serbia suffered for a full six centuries" (Milosevic 2001: 11). Milosevic makes this appeal in carefully camouflaged terms:

> Serbia has never had only Serbs living in it. Today, more than in the past, members of others peoples and nationalities also live in it. This is not a disadvantage for Serbia. I am truly convinced that it is its advantage.

> (Milosevic 2001: 10)

Milosevic ostensibly praises the increasingly multicultural character of Yugoslavia within which Serbian solidarity should coalesce. "Yugoslavia," he proclaims, "is a multinational community and it can survive only under the conditions of full equality for all nations that live in it" (2001: 10). Milosevic emphasizes that the Serbian people are thus hungry for the inspiration of modern-day democratic and political heroism rather than martial valor.

Collective memory of the battle, however, remains the inspirational theme of Milosevic's ceremonial address. As such, its latent significance consistently subverts the manifest meaning of the president's apparently democratic and politically inclusive language. The memory of Serbian defeat at Gazimestan invokes the memory of the Serbians' enslavement, in Milosevic's terms, based on their ethnicity. In this context, the stated meaning of Milosevic's rhetoric assumes sinister undertones. His motivational purpose in lingering over the Serbians' fate following this battle is to instruct his supporters, in conventional epideictic fashion, in honorable and dishonorable values. In Milosevic's narration, Serbian leaders of recent memory took the wrong lesson from the Battle of Kosovo: "Thanks to their leaders and politicians and their vassal mentality they felt guilty before themselves and others. Disunity among Serb officials made Serbia lag behind, and their inferiority humiliated Serbia" (2001: 10). The historical lesson of Gazimestan, as Milosevic conjures it, is that the Serbians' former disunity caused them to become slaves, a condition perpetuated by the "vassal mentality" of modern Serbian politicians. With such language, Milosevic "tapped into a broad vein of dissatisfaction among Serbs about their role in postwar Yugoslavia" (Sell 2002: 41; see also Doder and Branson 1999; LeBor 2004). His rhetoric of collective memory implies that Serbian solidarity in the present will allow them to cleanse the stain of their historical enslavement, to absolve the legacy of their sorely remembered submission, by submitting contemporary political processes to their will.

Milosevic's rhetoric is ominously totalizing. It asks listeners to act upon a series of dramatic inversions couched in inspirational ceremonial terms. What was done six centuries ago should be undone today. Divided then, we will unite now. If disunity made us subservient to unworthy masters in our past, then we should collectively master events in the present. Oddly enough, the Battle of Kosovo is an object of praise rather than blame in Milosevic's discourse: the slavery to which Serbians succumbed as a result of their defeat is an ever-present reminder inspiring them to achieve a strong and unified modern state. The mission of building that state, however nominally democratic or multicultural, assumes militaristic and exclusionary significance when set against this commemorative backdrop. The current Serbian cause becomes, in Milosevic's rhetoric, an extension of its military and ethnic history, wherein defeat must be answered with victory and inferiority replaced by superiority.

The operative dehumanizing implication of such rhetoric lies in the fact that its appeal for unity is (implicitly but powerfully) an appeal for division – from agents or institutions that have kept the Serbians divided and subservient (even "enslaved") for centuries. Indeed, Milosevic drapes his closing appeals for Serbian unity in martial symbolism. His profession that Serbians now require political and cultural heroism rather than military valor is quickly dispelled by his forewarning that although they are not presently engaged in "armed battles," "such things cannot be excluded yet" (2001: 11). The new social, political, and economic "battle" he describes remains a battle nonetheless. The binary logic underlying Milosevic's invocations of collective memory allows him to praise only the Serbian people; such praise simultaneously apportions blame to those groups with whom Serbians competed in greater Yugoslavia for social, political, and economic advantage – a logic which led infamously to programs of ethnic cleansing (see Cigar 2002; Cohen 2001; Djukic 2001). The politically destructive effect of such rhetoric, whether Milosevic or other power-holders espouse it, indicates that ceremonial invocations of the past are not merely ceremonial in nature. Oversimplified historical narratives appeal to present-day audiences by promoting a grossly simplified logic for understanding the troubles historically afflicting one's community and an equally reductive understanding of those that one may blame for perpetuating them in the present.

Politically constructive arts of praise and blame

Relegating blame to the past

Leaders' rhetoric of praise and blame rooted in communal memory may provide grounds for political reconciliation when it relegates blame to the past. This technique contrasts sharply with the aforementioned politically destructive uses of praise and blame, which consistently invoke collective memories of intrastate violence in order to justify the resumption or escalation of present conflicts. Public invocations of a conflict-ridden collective past, however, can be used to suggest telling differences, rather than similarities, between history and the present. Memory of conflict might be used not as an excuse for prolonging it but for defining violence as an outmoded historical condition – in the eyes of political, ethnic, or religious friends and enemies alike.

From a rhetorical perspective, Nelson Mandela's address to the people of Cape Town, on the eve of his presidential inauguration (9 May 1994), provides an irresistibly skillful and influential demonstration of such techniques. Mandela's advocacy, leadership, and policies have been documented copiously (see Benson 1994; Lodge 2006; Mandela 1995, 1993; Meer 1990; Meredith 1998; Sampson 2000); but the present discussion argues for the equally compelling but less fully considered merits of his epideictic rhetoric. Mere hours before his inauguration, Mandela describes South African history as an unceasing quest for a democratic constitution. His narrative recasts the country's history of repeated brutalities not as a justification for one party to inflict retributive violence on the other but as a trial that the country itself endured in order to create its constitution:

> Perhaps it was history that ordained that it be here at the Cape of Good Hope that we should lay the foundation stone of our new nation. For it was here at this Cape, over three centuries ago, that there began the fateful convergence of the peoples of Africa, Europe and Asia on these shores.
>
> (Mandela 1994)

Mandela's discourse moves swiftly, and allusively, past the long history of slavery, racially-inspired brutality, and apartheid that typified such "convergence" in order to conclude:

> We have fought for a democratic constitution since the 1880s. Ours has been a quest for a constitution freely adopted by the people of South Africa, reflecting their wishes and their aspirations. The struggle for democracy has never been a matter pursued by one race, class, religious community or gender among South Africans. In honouring those who fought to see this day arrive, we honour the best sons and daughters of all our people. We can count amongst them Africans, Coloureds, Whites, Indians, Muslims, Christians, Hindus, Jews – all of them united by a common vision of a better life for the people of this country.
>
> (Mandela 1994)

Mandela insists that the past should be collectively remembered only to the extent that it suggests ways of transcending history's most divisive legacies in the present. His discourse is not designed to commemorate incidents of violence and conflict; its purpose is to relegate their very memory to the past. Mandela's rhetoric depicts the country itself (a community comprised of previously divided populations) as an object of praise because it has supposedly overcome the conflict for which it was previously to be blamed (see Chapter 14 in this volume for a complimentary demonstration of this theme).

Hence, blame in the present does not follow from blame in the past. Mandela's rhetoric (and other epideictic performances that resemble it) works to neutralize cycles of blame between traditionally opposed groups by professing their common agency in both exacerbating and resolving intrastate violence. Mandela does so in pragmatic political terms:

> Democracy is based on the majority principle. This is especially true in a country such as ours where the vast majority have been systematically

denied their rights. At the same time, democracy also requires that the rights of political and other minorities be safeguarded.

(Mandela 1994)

Perpetrators and victims of violence are, for Mandela, equally to blame for division between formerly opposed parties and equally to praise for renouncing it, whether literally or symbolically. His charge to the country "needs unity of purpose. It needs in action. It requires us all to work together to bring an end to division, an end to suspicion and build a nation united in our diversity" (Mandela 1994).

Other late- or post-conflict leaders may also adopt this formulation in their rhetoric: all may be blameworthy, but for expressly historical animosities, which the community has overcome to create political accord in the present. The past does not justify continued hostilities between armed groups in the present but represents a tragic era for all that all should participate in working to overcome. In Mandela's phrasing:

We place our vision of a new constitutional order for South Africa on the table not as conquerors, prescribing to the conquered. We speak as fellow citizens to heal the wounds of the past with the intent of constructing a new order based on justice for all.

(Mandela 1994)

Such deft appeals to the past and praise for those who have mutually transcended it can reinforce the appeal of political accord, rather than violent opposition, in the present.

Inclusive blame and political transformation

Leaders such as Mandela, who employ an inclusive rhetoric of blame in order to further political transformation, contrast sharply with previously mentioned leaders whose rhetoric invokes collective memories in order to assign blame to others. Blame, in more politically productive appeals, may not be assigned to particular groups as a justification for treating them as enemies; the attribution of blame can represent a form of internal critique that alleviates indices of division. Vaclav Havel's New Year's address to the Czech Republic on 1 January 1990 represents a prime instance of such unconventional epideictic performances. As with Mandela, Havel's role in the Velvet Revolution and political statecraft have been analyzed in detail (see Bradley 1992; Keane 2000); but the significance of his epideictic rhetoric in resolving conflict has been less fully appreciated.

Upon entering office, Havel broke with previous communist customs of ceremonially announcing that Czechoslovakia was thriving; he instead emphasized that the nation was in dire economic, social, and political circumstances stretching back to its communist past. He began:

> For forty years on this day you heard, from my predecessors, variations
> on the same theme: how our country flourished, how many million
> tons of steel we produced, how happy we all were, how we trusted our
> government, and what bright perspectives were unfolding in front of
> us.
>
> (Havel 1997: 3)

But Havel quickly pivots away from the past, from this tradition of "forty
years," in order to draw a stark contrast with the present:

> Our country is not flourishing. The enormous creative and spiritual
> potential of our nation is not being used sensibly. Entire branches of
> industry are producing goods that are of no interest to anyone, while
> we are lacking the things we need.... Our obsolete economy squan-
> ders what little energy we have available. A country once proud of its
> educational standards now spends so little on education that it ranks
> seventy-second in the world. We have contaminated the soil, rivers,
> and forests bequeathed to us by our ancestors, and today we have the
> most polluted environment in Europe.
>
> (Havel 1997: 3)

This is a bruising litany of faults for an audience to receive on a normally
celebratory epideictic occasion; but conspicuously inclusive language –
repeated invocations of "our" and "we" – indicate Havel's larger rhetorical
strategy for resolving conflict.

Havel's discourse entreats sympathetic sectors of the public not to
regard such ills as wrongs done to them by a distant and alien power but
as sins they committed to their own collective detriment. He conveys this
insight simply but powerfully:

> It would be quite unreasonable to understand the sad legacy of the
> last forty years as something alien, something bequeathed to us by
> some distant relative. On the contrary, we must accept this legacy as a
> sin we committed against ourselves. If we accept it as such, we will
> understand that it is up to us all, and up to us alone, to do something
> about it. We cannot blame the previous rulers for everything, not only
> because it would be untrue but also because it could blunt the duty
> each of us faces today, that is, the obligation to act independently,
> freely, reasonably, and quickly.
>
> (Havel 1997: 4–5)

Havel's message is an unconventional appeal for solidarity: what we have
done to ourselves we may be inspired to undo, and be duly praised for it.
"Let us make no mistake," he insists: "the best government in the world,
the best parliament and the best president in the world cannot achieve

much on their own.... Freedom and democracy require participation and therefore responsible action from us all" (1997: 5). Collective blame, in a strange inversion, becomes a necessary precondition for adopting praiseworthy public attitudes of mutual "participation and therefore responsibility."

In Havel's rhetoric, acknowledging mutual blame or responsibility for previously exacerbating violence and discord simultaneously implies grounds for mutual acceptance and transcendence – even forgiveness – as the foundation of a new state. "The worst thing," Havel laments, "is that we live in a contaminated moral environment.... We learned not to believe in anything, to ignore each other, to care only for ourselves. Concepts such as love, friendship, compassion, humility, and forgiveness lost their depth and dimensions" (1997: 4). Throughout Havel's address, blame represents a basis of inclusion, however unfortunate its origins. Others do not embody the ills he bemoans, therefore justifying their dehumanization; the public itself uniformly shares those ills.

Inclusive blame for the poignantly remembered past ironically cultivates, in Havel's message, a recognition of common humanity rather than an excuse for denying others' human rights. In this fashion, Mandela and Havel's epideictic appeals exemplify how ceremonial performances of praise and blame can symbolically communicate reasons for creating a functionally unified political identity in periods of conflict resolution and political transformation (Chapter 11 in this volume analyzes vividly the emergence of such new identity). Such appeals contrast sharply with epideictic performances in which the objects of praise and blame are radically incompatible, and thus imply violently opposed identities and goals.

Conclusion

Epideictic rhetoric (or public discourses of praise and blame) provides insight into modes of speech that may demonstrably help or hinder the work of intrastate conflict resolution. Leaders and spokespersons with violent and peaceful agendas alike may seek to consolidate power and secure support for their causes with a rhetoric of praise and blame that exhorts supporters as well as likely recruits to uphold and defend specific values, norms, or actions and, in so doing, to counteract behaviors that threaten such precepts of communal identity and conduct. The rhetoric of praise and blame also illustrates techniques by which leaders and spokespersons appeal to collective memory as a potentially powerful resource of communal judgment and coordinated action. Epideictic performances routinely gesture to traditionally revered historical exemplars of praiseworthy and blameworthy civic attributes. Such seemingly ceremonial modes of discourse may notably influence the course of political events: even outside of conflict zones, the putative lessons of a community's shared past are omnipresent factors in institutional decision-making.

The present chapter has sought to contribute to literature on conflict resolution by uncovering useful principles with which to assess whether epideictic performances contribute to or detract from the work of political transformation. Such assessments may prove useful in suggesting templates with which to encourage new forms of public speech concerning the selective lessons of the past amidst violent conflict. The chapter has therefore focused on examples of epideictic rhetoric that produced especially demonstrable results in either ending or prolonging armed conflict.

Such especially demonstrative examples may serve policy-makers as evaluative ideals. Not every destructive rhetoric of praise and blame may produce genocide or ethnic cleansing and not every constructive epideictic appeal may inspire the comparatively encouraging results witnessed in South Africa or Czechoslovakia; but scrutinizing particularly destructive or constructive public discourses in this vein indicates especially clear rhetorical ideals against which to measure the relative merits of other discourses bearing similar rhetorical characteristics. In sum, this chapter's examination of instructive rhetorical exemplars is intended to help others pursue a simultaneously informed and adaptable framework for devising constructive discourses of praise or blame in present and future conflicts – a framework *informed* by proven examples yet *adaptable* enough to accommodate future insights gleaned from public discourses yet to be spoken.

References

Alexander, J.C. (2004) "Cultural Pragmatics: Social Performance between Ritual and Strategy," *Sociological Theory* 22: 527–573.

Aristotle. (2007) *On Rhetoric: A Theory of Civic Discourse*, 2nd edn., trans. G.A. Kennedy, New York: Oxford University Press.

Asmal, K. (1997) *Reconciliation through Truth: A Reckoning of Apartheid's Criminal Governance*, 2nd edn., New York: St. Martin's.

Benson, M. (1994) *Nelson Mandela: The Man and the Movement*, New York: W.W. Norton.

Bodnar, J. (1992) *Remaking America: Public Memory, Commemoration, and Patriotism in the Twentieth Century*, Princeton, NJ: Princeton University Press.

Boraine, A. (2001) *A Country Unmasked: Inside South Africa's Truth and Reconciliation Commission*, New York: Oxford University Press.

Bradley, J.F.N. (1992) *Czechoslovakia's Velvet Revolution: A Political Analysis*, Boulder: East European Monographs.

Chapman, A.R. and Merwe, H. van der (2008) *Truth and Reconciliation in South Africa: Did the TRC Deliver?*, Philadelphia: University of Pennsylvania Press.

Chase, R. (1961) "The Classical Conception of Epideictic," *Quarterly Journal of Speech* 47: 293–300.

Christie, K. (2000) *The South African Truth Commission*, New York: St. Martin's.

Cigar, N.L. (2002) *Indictment at The Hague: The Milosevic Regime and Crimes of the Balkan Wars*, New York: New York University Press.

Cohen, L.J. (2001) *Serpent in the Bosom: The Rise and Fall of Slobodan Milosevic*, Boulder: Westview.

Djukic, S. (2001) *Milosevic and Markovic: A Lust for Power*, Montreal: McGill-Queen's University Press.

Doder, D. and Branson, L. (1999) *Milosevic: Portrait of a Tyrant*, New York: The Free Press.

Edelstein, J. (2002) *Truth and Lies: Stories from the Truth and Reconciliation Commission in South Africa*, New York: New Press.

Gunaratna, R. (2002) *Inside Al Qaeda: Global Network of Terror*, New York: Columbia University Press.

Halbwachs, M. (1992) *On Collective Memory*, trans. L.A. Coser, Chicago: University of Chicago Press.

Hashim, A.S. (2006) *Insurgency and Counter-Insurgency in Iraq*, Ithaca: Cornell University Press.

Hauser, G. (1999) "Aristotle on Epideictic: The Formation of Public Morality," *Rhetoric Society Quarterly* 29: 5–23.

Havel, V. (1997) *The Art of the Impossible: Politics as Morality in Practice*, trans. P. Wilson, New York: Alfred A. Knopf.

Herrick, J.A. (2005) *The History and Theory of Rhetoric: An Introduction*, 3rd edn., Boston: Allyn and Bacon.

Judah, T. (2000) *The Serbs: History, Myth and the Destruction of Yugoslavia*, New Haven: Yale University Press.

Keane, J. (2000) *Vaclav Havel: A Political Tragedy in Six Acts*, New York: Basic Books.

LeBor, A. (2004) *Milosevic: A Biography*, New Haven: Yale University Press.

Lincoln, A. (1989) "Address at Gettysburg, Pennsylvania, November 19, 1863," in *Speeches and Writings, 1859–1865*, New York: The Library of America.

Lodge, T. (2006) *Mandela: A Critical Life*, Oxford: Oxford University Press.

Loraux, N. (1986) *The Invention of Athens: The Funeral Oration in the Classical City*, trans. A. Sheridan, Cambridge, MA: Harvard University Press.

McKnight, A.N. (2004) "Historical Trauma, the Persistence of Memory and the Pedagogical Problems of Forgiveness, Justice and Peace," *Educational Studies Journal of the American Educational Studies Association* 36: 140–158.

Mandela, N. (1993) *Nelson Mandela Speaks: Forging a Democratic, Nonracial South Africa*, New York: Pathfinder.

—— (1994) "Inauguration Speech," *Mandela Speaks*. Online, available at: www.anc. org.za/ancdocs/history/mandela/1994/index.html accessed 18 June 2008.

—— (1995) *Long Walk to Freedom: The Autobiography of Nelson Mandela*, Boston: Back Bay Books.

Margalit, A. (2002) *The Ethics of Memory*, Cambridge, MA: Harvard University Press.

Meer, F. (1990) *Higher Than Hope: The Authorized Autobiography of Nelson Mandela*, New York: Harper and Row.

Meredith, M. (1998) *Nelson Mandela: A Biography*, New York: St. Martin's.

—— (1999) *Coming to Terms: South Africa's Search for Truth*, New York: Public Affairs.

Milosevic, S. (2001) "Speech by Slobodan Milosevic at the Central Celebration Marking the 600th Anniversary of the Battle of Kosovo, Gazimestan, 28 June 1989," in H. Krieger (ed.) *The Kosovo Conflict and International Law: An Analytical Documentation, 1974–1999*, Cambridge, UK: Cambridge University Press.

Nuttall, S. and Coetzee, C. (eds.) (1998) *Negotiating the Past: The Making of Memory in South Africa*, Cape Town: Oxford University Press.

Olick, J.K. (ed.) (2003) *States of Memory: Communities, Conflicts, and Transformations in National Retrospection*, Durham: Duke University Press.

Penslar, D.J. (2005) "Herzl and the Palestinian Arabs: Myth and Counter-Myth," *Journal of Israeli History* 24: 65–77.

Perelman, C. and Olbrechts-Tyteca, L. (1971) *The New Rhetoric: A Treatise on Argumentation*, trans. John Wilkinson and Purcell Weaver, Notre Dame: University of Notre Dame Press.

Pericles. (1979) "Funeral Speech," in *The Speeches of Pericles*, by Thucydides, trans. H.G. Edinger, New York: Frederick Ungar.

Rogers, P. (2006) *Iraq and the War on Terror: Twelve Months of Insurgency, 2004/05*, London: I.B. Tauris.

Rotberg, R. (ed.) (2006) *Israeli and Palestinian Narratives of Conflict: History's Double Helix*, Bloomington: Indiana University Press.

Rothstein, R.L. (2006) *How Not to Make Peace: "Conflict Syndrome" and the Demise of the Oslo Accords*, Washington, DC: US Institute of Peace Press.

Sampson, A. (2000) *Mandela: The Authorized Biography*, New York: Vintage.

Sell, L. (2002) *Slobodan Milosevic and the Destruction of Yugoslavia*, Durham: Duke University Press.

Swedenburg, T. (1995) *Memories of Revolt: The 1936–1939 Rebellion and the Palestinian National Past*, Minneapolis: University of Minnesota Press.

Tuman, J.F. (2003) *Communicating Terror: The Rhetorical Dimensions of Terrorism*, Thousand Oaks: Sage.

Wiesel, E. (1977) *Ethics and Memory*, Berlin: Walter de Gruyter.

Wilson, R. (2001) *The Politics of Truth and Reconciliation in South Africa: Legitimizing the Post-Apartheid State*, New York: Cambridge University Press.

Young, J.E. (1993) *The Texture of Memory: Holocaust Memorials and Meaning*, New Haven: Yale University Press.

Zelizer, B. (1995) "Reading against the Grain: The Shape of Memory Studies," *Critical Studies in Mass Communication* 7: 214–239.

7   Peacebuilding, democratization, and transforming the institutions of war

Terrence Lyons

The liberal internationalist paradigm posits that peace, both between and within states, is based on market democracy and that constructing democratic political structures is key to sustainable peace (Mac Ginty 2006; Paris 2004). In the post-Cold War era, the terms of a peace agreement had to meet the expectations of the Western leaders who mediated and provided the resources to implement it and multi-party competition was a key component of these expectations. As part of the transition from war to peace, the legitimacy of a new dispensation of authority through electoral validation was essential. Ottaway and others are sharply critical of this "democratic reconstruction model" that imposes democratization agendas in the unpropitious cases following civil war and state breakdown (Ottaway 2003). International practice, however, continues to look to elections as the mechanism to mark the transition and endorse the new dispensation.

The literature on the politics of peace implementation has grown in recent years (Lyons 2005; Söderberg Kovacs 2007; De Zeeuw 2007; Manning 2008; Sisk and Jarstad 2008). Recent cases suggest that elections have sometimes succeeded in providing a mechanism for selecting new political leadership and institutions capable of preserving the peace and initiating democratization. This was the result in El Salvador, Nicaragua, South Africa, and Mozambique, for example. The outcomes, however, are not always so successful. In Angola the 1992 elections precipitated renewed conflict and the 1997 Liberian elections provided only a brief interregnum before another round of conflict. In other cases, such as Cambodia, Bosnia-Herzegovina, and Tajikistan, elections served more as a mechanism of war termination with only a secondary, limited, and arguably damaging, relationship to democratization. In Sri Lanka and Rwanda, the peace process collapsed before elections, making it difficult to assess the roles of processes to demilitarize politics. Finally, there are cases such as Uganda, Ethiopia, and Rwanda where a victorious insurgent army organized elections to consolidate its rule.

Elections to implement a peace settlement by themselves do not provide the basis for sustainable peace or for the transformation of insurgents into peaceful political players. There are no panaceas to protracted social conflicts. In cases where elections have been part of relatively successful peacebuilding, key processes to "demilitarize politics" were in place prior to the vote. It is not primarily the events on Election Day but rather the processes leading up to the election and the kinds of incentives and opportunities developed that encourage warring factions to shift their strategies from violence to electoral politics. Demilitarization of politics therefore helps transform the institutional basis of war into organizations that can sustain peaceful electoral competition.

The legacy of fear and voting for peace

Fear, polarization and power derived from violence and predation will shape the context of post-settlement elections unless politics is demilitarized during the transitional period prior to the election. Some scholars have advocated that post-settlement elections should be held much later in the transitional process, that powersharing pacts should be negotiated prior to elections to manage the uncertainty of the transition, or that electoral rules should be drafted to encourage inclusive regimes (Paris 2004). Pacts, powersharing, and electoral rules, however, require a degree of confidence in the process that is often lacking in these cases. The challenge therefore is to support processes to demilitarize politics rather than to put in place rules and agreements. If politics has not been demilitarized, additional time, pacts, or electoral systems are unlikely to overcome the legacies of fear and the power of organizations that developed during the war and that are therefore likely to dominate the campaign and win the election.

In contexts where the legacies of war remain dominant, voters often choose to use the limited power of their franchise either to appease the most powerful faction in the hope that this will prevent a return to war or to select the most nationalistic and chauvinistic candidate who can credibly pledge to protect the voter's community. Outside observers often regard these leaders as warlords or war criminals. To vulnerable voters, however, they are seen either as powerful protectors capable of defending the voter from rival military forces or as intimidators to be placated in order to preclude a return to the violence that they threaten to unleash if they lose. Civilian candidates and those who do not have a convincing answer to the issue of post-election security are unlikely to prevail. Post-settlement elections will be dominated by questions of peace and security.

In the 1997 Liberian elections, for example, fears that war would return led many voters to cast their ballots to appease the most dangerous candidate, ex-factional leader Charles Taylor. Supporters chanted: "He killed my ma, he killed my pa, I'm going to vote for him" (Ellis 1999: 109). In Angola in 1992, the insurgent UNITA similarly threatened a return to war if it did not win the election but this strategy backfired with the majority endorsing the incumbent MPLA government. Graffiti on the walls of several towns summed up the choice perceived by many Angolans: "MPLA steals but UNITA kills" (Vines 1993: 6). In Cambodia in 1993, the Khmer Rouge also threatened to return to war, but lacked the military strength to return the country to the full-scale conflict of the past.

In a second set of cases still distorted by the fears and structures of civil war, parties made appeals to protect their constituencies from other threatening parties. In Bosnia–Herzegovina in 1996, parties campaigned in their ethnically defined constituencies by promising to defend their nationality's interests and by heightening the danger of supporting anyone other than a nationalist (International Crisis Group 1996). Ethnic outbidding led to polarization and moderate or multiethnic parties did poorly in the first post-settlement election. In some cases, the best that such elections may be able to do is to reduce the gap between de facto power derived from military strength and *de jure* power based on constitutional and electoral processes. Longer term peacebuilding will be difficult in these circumstances and ending the violence may need to receive priority (in emphasis and sequencing) over democratization.

In a third set of cases, processes to demilitarize politics during the transitional period created a new institutional context by the time elections took place. In El Salvador and Mozambique, for example, politics had been relatively demilitarized prior to elections and voters therefore had less fear that war would return. Both the ruling ARENA party and the insurgent FMLN in El Salvador transformed themselves into effective political parties and demonstrated a willingness to compete on the basis of electoral politics rather than through violence. In Mozambique, relatively effective demobilization, the creation of strong interim institutions based on consultation and joint decision-making, and the support given to RENAMO to encourage it to make the transition from a military to a political organization reduced the strength of the institutions of war relative to the institutions of democratic governance by election day.

Demilitarization of politics

Protracted civil war and peaceful electoral competition are rooted in distinct sets of social institutions. Military-dominated regimes and insurgent forces, economies based on humanitarian relief, black market networks, and predation, as well as polarized social formations and identities shaped by insecurity and fear are all the result of, and the necessary institutional basis for, protracted civil war. Much of the attention in the literature focuses on the transition of insurgent groups but the transformation of military governments and ruling parties is often just as important, as illustrated by Camilla Orjuela and Tom Lodge in this volume. Civilian-oriented political parties, open economies and rule of law, civil society and diverse, multifarious identities based on security and trust are created by and support sustainable peace and democratization. The first steps of the transition from war to peace and the first post-settlement elections therefore are crucial because early precedents will shape which path key actors choose to follow. It is the process leading up to the elections, rather than the outcome of the vote, that is key to demilitarizing politics. As Call argues in the case of El Salvador, "the implementation of the accords, especially the transition of the FMLN to civilian life and into a political party, took place *in anticipation of* the constitutionally slated elections" (emphasis author's) (Call 2002: 388). Louis Kriesberg and Gearoid Millar in this volume also emphasize how the anticipation of future change in the distribution of power and resources contribute to the transformation of conflict strategies.

To demilitarize politics entails creating and reinforcing the incentives and opportunities for the institutions of wartime based on violence, insecurity, and fear to transform themselves into institutions of peacetime based on security and trust. These peacetime institutions, such as political parties and civil society, are critical to sustaining peacebuilding and democracy. Demilitarization of politics therefore is a process of institutional transformation that may or may not take place in the often brief period between ceasefire and post-settlement elections.

Incentives, opportunities, and the demilitarization of politics

To understand processes of post-settlement institutional transformation, it is useful to assume that the parties that enter into a peace process respond to incentives and assess opportunities based on expectations. As Shugart has argued, "decisions by regime and rebel leaders alike to seek a democratic 'exit' from a conflict are based upon rational calculations of the possibilities and limitations inherent in playing the competitive electoral game versus continuing the armed conflict" (Shugart 1992: 121). Successful demilitarization of politics shifts the incentives parties to the conflict face by both raising sanctions against returning to war while simultaneously increasing the incentives for working toward peace. Bermeo makes the point with regard to leaders, but the same challenges face organizations:

> Elites in emerging, post-war democracies face a double challenge. On the one hand, they must raise the costs of violent competition. On the other hand, they must lower the costs of electoral competition. The probability of stable democracy is a function of both these processes and the many variables that drive them.
>
> (Bermeo 2003: 163)

If appreciable progress on demilitarizing politics takes place during the transitional peace implementation period leading to elections, then key decision makers and institutions will alter their strategies and pursue electoral rather than military opportunities.

This perspective therefore emphasizes how parties and their leaders choose strategies in order to make the most of the fresh opportunities that arise during peace implementation; it does not require that individuals transform their perspectives or goals or have a change of heart. Top decision makers may perceive that the prospects for gaining and retaining power and resources are greater if they compete in elections than if they engage in violence and therefore transform their strategies and institutional bases in order to contend more effectively. In Mozambique, for example, both Renamo and Frelimo retained their desire to win political power and continued to view their competition as a zero sum game but shifted their strategies from violence to electoral competition. Similarly, Thania Paffenholz argues in this volume that the Communist Party of Nepal retained its fundamental goals while making a strategic shift from military to political means.

Major shifts in strategy such as a transformation from military to political forms of struggle tend to generate intense periods of intra-party debate and often result in schisms and break-away factions (Manning 2008, Kriesberg and Millar this volume). It is common (perhaps inevitable) that one set of leaders will be ready to make the shift while another set will not. Not every member of the leadership will assess opportunities in the same way. Every move toward peace strengthens some leaders and constituencies but also weakens others. The fundamental shift from pursuing military strategies to pursuing electoral strategies may result from a divided leadership finally reaching a tipping point where a thin majority alters its assessments of the efficacy of the two options.

Shaping such expectations through the demilitarization of politics has two interlinked aspects. The process entails building institutions capable of supporting democratization. Among the key institutions are effective, credible interim regimes (particularly electoral authorities), transformed militarized organizations and the construction of strong political parties, and joint decision making bodies to manage the demobilization and security sector reform process. These processes and institutions increase and make more credible the rewards for participating in and accepting outcomes of electoral competition while simultaneously reducing the perceived rewards for engaging in violence. An electoral commission that is acceptable by all main parties as legitimate will reduce fears that the other party will cheat. The processes by which security sector reform is conducted also contribute to the demilitarization of politics. If done well, these processes of security sector reform decrease both the incentives and capacity to return to war. These two aspects are interlinked and progress on one encourages the demilitarization process in the other. For example, building effective political parties increases the prospects for demobilization, as groups perceive that they can protect their interests through political rather than a military means and therefore are ready to lay down their arms. Processes to demilitarize politics simultaneously increase both the incentives and opportunities to play by the rules of non-violent electoral competition and decrease the incentives and opportunities to seek power by engaging in violence.

Interim administration

One component of demilitarizing politics entails building interim institutions that can generate precedents and support perceptions that peaceful electoral processes can work. Interim governments derive their authority from the extent to which they prepare the country for meaningful elections and turn power over to the winners. In the meantime, however, the country needs to be governed. Critical and contentious policy decisions must be made and implemented. The processes through which such policies are made will shape the expectations of the major actors and may either inspire confidence or ignite fears. Disputes are inevitable during the transition, as the broad (and often vague, if not contradictory) principles listed in the peace agreement must be made operational in a difficult atmosphere characterized by fear and distrust. As suggested by analysts of security dilemmas, a key to successful interim administration is to build institutional frameworks that bind the parties in self-restraint and mutual cooperation without increasing the risk of exploitation from a spoiler who does not comply (Posen 1993; Stedman 1997).

Institutions based upon on-going consultations, bargaining, and joint decision-making provide a framework for continuing cooperation and encourage the development of a constituency that supports such cooperation (Kelman 1999). Fortna (2003) develops similar findings in her examination of the durability of international peace agreements, arguing that such joint commissions provide an important signal of intentions. Parties engaged in such problem-solving processes may develop a sense of partnership (even if only tentatively and tactically) and perceive a joint interest in managing risk and marginalizing extremists and spoilers (including those within their own parties) who want to derail the peace process. A process of self-interested mutual adjustment of behavior may initiate a self-reinforcing cycle of increased cooperation and confidence (Rothchild 1995; Sisk 1996). Effective interim regimes constructed around sustained dialogue help manage the uncertainty of transitions and thereby encourage democratization (Przeworski 1986).

Interim electoral commissions provide a particularly important opportunity to demilitarize politics by building consultative mechanisms and norms that increase confidence in the peace process and the legitimacy of the post-settlement elections. With so much at stake, decisions on electoral plans and processes are, inevitably, highly contentious and electoral institutions become the focus of partisan struggles. In a context of high mistrust, parties fear that their opponents will capture the electoral commission and tilt the rules. Electoral administration that does not address the fears and mistrust of key parties, particularly recently warring and incompletely demobilized parties, may reignite conflict. If, however, collaborative institutions are developed to manage the electoral process during the transition, greater confidence in the peace process can be nurtured and the prospects for an election that promotes both peace and democracy enhanced (Lyons 2004).

In El Salvador, the 1991 peace accords set up the National Commission for the Consolidation of Peace (Comisión Nacional para la Conslidación de la Paz, COPAZ), a body with representation evenly split between the government and its allies and the opposition including the FMLN insurgents, with observer status for the United Nations and the Catholic Church. COPAZ was conceived as the major forum for verifying compliance and resolving disputes during the implementation of the peace agreements and was an important guarantee to the FMLN (since the insurgents did not have representation in the parliament at the time) (Fagen 1996; Byrne 1996). COPAZ debated and passed implementing legislation under the peace agreement, ranging from a new electoral law to constitutional amendments that redefined the role of the armed forces. Because the commission was evenly split between the government and the opposition, "hammering out compromises became a political necessity – and a newly acquired skill for many politicians" (Montgomery 1995: 233–234). COPAZ's structure led to slow and cumbersome decision-making, compelling endless rounds of negotiations among parties (Holiday and Stanley 1993: 427–429). From the perspective of building new norms to demilitarize politics, however, such continuous discussion is a strong asset. When problems arose over the electoral system, over delays in reforming the police, or when an FMLN arms cache was uncovered after the deadline for disarmament, COPAZ was able to keep the parties talking and to keep the process moving toward elections. While the transition was uncertain, interim institutions in which they had an effective voice managed their fears of losing everything.

> The course of the implementation of the accords was determined by a process of political bargaining [whereby] … political actors hammered out agreements and concessions on the various issues that reflected the evolving balance of power among the contending interests.
>
> (Wood 1996: 101–102)

The Abuja II peace process in Liberia (1996–1997), in contrast, represented a much more minimal framework for a ceasefire leading to quick elections with little ongoing bargaining or attention to building effective interim institutions that could serve as the basis for longer-term peacebuilding and democratization. The interim Liberian Council of State consisted of representatives of the major warring factions along with representatives of civil society organizations, but interim administration was parceled out to each of the many factions and the generally stalemated Council of State lacked the authority to coordinate. The rival parties rarely engaged in talks regarding the administration of the interim period or to build a sense of confidence in the peace process. Each instead sought to place loyalists in key locations within the bureaucracy where they could tap into resources and patronage. Rather than a process of political bargaining among the main Liberian parties, the peace implementation process was managed unilaterally by the West African peacekeeping force without consultation with the Liberian parties or people (Lyons 1999).

In a number of cases, the international community played significant administrative roles and provided fewer opportunities for joint decision making and bargaining among the ex-combatants. In Cambodia, the United Nations assumed a large role in the administration of the state, although the incumbent Cambodian Peoples' Party maintained its authority over many issues in part due to the lack of UN capacity to manage day-to-day affairs. The large international presence in Bosnia–Herzegovina played a decisive role in managing key areas of administration, including preparations for elections, although the Dayton Accords left other areas under the authority of local, ethnically based institutions.

These cases suggest that peace implementation should emphasize creating the spaces and building opportunities for the formerly warring parties to work together in joint decision making institutions. Continuous bargaining and regular processes of consultation may generate contentious debate and disorderly outcomes but such decision making processes demilitarize politics more than well designed and efficiently implemented administration that excludes the parties. Sustainable peacebuilding relies more fundamentally on altering the perceptions and expectations of the parties.

Transforming militias into political parties

It is extremely difficult for insurgents and military governments that derived their power from the conflict to play the role of competing political parties in a democratic system if they remain unreconstructed and organized as they were during the period of armed violence. Peace implementation processes and their ability to support the demilitarization of politics influence the transformation of militias into political parties. In the more successful cases of transition, particularly in El Salvador, Mozambique, and Nepal, processes to demilitarize politics encouraged military organizations to transform themselves into political parties able to operate effectively in an electoral context. In the less successful or failed cases, particularly Bosnia–Herzegovina, Angola, Liberia, and Tajikistan, insurgents and military regimes retained the ability to operate as military forces at the time of elections, thereby weakening the capacity of post-conflict elections to mark a transition to civilian rule.

Some militias do not make the transition and fade away while others resist losing power and act as spoilers. Not every military organization can or should be a political party. *La Unidad Revolucionaria Nacional Guatemalteca* (URNG) in Guatemala, the political party that developed out of the insurgency, has failed to win more than a handful of seats, as noted by Michael Allison in this volume. The Revolutionary United Front (RUF) in Sierra Leone collapsed as a political party but retained an institutional identity that focused on advocating for more generous assistance to ex-combatants (Richards and Vincent 2007). Under the Abuja II peace agreement, all Liberian military factions had equal representation in the interim Council of State. After the 1997 elections, however, it was clear that only Taylor's National Patriotic Party had significant support and that the others (ULIMO-J, ULIMO-K, LPC) were less significant. The United Tajik Opposition and the Islamist parties also played vastly reduced roles after failing to do well in the 1999 elections. Sustainable peacebuilding need not require that every military faction become an effective political faction.

In some successful cases, military organizations were transformed into political parties prior to the election. For example, the transformation of the insurgent Renamo from an armed insurgency into a viable civilian political party able to play a constructive role in a multiparty electoral process was critical to the successful Mozambique peace process (Manning 2002, Bartoli *et al.* this volume). UN Special Representative Ajello recognized that peace implementation required Renamo to become a political party and that the international community should fund this transformation: "Democracy has a cost and we must pay that cost" (Vines 1996: 146). After initial concerns from donors reluctant to fund a party with a particularly brutal reputation, a $19 million fund was established. Some of the delay in implementing the peace agreement was due to Renamo's desire to have more time to complete its transformation into a political party prior to voting. To fill the many posts in interim institutions, Renamo recruited new, better-educated officials who, over the period of the transition, became more influential at the expense of the old wartime leaders. The slate of parliamentary candidates represented this younger, civilian group and included few wartime leaders (Manning 2002).

The ruling Frelimo party went through its own transformation. As Bartoli *et al.* argue in this volume, both Renamo and Frelimo changed strategies and accepted a "redefinition of the political space." The party began as a liberation movement, drawing strength from diverse elements of Mozambican society during the struggle against Portuguese colonialism, then transformed itself into a Marxist–Leninist vanguard party with restricted membership after independence in 1975. The party transformed itself into a "democratic socialist" organization and then endorsed a multi-party constitution in 1990 (Simpson 1993). This transition created tensions within Frelimo and the "move from party-state to simple party, and

from Marxist–Leninist vanguard party to mass-based party affected both
the ideals and interests, for the leadership and the party base alike"
(Manning 2002: 125). It was this new political organization, rather than
the Marxist–Leninist party that had fought the civil war earlier in the
1980s, that made peace with Renamo and engaged in the post-settlement
elections.

In Angola, some observers expected UNITA to make the transition
from insurgency to political party in accordance with the Bicesse agreement with relative ease. A pre-election assessment characterized UNITA as
a "sophisticated, versatile organization with proven resilience and discipline" and concluded that:

> Given standard indicators for organizational effectiveness – chain of
> command, responsiveness of policy decisions to local as well as
> national demands, resilience and regeneration in the face of disrup-
> tions, etc. – UNITA ranked favorably against established political
> parties in Central and South America, the Caribbean, Central Europe,
> and the Balkans.
>
> (Henderson and Stewart 1991: 9)

But in the end UNITA did not transform itself and participated in the
elections as a military organization. UNITA leader Jonas Savimbi demonstrated he was an "all-or-nothing" player and held onto his determination
to accept nothing less than the presidency. Poorly designed and implemented demobilization programs, a weak UN peacekeeping operation,
and UNITA's ability to tap into resources such as diamonds to rearm and
remain in the field resulted in UNITA perceiving more attractive alternatives than accepting the role of loyal opposition following electoral defeat.

A sustained shift from violence to non-violence requires the transformation of the institutions of war into institutions that can sustain peace.
Renamo and Frelimo in Mozambique, the FMLN and ARENA in El Salvador, and the Communist Party of Nepal made this transition and played
crucial roles in supporting the shift from violence to electoral competition. In contrast, UNITA (and perhaps the incumbent MPLA regime) in
Angola, the NPFL and other militias in Liberia, the Khmer Rouge (and
perhaps the incumbent CPP) in Cambodia, and the Peoples' Democratic
Party (PDP) in Tajikistan did not.

Demobilization and demilitarization of politics

The demobilization of armed forces is a process at the heart of peace
implementation. For a successful, sustainable transition from war to peace,
the warring parties need to demobilize and create new, accountable security forces. Reducing the number of soldiers under the command of the
leaders of the conflicting parties will increase the prospects for effective

post-settlement elections by reducing the viability of returning to war. In addition, however, the process by which demobilization takes places has the potential to play an additional role in demilitarizing politics. As with electoral preparations, if demobilization is organized around joint problem solving and collaborative decision-making, then the process will promote new institutions appropriate for democratization as well as reducing the capacity for armed conflict. In other words, over and above the important part played by reducing the numbers of combatants, demobilization can serve as an opportunity to launch new institutional models, create precedents conducive to sustaining democratization, and establish new norms that support peacebuilding. A top-down or internationally led process of demobilization can meet the goal of reintegrating ex-combatants into civilian life. A process of demobilization that is based upon consultations and joint decision-making, however, will have the critically important additional benefit of building new institutions that demilitarize politics and thereby increase the prospects for sustainable peacebuilding.

Security sector reform is inherently a highly political process in a context where political power is shifting away from armed groups and violence and toward civil institutions and electoral politics. As Berdal argues, there is "interplay, a subtle interaction, between the dynamics of a peace process and the manner in which the disarmament, demobilization and reintegration provisions associated with that process are organized, funded and implemented" (Berdal 1996: 73). Successful demobilization will reduce the opportunities of those who might be inclined to act as spoilers and use violence to sabotage a peace process. As demobilization proceeds apace and as the dividends of peace deepen, actors may become trapped in a politics of moderation whereby the attractiveness of maintaining the peace rise, the rewards for returning to war shrink, resulting in a higher probability of successful peace implementation. In many cases, of course, the incentives that peace offers are insufficient for one or another faction to abandon violent strategies and spoilers emerge who have the potential to derail the transition to peace (Stedman 1997; Darby 2001; Newman and Richmond 2006).

Demilitarization of politics may result from a combination of effective political process and effective demobilization. What matters is that leaders and rank-and-file change expectations and perceive that they will not be vulnerable if they demobilize and disarm, rather than a precise number of soldiers reintegrated and weapons collected. When challenged that parties were hedging their bets and hiding weapons, UN Special Representative to Mozambique Ajello responded:

> I know very well that they will give us old and obsolete material, and they will have here and there something hidden. I don't care. What I do is create the political situation in which the use of those guns is not the question. So that they stay where they are.
>
> (Hall 1994: 24)

Demobilization therefore encourages the demilitarization of politics both by decreasing the means, and hence likelihood of a return to warfare and by increasing confidence in and hence the incentives to participate in a political process.

Conclusion

The demilitarization of politics perspective therefore focuses attention on the processes by which the former parties to the conflict relate to one another during the peace implementation process following civil war and how these interactions may promote the adoption of strategies that can support peacebuilding. At the time of the initial ceasefire, organizations made powerful by the war will dominate the political landscape. During the transitional period leading up to post-settlement elections, a new context can shift the incentives and opportunities organizations face and thereby encourage the transformation of institutions whose origins lay in violent conflict into institutions whose future lies in democratic competition. In this way, post-settlement elections are both the context for demilitarization of politics to take place and the event that will demonstrate the extent to which that transformation has taken place.

Post-settlement elections have become a ubiquitous component of civil war settlements, supported by the international community since the end of the Cold War. In recent years there has been a vigorous policy debate about whether elections are useful in such difficult cases as Afghanistan, Iraq, and the Democratic Republic of Congo. Yet elections remain a core component of the transitional plans in these cases. Despite the widely recognized limits to elections and the potential for elections to exacerbate tensions in post-settlement contexts, there seem to be few alternatives to this mechanism of peace implementation.

Post-settlement elections are often criticized for failing to advance democratization. This is often true but misses the potential for such elections to promote important war termination goals even if they fail to promote democratization. Policy makers seeking to address the challenges of post-settlement reconstruction cannot afford to make democratization their one and only goal and must accept that in many of the difficult cases war termination is the only available short-term option that provides at least the potential for long-term stability and eventual transition to democracy (Lyons 2002). In this way, moving forward with elections even in a context where politics remains militarized may be the "least bad" option.

Peace implementation should focus on what kinds of institutional transformations may take place in the period between the signing of the peace accord and the post-settlement election. In difficult cases like Angola, El Salvador, Cambodia, Mozambique, Bosnia-Herzegovina, Liberia, and Tajikistan – as well as Iraq, Afghanistan, and the Democratic Republic of

Congo – there will be few opportunities to promote peacebuilding and democratization through powersharing pacts, electoral system engineering, or delaying the elections until security is firmly established. Even these difficult cases, however, often have openings to advance the demilitarization of politics by encouraging the transformation of the institutions of war into political institutions that can support peace, as was seen in Mozambique and El Salvador.

For the international community, the peace implementation process following civil war presents a number of opportunities. Greater emphasis should be placed on the processes that shape how the parties to the conflict relate to each other during the transition rather than to elements in the peace agreement itself or international peacekeeping policy. By emphasizing the internal dynamics among parties and institutions during the interim phase rather than powersharing arrangements or international guarantees, the issue of what policies support successful implementation shifts. Rather than asking for additional provisions in the peace accord, trying to negotiate a post-election powersharing pact (a difficult challenge given the imperatives to negotiate a ceasefire), or promising an international security "guarantee" (a guarantee that is rarely credible), it is more useful to ask how the implementation process can strengthen inter-party patterns of cooperation, trust, and overcome insecurity. The peace agreement becomes the starting point for another series of negotiations, bargaining, and institution building rather than a blueprint to be enacted. The interim period will represent a fluid period during which parties and leadership change, expectations are formed, and the fears and interests that motivated the initial ceasefire agreement are transformed. The outcome of this period of continued bargaining and maneuvering for advantage provides the context for post-settlement elections more than the initial agreement or the international community.

To the extent that a process to demilitarize politics can be initiated, the precedents and institutional basis for sustainable peace and democratization can be supported. Donor support for strong and effective interim administrations, particularly those based on consultation and collaborative problem solving, can help create a new institutional context that bridges the structures of war to structures that can sustain peace and democracy. In particular, donors and international organizations should examine electoral commissions and recognize them as opportunities not only to administer good elections but also as opening for confidence building and potential models for new forms of cooperation and peaceful competition. The transformation of militarized institutions into political parties has enormous potential to bolster both the war termination and democratization agendas of post-settlement elections. Finally demobilization and security sector reform provide opportunities not only to reduce the potential for a return to war but also to build institutions that will encourage ex-combatants to change their evaluation of their future prospects and pursue electoral strategies. The process of implementing peace and promoting democracy following civil war is difficult but recent experience suggests that processes to demilitarize politics can – and must – begin during the transitional period.

References

Berdal, M.R. (1996) *Disarmament and Demobilisation after Civil Wars*, London: International Institute for Strategic Studies Adelphi Paper no. 303.

Bermeo, N. (2003) "What the Democratization Literature Says – or Doesn't Say – About Postwar Democratization," *Global Governance* 9: 159–177.

Byrne, H. (1996) *El Salvador's Civil War: A Study of Revolution*, Boulder, CO: Lynne Rienner.

Call, C.T. (2002) "Assessing El Salvador's Transition from Civil War to Peace," in S.J. Stedman, D. Rothchild and E.M. Cousens (eds.) *Ending Civil Wars: The Implementation of Peace Agreements*, Boulder, CO: Lynne Rienner.

Call, C.T. and Stanley, W. (2003) "Military and Police Reform after Civil Wars," in J. Darby and R. Mac Ginty (eds.) *Contemporary Peacemaking: Conflict, Violence, and Peace Processes*, Hampshire: Palgrave Macmillan.

Darby, J. (2001) *The Effects of Violence on Peace Processes*, Washington, DC: United States Institute of Peace Press.

Ellis, S. (1999) *The Mask of Anarchy: The Destruction of Liberia and the Religious Dimensions of an African Civil War*, New York: New York University Press.

Fagen, P.W. (1996) "El Salvador, Lessons in Peace Consolidation," in Tom Farer (ed.) *Beyond Sovereignty: Collectively Defending Democracy in the Americas*, Baltimore, MD: Johns Hopkins University Press.

Fortna, V.P. (2003) "Scraps of Paper? Agreements and the Durability of Peace," *International Organization* 57: 337–372.

Hall, B. (1994) "Blue Helmets, Empty Guns," *New York Times Sunday Magazine*, 2 January.

Henderson, R.E. and Stewart, E.B. (1991) *UNITA after the Cease-Fire: The Emergence of a Party*, Washington, DC: National Republican Institute for International Affairs.

Holiday, D. and Stanley, W. (1993) "Building the Peace: Preliminary Lessons from El Salvador," *Journal of International Affairs* 46: 415–438.

International Crisis Group (1996) *Elections in Bosnia and Herzegovina*, Europe Report no. 16. Online, available at: www.crisisgroup.org/library/documents/report_archive/A400148_22091996.pdf accessed 25 June 2008.

Kelman, H.C. (1999) "Transforming the Relationship between Former Enemies: A Social-Psychological Analysis," in R.L. Rothstein (ed.) *After the Peace: Resistance and Reconciliation*, Boulder, CO: Lynne Rienner.

Lyons, T. (1999) *Voting for Peace: Postconflict Elections in Liberia*, Washington, DC: Brookings Institution Press.

Lyons, T. (2002) "The Role of Postsettlement Elections," in S.J. Stedman, D. Rothchild and E.M. Cousens (eds.) *Ending Civil Wars: The Implementation of Peace Agreements*, Boulder, CO: Lynne Rienner.

Lyons, T. (2004) "Postconflict Elections and the Process of Demilitarizing Politics: The Role of Electoral Administration," *Democratization* 11: 1–27.

Lyons, T. (2005) *Demilitarizing Politics: Elections on the Uncertain Road to Peace*, Boulder, CO: Lynne Rienner.

Mac Ginty, R. (2006) *No War, No Peace: The Rejuvenation of Stalled Peace Processes and Peace Accords*, New York: Palgrave Macmillan.

Manning, C.J. (2002) *The Politics of Peace in Mozambique: Post-Conflict Democratization, 1992–2000*, Westport, CT: Praeger.

Manning, C.J. (2008) *The Making of Democrats: Elections and Party Development in Bosnia, El Salvador, and Mozambique*, New York: Palgrave Macmillan.

Montgomery, T.S. (1995) *Revolution in El Salvador: From Civil Strife to Civil Peace*, New York: Westview.

Newman, E. and Richmond, O. (eds.) (1996) *Challenges to Peacebuilding: Managing Spoilers during Conflict Resolution*, New York: United Nations University Press.

Ottaway, M. (2003) "Promoting Democracy after Conflict: The Difficult Choices," *International Studies Perspectives* 4: 314–322.

Paris, R. (2004) *At War's End: Building Peace after Civil Conflict*, Cambridge: Cambridge University Press.

Posen, Barry R. (1993) "The Security Dilemma and Ethnic Conflict," in M.E. Brown (ed.) *Ethnic Conflict and International Security*, Princeton, NJ: Princeton University Press.

Przeworski, A. (1986) "Some Problems in the Study of the Transition to Democracy," in Guillermo O'Donnell, Philippe C. Schmitter and Laurence Whitehead (eds.) *Transitions from Authoritarian Rule: Comparative Perspectives*, Baltimore, MD: Johns Hopkins University Press.

Richards, P. and Vincent, J. (2007) "Sierra Leone: The Marginalization of the RUF," in J. de Zeeuw (ed.) *From Soldiers to Politicians: Transforming Rebel Movements after Civil War*, Boulder, CO: Lynne Rienner.

Rothchild, D. (1995) "Bargaining and State Breakdown in Africa," *Nationalism and Ethnic Politics* 1: 54–72.

Schedler, A. (2006) *Electoral Authoritarianism: The Dynamics of Unfree Competition*, Boulder, CO: Lynne Rienner.

Shugart, M.S. (1992) "Guerrillas and Elections: An Institutionalist Perspective on the Costs of Conflict and Cooperation," *International Studies Quarterly* 36: 121–151.

Simpson, M. (1993) "Foreign and Domestic Factors in the Transformation of Frelimo," *Journal of Modern African Studies* 31: 309–337.

Sisk, T.D. (1996) *Power Sharing and International Mediation in Ethnic Conflict*, Washington, DC: United States Institute of Peace Press.

Sisk, T.D. and Jarstad, A. (eds.) (2008) *From War to Democracy: Dilemmas of Peacebuilding*, Cambridge: Cambridge University Press.

Söderberg Kovacs, M. (2007) *From Rebellion to Politics: The Transformation of Rebel Groups to Political Parties in Civil War Peace Processes*, Uppsala University Report no. 77.

Stedman, S.J. (1997) "Spoiler Problems in Peace Processes," *International Security* 22: 5–53.

Vines, A. (1993) *One Hand Tied: Angola and the U.N.*, London: Catholic Institute of International Relations.

Vines, A. (1996) *Renamo: From Terrorism to Democracy in Mozambique?*, London: James Currey.

Wood, E.J. (1996) "The Peace Accords and Postwar Reconstruction," in James K. Boyce (ed.) *Economic Policy for Building Peace: The Lessons of El Salvador*, Boulder, CO: Lynne Rienner.

Zeeuw, J. de (ed.) (2007) *From Soldiers to Politicians: Transforming Rebel Movements after Civil War*, Boulder, CO: Lynne Rienner.

8 Insecurity and opportunity in conflict settings

Gavan Duffy

In this volume, we set before ourselves a central problem of the contemporary world – a world in which culturally and ethnically distinct communities increasingly impinge upon one another. We investigate the parameters of constructive conflict transformation (Kriesberg 2007). We pose this question: short of the unilateral capitulation of one group of partisans to its rivals, under what conditions do adversaries forego violent confrontation in favor of negotiation and compromise?

This question contains a presumption – the presumption of rationality. It precludes answers that refer to the putative irrationality of violent action. It implicitly dismisses any account that would characterize those who resort to violence as "evil-doers," "fanatics," "crazies," or the like. To the contrary, our question presupposes that group leaders would forego violent tactics if conditions indicated to them that violence would not serve their ends. It thereby presumes the rationality of those who employ violent conflict means. That is, they are presumptively open to persuasion.

My hunch, and also my hope, is that this presumption of rationality (a presumption that conflict analysts nowadays widely accept) more or less accurately reflects reality. If it does not, there can be no route to peace except through the surrender of the vanquished. Fortunately, we have many demonstration proofs. Longstanding, exceedingly violent community conflicts occasionally end through settlements negotiated and implemented by political leaders. This assures us that leaders of violent conflicts can in principle reason with one another and arrive at mutually acceptable accommodations. Peace is possible.

The common tendency to doubt the rationality of those who employ violent conflict tactics arises naturally enough. After all, political elites have long employed the practice of mobilizing their followers for fighting by distributing to them "solidary incentives" (Duffy and Lindstrom 2002). That is, they encourage participation in conflicts by exploiting their constituents' personal identification with the group. Leaders issue communications to followers that glorify their own group as they vilify their adversaries. It requires no great inferential leap to conclude that one cannot reason with an adversary when one's political leaders repeatedly characterize that adversary as sub-human or inherently evil.

Because they are both effective and relatively costless to distribute, solidary incentives appear widely across conflict settings. State leaders typically enjoy access to the resources needed to distribute material benefits selectively to those who participate in defense of their regimes. Yet, even they find it advantageous to distribute solidary incentives, as they cast their adversaries as a "great Satan" or part of an "axis of evil."

Vivian (this volume) details the rhetorical strategies political leaders use in distributing solidary incentives. Cataloguing these strategies seems a useful endeavor. It would boost the likelihood that we will recognize their future employment and more readily distinguish leaders' instrumental rhetoric from their actual motives. As analysts interested in understanding conflict and the use of violent means, we compel ourselves to examine the motives behind the rhetoric.

Insecurity

Although likely not their sole motivating force, security concerns underlies a large proportion of political conflicts. Because fighting is a highly risky undertaking, political leaders generally do not choose violence unless they believe themselves and/or their constituents threatened by an adversary. I intend a rather broad conception of security here, one not limited to threats of physical force. For instance, an adversary may threaten one's livelihood, one's freedom to associate or worship, one's access to education, one's access to resources, etc. In short, a security threat is a threat to self-determination in all its manifest forms.

Beneath the surface rhetoric, feelings of insecurity among the elites and mass constituencies of one or more communities can be found in most conflicts. The conflict in Northern Ireland exemplifies this well. A wide variety of explanations have been offered for this conflict, such as religious differences, cultural distinctions, British imperialism, economic inequality and deficiencies in institutional design. After a careful and detailed critical review of these and other explanations for the Northern Irish "Troubles," McGarry and O'Leary (1995: 348) portray Northern Ireland as "the site of twin nation-building failures." The unionists have failed to integrate themselves into the British state and the nationalists have failed to integrate themselves into the Irish state. Moreover, the conflict represents, in miniature, the historic conflict between the competing nationalisms of Ireland and Britain.

The failures of these sovereignty claims produced a great deal of insecurity all around. Nationalists felt insecure because, as a minority within Northern Ireland, they believed themselves systematically oppressed by the unionist majority. Unionists, for their part, felt insecure because they were a minority on the island. Until very recently, the Irish Constitution claimed jurisdiction over Northern Ireland. Unionists and loyalists also feared that the British may eventually jettison them from the United Kingdom. Ireland felt insecure because the British, formerly their colonial rulers, maintained a foothold on the island. Finally, although its representatives consistently deny it, the British state felt insecure and wished to maintain its foothold in Ireland, because the island could be used as a staging ground from which to launch an invasion of Britain. The Republic of Ireland's choice to remain neutral in World War II exacerbated this insecurity.

Other issues animated the struggle in Northern Ireland, of course. Religion, class and nationality were certainly at issue and doubtless still are. The suggestion is only that, at base, this conflict has concerned security. Other issues that have arisen doubtless motivated the participation of many. As leaders derogate their opponents, they stir religious animosities, rail about economic inequalities across communities and decry the violent, colonial and/or oppressive historical actions of their rivals. These representations encourage insecurity among their mass constituents. Simultaneously, they encourage individual constituents to develop what Kurt Lewin (1948) termed "a sense of common fate" with others in the community. In delivering solidary incentives, leaders purposefully foster the sense of insecurity among their followers and ready them for direct, confrontational action.

Insecurity, then, is a layered affair. At the surface, one finds popular representations of insecurity replete with references to the heroism of valiant defenders of the in-group and to atrocities committed by the out-group. Beneath this level lies the residue of leaders' distributions of solidary incentives that underpin the surface narratives of heroism and atrocity. These are popular internalizations of leaders' attributions of evil intentions to adversaries and also of leaders' glorifications of the in-group. At the deepest layer one finds the core problem – the insecurity that motivated leaders' distributions of incentives and the emergence of narratives of heroism and atrocity.

Insecurity issues at this deepest level deserve the bulk of our analytical focus. We should distinguish these issues sharply from the attributions that comprise more surface layers. The narratives and attributions of the surface levels certainly help to reproduce conflicts and can even exacerbate them. They are consequently worthy of study, if only to develop practical measures to counter their ill effects. But they are more consequences of adversarial contention than causes. One more often finds insecurity's cause in the desire to achieve, or in the fear of losing, group self-determination.

Leaders are unlikely to give up violent confrontation unless they see the prospect of attaining or retaining security in this sense. Even then, the insecurities that they themselves spread through their rhetorical representations to constituents may limit their ability to make conciliatory moves, even if they perceive a real prospect of securing group self-determination. Nevertheless, our interest in transforming lethal conflicts into less violent forms of political contention motivates us to examine insecurity more closely.

Insecurity has a curious property – in certain contexts it breeds further insecurity. I refer here to the "security dilemma" first described by Herz (1951) and Butterfield (1951) and subsequently treated extensively as a major concern in much "neo-realist" scholarship in international relations. The idea is rather simple. Neo-realists presume that, because no institution exists to police the activities of states, the international system is essentially anarchical. Consequently, they believe in "self-help" – that each state is responsible for its own survival and thus also its own defense. Now, consider state A and assume it to be non-aggressive and peace-loving. Suppose further that state A nevertheless believes itself vulnerable to external attack. To prevent such an attack, state A builds up its arms and military personnel. This, it believes, will discourage external attack. However, now consider state B, which we will assume to be just as non-aggressive and peace-loving as state A. Suppose state B observes state A's military buildup. It might well misperceive the intention behind state A's activity. It might even construe state A's buildup to be so threatening that it decides to strike state A preemptively. This is the security dilemma – in addressing its own perceived insecurity, state A unwittingly renders itself more insecure.

Immediately, intrastate conflict appears an inappropriate domain in which to apply the security dilemma analytically. The dilemma can arise only in anarchic contexts, where political units (typically ethnic groups in intrastate settings) must fend for themselves (self-help). To the extent that incumbent regimes lack governance capacity, the political context is effectively anarchic and groups must engage in self-help. Intrastate security dilemmas most likely arise, then, in situations in which intergroup animosities fester within the context of a regime without, or with vanishingly little, capacity.

Posen (1993) first proposed the intrastate ethnic conflict application of the neo-realist security dilemma. He argued that the dilemma offered analytical leverage in accounting for events in the Serbo-Croatian conflict that emerged as Yugoslavia weakened. He contrasted the Serbo-Croatian rivalry with relations between Ukrainians and ethnic Russians in Ukraine after the Soviet collapse, where the relative absence of great ethnic antipathies and the proximity of Russian military forces mitigated ethnic insecurity.

Several ethnic conflict applications of the security dilemma have appeared since Posen's. Kaufman (1996a; 1996b) uses it in comparisons of the Serbo-Croatian conflict, the fight between Azerbaijan and Armenia over Nagorno-Karabakh and the brief conflict in Moldova between Moldovan nationalists and ethnic Russians. His comparisons indicate that ethnic war arises from interactions between: (*a*) longstanding ethnic animosities; (*b*) mass mobilization through distributions of solidary incentives (my term, not his); and (*c*) the security dilemma.

Melander (1999) finds support for the security dilemma in a quantitative study of 85 conflicts in the 1990–1994 period that were undergoing transition from Leninism. He also conducts qualitative studies of two simultaneous conflicts in Bosnia–Herzegovina – between ethnic Serbs and ethnic Croats and between ethnic Serbs and the Bosnian state. Only the former conforms to the security dilemma.

Roe (1999, 2000, 2002, 2005) takes as his primary cases two instances of ethnic fighting in the early 1990s: (*a*) the brief flare-up between Hungarians and Romanians in Transylvania in 1990; and (*b*) the conflict between Serbs and Croats in the Krajina region of Croatia. Roe subcategorizes instances of what he terms the societal security dilemma on the basis of their relative "tightness." Tight security dilemmas closely resemble the original formulation taken from neo-realist international relations theory. Regular security dilemmas, to the contrary, do not rely on misperceptions of group intentions, as in tight security dilemmas. Security is constant-sum in regular dilemmas, in that security for one group implies a measure of insecurity for the other. In loose security dilemmas, in contradistinction to the other two, groups do not seek security solely but may also be power-seeking. Roe contends that the relative tightness has implications for third parties, as external intervention is more likely to succeed in conflicts with tighter dilemmas.

I do not challenge the substance of these works. I stipulate that each offers insights into a class of conflicts of which the particular cases they analyze are representative. However, I do question the generality of this approach. The analyses of Posen, Kaufman, Melander and Roe all center on ethnic conflicts in post-communist societies. Perhaps this should not surprise us. The premises of the security dilemma fit only those conflict contexts in which the state has effectively collapsed. But this feature is absent from the vast bulk of conflict contexts. Beyond the post-communist cases, Lake and Rothchild (1996) identify Somalia and Liberia as cases for which the logic of the security dilemma may have some analytic leverage. But these two cases add precious little to the security dilemma's empirical scope.

Most violent intrastate conflicts take place where states are weak, but rarely are they so weak that one can consider the political environment effectively anarchic. The very weakness of these states (in terms of their ability to deliver services and maintain an operating infrastructure) makes them susceptible to challenge from internal groups and prompts their repressive actions against those groups (Thomas 1987). This is hardly anarchy. Most intrastate conflicts are consequently incompatible with the presumptions of neo-realist analysis generally (Job 1992: 17–18) and with the security dilemma framework in particular.

Quite apart from this limitation of the effort to apply this element of neo-realist international relations theory to intrastate conflicts, the security dilemma predominantly concerns the threats that groups perceive. It does not treat the other side of the coin at all – the opportunities that they perceive.

Opportunity

The security dilemma can be seen as a special case subsumed within the more general notion – a "political opportunity structure." This construct emerged from the social movement literature (McAdam 1996). It has since found application in the "contentious politics" research program of Sidney Tarrow, Doug McAdam, Charles Tilly and their associates. The notion also elaborates the "opportunity/threat" variable that Tilly (1978) included in his mobilization model, modified to recognize (as Butterfield and Herz recognized for the security dilemma) that what matters is not the objective opportunities and threats that face a group (or state, in the international case), but that group's (state's) perception or framing of those opportunities and threats (McAdam *et al.* 2001: 45). The political opportunities of a group refer to the perceived features of the political environment external to the group that affect the group's expectations for the success or failure of collective action (Tarrow 1998: 76–77).

A political opportunity *structure*, on the other hand, refers to features of the regime that contextualizes contentious interaction. There is no standard list of factors or variables that comprise a political opportunity structure (Tarrow 1996: 41–42). For lethal conflicts, Tilly and Tarrow (2007: 57) consider these relevant: (*a*) the number of independent power centers in a regime; (*b*) its openness to new actors; (*c*) the stability of political alignments; (*d*) whether it prohibits or facilitates contacts with influential external allies and supporters; (*e*) whether it represses or facilitates the collective actions of challengers; and (*f*) any decisive changes in features *a–e*. For analytic simplicity they capture these features in two dimensions: a regime's capacity and the extent of its use of democratic processes.

For Tilly and Tarrow (2007: 55), capacity refers to "the extent to which governmental action affects the character and distribution of population, activity, and resources within the government's territory." Thomas' (1987) distinction between a state's despotic power and its infrastructural power has relevance here. The capacity component of a political opportunity structure refers not to a state's capacity to dominate or oppress groups within its jurisdiction, but rather to its capacity to provide the public goods – infrastructure – requisite for orderly and productive economic and social activity. Regimes that lack infrastructural power often turn to despotic power when challenged internally.

Democracy means "the extent to which people subject to a given government's authority have broad, equal political rights, exert significant

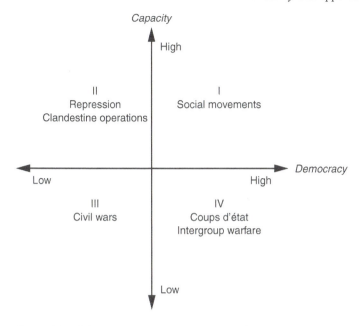

Figure 1 Modal forms of contention, given political opportunity structures presented by regimes (source: adapted from Tilly and Tarrow 2007).

direct influence ... over government personnel and policy, as well as receive protection from arbitrary action by governmental agents...." (Tilly and Tarrow 2007: 55). Essentially, "democracy" refers to the opportunities of groups and individuals in society to express their aspirations freely, without fear of reprisal, whereas "capacity" refers to the opportunities of groups and individuals to realize those aspirations, at least occasionally, as a consequence of state action.

By distinguishing regimes as having high or low values on capacity and democracy, Tilly and Tarrow produce the 2x2 category scheme depicted in Figure 1. Because they typically can and do act to repress opponents, undemocratic regimes with high capacity (quadrant II of Figure 1) tend to suppress their rivals or drive them underground, where they resort to clandestine operations. Owing to their shaky hold on power and their typically illiberal policies, civil wars more likely appear in undemocratic regimes with low capacity (quadrant III). The drive for order motivates coups that typically appear in democratic, low capacity regimes (quadrant IV). Because they often cannot adjudicate them (or enforce judgments when they do adjudicate them), these regimes also provide opportunities for linguistic, religious and/or ethnic animosities to develop into inter-group warfare. Finally, because they provide opportunities for views to be heard, because they protect minorities, because they enjoy (justly or not) reputations for fairness and because they have the capacity to provide public goods, high-capacity democratic regimes (quadrant I) tend to produce social movements that do not employ violent tactics (Tilly and Tarrow 2007: 56–57). Of course, these represent only the typical form of contention for regimes with particular levels of capacity and democracy. Any form of contention might arise anywhere in the matrix of Figure 1. But, it follows from these modal forms that, *ceteris paribus*, the simultaneous promotion of regime capacity and regime democratization in conflict settings would enhance the likelihood of long-lasting peace.

The security dilemma analysis fits this framework poorly. Borrowed as it is from the neo-realist understanding of world politics, the security dilemma is predicated upon the presumption of anarchy. Because there is no regime in the context of the hypothetical security dilemma, the idea of altering the political opportunity structure, bolstering regime capacity and regime democracy to encourage peaceful forms of contention, cannot be conceptualized. The best that can be said for the security dilemma approach is that it represents a special case within the political opportunity structure approach. It pertains only to a subset of conflicts in low-democracy, low-capacity regimes (quadrant III) – but only those in which capacity approaches non-existence.

Only two pathways to peace are conceivable from the security dilemma analysis: (*a*) the pathway neo-realists conceive for the international system – the creation and maintenance of a balance of power; and (*b*) the imposition of a supervening authority that can forcefully implement a cessation of hostilities and subsequently police the political environment to prevent its re-emergence. In the context of contemporary ethno-territorial conflicts, this is an exceedingly limited and unhelpful set of options. The first pathway would simply maintain conflict, ensuring no resolution. Peace might ultimately come as participants weary of the fighting, but the interim costs in human lives and delayed economic progress would be enormous. The second pathway would simply drive the adversaries underground. The conflict would not be resolved but would instead become latent (Duffy and Frensley 1991), restarting when the authoritarian lid is removed. The security dilemma approach, because it presumes anarchy, literally cannot conceive of pathways to peace that involve the expansion of opportunities for effective democratic participation and self-expression.

Illustrations

What can political opportunity structures tell us about conflicts? Consider by way of illustration the conflict in Northern Ireland. While this conflict has solidary roots that stretch back to the Middle Ages, the modern conflict began in 1968. The Northern Ireland Civil Rights Association (NICRA) headed a social movement that, emulating (McAdam *et al.* 2001) the US civil rights movement, marched for equal rights for Catholics in Northern Ireland. Although there were instances of police over-reaction, the movement itself was by-and-large peaceful and overt. We would expect contention to take the form of relatively peaceful social movements in such quadrant I high-capacity, high-democracy political environment.

Britain had played a relatively even-handed role during the NICRA campaign. The British Army worked to interpose itself between groups in the streets in efforts to maintain the peace. Things changed dramatically on Bloody Sunday, 30 January 1972, when British soldiers fired into a group of civil rights protesters in Derry, killing 14 and wounding 12 more. Later in 1972, the British suspended the Northern Irish parliament and began to rule directly from London (Duffy and Frensley 1991). These changes in British policy altered the political opportunity structure in Northern Ireland. The regime transitioned from high-capacity, high-democracy (quadrant I) to high-capacity, low democracy (quadrant II). In response to this new, repressive environment, social movement tactics instantly lost their feasibility. The ranks of the Provisional IRA consequently swelled and a generation of clandestine violence ensued.

The African National Congress (ANC) decision to employ violence in its struggle in South Africa similarly transits from quadrant I to quadrant II. From Lodge's account (this volume) it is clear that most of the ANC would have preferred to maintain itself as a non-violent social movement. But, the South African regime chose to repress the movement, driving it underground and motivating its turn to violent tactics. Its refusal to accommodate the aspirations of the majority of its people betrayed South Africa as a high-capacity, low-democracy (quadrant II) regime, despite the democratic trappings of its political institutions.

The Brazilian case that Serbin (this volume) analyzes bears some similarity to the Northern Irish and South African cases, in that a quadrant I regime transitioned to quadrant II and then back again to quadrant I. It differs in that the regime in Brazil was more successful in suppressing its adversaries than were the regimes in Northern Ireland and South Africa. As in these cases, the state exercise of repressive force in Brazil eliminated opportunities for democratic expression and any hope for the realization of group goals except through violence and militancy.

In all three cases, one question leaps out. Why would regimes choose to adopt repressive measures, pushing stable quadrant I societies into the relatively unstable quadrant II? In the South African case, racism was surely a factor. However, the prominence of Marxist elements in Northern Ireland's NICRA, in Brazil's ALN and in South Africa's ANC suggests that these regimes may have adopted repression at least in part at the behest of allies in the Cold War, which contextualized much political contention in the post-war period. Cold War considerations often led external powers to lend support to those regimes that furthered those powers' Cold War aims. As a by-product, this support qualitatively altered political opportunity structures across a wide variety of regimes. This often resulted in assistance to despotic regimes, presenting obstacles to just and peaceable outcomes.

Hopefully, contemporary external concerns about terrorism will not similarly affect political opportunity structures. Sometimes, an enemy of one's enemy is not one's friend in the longer term.

The outcome differed in Brazil, compared to outcomes in Northern Ireland and South Africa. Peace in Northern Ireland and South Africa was negotiated. Peace in Brazil, however, was fait accompli, as the regime had entirely suppressed the opposition forces. Serbin's account of the failed expectations of those revolutionaries who emerged from Brazilian jails illustrates the effect of political opportunity particularly well. These regime opponents expected upon their release to rejoin their comrades in clandestine action, but found them engaged instead in electoral politics. By pursuing its policy of re-democratization, the regime effectively created both opportunities for the opposition to express itself freely and institutional mechanisms to institute even the policies of the left, so long as they could convince a majority to go along.

The account by Bartoli *et al.* (this volume) of the transition to peace in Mozambique presents a rosy picture in which Mozambicans "played the cardinal role in ending their war by choosing peace and creating the political conditions for political inclusiveness." Bartoli *et al.* justly celebrate this turn of events and point hopefully to the creation of a growing civil society in Mozambique. From their account, it appears as though Mozambique has transitioned from quadrant III (low-capacity, low-democracy) to quadrant IV (low-capacity, high democracy).

Allison's portrayal of Guatemala (this volume) indicates that it too has transitioned from quadrant III to quadrant IV. Although, like Mozambique, Guatemala has democratized substantially, its levels of poverty and non-political violence are troubling indicators of state incapacity. The ultimate success of both Guatemala and Mozambique, then, depends upon the ability of each regime to move from quadrant IV to quadrant I. Democratic advances in each setting may go for naught if these regimes fail to acquire the capacity to meet popular aspirations across social groupings, at least occasionally. Each regime must be able to deliver the infrastructural resources these groups need in order to advance themselves. If there is little pie to divide, each group will have an incentive to take all the pie for themselves. In that eventuality, democratic forms and pluralistic practices are left by the wayside. External donors can prevent this by facilitating projects that enhance the infrastructural capacity of democratizing states.

The political opportunity framework suggests that prospects for sustained peace are maximal where regimes transit to quadrant I. From this perspective, then, we should be more concerned about the prospects for peace in Guatemala and Mozambique and more confident about those prospects in Northern Ireland, Brazil and South Africa.

Transformation

How then shall we answer our question? When do conflicts undergo "constructive transformations?" Short of the unilateral capitulation of one side to the other, under what conditions do adversaries forego violent confrontation in favor of negotiation and compromise? How should external parties design their interventions in order to maximize the prospects of a lasting peace?

Although we have described some settings (Brazil, South Africa and Northern Ireland) that deviate from it, my sense is that intrastate conflicts typically arise in quadrant III contexts. The political opportunity perspective suggests that efforts be directed toward the promotion of transitions of these regimes to quadrant I. Anyone interested in fostering negotiation and compromise as alternatives to violence, then, should be interested in enhancing regime capacity and democracy. Violent forms are selected least often under quadrant I conditions: high regime capacity and high regime democracy.

It cannot be over-emphasized that enhancing democracy means more than simply implementing free and fair elections, although this too is necessary. Open electoral competition for public offices encourages groups to declare their positions and intentions publicly. This promotes the transparency of intentions across groups and thereby diminishes the likelihood of fighting. However, by themselves, democratic elections might only legitimize the oppression of minorities by majorities.

Roland Paris for this reason suggests that "peacebuilders should delay liberalization and limit political and market freedoms in the short run, in order to create conditions for a smoother and less hazardous transition to market democracy – and durable peace – in the long run" (Paris 2004: 188). Effectively, then, Paris advances the view that post-conflict regimes should first transition from quadrant III to quadrant II and then later transition to quadrant I. However, whichever group controls the state apparatus in the quadrant II period could easily exploit limited freedoms and enhanced state capacity to repress its rivals. It would be difficult for any group in that position to avoid the temptation.

Nevertheless, Paris has a point so far as elections are concerned. If, by "enhancing democracy," we merely mean instituting majority rule, then elected majorities might well exploit their majority position to control state instrumentalities and with these dominate minorities. However, if democracy is enhanced in ways that protect minorities, the difficulties that motivate Paris' recommendation vanish. Institutional design features, such as federalist power devolution, legislative supermajorities, or a power-sharing executive, can ease the perceived insecurity of minorities. Designs that encourage multi-partyism, such as proportional representation and parliamentary executives, promote coalition formation and thereby provide groups incentives to cooperate with one another to achieve their political ends.

Other steps can be taken to promote the protection of minorities from arbitrary government actions. Apart from legal guarantees of free speech, free assembly, and the like, formal requirements for diversity in the composition of public bureaucracies – particularly police bureaucracies – can help prevent the emergence of oppressive governments. Judicial reforms are particularly important, both for promoting post-conflict reconciliation and for providing authoritative dispute resolution forums. For these institutions to be effective, they require legitimacy from the perspective of ordinary people across social groupings. Externally funded rule-of-law promotion efforts sometimes attempt to impose onto underdeveloped post-conflict societies the legal norms of the developed world (Amisi and Duffy 2007). Donors should recognize that judicial reforms are not meant simply to provide transparency and predictability for business practices but also have important reconciliation, dispute resolution and state-building purposes. Incorporating longstanding jurisprudential traditions in the design of post-conflict legal institutions will be crucial if post-conflict governments are to attain the respect of the people and key groups in society.

Enhancing democracy allows groups to express their aspirations freely and to engage other groups in negotiations for the resources needed to realize those aspirations. But those resources cannot be realized if the regime lacks the capacity to deliver them or at least to provide the infrastructural conditions necessary to attain them. Enhancing capacity also dampens violent confrontation by providing security. To the extent that the regime can police its territory, constituents need not engage in "self-help" to secure themselves. High capacity regimes can ensure that everyone plays by the rules. None of this matters, of course, unless the rules are fair and fairly applied.

Generally, the idea is to establish conditions conducive for the creation of a modus vivendi between conflicting groups. However helpful they might be, the promise of democratic conditions will rarely suffice to motivate conflict leaders to lay down their arms. In creating a political opportunity structure conducive to peace through the enhancement of capacity and democracy, one addresses only the core insecurity – the fear of losing or not attaining group self-determination. A third enhancement is needed, beyond the enhancements of capacity and democracy – the enhancement of trust.

Remember that leaders' distributions of solidary incentives have created additional layers of insecurity around this core. Retracting solidary incentives is a bit like putting toothpaste back in the tube (Duffy and Lindstrom 2002). Unraveling those layers of insecurity will take time and involve great hortatory efforts on the part of group leaders, key figures in the community and external figures interested in promoting peace. Vivian (this volume) discusses the rhetoric of political reconciliation.

Sens (2006), a member of the Independent International Commission on Decommissioning (IICD) in Northern Ireland, describes such an effort in Northern Ireland. Political leaders work toward creating a "parity of esteem" across the communities. Political and civic leaders find ways to indicate the unacceptability of cross-group demonization. They work to end name-calling and labeling opponents (e.g. terrorist, colonist). They endeavor to prevent hard-liners within their respective communities from hijacking policy by portraying moderation as betrayal.

Truth commissions can be useful in this regard, as can confessional exhortations. Galtung's idea of peace journalism is relevant here. Journalists interested in telling truth in the service of pro-social ends can, if sensitized to the problem, contribute valuably to the enhancement of trust.

Trust can be enhanced also by opening negotiations to non-combatants. I am reminded by Bertha Amisi that, too often, conflict negotiations take place only between the armed combatants. This practice effectively excludes major stakeholders in civil society. It conveys the message that interests attain political leverage only by means of the display and use of arms. Consequently, it encourages war-making over peace-making. Opening negotiations to non-combatant stakeholders, particularly to women but also to confessional groups, trade groups, and others, facilitates the consideration of issues and collective aspirations broader than those over which the groups fight. It may also introduce cross-cutting cleavages at the negotiation table that could be conducive to peace. Combatants more likely find mutual accommodations easier to the extent that important groups within constituencies across conflicting groups push for them. Opening negotiations to non-combatants can help produce the benefits to "the streets" that Atashi (this volume) discusses, improving the likelihood that peace will be sustained.

Although external advice ought to be considered, final decisions regarding the pace and order of institution-building in any post-conflict setting are best left to the people who will live with their consequences. Because conditions will vary widely across settings, no specific steps can be offered here – or anywhere, for that matter – about the steps to take to reach stable peace. We can speak only in generalities and with the understanding that local conditions make some routes to peace more propitious than others.

In quadrant III post-conflict regimes, enhancements of capacity and democracy should be more-or-less simultaneous. Enhancing democracy before enhancing capacity can produce a political environment in which each group can express its aspirations freely, but the regime is unable to provide infrastructural support to make those aspirations achievable across groups. If democratic reforms do not produce better lives, they themselves will be short-lived. Where infrastructural resources are scarce, pluralist negotiations may fail to yield mutually satisfactory allocations across groups. Under such conditions, pressure will mount for authoritative distributions of resources. Enhancing capacity before enhancing democracy favors those groups who control the regime's instruments of power. Unless outside actors manage resource allocation decisions, enhancing capacity before democracy produces incentives for incumbents to exclude the opposition or even to repress it before it can become an electoral force. In that eventuality the opposition is driven underground, possibly to engage in clandestine violence.

Trust should also be enhanced as capacity and democracy are enhanced. Without enhancing trust, there will be very little opportunity to generate the coordination needed across groups to effect the enhancements of capacity and democracy. Transforming conflicts from the practices of violence to those of negotiation and compromise surely requires as a precondition the recognition among leaders across groups that violent means will not attain for their constituents the security they desire. Beyond this, however, transformation requires the construction and communication of a vision of a secure and more just future across conflicting groups. At the same time, leaders who wish to actualize this vision must engage in efforts to rehabilitate their adversaries in the eyes of their constituents.

The tasks of enhancing democracy and capacity are difficult ones at best. Nation building is not for the faint of heart. But this last task, the task of enhancing trust, I take to be the most difficult by orders of magnitude. We know how leaders distribute solidary incentives as a relatively costless method of mobilizing followers for conflict action. We know even the psychological processes (concerning identification and causal attribution) that make solidary incentives effective for changing the behavior of individual followers. We know precious little, however, about how best to retract solidary incentives and reverse those psychological processes. Some may find too pessimistic the view that solidary incentives lose their effectiveness only through cohort replacement. Only after one or two generations is trust restored, and even then not completely. I fear, however, that the view is more realistic than pessimistic.

Conclusion

If, at base, conflicts revolve around security issues, it makes a great deal of sense to consider the conditions under which groups feel secure. The political opportunity approach suggests that these conditions are met when: (*a*) groups enjoy opportunities to express their aspirations in the context of democratic institutions without fear of reprisal; and when (*b*) the regime has the infrastructural capacity to create the conditions under which those aspirations become attainable. Under these conditions, political contention between groups takes the form of peaceful social movement, not civil war or clandestine violence.

As we have seen, the political opportunity approach offers a much richer understanding of security than offered by the security dilemma account. In particular, because it presumes an anarchical political context that rarely, if ever, exists, the security dilemma account cannot conceive of strategies to achieve peace that involve the construction of regimes that promote free expression (with the protection of minorities) and provide the infrastructural support to allow people, across ethnic, confessional, linguistic, or other social divisions, to make better lives for themselves.

One should not conclude from this chapter that the political opportunity approach offers a smooth pathway from conflict to peace. In fact, it only helps us obtain analytical leverage on the nature of the problem in any particular conflict setting. Heavy conceptual and political lifting is required to forge institutional arrangements that all parties believe just and fair. Even more burdensome for those who wish to transform conflicts is the necessary reconciliation work. By this I mean not only finding just remedies for excesses committed during conflict, but also finding ways to retract solidary incentives and to reinterpret the stories of heroism and atrocity that leaders use to mobilize their followers and that reinforce among followers a sense of insecurity. However difficult this might be, we have no reasonable alternative.

References

Amisi, B. K. and G. Duffy. (2007) "New Rules for the Rule of Law? External Actors and Rule of Law Development in Post-Conflict African Societies," paper presented at the Annual Meeting of the International Studies Association, Chicago, March 2007.

Butterfield, H. (1951) *History and Human Relations*, London: Collins.

Duffy, G. and N. J. Frensley (1991) "Community Conflict Processes: Mobilization and Demobilization in Northern Ireland," in J. W. Lamare (ed.) *International Crisis and Domestic Politics: Major Political Conflicts in the 1980s*, New York: Praeger, 99–135.

Duffy, G. and N. Lindstrom (2002) "Conflicting Identities: Solidary Incentives in the Serbo-Croatian War," *Journal of Peace Research*, 39: 69–90.

Herz, J. (1951) *Political Realism and Political Idealism*, Chicago: University of Chicago Press.

Job, B. L. (1992) "The Insecurity Dilemma: National, Regime, and State Securities in the Third World," in B. L. Job (ed.) *The Insecurity Dilemma: National Security of Third World States*, Boulder: Lynne Rienner, 11–35.

Kaufman, S. J. (1996a) "Spiraling to Ethnic War: Elites, Masses and Moscow in Moldova's Civil War," *International Security*, 21: 108–138.

—— (1996b) "An 'International' Theory of Inter-ethnic War," *Review of International Studies*, 22: 149–171.

Kriesberg, L. (2007) *Constructive Conflicts: From Escalation to Resolution*. 3rd edn., Oxford: Rowman & Littlefield.

Lake, D. A. and D. Rothchild (1996) "Containing Fear: The Origins and Management of Ethnic Conflict," *International Security*, 21: 41–75.

Lewin, K. (1948) *Resolving Social Conflicts*, New York: Harper & Row.

McAdam, D. (1996) "Conceptual Origins, Current Problems, Future Directions," in D. McAdam, J. D. McCarthy and M. N. Zald (eds.), *Comparative Perspectives on Social Movements*, Cambridge: Cambridge University Press, 23–40.

McAdam, D., S. Tarrow and C. Tilly (2001) *Dynamics of Contention*, Cambridge: Cambridge University Press.

McGarry, J. and B. O'Leary (1995) *Explaining Northern Ireland: Broken Images*, Oxford: Blackwell.

Melander, E. (1999) *Anarchy Within: The Security Dilemma between Ethnic Groups in Emerging Anarchy*, Report no. 52, University of Uppsala, Department of Peace and Conflict Research.

Paris, R. (2004) *At War's End: Building Peace after Civil Conflict*. Cambridge: Cambridge University Press.

Posen, B. R. (1993) "The Security Dilemma and Ethnic Conflict," *Survival*, 35: 27–47.

Roe, P. (1999) "The Intrastate Security Dilemma: Ethnic Conflict as 'Tragedy?'" *Journal of Peace Research*, 36: 183–202.

—— (2000) "Former Yugoslavia: The Security Dilemma that Never Was?" *European Journal of International Relations*, 6: 373–393.

—— (2002) "Misperception and Ethnic Conflict: Transylvania's Societal Security Dilemma," *Review of International Studies*, 28: 57–74.

—— (2005) *Ethnic Violence and the Societal Security Dilemma*, London: Routledge.

Sens, A. D. (2006) "A Commission to Decommission Paramilitary Arms: Northern Ireland's Example," *World Policy Journal*, 23: 75–85.

Tarrow, S. (1996) "States and Opportunities: The Political Structuring of Social Movements," in D. McAdam, J. D. McCarthy and M. N. Zald (eds.), *Comparative Perspectives on Social Movements*, Cambridge: Cambridge University Press, 41–61.

—— (1998) *Power in Movement: Social Movements and Contentious Politics*, 2nd edn., Cambridge: Cambridge University Press.

Thomas, C. (1987) *In Search of Security: The Third World in International Relations*, Boulder: Lynne Rienner.

Tilly, C. (1978) *From Mobilization to Revolution*, New York: McGraw-Hill.

Tilly, C. and S. Tarrow (2007) *Contentious Politics*, Boulder: Paradigm.

9 Globalization and the transformation of conflict

Galia Golan and Adir Gal

Introduction

Globalization in its various forms (social, cultural, and political as well as economic), has often contributed negatively to conflict. By creating hardships leading to grievances, by disrupting social cohesion or arousing xenophobia and fundamentalism in reaction to outside influences, or by sustaining, even escalating violence through the flow of resources (currencies, weapons, personnel), globalization has served to perpetuate armed conflict. Various aspects of globalization often impact upon the protagonists in conflict, contributing to transformation or resolution of conflicts. They may affect conditions that promote transformation, such as a mutually hurting stalemate, awareness of possible solution, elimination of asymmetries, neutralization of spoilers, or other factors. We examine four kinds of non-state actors, related to globalization, which may affect conflict transformation: the media, diasporas, non-governmental organizations and the private sector.

The media

In the era of the "new media," media technologies (satellite television, wireless, video, Internet) have assumed a greater importance than at any time in history. They are often viewed as such an integral part of conflict that they may be an actor themselves, a third party, possibly no less important than the direct protagonists of a conflict. In the wars of today, winning over the minds of the people may be as important as winning the military battle, thereby according the media a significantly new role (Smith 2007). Media frame the narrative of a conflict, convey the issues, positions, demands of the protagonists, influencing public support or opposition as well as recruitment. Even for those involved in a conflict, the media may be a major source of information. The media may also be a tool, for signaling or communicating between parties to a conflict, or actually serving one party.

Given these various roles, the media can contribute to ending violence, often by focusing on non-violent solutions or presenting alternative methods. They can provide coverage for voices of moderation, propose solutions and point out common ground, even urge negotiation. They may clarify issues to prevent misunderstanding or counteract disinformation and incendiary rumors, highlight the costs of conflict, depolarize and humanize the conflict. Such measures can create or strengthen pressures for negotiations or the abandonment of the use of violence. In these tasks, the media may strengthen the weaker party, correcting asymmetry and thereby, possibly, providing an alternative to violence for the securing of its goals or response to its grievances, whether through pressure or simply public support.

In the anti-apartheid struggle in South Africa and in China (Tiananmen Square), global telecasts were instrumental in attracting attention and support (as well as participants in China) for the non-violent campaigns. In the latter, dissidents were able to use the media due to the large presence of foreign press and thanks to satellite technology for the Gorbachev visit. While this aided the non-violent struggle, ultimately the massive international coverage and interest did not prevent the Chinese government's use of violence to end the demonstration. According to one analysis, however, contrasting the Tiananmen Square protest with a similar pro-democracy protest nine years earlier in South Korea, globalization did prevent demonstrator violence. In the earlier conflict there was little presence of international media, no direct broadcasting, satellite link-ups and the like and, therefore, little international attention, understanding or sympathy for the protest. That pro-democracy protest ultimately deteriorated into student violence. In contrast, according to Becky Shelley, "the international media, particularly through the medium of instantaneous broadcasting set the agenda, created [*sic*] mass public opinion on a global scale, and influenced [*sic*] the actors in the drama" (Shelly 2001: 171). With the confidence engendered by the international support and the broad participation that grew from the coverage, students in Beijing did not revert to violence, as, according to Shelly, had their precursors in Korea.

Still more direct measures may be taken by the media, such as relaying negotiating signals between protagonists, bringing them together, through videos or satellite "meetings" of protagonists in different locations, or live television "shows" aimed at mediating between warring parties. An example of the last was Ted Koppel's 1988 Nightline program in Jerusalem, during the intifada, in which Koppel brought leading Palestinian and Israeli political figures together (with a small wall between the two sides) to discuss possible solutions. While Koppel did not succeed in his effort to elicit mutual recognition from the two sides, he did succeed in having them clarify differences and possible areas of agreement (Ashrawi 1995: 48–50). Perhaps more importantly, the program provided access for very broad audiences to hear both sides, including what for many of the viewers was their first encounter with moderate voices from the opposing side. A similar media effort was organized in Burundi. During official peace talks, politicians from different groups were brought together for a radio round-table dealing with the issues of the conflict. Serving a somewhat similar purpose, but in a different form, joint reporting teams have been organized in Macedonia, consisting of Macedonians, Albanians, Turks and Roma, and their products are published in identical form in all the news-papers (Melone *et al.* 2002).

As we shall see below, a number of international NGOs are involved not only in bringing together and training journalists from conflict areas but actually producing conflict resolution programs, one of which has been credited with bringing pressure on the Liberian government for accounta-bility during the civil war (Hieber 1998). The most well-known media group of this kind is Common Ground Productions (created by NGO Search for a Common Ground), and perhaps the most well known vehicle is the radio station it initiated in Burundi, Ijambo (Wise Words). Ijambo employs a multi-ethnic staff that, among other things, seeks to counter the anti-Tutsi propaganda coming from a pirate station in the Congo. Ijambo's primary messages are that Hutu and Tutsi can live together, and that the shooting should stop; they feature a program entitled "People Are Calling for Peace" (Verhoeven no date). Similar work is being done in Angola to promote a message of non-violence.

While Johan Galtung and journalists Annabel McGoldrick and Jake Lynch, as well as a number of NGOs, have offered explicit proposals for peace journalism (Galtung no date; Reljic 2002), the opposite approach has also been suggested: to treat conflict like crime, i.e. oppose it and, also, shut down hate radio and that of radical elements (Gilboa 2000). In 1997 there was a proposal for the creation of a "UN Information Interven-tion Unit" to monitor information provided in crisis areas, broadcast peace promotion material, and, in extreme cases, jam broadcasts of hate and war propaganda material. This use of force to stop force (attempted by NATO bombings of media stations in Serbia) has not, however, been particularly effective for stemming violence.

The Internet is far more difficult to censor, but, like other media, it too can be employed in the service of conflict transformation. The Inter-net, like the media in general, can empower the weaker side, but it can also empower the individual. It does so not only by providing informa-tion, which is indeed a source of power, but also by providing participa-tion and expansion of the public sphere beyond space and time. Through the Internet, one can not only express grievances, but also create a virtual community of supporters. In the Chiapas case this enabled continuation of the struggle through peaceful means (Froehling 1997). Alternative solutions, options and recommendations can be aired and, given the interactive nature of the Internet, these can be debated directly and in real time. Bitterlemons.org features comments on topical issues by two Israelis and two Palestinians weekly, with broader participation in the international version, bitterlemonsinternational.org. Internet exchanges can, of course, be virtual wars ("netwars") rather than net cooperation, but the Internet "brings together different levels of conflict and authority on the same virtual stage, thus flattening and effectively equalizing those levels and facilitating a discourse between formerly separated levels," according to the researcher of the Moluccan conflict Birgit Brauchler (2003). Moreover, one can engage in on-line dispute resolution, with technology becoming a party to the dispute. Voices of moderation can engage protagonists directly, often from the diaspora, as we shall see below. Thus, while cyberspace can be used for incitement and actual Internet warfare (e.g. bombarding sites to clog them, crashing servers), it is presumably better to have virtual rather than actual warfare, delaying if not actually eliminating the use of "real" violence. One such instance, for example, was the netwar that replaced actual violence between the groups supporting and opposing President Estrada in the Philippines (Ortis and Evans 2003).

The Internet may be an actor itself, for good as well as bad. In a situation of heavy censorship of traditional media, the Internet became the major if not only scene for democratic opposition in Indonesia, playing a major role in the overthrow of the Suharto regime. Researchers David Hill and Krishna Sen credit an e-mail list, "Indonesia-L," moderated by an American in Maryland, providing hard news on Indonesia from around the world, along with commentaries, opinions, exchanges and the like, unedited, mainly in the Indonesian language. After tremendous growth of the site itself, some hundreds of mailing lists relating to Indonesia emerged, most of them linked to Indonesia-L and generally functioning together as a forum for news, opinions and discussions, from local and international sources – and a clear reminder of the regime's censorship. As such, it was the major factor in the information war against the dictator. According to Hill and Sen, on the eve of the post-Suharto elections, Indonesian Internet guru Onno Purdo

> Called upon the "community" to use the Internet to express their opinions rather than go out on the streets and face the military. The Internet in Indonesia had become the space from which educated middle-class liberal democrats could become guerilla combatants in defense of democracy and against the military.
>
> (Hill and Sen 2002: 175)

Diasporas

Globalization has greatly changed the role of diasporas as well. While the movement of people from place to place is hardly new, immigration has become an ever growing phenomenon both because of the hardships created in some countries, the growing gaps between rich and poor, agrobusiness displacements and overcrowding of cities, as well as simply greater mobility resulting from globalization. More and more people are emigrating to improve their living standards. Without necessarily stopping the flow of immigrants, increasing restrictions by receiving countries have led to a burgeoning business in the illegal movement of persons – trafficking of all kinds. There is a growing presence of foreign workers (legal or otherwise) alongside more traditional immigrants. Refugees, political asylum seekers, and what may be called "conflict generated diasporas" often constitute a different type of diaspora joining more traditional immigrant communities, possibly bringing a different type of activity. Whether the result of intrastate strife or the disruptions brought by economic and social change, there are larger and larger communities of persons living beyond the borders of their homeland today.

Aside from the numbers, what is new about this phenomenon is the role that globalization has enabled these communities to play. The freeing of currency transfers has rendered remittances sent to the homeland an integral part of the economy of some receiving countries – in some cases greater than their total investment from abroad (FDI). The changes in communications (Internet, satellite television, videos etc.), inexpensive telephone and travel, greatly facilitate and thus increase direct contact between diaspora and homeland, providing immigrants with the possibility of playing an active role from some distance or through frequent travel to their former countries. Moreover, these same facilities – in particular the Internet but also inexpensive travel – provide the possibility for the creation of global communities of diasporas, holding transnational meetings, coordinating efforts and also working with different diasporas. Local protagonists may mobilize, engage and benefit from their diasporas.

Operating in their new roles, with enhanced opportunities and means, diasporas are often viewed as more militant than those left behind in the home country, and therefore more likely to contribute to the creation or prolongation of conflict (Ostergaard-Nielsen 2005). Thus, a positive role for diasporas in transforming violent conflict may be more potential than actual. Nevertheless, there are a number of ways in which they may have a positive effect. Virtually everything that globalization has made possible (or easier) for diasporas to do in support of violence could be shifted to support for peaceful action. In simplest terms diasporas could cease the provision of money, arms and support for violence, and, instead, use their resources and influence to press for non-violence and political action. Perhaps surprisingly, one such case was that of the Tamils. The changed atmosphere in North America after 9/11 led influential diaspora figures, fearing for their own standing, to urge the LTTE to abandon military struggle and enter negotiations (Fair 2005). Funding was also reduced, and there were visits by diaspora representatives in an effort to persuade LTTE leaders to use political means. Thus the diaspora was directly credited with being one of the major factors that led to the LTTE's unilateral ceasefire in December 2001.

Diasporas can support those groups, factions or leaders in the homeland that propose peaceful means, using the media, especially the Internet, satellite television, videos and the like, in much the same way as diasporas have done in support of opposite policies. The Chinese diaspora provided this kind of support in connection with the Tiananmen demonstrations. Many diasporas maintain contacts with civic and governmental figures in the homeland; indeed sometimes they may have greater access than local people. There is even a case of Turkish Kurds in London canvassing voters long distance to urge participation in the Turkish elections in favor of a party that had complained that it lacked access to local public campaigning, while in other cases diaspora members have returned home to run in elections, for example in Iraq (Ostergaard-Nielsen 2005).

In many cases, leaders themselves are in the diaspora, from which they can use their influence to change policies toward their homeland as well as guide donors and international bodies to support only non-violent groups. Such a role by the diaspora, coupled with lobbying in the host country, has become an almost integral part of the "new wars" of the global era. An example of a successful lobby for peaceful change is that of Irish Americans. Always an active diaspora, the Americans for a New Irish Agenda (ANIA) played a direct and significant role in bringing about an end to the violence in Northern Ireland both by shifting Irish American support from financing arms to pressing for peaceful means, and by persuading President Bill Clinton to allow Sinn Fein leader Gerry Adams to come to the US. Irish Americans have been credited with the IRA's 1994 ceasefires that accompanied or followed visits by ANIA delegations (Guelke 1996). The success of ANIA has been attributed to the fact that the Irish American diaspora had changed from a group of non-influential politicos to a group of rich and therefore powerful businessmen (Cox 1997).

Given the fact that diasporas tend to be educated, as well as financially better off than their former compatriots, they may also be a source of alternative solutions, or expertise, for negotiations. In Somali peace talks between warring political factions, and also in the case of the PLO, experts from the diaspora have provided significant assistance to negotiating teams, though they did not necessarily play a critical role in getting the protagonists to the negotiating table. In the case of Burundi, diaspora experts (Dutch-Burundians) were said to have made a big difference in the peace negotiations in that country (African Diaspora 2006). Outside the area of conflict, globalization has greatly facilitated the possibility for diasporas to be involved directly in bringing protagonists together, by organizing meetings outside the homeland, dialogues, joint activities or actually mediating between protagonists. Such encounters have been organized by American Jewish groups, for example, Americans for Peace Now

(APN), sometimes in cooperation with Arab-Americans or working with organizations from both sides within the homeland. APN and the Association of Arab-Americans have conducted joint surveys of their diasporas to demonstrate diaspora support for peace, thereby trying to influence the warring parties in Israel and Palestine to seek peaceful solution of the conflict. Diasporas can contribute not only politically and financially to the strengthening of peace-oriented groups in the homeland, but, also, through collective remittances and projects, diasporas can contribute to the local economic situation. This in turn may serve to create or strengthen social cohesion in the homeland, possibly reducing factors connected with the outbreak of violence and recruitment. According to a Danish study, this has been the case in some areas of Africa (Mohamoud 2006).

Diasporas are not homogeneous, however, and the same broad diaspora may play both negative and positive roles, often reflecting conflicting views within the homeland, and playing out these differences in the host country as well as transnationally, in cyberspace and the media. A study of Turkish Kurdish groups in the diaspora has concluded that the groups with the closest contact to civil society actors in the homeland are the most moderate, urging compromise (Ostergaard-Nielsen 2005). In view of this, and given the importance of diasporas, one way of promoting transformation of the movements in the homeland has been to work on the differences of opinion within the diaspora, such as the sustained dialogues between opposing Ethiopian diaspora groups, organized by George Mason University between 1999 and 2003 (Lyons 2004). A diaspora group like APN in fact divides its work almost equally between trying to moderate opinion in the Jewish diaspora itself, lobbying the US government to press for peace negotiations in the region, and sending financial assistance to the peace movement in Israel. Many Jewish–Palestinian dialogues have been organized within diasporas, in Brazil, Great Britain, the US, France and others, designed first to change opinion within the diaspora, with the result in many cases of somewhat increased diaspora support for those promoting political solutions in Israel and Palestine. The African Diaspora Policy Center has organized joint conflict resolution training workshops for diaspora participants from Eritrea, Ghana, Liberia, Rwanda, Sierra Leone, Somalia, Sudan and Ethiopia. Of an entirely different nature, Moluccan diaspora activities (including violence) in support of protagonists in the homeland were significantly curbed in a novel way in Holland. The Dutch government offered hundreds of members of the diaspora round-trip visits to Molucca, to see the situation for themselves, and also jobs in Holland. This reportedly brought an end to the violent actions in the host country (Soetres 2007).

Non-governmental organizations

Globalization has also contributed to the expansion if not actual creation of civil-society organizations, within countries and globally. Civil society has developed in many countries in order to cope with the problems and tasks created by the new economy and reduced role of government, while greater exposure via the media has led to local organizing for the achievement of rights and benefits existing elsewhere. In addition, often in response to the globalization of mass culture, and also to the surge of immigration, NGOs have increasingly been organized around identities. A global civil society has emerged with links between local NGOs; communications, the Internet in particular, are credited with creating virtual INGOs, namely separate NGOs coordinating or cooperating with each either, in addition to actual INGOs, i.e. groups organized on an international basis.

There is much criticism of NGOs, connected mainly with problems of supervision, accountability, internal functioning, or the fact that they may serve certain interests, not always of a positive nature. Yet, the burgeoning of NGOs and INGOs may be considered a positive development not only for fulfilling many needs (eliminating grievances) and expanding democracy or social cohesion, but also more directly for contributing to conflict transformation. There are hundreds of groups and thousands of projects of local and international civil society striving to transform conflict, using a wide variety of tools. The major task, specifically, is to bring protagonists to engage in negotiation and/or political solutions. Success has not been frequent, nor have negotiations necessarily resulted in an end to the conflict or prevented reversion to violence. Nonetheless, globalization has played a role not only in the growth of this sector but also in the way that it can operate regarding the effort to transform conflict.

Through direct funding, personnel on the ground, training, advice and other types of assistance – all facilitated by the access provided by communications and inexpensive transportation – external NGOs play a major role in activities in conflict areas. American Women Waging Peace, for example, provides training materials to local women's NGOs all over the globe, while international NGOs like Oxfam-Novib provide funding as well as workshops, conferences and meetings for the training of groups in conflict, globally. NGOs can bring protagonists out of the area of conflict, for mediation, track two and dialogue in safe surroundings. International Alert, the National Democratic Institute, and Parliamentarians for Global Action, along with a number of church groups have organized conferences and shuttled Burundian decision-makers, members of the opposition and resistance leaders out of the country for meetings and dialog (Rotberg 1996). Numerous groups (from Harvard University to Pugwash Conferences) have done the same for Palestinians and Israelis, Kashmiris, Indians and Pakistanis, as well as other groups, sometimes including members of the military and persons associated with groups using or advocating violence.

On the ground, NGOs can alter asymmetry, strengthening weaker parties, providing or strengthening the voice of those advocating peace, often by working with opinion-makers. The Search for Common Ground is but one example of NGOs with this particular purpose. Working at the grass roots level, or assisting grass roots organizations, NGOs may build popular support for peaceful means, thereby perhaps impeding recruitment for violence and providing a basis for non-violent solutions. The Swedish church-based NGO Life and Peace Institute (LPI), for example, is one of many conducting grass roots work in a number of African countries and elsewhere. With longer-range goals in mind, NGOs may engage in educational efforts as well as work with children, such as the work conducted by Seeds of Peace which brings children from conflict areas to summer camp/workshops in America, frequently maintaining activities also upon the return to home countries.

More specifically NGOs can serve as conduits or messengers for the battling parties, where direct communications are not available or acceptable, possibly becoming a bridge between parties. Similarly, they can provide channels not only for funding (from the EU for example) for activities geared to conflict resolution, along with links to other groups that may be of assistance, but they can also provide ideas, alternative solutions and different perspectives (including perceptions of the enemy) that might bring protagonists to change their tactics or positions. Potential spoilers might also be changed or neutralized in this way. An example of the latter is the work done by Refugees International, assisting local Burundi NGOs working among returning refugees. The classic example of the role of globalization in creating international civil society, Jodi Williams' International Campaign to Ban Land Mines, clearly demonstrated the power of NGOs, armed with fax, Internet and other tools, to rally international awareness and support or pressure to end violence. The Free Burma Coalition and the International Federation for East Timor were two examples of similar means applied to conflict.

As with other non-state actors, it is not always easy to discern which if any of these possible roles has actually worked or contributed to ending violence, whether directly or by affecting the various factors that produce solutions. Yet there are examples, or claims, of successful NGO work directly affecting the abandonment of violence. As noted above, diaspora intervention in some cases through their fund-raising NGOs is credited at least in part with the LTTE decision for a ceasefire and negotiations in 2001–2002; there is also the claim that the ICRC played a critical role in achieving the earlier talks in 1995. Going beyond its humanitarian mandate, albeit cautiously, the ICRC mediated between the Sri Lankan government and the LTTE, helping in establishing the initial contact, passing confidential messages and creating the modalities for the peace talks (Rotberg 1996). The Swedish LPI is said to have played a critical role in bringing the sides together in the Somali peace talks, while the Center for Strategic Initiatives of Women was instrumental in bringing about successful dialogue between warring clans in Somalia (Paffenholz 2004). In the Nagorno-Karabakh conflict, women in the local branches of the Helsinki Citizen's Assembly won the Olaf Palme prize for their work in reducing ethnic strife, along with their practical work (together with other NGOs) in organizing prisoner exchanges (Van Tongeren *et al.* 2002). An Italian contingent of the international Catholic-lay NGO Community Sant'Egidio played a similar role in Mozambique, using mediation and facilitation of dialogue so that the warring parties began talking instead of fighting (Paffenholz 2004).

Also as noted regarding diasporas, the American-Irish ANIA played what may have been a critical role in the IRA ceasefires and eventual agreement to negotiations that led to the Good Friday accord, while a large number of local and international NGOs were involved in conflict resolution workshops, dialogues and the like that paved the way for the negotiations – and acceptance of the agreement and the subsequent decommissioning. Linking conflict resolution NGOs, a Northern Ireland based Moldovan group (Moldovan Initiative Committee of Management) was one of many NGOs defusing the conflict between Moldavians and Transdniestr fighters, leading to the ceasefire in April 1992. They worked with leaders and negotiators of the two communities, organizing study trips to Northern Ireland, with the aid of the Center for Conflict Resolution of the University of Kent and the German Berghof Research Center for Constructive Conflict Management). These were just a few of the NGOs credited with unlocking the peace process in Moldova (Van de Veen 1999). Many NGOs brought Israelis and Palestinians closer to negotiations, through dialogues, track-two, and any number of conflict resolution methods, but it was the initiative of the Norwegian Institute for Applied Social Science (FAFO) that actually brought about the track two talks that led to the Oslo Accords of 1993.

NGOs have not totally replaced inter-governmental and third country mediation or intervention. Indeed one researcher has established that the key to agreement to abandon violence in civil wars is in fact the offer of security guarantees by an outside power (Walter 1997). If this were the case, the end of the Cold War rather than globalization would be the significant enabling factor. Nevertheless, globalization has created conditions for an unprecedented number of non-governmental groups to work for conflict transformation in far flung areas, greatly expanding their potential and actual contributions, particularly with regard to conflicts in which governmental bodies have failed or would not be acceptable to the protagonists, or are themselves unwilling to act.

An apparently quite effective form of conflict transformation by NGOs may be seen in connection with the economic sphere, using the resources of globalization to eliminate the livelihood of violent groups. The efforts of the international NGO Global Witness with regard to the Khmer Rouge in Cambodia are a notable example. In the early 1990s, private companies, mainly in Thailand but also Laos, were providing financing for the Khmer Rouge by illegally purchasing timber (and also gemstones). According to Global Witness, "in early 1995 [the Khmer Rouge] were making between $10 to $20 million per month from illegal sales of timber farmed around the whole northern and western border" of Cambodia (BBC 1998). Since both the Cambodian and Thai governments, along with leading politicians, were involved in the illicit trading (financing the governmental side of Cambodia's civil war as well), little was done to stop the transactions. In 1995–1996, Global Witness led a campaign to end Khmer Rouge timber exports. Their pressure brought international donor states and organizations (such as the IMF, World Bank) to threaten sanctions (including suspension of aid) if the governments of Thailand and Cambodia did not close their borders to the timber trade (Le Billion 2000). Compliance led to both reduced fighting over timber and to reduced finances for the Khmer Rouge, weakening the group to the point of shortages in ammunition and medication, ultimately bringing the violent conflict in Cambodia to an end.

Similarly, a multi-NGO campaign called Fatal Transaction was launched against "blood diamonds," exposing the practice and calling upon governments and companies involved in the diamond trade to take measures to ensure that no diamonds were purchased from these sources. Under the pressure of the campaign, a large number of companies, including De Beers, (which held up to 65 percent of the supply of raw diamonds at the time), abandoned the illicit purchases that were financing violent conflict in Sierra Leone, Angola and the Democratic Republic of Congo. Following Fatal Transaction, the diamond industry in cooperation with governments and NGOs participated in the "Kimberly Process," that created an international system of Certificate of Origin. The certification system placed significant barriers to conflict diamonds, lowering the previously manipulated price on world markets, thereby reducing revenues for insurgent groups (Koyame 2005).

The private sector

One of the major aspects of globalization is the growth of businesses as major world actors, sometimes no less important than states themselves given their influence not only over world markets but also over state systems and practices, as well as sub-state entities. In certain circumstances business may benefit from instability and weak governments, often contributing to conflict not only by disrupting social cohesion and local economies, but also by exploiting markets and control of natural resources. In particular private military companies have become a mainstay of globalization, representing the "outsourcing of war" and becoming directly involved in conflict. Yet, just as with other non-state actors, there can be other roles for the private sector, including a positive, even direct, role for the transformation of conflict, given certain conditions or incentives.

In the new global environment of human rights concerns, and the scrutiny and criticism that accompanies this, business executives may acknowledge an ethical obligation or corporate social responsibility for conflict transformation. In the interests of maintaining goodwill and credibility among clients, this obligation may go so far as an interest in avoiding association with or contribution to violence. For example, combating negative practices associated with globalization, BP and other oil companies have established a set of "voluntary principles" for human rights compliance, and insist that local sub-contractors also sign on to these principles (Committee 2002). As we have seen above, companies may have to deal with pressure from NGOs, especially transnational actors, to act positively. Enhanced by globalization (through communications technology, litigation, agitation, networking and the like on the part of NGOs) such pressures can impose intolerable costs upon a firm or lead to divestment. These too may encourage a company to curb the practices that contribute to violence. As we have seen, De Beers, for example, was negatively affected in this way when the NGO campaign publicized the fact that the company's efforts to maintain high diamond prices were actually financing conflicts in Africa. To avoid this association with violence, De Beers stopped its illegal trading in the three African countries, foregoing its interest in price manipulation, and even became proactive in support of the Certificate of Origin system. Private banks, too, have been pressured to prevent their services from being used to support a war economy. Swiss banks, for example, have responded with restrictive banking rules and greater vigilance in this direction (Haufler 2001). Thus, dissociation from violence and efforts to curb resources fueling conflict might benefit a company's reputation and therefore profits, creating a positive incentive for action that promotes conflict transformation. Additionally, there are companies that prefer stability, eschewing regime change and crises that might change the rules of the game they have obtained (benefits in taxation and so forth) or threaten trade patterns, deliveries, markets and the like.

There are other ways in which businesses can act to transform conflict. To a large degree a company's capacity to contribute to transformation of conflict is based on its standing with the local population. Often they are able to collaborate with local groups, other businesses and local or national authorities. Through social and economic projects in conflict areas, companies can participate positively in local development, creating jobs, social cohesion, and human security. These in turn may not only make it more difficult for warring parties to recruit and find support for combat, but also, possibly, eliminate the grievances propelling a conflict. The attraction of gaining this outside investment and aid – which would be available only in a stable environment, might also serve as incentive for protagonists to reduce or abandon violence. At the least, such an incentive might be a significant addition to other factors contributing to the decision to abandon violence. More directly, companies can actually bring warring sides to the negotiating table, possibly by providing economic incentives for dialogue. The Lonrho Corporation, for example, pledged support to the rebel organization Renamo in Mozambique if it agreed to a ceasefire, thereby contributing significantly (some might say buying) to the group's support for the transition to peace (Haufler 2001).

Given the extensive involvement of many corporations today in philanthropy, particularly local social and economic projects (for tax purposes but also to establish good will), firms often become familiar with and trusted by local communities and thus in a position to mediate conflicts. They may advocate and encourage conflict resolution, speaking out in favor of dialogue. In one case, when Talisman Energy in Sudan was accused of human rights violations and assisting government oppression, the corporation demanded of the firm in Sudan that it conduct monitoring of its own and report on violations such as forced removals and displacement of whole populations and human rights violations. (Haufler 2001). The company did not comply, but in another case, in Mozambique, the CEO of Lonrho became personally involved in the peace process, using shuttle diplomacy and building up Renamo's confidence to enter negotiations (Vines 1998). These types of effort often benefit from the ability of companies to create their own communications networks, and also to sponsor or underwrite those involved in or advocating political rather than military solutions, usually with greater means or resources than those available to other non-state actors. In southern Sri Lanka, for example, businesses, together with the Tamil diaspora, organized and financed a campaign, Sri Lanka First, promoting a ceasefire and supporting the peace talks that took place between the LTTE and the government (Sri Lanka Peace no date). In the escalating conflict over dam projects in India and China, the engineering firm ABB participated in the World Commission on Dams that worked with all parties involved to resolve the growing conflicts over the various mega-projects.

Perhaps surprisingly, even private security companies – generally blamed for directly prolonging violent conflict, can play a constructive role. While operating for profit, they are lawful businesses that offer the gamut of services that weakened or failed states, or even international bodies are unable or unwilling to offer. Often they operate as peacekeepers, ensuring safe areas or protecting refugees, or provide training for peacekeepers. The US based Military Professionals Resources Inc. (MPRI), for example, undertook peacekeeping functions and training in Croatia (early 1990s) and Bosnia (1995) (Avant 2002). Of course, these companies can also use force in the service of one side in order to compel the other side to abandon violence and agree to negotiate. Typically this occurs when governments use the private security company against rebellious groups, as in Sierra Leone where the South African company, Executive Outcomes (EO), subdued the RUF rebels, contributing to the process that brought the RUF and the government to the negotiating table. While this was a positive effect, EO was reportedly paid by a controlling interest in the diamond mines previously under the RUF (Montague 2002). Moreover, the use of violence to end violence may not be the most beneficial way to transform conflict.

Economic sanctions are another means that not only states (and cities – another non-state actor in the era of globalization) but also companies can employ to transform conflict, similarly to the role that can be played by pension funds, financial institutions, and the various other sources of investment dominating the global economy. Closing down operations, withdrawing funds, refusing to buy or sell, especially in conflicts fuelled by natural resources, may all be vehicles for leveraging cessation of violence. Groups dealing in lootable natural resources such as diamonds, timber, gemstone and tobacco, are almost totally dependent upon trade with multinational corporations. Thus, although violent groups have a tendency to adjust quickly and to find alternate means of economic support or trading partners, sanctions can reduce the violence and create fertile ground for negotiations. In Angola, for example, sanctions by multinational businesses led to a 50 percent drop in UNITA's revenues from diamonds, from $150 million a year to $75 million, severely limiting the organization's ability to continue fighting (Tamm 2002). In the case of Sierra Leone, sanctions on Liberia, the country through which Sierra Leone's diamonds were traded, together with the establishment of the Certificate of Origin system, effectively cut off RUF's financial resources, leading in November 2001 to the signing of the Abuja Ceasefire Agreement. In Cambodia economic sanctions (that resulted from the NGO campaign) and the disruption of the illegal trading in timber were instrumental in the depletion of Khmer Rouge power. Thus the power of the private sector can be used positively for the transformation of conflict.

Conclusion

The negative effects of globalization, including the often negative contributions of the new or enhanced roles of non-state actors with regard to conflict have only been sparsely mentioned. It may well be the case that these negative contributions, such as support for violent conflict, are in fact greater than the positive, particularly on the part of diasporas or the private sector. Yet, some positive aspects of globalization, in general, and the role of the non-state actors, in particular, can and have contributed to conflict transformation. Globalization has provided important tools through the expanded capabilities of the non-state actors for bringing warring parties to the negotiation table. Working directly or indirectly, the new media (especially the Internet), diasporas, NGOs and the private sector, including even those involved in the new war economy such as private military organizations, have all in fact positively effected transformation of conflicts in a wide variety of cases and in a variety of ways. Judging from the many examples of such positive effects, this work may be accomplished unilaterally but it is particularly effective when conducted in a collaborative manner between some or even all of the non-state actors: NGOs working with or as part of diasporas, employing new media (satellite television or the Internet), while influencing or benefiting from private investment; working with protagonists and their supporters at home or abroad, directing or controlling resources, responding to grievances, or providing the means for conflict resolution. Such collaboration itself is facilitated if not actually created by globalization. Inasmuch as it is safe to assume that globalization is here to stay, it would be wise to look to these positive ways in which globalization can and does contribute to the transformation of violent conflict, by affecting both the parties involved and the environments in which they live and operate, the means by which they can and do operate, and the incentives and possibilities for resolving differences.

References

African Diaspora Policy Center (2006). Conference Report, Diaspora and Peacebuilding in Africa, Amsterdam.

Anderson, J. (2000). New Media and Globalization in the Internet Age Keynote Address, MEViC Inaugural Conference: People across Borders. Online, available at: www.mevic.org/keynote.html.

Ashrawi, H. (1995). *This Side of Peace: A Personal Account.* New York, Simon and Schuster.

Avant, D. (2002). "Privatizing Military Training." *Foreign Policy in Focus,* 7 (6).

Avant, D. (2005). *The Market of Force: The Consequences of Privatizing Security.* London, Cambridge University Press.

BBC (1998). "Khmer Rouge Approach Last Stand." 16 April. Online, available at: http://news.bbc.co.uk/2/hi/south_asia/79176.stm.

Brauchler, B. (2003) "Cyberidentities at War: Religion, Identity, and the Internet in the. Moluccan Conflict." *Indonesia,* no. 75.

Committee for Conflict Transformation Support (2003). "Economy, Conflict and the Private Sector: Seminar Report." *Newsletter 19.* Online, available at: www.c-r.org/ccts/ccts19/seminar.htm.

Cox, M. (1997). "Bringing in the 'International': The IRA Ceasefire and the End of the Cold War." *International Affairs* 73 (4): 671–693.

Fair, C. C. (2005). "Diaspora Involvement in Insurgencies: Insights from the Khalistan and Tamil Eelam Movements." *Nationalism and Ethnic Politics* 11(11): 125–156.

Froehling, O. (1997). "War of Ink and Internet in Chiapas, Mexico." *Geographic Review* 87 (2): 291–307.

Galtung, J. (no date). "Media: Peace Journalism." Online, available at: www.crnet-work.ca/programs/PeaceJournalism.htm.

Gilboa, E. (2000). "Mass Communication and Diplomacy: A Theoretical Framework." *Communication Theory* 10 (3): 275–309.

Guelke, A. (1996). "The United States, Irish Americans and the Northern Ireland Peace Process." *International Affairs* 72 (3): 521–536.

Haufler, V. (2001). "Is There a Role for Business in Conflict Management," in Chester A. Crocker, Fen Osler Hampson and Pamela Aall *Turbulent Peace: The Challenges of Managing International Conflict.* Washington, DC, United States Institute for Peace Press: 659–675.

Hieber, L. (1998). "Media as Intervention." *Track Two* 7 (4). Online, available at: http://ccrweb.ccr.uct.ac.za/archive/two/7_4/p16_intervention.html.

Hill, D. and Krishna, S. (2002). "Netizens in Combat: Conflict on the Internet in Indonesia." *Asian Studies Review* 26 (2): 165–188.

Koyame, M. (2005). "United Nations Resolutions and the Struggle to Curb the Illicit Trade in Conflict Diamonds in Sub-Saharan Africa," *African Journal of Legal Studies* 2 (1): 80–101.

Le Billon, P. (2000). "The Political Ecology of Transition in Cambodia 1989–1999: War, Peace and Forest Exploitation." *Development and Change* 31 (4): 785–805.

Lyons, T. (2004). "Engaging Diasporas to Promote Conflict Resolution: Transforming Hawks into Doves." Working paper, Washington Policy Seminar: 1–22. Online, available at: www.tamilnation.org/conflictresolution/lyons.pdf.

Melone, S., Georgios, T. and Ozsel, B. (2002). "Using the Media for Conflict Transformation: The Common Ground Experience." *Berghof Handbook for Conflict Transformation.* Berlin, Berghof Research Center for Constructive Conflict Management: 1–15.

Mohamoud, A. A. (2006). "African Diaspora and Post-Conflict Reconstruction in Africa." Copenhagen, Danish Institute for International Studies: 1–14.

Montague, D. (2002). "The Business of War and the Prospects for Peace in Sierra Leone." *The Brown Journal of World Affairs* 9 (1): 229–237.

Ortis, C. and Evans, P. (2003). "The Internet and Asia-Pacific Security: Old Conflicts and New Behavior." *The Pacific Review* 16 (4): 549–572.

Ostergaard-Nielsen, E. (2005). *Diasporas and Conflict Resolution – Part of the Problem or Part of the Solution?* Copenhagen, Danish Institute for International Studies.

Paffenholz, T. (2004). "Designing Transformation and Intervention Process" in Alex Austin, Martina Fischer and Norbert Ropers (eds.) *Transforming Ethnopolitical Conflict.* Berlin, Berghof Research Center for Constructive Conflict Management: 1–16.

Reljic, D. (2002). "The News Media and Transformation of Ethnopolitical Conflicts," in Martina Fischer, Hans J. Gießmann and Beatrix Schmelzle (eds.) *Berghof Handbook for Conflict Transformation.* Berlin, Berghof Research Center for Constructive Conflict Management: 1–16.

Rotberg, R. I. (ed.) (1996). *Vigilance and Vengeance: NGOs Preventing Ethnic Conflict in Divided Societies.* Cambridge, World Peace Foundation.

Shelley, B. (2001) "Protest and Globalization: Media, Symbols and Audience in the Drama of Democratization," in *Democratization* 8 (4): 155–174

Smith, R. (2007). *The Utility of Force: The Art of War in the Modern World.* New York, Alfred A. Knopf.

Soeters, J. (2007). Military Transformations and Peace Support Operations Lecture. Hebrew University of Jerusalem, Jerusalem. 18–21 June.

Sri Lanka Peace. The Official Website of Sri Lankan Government's Secretariat for Coordinating the Peace Process. Online, available at: www.peaceinsrilanka.org/peace2005/Insidepage/Partners/SLF/SLF.asp.

Tamm, I. J. (2002). "Diamonds in Peace and War: Severing the Conflict-Diamond Connection." *WPF Report no.30*. Cambridge, MA: World Peace Foundation.

Tongeren, P. van, Veen, H. van de and Verhoeven, J. (eds.) (2002). *Searching for Peace in Europe and Eurasia*. London, Lynne Rienner.

Veen, H. van de (1999). "Introduction: Better Media, Less Conflict." In P. van Tongeren (ed.) *People Building Peace: 35 Inspiring Stories From Around the World*. Utrecht, European Centre for Conflict Prevention. Online, available at: www.gppac.net/documents/pbp_f/5/2_intro.htm.

Verhoeven, J. (no date). "Radio Ijambo Bridges the Ethnic Divide in Burundi." In P. van Tongeren (ed.) *People Building Peace: 35 Inspiring Stories From Around the World*. Utrecht, European Centre for Conflict Prevention. Online, available at: www.gppac.net/documents/pbp_f/5/2_intro.htm.

Vines, A. (1998). "The Business of Peace: 'Tiny' Rowland, Financial Incentives and the Mozambican settlement." *Accord*, issue 3. Online, available at: www.c-r.org/our-work/accord/mozambique/business-peace.php.

Walter, B. F. (1997). "The Critical Barrier to Civil War Settlement." *International Organization* 51 (3): 335–364.

10 Mozambique – Renamo

Andrea Bartoli, Aldo Civico and Leone Gianturco

Introduction

Mozambique is now at peace. But peace did not come easily to the country. It came in a long, violent, and destructive struggle. Mozambique gained its independence through a war against its colonial ruler, Portugal, which had taken administrative control of the country and implemented vicious processes of race stratification and economic exploitation. Even after independence, regional powers actively intervened in Mozambique's internal affairs and contributed to the destabilization of the country. Most critically, Mozambique faced a 16-year civil war that ravaged its people.

Today, Mozambique is a unified and democratic country and is playing a significant role in ensuring peace and security in southern Africa. This is a remarkable achievement for a country in which war had left more than one million dead and four million as refugees or internally displaced persons. While Mozambique must still address present challenges, especially natural disasters that are made worse by the lack of adequate infrastructures, the civil war is over and the prospect for the successful continuation of the state formation process is favorable (Hume 1994).

Mozambique's success is due in major part to the interruption of a long cycle of violence and the introduction of peace negotiations between the Frelimo (Frente de Libertação de Moçambique) government and Renamo (Resistencia National Moçambicana). Through the talks, Renamo became a political party, abandoned its military struggle and became part of new political institutions. Frelimo, too, underwent a profound transformation. The shifts were encouraged by macro-level political change (especially the end of the Cold War and the subsequent global and regional realignment of power structures) that permitted a "re-imagining" of the Mozambique conflict and the movement toward reconciliation. Still, the process defied the conventional wisdom of post-conflict peacebuilding and set the stage for transformations based on important endogenous process (Terrence Lyons in this volume).

The ability of the Mozambicans and specific members of the international community to broker an end to the civil war rested on the dynamic interplay of several critical components. The transformation of the conflict may be understood by exploring factors including the openness of Frelimo to political change, the redefinition of the Mozambican polity, the active facilitation of third parties, the state of the Mozambican security system, the importance of effective leadership, and the role of traditional and tribal mechanisms of redress. Taken together, an overarching theme of the Mozambique peace process is the idea of direct ownership of the process by the very people it sought to serve. Conflict transformation in Mozambique happened in the streets and villages, as well as in other countries. And in many ways, the process is still continuing. While the risks of political instability are still palpable, especially around the possibility of a truly inclusive and representative polity, the transformation in Mozambique remains a critically important case study of successful peacebuilding.

Mozambique and the historical legacy

Mozambique was the subject of long colonial control by Portugal, which left the majority of its population facing deprivation and misery. By the time it achieved independence, Mozambique was one of the world's poorest and least developed former colonies: It lacked infrastructure; faced a chronic deficit in its current-account balance; maintained a substantial debt burden; faced agricultural dualism between the modern and the subsistence sectors; and had little human capital. Until the advent of former Prime Minister António de Oliveira Salazar, Portugal was not in a position to build the Mozambican economy. After nearly four centuries of neglect, the Berlin Conference prodded the Portuguese into bringing effective control over their territorial claims, but the European nation lacked the capital and technical capability to firmly establish an effective presence in the colony (Gentili 1995; Alden 2001).

The other major reason for Mozambique's lack of development was its geographical position. The country runs primarily north–south, yet nearly its entire infrastructure was established along east–west lines. This orientation of development, including railroads, ports and highways, was designed to serve as an outlet to sea for landlocked Rhodesia, Malawi and the Transvaal.

On the social side, Portuguese colonialists implemented race separation, with devastating consequences. The system was different from institutionalized South African apartheid, but was equally discriminatory. The Portuguese settlers, while imposing forced labor (*chibalo*) and other restrictions, prevented black Mozambicans from developing skills. Employees in the local industries were mainly whites or *assimilados*, even in the lower rungs of the employment ladder. *Assimilados* applied to Mozambican natives who could speak and write Portuguese and subscribed to Portuguese cultural norms and "civil" behavior. Until the early

1960s, it had a legal basis in Mozambique; the proportion of the African population which attained *assimilado* status was below 0.5 percent. Such policies, combined with state repression, made the creation of a black middle class virtually unthinkable. Whites were privileged, while Asians (primarily Pakistanis, Indians and Chinese), handled trade and other tertiary activities and fared well. Black people had a very low per capita income, little education and very poor health. Of the ten million black Mozambicans, 97 percent were illiterate (Munslow 1983; Newitt 1995), while 70 percent lived out of reach of any form of health care (Unicef 1989: 19).

Complicating Mozambique's precarious post-colonial situation was the demand that the Frelimo government take sides in the Cold War environment. Many of its higher ranking citizens had studied in socialist Algeria or Julius Nyerere's non-aligned Tanzania, while others maintained Marxist convictions. In 1975, the victory of Frelimo was regarded with alarm by the rulers of South Africa and Rhodesia, who had been Portugal's allies. The newly independent socialist state represented a threat to these "white" neighbors, who eagerly acted as the anti-communist watchtowers in Southern Africa.

Rhodesia and South Africa adopted aggressive military and external policies to destabilize Mozambique. For instance, South African mine owners dramatically reduced the number of Mozambicans allowed to be employed as cheap labor. The drop in employment halved the gold receipts that had, until 1975, helped to control Mozambique's chronic current-account deficit. This change, together with a deliberate policy of diversion of commercial traffic from the port of Maputo to other South African ports (Coscione 2007: 338), reduced Mozambique's earnings to one-third of its prior revenue.

Frelimo's Mozambique is not the case of a "failed" or "collapsed" state. As internal conflict broke out in 1976, a year after independence, the state barely existed. Nor was Mozambique a "predatory" state unwilling to create and distribute public services, such as health and education. Indeed, the history of the early years following independence saw the opposite behavior. In addition, there was no "fragmentation of state structures" (with the rise of local power centers such as Zaire). Rather, excessive centralization was among Mozambique's problems. Yet, what else was there to do when, in 1975, 90 percent of Portuguese settlers had left (together with their skills) and there was a need to drive the economy? The "cement" chosen to enhance Mozambican nationalism was Socialism.

The enmity system

In March 1976, as Rhodesia's liberation war intensified, the Frelimo government, which supported Zimbabwe's Robert Mugabe, implemented UN-ordered trade sanctions against Rhodesia in the name of solidarity with the Zimbabwean people. This event triggered a Rhodesian counteroffensive. While its external backers were mainly Portuguese who had their properties nationalized after independence, several of Rhodesia's fighters were Mozambicans – former Frelimo members who had been expelled by the party. Some claimed to have escaped from "re-education" camps – rural prisons established after independence in Mozambique – after having been imprisoned under minor charges. It is difficult, however, to trace an objective reconstruction of Mozambican dissidence. Some authors point out that the weak "adhesion" to Frelimo of some of its members was merely the result of corruption. Others blame Frelimo's ethnic and regional polarization, while still others highlight the historical marginalization of specific groups in Mozambique.

Renamo began its activities by destroying physical infrastructure, such as roads, bridges, and factories. At the outset, the organization's scope was limited: it had an estimated 1,000 members (Flower 1987) and the existing international environment discouraged many from taking Renamo seriously. The organization seemed to be "an ad-hoc dissident movement that would fade out with the independence of Zimbabwe" (Alao 1994: 52). Actually, major damage was to come after 1980, with Renamo's "change of sponsors."

In 1980, with the independence of Zimbabwe, Renamo fell under the protection of the South African military and civil intelligence. At the same time, Renamo and its backers unleashed an enlarged military offensive comprised of attacks on civilians, raids on buildings in small towns, and the destruction of various infrastructures. This activity was complemented by South Africa's direct military raids in southern Mozambique (Finnegan 1992: 32). The apartheid regime was anxious to end Frelimo's support for the African National Congress (ANC), and increase the degree of economic dependence on South Africa by all its neighboring countries.

By 1982, Renamo had approximately 5,000 soldiers operating throughout Mozambique with increasing success. Its practices often included killing innocent civilians and other brutality. But as we will see later on, violence cannot be exclusively ascribed to Renamo.

The intensification of war activities after 1981 jeopardized Mozambique's overall situation, therefore undermining its economic system. The attacks were mainly against civilians or economic targets – there was very little direct battle between the armies.

Protracted war caused death, disability, insecurity, displacement, and the devastation of economic activity and social infrastructures. It led to the spread of disease, famine, starvation, and physical and psychological damage, and left a terrible legacy: millions of landmines. War casualties, however, are difficult to disentangle from other deaths. The International Federation of Red Cross and Red Crescent Societies' (IFRCS) estimate of 100,000 war casualties in Mozambique (1992) surely comprises indirect loss of life, as reportedly there were very few direct military actions that year. While no reliable source has estimated the number of people whose disabilities were caused by the war, or the number of years that were lost or disrupted due to physical or mental disability or disease, anecdotal evidence indicates that at least every Mozambican family included a person killed, injured or maimed because of the war and/or its consequences.

Displacing and controlling the population

The struggle for "population control" in Mozambique involved many violent and arbitrary measures. It included forced relocation, such as Frelimo's "villagization." Called the "*Operação Produção*," the process arbitrarily regrouped people who had been "recuperated from Renamo" into enormous and ill-equipped accommodation centers. On its side, Renamo demanded the forced relocation of entire villages to generate compulsory labor (mainly porters) and recruit members.

Recruitment to Renamo often coincided with kidnapping. Many of the forcibly recruited Renamo "conscripts" showed fatalistic acceptance. Frelimo's propaganda highlighted the plight of many kidnapped youths, some of whom were allegedly forced to kill relatives to show loyalty to the Renamo "cause." However, as some commentators have maintained, recruitment by Renamo was often a more complex matter. While some people in the "risk" areas immediately abandoned their homes and moved to small towns under Frelimo control, and benefitted at times from international aid, the remaining segments of the population decided to stay and abide Renamo's "rule" or influence, in the face of retaliation by government soldiers.

Considering the conditions of its early stages, the variables of the Mozambican conflict (state weakness, colonial legacy, hostile neighbors) appear to be largely exogenous. However, while these conditions were necessary for war, they are not sufficient to account for the persistence of the conflict. As war endured, the determinants of the protracted Mozambican conflict appeared to be predominantly of an endogenous nature.

First, the socialist economic model introduced in 1977 with the backing of the Eastern Bloc quickly failed. Also, the negative heritage of colonialism, including the existence of a largely unskilled population, played a part. Similarly, there was a post-independence collapse of the rural trading network due to the massive out-migration of small-time Portuguese businessmen who had guaranteed the system. These demographic and economic shifts offer a partial explanation for the breakdown of rural production, as peasants had nothing to buy with money earned from work in the fields.

Frelimo's strategy of "transforming Mozambican society" did not prove successful in modifying the inherited colonial structures or enhancing economic growth. Efforts were concentrated in state-run farms and other "grand" projects, and not in substituting the former commercial network in the countryside or enhancing household agricultural production.

Another important factor was the redistribution of land following the creation of the state-run farms, important pillars of Frelimo's "modernization" strategy. In Mozambique, land was state property. Territories left over by the Portuguese had already been informally "alienated" by peasants between 1974 and 1977. Subsequently, these people were compelled to give their holdings to the state farms, or *machambas estatais* (Hermele 1998). Not surprisingly, passive resistance by peasants toward the new government policies accelerated the failure of the "grand" projects.

"Modernization" versus tradition

In the early years following independence, the rural population viewed Frelimo as a potential vehicle for change. It seemed to have the power to actualize the people's "desire of freedom" (Abrahamsson and Nilsson 1995). This included the abolition of forced labor (*chibalo*), access to health and education (which had been denied during the colonial era), as well as access to fertile land and to non-agricultural consumer goods. Frelimo addressed the most glaring inequalities: school enrollment doubled in less than five years for primary and secondary schools and the new national health system included quadruple the number of medical personnel. The international acclaim that Frelimo garnered for its ambitious mass literacy and vaccination campaigns was indeed deserved.

Hence, for some time, Frelimo was supported by national euphoria for independence and appeared able to guarantee social stability and freedom. But many of its members misinterpreted the people's enthusiasm, regarding it as a "revolutionary ebullience." Subsequently, Frelimo's legitimacy, especially in the rural world, began to crumble. As someone remarked,

> In Mozambique, differently from the Angolan situation, it was not only Frelimo's disregard towards the rural world to provoke the crisis and to open the way to the rebellion, rather the latter was a combination of the neglect of the economy and the will of exerting a political control.
>
> (Raison 1993: 1073)

By 1981, 1.8 million Mozambicans had been forced into 1,266 communal villages (Human Rights Watch 1992: 67). This nurtured hostility and suspicion toward Frelimo in the rural areas that led to increased support for Renamo.

Other major impositions, stemming from the ideological dogmatism of Frelimo's "modernization paradigm," irritated the Mozambican population. Among the changes were the:

- creation of the "re-education" camps (first created in 1975, they gathered political opponents, ordinary criminals, Jehovah's witnesses, unemployed vagrants and all people labeled as marginal);
- massive deployment of some 300,000 "unproductive" street people to northern rural areas (the 1983 "*Operação Produção*");
- quasi-forced charters of young adolescents to Cuba;
- travel restrictions inside the country (a "pass" named *guia de marcha* was in force from 1984 to 1990);
- banning of traditional healers (*curandeiros*);
- marginalization of the traditional authorities.

The aim of the "modernization" paradigm, besides the abolition of colonial systems, was to "wipe out" traditional social structures in rural areas. The effort to forcibly suppress important parts of the social and cultural universe in Mozambique weakened the existing social order and fostered instability (Lundin 1995: 435). In reaction, Renamo committed itself to restoring traditional authorities. At first, this move may have seemed insignificant, but it resulted in a critical alliance between Renamo and traditional figures (Geffray 1990). In a sense, Renamo astutely recognized the popular shift toward the values and models of the past (Cabaço 1995: 94). Too easily, the African continent is labeled as a place where people strive for authoritarian rule, as if the existence of tribal chiefs implies support for authoritarianism. Indeed, as Basil Davidson put it, it was participation and not authoritarian rule that guaranteed stability in the pre-colonial era (Davidson 1992).

As a quasi-totalitarian Mozambican state denied access to political entitlements and protection from dangerous policies, such as arbitrary imprisonment, Renamo took advantage of public dissatisfaction to attract sympathies and establish legitimacy among the people (Alao 1994).

The Mozambique peace process

The peace process was launched when Mozambicans asked, for the first time, that an international non-governmental organization, the Rome-based Community of Sant'Egidio (Galia Golan and Adir Gal in this volume), lead a mediation effort. For more than two years, the Community engaged in an integrative model of intervention that constructively linked official and unofficial diplomacy. The work is now studied as an intriguing development within the conflict resolution field (Dayton in this volume).

The strength of the Mozambique peace process rested on the governing party's openness to change, which allowed for the transformation of Renamo from a military force into a political one. These processes of transformation were mutually reinforcing (Terrence Lyons in this volume) and culminated with a series of institutional modifications, including joint commissions and elections.

The stability of the peace process related to the successful redefinition of the polity, which had been exclusivist under the Frelimo regime. The polity became much more inclusive and representative after the signing of Mozambique's General Peace Agreement (GPA), with not only the rebel faction but the governing party accepting a redefinition of the political space. If we use Edward Azar's ten general propositions that characterize intractable conflicts, we can see that Mozambique is almost a classic example of how protracted social conflicts can be resolved when both sides employ innovative political solutions (Azar 1986).

Renamo's transformation began in Rome well before the peace process was implemented through the United Nations Operation in Mozambique (ONUMOZ) peacekeeping operation led by Aldo Ajello between 1992 and 1994. The transformation was imagined and practiced in the negotiations that led to the GPA, where Renamo acted as a political party, dealt with complex diplomatic issues, and contributed to the redefinition of the polity.

The elections that followed the peace agreement sanctioned this transformation and made it sustainable. Also, the Electoral Commission's President, Dr. Brazao Mazula, a well-respected independent, navigated the difficult waters of the first election and contributed to the perception that a new form of political representation was possible.

Changes in Frelimo's rhetoric also supported the peace process. The government, for example, stopped describing Renamo as a group of bandits with whom communication was banned and began referring to it as a group of compatriots. This change, found in the first Joint Communiqué of the parties, was not cosmetic: it represented a profound shift in the general perception of Renamo by the population.

New opportunities for progress were also made possible by the poor state of Mozambique's security system and important political developments at the global and regional levels. As threats against all actors in the region de-escalated, the processes of political dialogue and joint redefinition of the polity took hold.

A number of third-party actors, intervening as facilitators, guarantors, observers, mediators, and partners, also assisted in the peace process. However, it is a deep conviction of the authors that the second-most important reason behind the success of the peace agreement in Mozambique and of the transformation of Renamo was the capacity to generate direct ownership of the process among the players.

Third-parties were, by character or by choice, weak; they did not have the capacity (or the will) to forcefully influence either party or the process. This "weakness" led to the paradoxical result that the parties had to be committed to the process and to one another because they were not forced into it. The final test of the transformation rested in their capacity to develop direct partnerships.

The strategies used by the protagonists to end their reliance on violence were primarily political and diplomatic. There was no military solution to the security threat that Renamo posed, while the capacity of Renamo to successfully govern the country would have been questionable. As Renamo leader Alfonso Dhlakama put it,

> We could have won but then what would have happened? Frelimo would have never surrendered. They would have gone to the mats, they would have stayed in the bush and fought. It would have been very hard for Renamo to keep the country together.
>
> (Bartoli 2007)

These preliminary observations underscore the role of leadership on both sides. Leadership was key to keeping Renamo together even when some of its members wanted to continue the military struggle and avoid the political process. It was Renamo's leaders who helped the group manage its political transformation. Yet, the quality of this leadership must be carefully examined. Some observers have identified in Dhlakama a strong and almost authoritarian leader, but the negotiations were held primarily by Raul Domingos, who is no longer a member of Renamo. Leadership was a dynamic process, at times challenged by the speed and degree of change required. On the Frelimo side there is no doubt that strong and effective political leadership, provided by Joaquim Chissano and Armando Guebuza, allowed the government to engage in an open and effective political dialogue with the enemy. The leaders of Frelimo clearly expressed a capacity to "keep the party together."

In Rome on 4 October 1992, Chissano and Dhlakama signed the GPA and announced to the country that the war was over. Everyone in Mozambique listened on the radio and started celebrating in the streets. In certain areas, the rejoicing lasted several days and included dancing in public. Peace came to Mozambique under the forward-looking leadership of both parties. Regular Mozambican citizens believed the leaders and supported them, making the transition possible. The peace was a Mozambican fruit, helped to ripen by wise and effective diplomatic hands.

The General Peace Agreement (GPA)

After 16 years of war, both parties were exhausted and under pressure to negotiate a ceasefire. In 1992, Mozambique was one of the poorest countries in the world (CIA 2005), and abandoned by its former ally – the Soviet Union. Neither Frelimo nor Renamo had the resources or the willingness to continue the war. Indeed, the government itself had already initiated the process of transformation with the new constitution in 1990.

The GPA was the result of a long process of negotiation for which Mozambicans themselves must take credit. The agreement was highly political, less a "legal" document and more a "constitutional" reference point for the incorporation of Renamo into the political process. Through Chissano's leadership, Frelimo accepted a redesigning of Mozambique as a state and relinquished the monopoly of power it previously enjoyed (Bartoli 1999b). Still, unlike many agreements in the post-Cold War era that called for power-sharing arrangements, the GPA gave Frelimo the presidency of the republic and all relevant governing roles, while Renamo became an opposition party in parliament.

All parties involved in the negotiation process agreed that it was necessary to stop the war to pave the way for political transformation and the self-representation that Mozambicans had never before enjoyed. Fundamentally, it was a way of entrusting Mozambicans with their own destiny. This path led to a peace agreement that spurred a political process based on a clear dichotomy consonant with traditional values: the time of war and the time of peace. For Mozambicans, it was crucial to focus their individual and collective energies toward peace and ensure that peace was embedded in the agreement. They owned the process and made decisions within it.

The GPA allowed Mozambicans of opposite parties to resolve their differences through political rather than military means, set a precedent for future political relations within Mozambique, and served as a constitutional framework. The agreement was intended to conform to international human rights norms; fundamentally, it was understood as a reorientation of the polity that would reference human rights in the process of stabilization and development, rather than actually provide them.

The GPA provided a comprehensive framework for the transition to democracy by addressing the:

- assembly and demobilization of troops;
- formation of new armed forces;
- reintegration of demobilized military personnel into civil life;
- resettlement of refugees and displaced persons;
- process of holding the first democratic multiparty elections.

The GPA offered amnesty, helping to create a discontinuity between war and peace. All prisoners were released (Protocol VI) and a general amnesty was granted to all Mozambicans in violation of the law and the normative practices of the government. The act was applied to all those in prison for political reasons, and those who were operating with and for Renamo (Lundin 2004).

For several years after the end of the war and the signing of the GPA, Mozambique experienced unprecedented economic growth with a 10 percent rise in its Gross Domestic Product (GDP). Though the GPA did not include provisions that addressed economic development, experts now suggest that it may be useful to emphasize national economic goals to strengthen the resolve of parties to abandon military struggles in favor of political ones.

The use of post-conflict traditional strategies of incorporation and reconciliation

Although human rights were always in the background of the Mozambique peace talks, a truth commission was never established to address actors' prior violent activity or to prosecute war criminals. The GPA represented the reality Mozambicans preferred: to accept those involved in war crimes into their own communities, rather than follow Western norms for handling the consequences of war. Later, Mozambicans blamed the war, not specifically Renamo or Frelimo, for the country's long suffering. This strategy – the emphasis on political agreement to assure peace rather than on justice to prosecute the main perpetrators of war crimes – is often derided by many in the international community. Yet, at least in the case of Mozambique, it is clear that a negotiated political settlement that reduces violence will also contribute to a dramatic reduction of human rights abuses (Bartoli 1999b). Also, respect for political autonomy and creativity may allow for peace and reconciliation to be achieved under means other than legal methods (Lundin 2004). Now Mozambique has a low level of violence, which is perhaps linked to its ability to re-incorporate former combatants using traditional mechanisms.

Mozambicans did not believe that trials would promote reconciliation. Instead, they invested in the structures of their traditional African society. Emblematic has been the use of African cultural means to reconcile and insert former soldiers into rural communities (Lundin 2004). Still, the flood of demobilized soldiers reintegrating into peace-time society, along with the spontaneous return of hundreds of thousands of refugees from neighboring countries, created a deep feeling of conflict fatigue among the population (Armon *et al.* 1998).

Furthermore, Alcinda Honwana's article, *Sealing the Past, Facing the Future*, emphasizes that the urge for peace and reconciliation in Mozambique may only succeed if individual traumas and communal rifts stemming from the war are addressed. Recognizing the costs and limitations of state- and internationally-sponsored healing initiatives, she argues that rehabilitating Mozambique's ravaged social fabric will depend on cultural and institutional resourcefulness at the local level (Honwana 1998).

Cultural understandings of health, trauma and healing are important because they are often are very location-specific. In the Mozambican context, for instance, good health is traditionally defined as a harmonious relationship between human beings, their natural surroundings and their ancestors. The social world (comprising the spirits and the living) and the physical world are united within a larger cosmology. The breakdown of this harmonious state is seen as the result of the malevolent intervention of *valoyi* (witches and sorcerers) or a sanction by the ancestral spirits for incorrect social behavior. Illness is therefore considered a social, rather than a physical, phenomenon (Honwana 1998). Such models of health contradict traditional Western approaches in which individuals and their social context, the body and the mind, are often perceived as separate, distinguishable entities.

These observations are relevant when we focus on the transition of Renamo from a military force to a political actor. This transformation played out in the realm of power politics as well the hearts and minds of Mozambicans who were able to distribute responsibility and blame very differently than Western observers would have predicted. This is why the practical and moral case for accommodating customary modes of healing and reconciliation, especially at the local level, is strong (Honwana 1998).

Peace consolidation and recent developments

There is little doubt that in Mozambique, peace has created conditions for economic, social and political development (Bartoli 1999b). The positive result was largely based on the ability of political leaders to articulate and deliver a policy of reconciliation that was open to structural institutional changes. This policy also reflected the desire for peace among the great majority of Mozambicans (Bartoli 1999a).

The results are, so far, extraordinary: the peace process was successful, violence is minimal, and economic growth has been significant. Although the signing of the GPA formally ended the war, the events that followed have also driven its long-term success. Implementation of the GPA, overseen by the ONUMOZ, was the fourth phase in the peace process that concluded with the holding of multi-party elections in October 1994. During this phase, ONUMOZ helped build Renamo's confidence and allowed it to transform itself into a political party (Armon *et al.* 1998).

Mozambique has conducted three democratic presidential elections since then, all of which were accepted as legitimate by the international community. The success of the electoral process was based on the Mozambicans' ability to create institutions, such as the National Elections Commission, that upheld the interests of the people. The National Information Commission monitors the conduct and activities of the government's security system and serves as an information service with regard to political rights. The National Police Affairs Commission was responsible for monitoring the conduct and activities of the Mozambican police. Finally, the National Commission on Territorial Administration was composed of government and Renamo delegates (Alden 2001).

The results of the first democratic presidential elections of 1994 gave Chissano 53.3 percent of the vote and Dhlakama 33.7 percent. The high level of voter participation and the peaceful conduct of the elections exemplified, politically and symbolically, Mozambique's passage from war to peace (Bartoli 1999b), as well as its newfound respect for human rights.

Other post-conflict improvements allow hope for the stable development of the country, though they pose new challenges for Mozambican society and the international community. Closer analysis of the political restructuring of Mozambique reveals that there were significant fractures in the newly built democratic edifice. At the national level, the nature of the transition to democracy had been – as in the classic cases in Latin America – an elite affair driven by a reformist clique centered around Chissano, who used his power to initiate a negotiated end to the civil war and, concurrently, install a liberal constitution and ultimately conduct elections (Alden 2001). After the 1994 elections, Mozambicans had to get used to the idea of pluralism and democracy, while democracy itself had to be extended from the urban elitist level to the local level.

Also, the building of peace in Mozambique depends on how the reconstruction process addresses the profound social divisions, political alienation and poverty that sustained the war for so many years. It is particularly crucial that reconstruction meets the needs of Mozambique's poor, isolated rural populations that have so far seen few tangible benefits of peace. The resettlement of some six million displaced people and refugees continues to be a cause for concern, raising the specter of severe and persistent land disputes (Rupiya 1998).

The opening of Mozambican society marked a turning point for civil society in the country. In 1990, the Ministry of Cooperation in Mozambique identified 12 local NGOs with sufficient resources to participate in the founding of an NGO network; by 1993 it had registered 87, and three years later, well over 100 (Bennet 1995). In 1998, the Scandinavia-supported Forum Nacional das Organizaxoes Nao-Governmentais Mocambicanas claimed a membership of 292 groups (Alden 2001). Mozambican NGOs have come to operate in spheres as diverse as business, historical preservation and the environment (Alden 2001). The country has witnessed more freedom for diverse religious practice and the media. The changes also resulted in the abolishment of the death penalty.

In the face of overwhelming odds, and with extensive involvement by international donors, this risky manifold process produced positive results. From 1992 to 2002, Mozambique enjoyed its first decade free of armed conflict since gaining its independence in 1975. It has provided the United Nations with its only real success story in Africa. According to Human Rights Watch, "Mozambique continued to consolidate peace and reconciliation" (Bureau of Democracy 2004).

Finally, the Mozambique government continues to cooperate with international organizations to remove the land mines planted during the war years. The work is imperative: According to the National De-mining Institute (IND), more than 229 persons were killed in Mozambique landmine accidents between 1997 and 2002 (Bureau of Democracy 2004).

Conclusion

Researchers, independent observers and non-governmental organizations agree that despite natural setbacks to the creation of a more democratic and open society, there are many indications that, under the right conditions and with continuing support from the international community, Mozambique will not only sustain peace but also build upon its achievements to strengthen its democracy and guarantee wider respect for human rights.

In its first decade after the peace accords were signed and democracy formally established as the basis of post-war politics, Mozambique has enjoyed a period of unprecedented peace and macroeconomic prosperity (Manning 2002).

> After the signing of the GPA, Mozambique stood out as one of the more stable and peaceful countries in southern Africa and as the United Nations' only post-conflict success story in Africa. There had been no return to armed conflict or significant political violence and neither of the two major parties had questioned the essential terms of the political settlement.
>
> (Manning 2002)

Still, the setbacks mentioned above indicate the importance of constant attention and supervision by all involved. Nominal victories on the human, political and economic fronts and the "set of formal processes and institutions created at the outset are the starting point, rather than the culmination of the democratization process" (Manning 2002).

Mozambique has gone from being one of the poorest countries in the world to being the most successful example of state transformation in Africa and arguably elsewhere. While international support was important in the process, Mozambicans themselves played the cardinal role in ending their war by choosing peace and creating the political conditions for political inclusiveness. Without these choices and commitment, little could have been achieved, as witnessed in the cases of Angola and Sierra Leone. Although human rights were neither mentioned nor included in the GPA, the Mozambican pledge to uphold peace and democracy has opened its society, which in turn has sparked the birth of a nascent civic society that is still growing today.

The case of Mozambique is peculiar in its nature and outcome: its success was largely dependent on its idiosyncratic culture and traditions, which enabled healing and reconciliation. Where local traditions fell short or could not provide answers amid development of the newly unified society, Mozambicans embraced the Western framework of societal development and committed themselves to adopting parliamentary politics and respecting basic human rights. This synthesis proved extremely successful and is still operational today.

References

Abrahamsson, H. and Nilsson, A. (1995) *Mozambique, the Troubled Transition: From Socialist Construction to Free Market Capitalism*, London and Atlantic Highlands, NJ, Zed Books.

Alao, A. (1994) *Brothers at War: Dissidence and Rebellion in Southern Africa*, London and New York, British Academic Press.

Alden, C. (2001) *Mozambique and the Construction of the New African State: From Negotiations to Nation Building*, New York, Palgrave.

Armon, J., Hendrickson, D. and Vines, A. (1998) "The Mozambican Peace Process in Perspective," *Accord*, issue 3.

Azar, E. (1986) "Protracted International Conflicts: Ten Propositions," in Azar, E. and Burton, J. (eds.) *International Conflict Resolution: Theory and Practice*, Boulder, Lynne Rienner.

Bartoli, A. (1999a) "Mediating Peace in Mozambique: The Role of the Community of Sant'Egidio," in Aall, P., Crocker, C. and Hampson, F. (eds.) *Herding Cats: The Role of Mediation in Multiparty Crisis*, Washington, DC, United States Institute of Peace Press.

Bartoli, A. (1999b) "Providing Space for Change in Mozambique," in Herr, Robert and Herr, J. Z. (eds.) *Transforming Violence: Linking Local and Global Peacemaking*, Scottdale, PA, Herald Press.

Bartoli, A. (2001) "Forgiveness and Reconciliation in the Mozambique Peace Process," in Helmick, R. G. and Petersen, R. L. (eds.) *Forgiveness and Reconciliation*, West Conshohocken, Templeton Foundation Press.

Bartoli, A. (2005) "Learning from the Mozambique Peace Process: The Role of the Community of Sant'Egidio," in Ronald, F. (ed.) *Paving the Way: Contributions of Interactive Conflict Resolution to Peacemaking*. Lanham, MD, Lexington Books.

Bennet, J. (1995) *Meeting Needs: NGO Coordination in Practice*, London, Earthscan.

Bureau of Democracy, Human Rights, and Labor (2004) *Country Reports on Human Rights Practices 2003: Mozambique*, Washington, DC, Bureau of Democracy, Human Rights, and Labor.

Cabaço, J. L. (1995) "A Longa Estrada da Democracia Moçambicana," in Mazula (ed.) *Moçambique: Eleições, Democracia e Desenvolvimento*, Maputo, Inter-Africa Group.

CIA (2005) *CIA World Factbooks: Mozambique*, Washington, DC, CIA.

Coscione, S. (2007) *Country Programme Mozambiqu: The Achievement of SADC Macro-economic Convergence Targets: Assessment of Performance Reviews and Implementation Plans*, Gaborone, Botswana, Southern African Development Community (SADC) Secretariat.

Davidson, B. (1992) *Africa in History*, London, Orion Books Ltd.

Finnegan, W. (1992) *A Complicated War: The Harrowing of Mozambique*, Berkeley, University of California Press.

Flower, K. (1987) *Serving Secretly: Rhodesia into Zimbabwe 1964–81*, London, John Murray.

Geffray, C. (1990) *La Cause des Armes au Mozambique: Anthropologie d'une Guerre Civile*, Paris, Editions Karthala.

Gentili, A. M. (1995) *Il Leone e il Cacciatore* Roma, Carocci, La Nuova Italia Scientifica.

Hermele, K. (1998) *Land Struggles and Social Differentiation in Southern Mozambique: A Case Study of Chokwe, Limpopo 1950–1987*, Uppsala, Scandinavian Institute of African Studies.

Hirsch, J. L. (2001) *Sierra Leone: Diamonds and the Struggle for Democracy*, Boulder, CO, Lynne Rienner.

Honwana, A. (1998) "Sealing the Past, Facing the Future: Trauma Healing in Rural Mozambique," *Accord*, issue 3.

Human Rights Watch (1992) *Conspicuous Destruction: War, Famine and the Reform Process in Mozambique*, New York, Human Rights Watch.

Hume, C. (1994) *Ending Mozambique's War: The Role of Mediation and Good Offices*, Washington, DC, United States Institute of Peace Press.

Lundin, I. B. (1995) "Traditional Authority in Mozambique," in Lundin, I. B. and Machava, F. J. (eds.) *Decentralisation and Municipal Administration: Descriptions and Development of Ideas on some African and European Models*, Maputo, Friedrich Ebert Stiftung.

Lundin, I. B. (2004) "The Peace Process and the Construction of Reconciliation Post Conflict – The Experience of Mozambique," presented in Barcelona under the international seminar Experiences of Penal Alternatives in Peace Process.

Manning, C. L. (2002) *The Politics of Peace in Mozambique: Post-Conflict Democratization, 1992–2000*, Westport, CT, Praeger.

Munslow, B. (1983) *Mozambique: The Revolution and Its Origins*, London, Longman Group.

Newitt, M. D. D. (1995) *A History of Mozambique*, Bloomington, Indiana University Press.

Raison, J.-P. (1993) "Mozambique," in Lacoste, Y. (ed.) *Dictionnaire de Geopolitique*, Paris.

Rupiya, M. (1998) "Historical Context: War and Peace in Mozambique," *Accord*, issue 3.

UNICEF (1989) *Children on the Front Line*, New York, Unicef.

11 Revolution deferred: from armed struggle to liberal democracy

The African National Congress in South Africa

Tom Lodge

Introduction

Organized violent opposition to the white minority government in South Africa lasted for more than 30 years, between 1961 and 1994, with the African National Congress (ANC) assuming a leading role. This chapter will focus on the ANC's development. It will discuss its decision to adopt violent tactics. It will then assess the factors that sustained its campaigning. Finally it will address the dynamics that caused the ANC's turn-away from violence as well as the considerations that shaped the political settlement.

Formed in 1912, the ANC began to build a mass membership during World War II and local branches began to embrace more militant kinds of activity. At this time several ANC leaders were also members of the Communist Party. Communists and a group of young self-professed "Africanists" who formed a Youth League influenced the embrace of more aggressive tactics. The ANC, in 1949, adopted a "Program of Action" of strikes, boycotts and civil disobedience toward a goal of African "self determination." The Communist Party was banned in 1950. Thereafter its members would work within the ANC helping to ensure that though the ANC itself remained an exclusively African body it formed multiracial alliances with sympathetic groups in other communities. The ANC's Freedom Charter, adopted in 1956, referred to a democratic future in which all races would enjoy equal rights. By 1960, though, a decade of mass-based militant resistance helped to convince a number of ANC principals, including Nelson Mandela, that the organization had exhausted all peaceful options. Mandela was one of a triumvirate of Johannesburg based leaders who predominated in the direction of the organization, together with his fellow lawyer, Oliver Tambo, and Walter Sisulu, an estate agent. Sisulu and Mandela had been privately discussing the possibilities of a guerrilla insurgency since the mid-1950s. The ANC's president, Chief Albert Lutuli was a more committed adherent of what he called "the non-violent passive resistance technique." He believed that the ANC stood "for the outlawing of war and violence as instruments for settling disputes" (Pillay 1993: 50, 107, 154).

In 1959 a breakaway movement, the Pan-Africanist Congress (PAC), constituted itself as a more radical alternative. The Pan-Africanists emphasized African racial identity and criticized the Communist Party for "watering down" the ANC's nationalist predispositions. In fact, the Communist Party's influence was most evident in the mild socialism of the Freedom Charter. In 1960 the PAC committed itself to resisting the pass laws. In Sharpeville on 21 March 1960, a crowd of 5,000 assembled outside the police station. After a tense standoff the police fired and killed 80. In the national tumult that followed the government banned both the PAC and the ANC.

Why did the ANC turn to violence?

Why did the ANC turn to violence in mid-1961? In Nelson Mandela's autobiography the decision to use violent tactics followed the state's forcible suppression of a three-day worker "stay at home" (Mandela 1994: 259), a protest intended to demonstrate popular support for the ANC's call for constitutional negotiations. Turn-out was impressive, but for Mandela and his colleagues it was the government's reaction that mattered. A massive army and police deployment in the main African townships and 10,000 arrests under new detention laws "raised the question of whether we can continue talking peace and non violence" (Pogrund 2000: 99).

In fact, discussion of the possibility of the ANC and its allies embarking upon an "armed struggle" began earlier. Members of the South African Communist Party (SACP) began considering the adoption of violence in mid-1960. Some of them claimed later that a party conference in December 1960 authorized preparations for guerrilla combat. SACP delegates attending an international conference in Moscow in July 1960 extracted a Chinese promise to provide military training.

From time to time during the 1950s, ANC-led campaigns had featured a violent undertow; for example, in 1957 ANC rural activists in Natal set fire to sugar cane fields (Magubane *et al.* 2004: 53). ANC leaders believed they could harness such rebellious predispositions and that if they did not they might be supplanted by more aggressive rivals. In 1960, the Sharpeville crisis encouraged perceptions that the state was vulnerable. The shootings were followed by protests in every major town. Declaration of a State of Emergency prompted an exodus of foreign investment: as *The Economist* observed at the time "Only a madman would buy South African shares" (Suzman 1993: 52). Several ANC leaders, including Nelson Mandela, had at least speculated about the possibility of an armed offensive against apartheid for several years, but they encountered considerable opposition to such a course. In mid-1961 at meetings of the ANC's leadership, Mandela had to work hard to overcome objections. Chief Lutuli maintained his moral reservations about using arms and the SACP's Secretary General, Moses Kotane was also skeptical, believing that violence was premature. Eventually and with mixed feelings, the ANC's principals consented to sanction the establishment of a new military organization, *Umkhonto we Sizwe* (Spear of the Nation). It would function separately from the ANC and would be co-sponsored by the SACP. For the time being, *Umkhonto* would engage only in very carefully controlled sabotage operations avoiding any casualties. This restraint may have been partly in deference to Lutuli's reservations, but Mandela 30 years later recalled that all were in agreement that non-lethal sabotage "offered the best hope of reconciliation afterwards" (Mandela 1993: 272).

Was the turn to violence strategically sensible? One line of reasoning is that in opting for conspiracy and sabotage, the ANC neglected other essential activities. Mandela himself was to make this point. He wrote in prison in the mid-1970s that in establishing *Umkhonto* "we ... drained the political organizations of their enthusiastic and experienced men, (and) concentrated our attention on the new organization" (Mandela 1976).

Academic critics of the ANC's decision have taken the argument further to contend that ANC rank and file were unready for armed confrontation and that the repression it would invite would discourage any other political assertion. One of Mandela's friends and contemporaries, the social psychologist Fatima Meer, a few years after Mandela's arrest suggested that generally black South Africans were politically immobilized as a consequence of the structural characteristics of the South African social system: the measure of economic security it offered and the migratory labor system which for men created contending focuses of loyalty between town and countryside and deflected their aggression inwards so that it became "irrationally dissipated in the neighbourhood and family" (Meer 1971: 141–143). In a similar vein, Edward Feit has argued that to succeed in its first campaign, *Umkhonto* would have needed to disrupt order on a much wider scale, "beyond a level the government could control" (Feit 1971: 75). On the whole, Feit suggests, for many black South Africans even the authoritarian order maintained by the government represented a form of security.

A rich autobiographical literature encourages analytical emphasis on the role of individual agency in prompting and shaping the ANC's embrace of violence. However the turn to armed struggle can be explained in more impersonal structural terminology. Both leadership and rank and file *Umkhonto* members tended to be drawn from well-educated African professionals and from trade unionists, groups who were particular targets of government policies during the 1950s, partly because during this period the African urban middle class was becoming more visible and African industrial workers were becoming more assertive. African politicians enjoyed access to fresh resources, including money from foreign sympathizers and the possibility of projecting their ideas through popular news-papers. Pan-African decolonization in the rest of Africa helped to nurture rising expectations, and the ANC's transformation from being a genteel lobby at the beginning of the 1940s to becoming a structured popular organization also helped to foster political ambitions. Early in the 1950s, Mandela startled older ANC notables by telling them that one day he would become South Africa's first black Prime Minister.

What helped to sustain political violence?

The ANC began sabotage operations on 15 December 1961. More than 200 attacks followed in the next three years. Targets varied – railway signal systems, electrical sub-stations, and official buildings – but in general the actions were planned to avoid bloodshed, though on their own initiative local units did kill or try to kill policemen and informers. On 16 December, an important nationalist anniversary for Africans and Afrikaners, *Umkhonto* distributed a leaflet expressing the hope that the sabotage would "bring the Government and its supporters to their senses before it is too late ... before matters reach the desperate stage of civil war" (Karis *et al.* 1977: 717). The police arrested most of *Umkhonto*'s national command in August 1963 though they had apprehended Nelson Mandela one year earlier, shortly after a journey he had made across Africa to Europe to raise foreign support. Several African governments together with China and the Soviet Union agreed to provide training facilities. Preparations for guerrilla warfare began early with the recruitment and dispatch of men for military instruction.

In early 1962 members of the High Command drafted a strategy for "protracted war." This clearly took its inspiration from Castro's victory in Cuba and from Guevara's *foco* theory in which a limited guerrilla offensive can manufacture the conditions that are needed for a revolutionary upheaval. In *Umkhonto*'s "*Mayibuye*" scheme, military operations would begin with the landing in rural locations "by ship and air" of four guerrilla bands, each numbering 30 men. These would combine with locally recruited auxiliaries who would be armed through sea-based deliveries. The plan envisaged "massive assistance ... from the whole of the African continent and the Socialist World" (Karis *et al.* 1977: 762). Effectively it assumed the willingness of sympathetic eastern bloc governments to supply naval support.

Though *Umkhonto* encountered no difficulties in recruiting potential trainees and sending them abroad, other aspects of the plan were woefully impractical. The fully trained guerrillas were meant to find in each of the four areas initially chosen for operations "at least 7,000 men ready to join the guerrilla army" (Karis *et al.* 1977: 764). In fact, *Umkhonto* was mainly an urban organization, and ANC organization was non-existent in each of the four locations targeted for the first phase of campaigning. In any case even governments that in the early 1960s were prepared to arm the ANC were most unlikely themselves to supply the logistical support envisaged in "*Operation Mayibuye.*" Most of the recruits who underwent training in China, Eastern Europe and Africa were going to remain outside South Africa for a very long time. Meanwhile by 1965 about 800 or so ANC members were serving prison terms alongside Nelson Mandela on Robben Island, probably most of the *Umkhonto* membership inside South Africa.

For the next ten years, *Umkhonto* would have virtually no presence within South Africa. Various efforts were made by surviving activists to rebuild the ANC. Between 1966 and 1969, Nelson Mandela's wife, Winnie Mandela led a group of cells that planned arson attacks on a railway shunting yard, a conspiracy that from its inception had been watched closely by the police. The external ANC made several efforts to infiltrate organizers through merchant shipping. In 1967 and 1968, joint *Umkhonto*–Zimbabwe African People's Union operations attempted to infiltrate groups across the Wankie Game Park in Rhodesia.

A few ANC networks composed of 1950s veterans and augmented by released political prisoners continued to function, recruiting and circulating photocopied leaflets. From 1974 contact resumed between these groups and the ANC's external organization through ANC officials stationed in Botswana, Swaziland and Lesotho. In 1975 the Johannesburg and Durban groups began transporting recruits to Swaziland for military training in the Soviet Union.

These rudimentary arrangements were just about sufficient for the ANC to assume an auxiliary role in the massive rebellion that broke out the following year. For in 1976, nationwide riots by schoolchildren put South Africa's rulers on the defensive. In fact, limits to their power were evident at the start of the decade. Growth contracted as manufacturing directed at local consumers reached its limits. During the 1960s rapid African advance into semiskilled manufacturing work gave black workers new leverage. Wildcat strikes in 1973 reconstituted a combative trade union movement. Mass literacy provided the cultural basis for the formation of a new generation of political organizations, inspired by the US black power movement and led by expanding numbers of graduates from the segregated universities.

The collapse of Portuguese colonial power in neighboring Mozambique had, from 1974, supplied fresh militant inspiration. As Black Consciousness percolated down to secondary schools, it found ready adherents. A regulation that half the curriculum should be taught in Afrikaans provoked the Soweto Students Representative Council into launching demonstrations on 16 June 1976. The police fired into a crowd of children. Quickly the revolt spread to 50 towns. In a year of street battles and classroom boycotts, at least 575 protesters died. Several thousand more left South Africa, many to join the ANC. Though before the revolt the ANC had begun to recruit amongst the students who were to constitute the leadership it did not exercise any real influence over its direction.

However, *Umkhonto* units, fresh from their Soviet training, began operations in Soweto during the rebellion.

Official response mixed reform with repression. In 1979 legislation conceded rights to black trade unions. Other measures attempted to solicit support from urban Africans. By the 1980s, though, urbanized Africans were more likely to acknowledge the authority of the ANC exiles. In Africa the ANC had constructed a formidable bureaucracy including an army. Presided over by Oliver Tambo, the organization was still led by 1950s veterans and the SACP remained decisive in shaping strategy. Communists perceived themselves to be engaged in a struggle for "national democracy," a transitional phase before a fully socialist society. "National liberation" represented a profound systemic alteration of a kind that could only follow "seizure of power." How to achieve this objective became clearer in the late 1970s. Now there were new opportunities for legal activity. A visit to Vietnam underlined the importance of building an organizational base through a non-violent political struggle in which the general population could participate. In turn, this political movement would later provide a platform for a People's War. So, for the time being, the ANC should foster a broad front from existing legal organizations to promote the widest kinds of political struggle.

Meanwhile *Umkhonto* "armed propaganda" would make the ANC visible. From 1976 the guerrillas became increasingly conspicuous. Operations were directed at targets chosen for their psychological impact in or near the main cities. A successful rocket attack on the Sasolburg synthetic fuel refinery in June 1980 represented *Umkhonto* operations at their most elaborate.

Despite such spectacles the warfare was symbolic. Up to 1985, *Umkhonto* mounted fewer than 100 attacks a year. Command structures remained external and there were never more than 500 *Umkhonto* soldiers deployed inside South Africa. The insurgents' conduct reflected their training. In particular, cadres were warned of the dangers of "militarism," the isolation of military from political activity. ANC leaders opposed indiscriminate terrorism and up to 1984 the basic intention of *Umkhonto*'s activity was not to mount a serious military challenge, but rather to enhance the ANC's popular status and win for it a mass following. By the end of 1983, the formation of a "United Democratic Front" suggested that *Umkhonto*'s "armed propaganda" had succeeded in its essential objective.

Reforms prompted the Front's establishment. Elected African municipalities were established in 1982. The following year a new constitution replaced the existing exclusively white House of Assembly with a "tricameral" legislature in which colored and Indian voters would be represented separately though Africans remained excluded. On 8 January 1983, Oliver Tambo announced it to be "The Year of United Action." All democratic forces, Tambo urged, should merge "into one front for national liberation." The United Democratic Front (UDF) assembled eight months later. The UDF's leadership included many veteran ANC notables and increasingly it assumed the authority of an ANC surrogate over a network of 600 organizations. These included local "civic" organizations that had recently mushroomed in black townships in struggles to win improvements in services. The UDF's proclaimed purpose was to challenge the constitutional reforms. Soon, though, its affiliates were swept up in a tide of insurrectionary opposition to the extremely corrupt local governments in African townships, sparked by heavy rent increases for public housing.

The rebellion began with rent strikes in the townships around Vereeniging, south of Johannesburg. A march on municipal offices swiftly degenerated into rioting and the killing of the local mayor. Soldiers restored order, but the rebellion proliferated, its explosive energy attributable to the combination of inflation and unemployment. Most black 18–24 year olds were unemployed in 1986 and inflation was accelerating. Economic recession coincided with the government's efforts to legitimize its authority. The rent strike remained one of the UDF's more effective weapons, enduring through a state of emergency that between 1986 and 1988 succeeded in halting most of the open forms of militant politics. As the ANC's strategists had hoped, the UDF's activist culture was informed by a rediscovery of Congress traditions and inspired by the martial theatre of *Umkhonto*'s armed struggle. At the ANC's Consultative Conference, held in Zambia in June 1985, ANC leaders announced it was time to move to a People's War that would end with "seizure of power." Now, "the risen masses" would be turned "into organized groups of combatants" while an externally trained "core" would function as an "officer corps" (African National Congress 1985a and 1985b).

Over the next 18 months, *Umkhonto* stepped up operations. In 1986 guerrillas struck 228 times. The escalation probably reflected wider weapon distribution: at the beginning of 1987 for example, teenage "comrades" protecting rent boycotters often possessed side arms, evidence that guerrillas were indeed equipping local "mass combat units." This may help to explain attacks on targets such as shopping arcades, though in October 1988 the ANC released a statement forswearing attacks on civilians. In 1989, the final year of *Umkhonto* operations, the number of attacks peaked at 300.

By then the ANC's commitment to arms had a long history. Early on, prospects for a generalized rebellion in South Africa appeared remote. Between 1964 and 1975, the year it began to rebuild its internal organization, the ANC's survival depended upon the quasi-official status it received from certain African governments, a "representative" authority that enabled it to maintain base facilities in Tanzania and Zambia. As organized anti-apartheid resistance expanded in the wake of the schoolchildren's uprising, it became easier for the ANC to build a disciplined following inside South Africa but even so up until the end of armed operations, most of the ANC's organization was located outside South Africa.

To a very large extent, then, externally derived resources sustained revolt. These resources included accommodation from African governments. Between 1977 and 1989 Angola supplied military facilities. Angolan willingness to provide camps was especially important because it was exceptional. Until 1969 the Tanzanians had hosted *Umkhonto* but were dissuaded from further hospitality of this kind by South African pressure though the Tanzanian government then granted land for the ANC to construct a training college. Meanwhile, Mozambique allowed the ANC to reinforce guerrillas across its territory and until 1984 *Umkhonto*'s operational command located itself in Maputo. The Botswana authorities ignored guerrillas crossing its territory. This sort of cooperation was indispensable in enabling the ANC to develop a significant presence inside South Africa.

Soviet support was also crucial. The Soviet Union provided the main training facilities for *Umkhonto* from 1969 until the opening of the Angolan camps in 1977. Soviet advisors helped train soldiers in African camps as well. The Soviet government began giving the ANC substantial financial help from 1963, $300,000 that year and tens of millions over the next three decades. As importantly, the Soviet Union supplied weaponry. Education and scholarships represented another critical resource supplied by communist administrations. Nordic governments funded the ANC's Tanzanian college and the Dutch also financed educational and welfare work. Soviet assistance was probably partly prompted by great power competition in Africa, though Southern Africa was never a region of particular concern to Soviet strategists.

During the 1980s, public sympathy for the ANC in Western Europe and in North America prompted European governments to impose financial sanctions upon South Africa. Similarly a "divestment" movement in the US gathered momentum on campuses and in churches through the decade, acquiring decisive weight when its goals were taken up the Congressional Black Caucus. The British Anti-Apartheid Movement (AAM), growing out of an early trade boycott campaign that began in 1959, was the first base of what was to develop into a remarkable pan-European new social movement, often drawing into its national leaderships key members of political and social elites. The AAM was usually loosely linked with political parties, though its main bases were the expanding populations of university students, the prime constituency for a range of single-issue pressure groups that emerged in the 1960s. ANC exiles often played a major role in setting up the AAM, particularly in Britain and Ireland, the two countries where the movement was strongest. Here, the existence of a South African diaspora, often white, generally well educated, and comfortably established in elite professions, helped the ANC make useful connections. The ANC's commitment to "multiracial" politics in the 1950s ensured that when its members went into exile they would be accompanied by people with ready access to middle class occupations and influential social networks. In 1969, the ANC allowed whites, Indians and coloreds to join the external organization, formalizing what was already a very close association between its own leadership and non-African allies. White, Indian and colored members of the Communist Party had joined *Umkhonto* at its inception. The Anti-Apartheid Movement represented an important base of support for the ANC during its insurgent phase but as a generally liberal constituency it may have also influenced the ANC to limit the scope and intensity of violence, through eschewing terrorism for example.

The 1976 Soweto uprising created new opportunities for organizing armed insurgency. Because of the range of resources available to the ANC, its leadership was able to exploit these opportunities much more effectively than any of its rivals. Broader structural developments helped to sustain the rebellion. Arguably earlier armed rebellions failed to elicit widespread public participation because even black South Africans experienced a measure of economic security. By 1980, for the South African authorities, ensuring security and order was very difficult. In contrast to the 1960s when real GDP growth averaged around 6 percent, by the 1980s GDP growth had contracted to around 1 percent a year. Stagnant employment meant that every year increasingly large numbers of school leavers joined the unemployed. Most of these unemployed were relatively well educated young people, for secondary education had expanded very quickly through the 1970s, more than tripling its enrolments between 1975 and 1984. Among 16 to 24 year olds it is likely that only a small minority succeeded in finding work. This generation was more open to modern political ideas and less likely to find authority intimidating, having no personal memories of the political repression of the 1960s. They were less respectful, not just of the authorities but of older people in general, and often they were ready to use violence as "a means of procuring scarce material resources" (Seekings 1993: 15). It was these disaffected youthful cohorts that supplied the ANC with its recruits. A rising tide of politically and criminally motivated violence accompanied most instances of political protest. Between 1976 and 1994, policeman, soldiers and activists killed around 24,000 people. Only a few hundred of these deaths could be directly attributed to *Umkhonto* activity.

De-escalation and the turning away from violence

At their peak, *Umkhonto*'s activities scarcely threatened South African security. In 1986, the ANC circulated a sober assessment. "Despite all our efforts we have not come anywhere near the achievement of the objectives we set ourselves." ANC structures inside South Africa remained too weak to supply reliable support for *Umkhonto* (African National Congress 1986). Police continued to anticipate with precision the arrival of trained guerrillas from across the border, an indication of their success in infiltrating *Umkhonto* command structures. In the field the average survival period for guerrillas was six months, according to an *Umkhonto* officer's estimate (Barrell 1990: 60). Meanwhile South African "destabilization" of neighboring countries disrupted *Umkhonto* supply lines. In April 1989 the ANC was compelled to move its guerrilla bases back to Tanzania from Angola, a consequence of the Namibia–Angola Peace accord. By this time it was obvious to most ANC leaders that, in Secretary-General Alfred Nzo's words, the ANC did "not have the capacity to intensify the armed struggle in any meaningful way" (Waldmeir 1998: 121).

From 1986 onwards, ANC spokesmen began to refer to the prospect of a negotiated accession to power. In September 1985, a meeting between ANC leaders and South African businessmen in Zambia represented an encouraging signal that powerful interests inside South Africa were willing to contemplate a change of regime. Here Thabo Mbeki, the head of the ANC's international office, explained the ANC's policies: "monopoly capital," including the press would fall under public control but "beyond that private capital would exist." However nationalization might be Zambian style, with a 51 percent state holding, leaving plenty of room for big companies. Within a few months, ANC references to negotiations were implying a very different form of political transition to the "seizure of power" envisaged in the ANC People's War strategy. By January 1986, a senior ANC leader was telling the *Observer* that the objective of the "offensive" was "breaking up the power structure." "We are not talking of overthrowing the government," he conceded, "but (of) turning so many people against it that it would be forced to do what Ian Smith had to do" (Phillips 1988: 47). With a proliferation of contacts between the ANC and representatives of different interest groups within South African, the likelihood of such a scenario was becoming more plausible.

In December 1985, from prison, Nelson Mandela initiated an increasingly ambitious schedule of talks with members of the government. In mid-1986, ANC leaders offered a qualified endorsement of negotiating terms developed by the British Commonwealth's Eminent Persons Group. Meetings between the ANC and the British and American governments in 1986 and 1987 and the embrace of sanctions by American policy makers similarly encouraged perceptions that negotiations represented a viable route to "national democracy." "National Democracy" itself began to be re-framed so that it represented a much less alarming prospect for white South Africans than the transitional order envisaged by communists as late as 1986 when their members were still envisaging a mainly state controlled economy (Suttner and Cronin 1986: 178). A set of constitutional guidelines and economic principles published by the ANC in mid-1988 suggested a political system that would retain many existing laws and personnel. Economic prescriptions omitted any specific commitments to nationalization.

Shifts in the ANC doctrine were matched by a turnabout in South African government strategy prompted by the mounting costs of backing an insurgent movement in Angola and defending a quasi-colonial admin-istration in Namibia. South African soldiers withdrew from Angola in 1988 after Pretoria agreed to cease supplying and reinforcing UNITA in return for the removal of ANC bases from Angola. Shortly afterwards, Namibian politicians began to negotiate a constitutional settlement that would bring into power the ANC's ally, SWAPO. Meanwhile, sanctions by formerly friendly governments as well as the Republic's exclusion from financial markets appeared much more immediately alarming than the increasingly untenable vision of a Soviet-sponsored revolutionary advance enveloping the sub-continent, the major threat traditionally perceived by official South African strategists. By 1989, with the blocking of South African access to international capital markets, the government was in severe financial trouble.

New leadership brought fresh vision. On 2 February 1990, President F.W. de Klerk opened parliament. In composing his address for this occa-sion, De Klerk was influenced by at least three considerations. He knew from the recent election that most whites favored political reform that would incorporate black South Africans as fellow citizens. Second, the fall of the Berlin Wall "created an opportunity for a much more adventurous approach than had previously been conceivable" (De Klerk 1998: 161), in particular an ANC without any further prospect of Soviet support might be a much weaker adversary, one that the government and its allies might realistically compete with in open electoral competition. Friendly exchanges with conservative administrations in London and Washington helped convince De Klerk that liberalizing South African politics would win him strong diplomatic support. Accordingly, in parliament he announced a series of measures that effectively reversed history. The gov-ernment would legalize all prohibited organizations. Political prisoners would be freed. The authorities would release Nelson Mandela without conditions. Mandela walked through the gates of Victor Verster prison nine days later. Within three months, the first formal talks between the government and the ANC secured indemnities for returning exiles and in August the ANC agreed to a suspension of its armed struggle "in the inter-est of moving as speedily as possible to a negotiated political settlement."

For the ANC, pragmatic considerations were important in shaping its conciliatory response to De Klerk. Its leaders were aware of the limitations of what it could achieve militarily and they were in any case under pres-sure to negotiate with Pretoria from their African hosts, particularly the Zambians, who had their own reasons for favoring a South African settle-ment. But there were longer term and more subtle considerations that affected the ANC's willingness to negotiate. The extent to which ANC leaders ever really believed that an insurrectionary seizure of power could be accomplished – or even wanted it – was questionable. When senior ANC officials encountered sympathetic North Americans and Western Europeans they often used a liberal language that contrasted rather sharply with the uncompromising phraseology that characterized the organization's internal strategic propositions. For example, the American researcher Steve Davis was told by one "top ANC veteran" in Tanzania that before the arrival of the 1976 activists, "we were tolerant, non-violent, convinced we could reason with whites." The older generation, Davis learned, "committed only to a controlled armed struggle" and was fearful of younger militants' vision: "This is our fear: the whole-scale burning of the country. We want to avoid that. We are not mad. It's easy to destroy, much harder to rebuild" (Davis 1987: 61–62). Nelson Mandela's reassertion of leadership over the movement after his release certainly reinforced moderate sentiment within the ANC Executive: by the mid-1990s, Mandela was arguing that "the purpose of armed struggle was always to bring the government to the negotiating table" (Mandela 1993: 578).

Reservations about violence may have strengthened with the progress of the ANC's insurgency. Its own success in exerting its political leadership over the rather wider rebellion orchestrated by the UDF meant that increasingly it was allied to groups that were dismissive about the prospects of guerrilla warfare. Certain key UDF leaders were unconvinced that guerrillas could capture power and their own vision of a massive mainly non-violent movement compelling the government to concede change seemed increasingly plausible as the black trade unions became better organized and more politically assertive. Finally, the ANC's success in animating through the anti-apartheid movement a liberal constituency of supporters and sympathizers in Western countries including the US meant that its allies included powerful groups predisposed in favor of a peaceful constitutional settlement.

What sustained the transformation?

In a hurting stalemate ANC leaders found compelling reasons to end guerrilla warfare: as one contributor to its journal, *Sechaba*, noted, "we are confronted with conditions in which an absolute victory is impossible" (Mashinini 1988: 27). Their decision was unpopular with *Umkhonto* rank and file, though, and political violence did not end with the "suspension" of armed struggle. Indeed it intensified: most victims of political conflict between 1976 and 1994 were killed after the ANC's agreement to halt operations. In the next four years, 14,000 people were killed in so-called "black on black" violence. Most of these deaths were in Natal province and were a consequence of competition for territorial control between UDF/ANC supporters and adherents of the *Inkatha* Freedom Party. Founded in 1975, *Inkatha* was a movement constructed around the patrimonial politics of the Kwa-Zulu homeland. Presided over by Chief Mangosuthu Buthelezi, the movement benefited from Buthelezi's lineage within the Zulu royal house. This helped *Inkatha* to build a strong following in the countryside as well as among Zulu migrant workers. Hostilities developed between

Inkatha and Congress supporters in 1980 after *Inkatha*'s brutal suppression of a school boycott. Bloody feuding between *Inkatha* and UDF supporters began shortly after the UDF's establishment. After 1990, the prospect of universal suffrage elections supplied fresh incentives to control territory in the one province in which the ANC was likely to encounter serious competition for African support.

The achievement of a negotiated constitutional settlement in 1994, and the ending of political violence thereafter, were all the more impressive when considered against this background. The achievement must be qualified by the consideration that the violent behavior through which political rivalries were expressed did not end in 1994. Since then South Africa has experienced extraordinarily high rates of violent crime. One explanation for this is that violent criminality is a response to "structural inequality" with "its roots in the sometimes seamless interface of youth involvement in criminal and political violence of the preceding era" (Gordon 2006: 89). Despite annual growth rates of around 5 percent in 2008, current levels of unemployment are between 28 and 40 percent.

Even so, ending political strife was an important step in transforming South Africa into a more orderly society. One factor in the success in reaching a settlement was the availability of models for "pacted" democracies in the aftermath of protracted conflicts supplied by Latin American transitions. From these experiences the South Africans borrowed a range of institutional devices including power-sharing, amnesties, a truth commission, employment and pension guarantees for civil servants. Electoral reform was an especially important measure. Proportional representation, in particular, downgraded the significance of controlling territory and supplied incentives for parties to compete for support beyond the boundaries of their base support, effectively drawing them into the more moderate ideological center.

The ANC's ability to demobilize its following and to check its more militant impulses was indispensable in both the achievement of a settlement its maintenance thereafter. How was this accomplished? First of all, leaders themselves needed to revise and lower their expectations of change. A negotiated settlement precluded the social reforms that the ANC had looked forward to since its adoption of a Freedom Charter in 1956. Interaction between business groups and key ANC leaders between 1990 and 1993 helped to shift the ANC's economic thinking away from its traditional Keynesianism toward neo-liberal orthodoxies. Left wingers within the ANC's leadership were also influenced by the collapse of "existing socialism" in Eastern Europe which had served as a source of inspiration to many of them for a very long time.

Second, between 1990 and 1994 the ANC succeeded in building a structured organization with a local presence all over the country except in rural Northern Natal, *Inkatha*'s heartland. Nelson Mandela's charismatic authority was one critical ingredient in its ability to extend its support base beyond the activist community that had sustained insurrectionary politics. Another contributory factor was funding. In 1990 the ANC received about R80 million in donations, mainly from Sweden. In the following years, the range of government donors and the quantities of foreign derived funding would increase. These resources paid for an organization that would employ several hundred full-time officials and provide local positions for members of nearly 1,000 local branches. Employment and the status associated with elected political positions all helped to channel activist energy. Meanwhile *Umkhonto* did not disband. Retaining *Umkhonto* through the negotiations helped reassure ANC followers that leaders would not "sell out" or backtrack from "national democratic" commitments. Within South Africa, *Umkhonto* continued to recruit in anticipation of the plans for its incorporation into a reconstructed South African National Defense Force. In 1994, some 33,000 *Umkhonto* cadres joined the army, probably three times as many as had returned from East Africa.

The enlargement of the ANC's organized following that accompanied its reconstruction as an open political organization helped to change its character. This was not least because it developed a presence in many parts of the country in which historically it had been absent – in many of the former homelands, for example. Though its 500,000 or so members were still mainly urban, as the ANC's popular following historically had been, it now commanded a substantial rural membership. When the ANC started preparing for elections it was to discover that the areas in which it was most overwhelmingly popular were often in the countryside. Here quite often, ANC branches and regional leaderships would be led by homeland notables, with ANC organization resting upon a sub-structure of youth cohorts mobilized around local "big men" reproducing customary patterns of patronage. Such a pattern was characteristic of certain parts of Mpumalanga where ANC membership was swollen by bulk sales of party cards to township traders. In the Transkei, the homeland civil service followed the lead of the homeland's ruler, General Bantu Holomisa, in affiliating to the ANC. This sort of following was much more likely to defer to leadership authority than the young Jacobins from the UDF's street battles. Meanwhile, within the cities, COSATU affiliated trade unionists played a major role in helping the ANC establish its organizational structures and imposing their own discipline upon them. Trade Unions played an essential role in helping the ANC to mobilize the demonstrations of mass militancy it required for leverage at certain points during the negotiations; as crucially it also enabled the ANC to end such demonstrations when it needed to.

Then, after the 1994 election, public office and public service would remove layers of leadership from the activist community. National and regional parliaments provided several hundred positions for ANC officials, and in 1995 the desegregation of around 800 municipalities provided several thousand more partly paid posts. Within ten years, the public service would be predominantly African. Many of the new public managers were people with activist credentials. They were now reassembling as a new and rapidly expanding African middle class, often changing residential location with their new social identity, moving out the townships and into the suburbs.

Finally, in its first two terms of government, the ANC's success in meeting its supporters' expectations helps to explain the sustaining of the settlement since 1994. Successive ANC victories in well-managed and fair elections suggest that despite the continuation of high levels of inequality and increasing unemployment, ANC-led administrations have addressed certain key needs. In 1993 pollsters commissioned by the ANC before the first election discovered that with respect to most Africans, aspirations and hopes were quite modest: the top issues identified by survey respondents were bringing down unemployment, ending political violence, more housing and better services. Generally the ANC promised what it could realistically hope to deliver, a million low-cost houses, job creation through public works, peace, clean water and domestic electrification. In fact, public works programs have at best supplied a few hundred thousand temporary jobs, but in other respects Nelson Mandela's and his successor's administrations fulfilled, or nearly fulfilled their pledges. They also substantially increased the scope and levels of welfare entitlements, quadrupling the numbers of pension recipients for example. In reality poverty has not reduced significantly since apartheid. However, through the real-location of public resources expenditure, from middle class communities to poorer neighborhoods and from the cities to the countryside, the ANC for a while at least, succeeded in building confidence and trust in government.

References

African National Congress, 1985a, *Documentation of the Second Consultative Conference*, Lusaka.

African National Congress, 1985b, *National Consultative Conference, June, Report, Main Decisions and Recommendations of the Second National Consultative Conference*, Lusaka.

African National Congress, 1986, *1987: What Is To be Done?*, document distributed by the ANC Politico-Military Council to regional command centers, October.

Barrell, H. 1990, *MK: The ANC's Armed Struggle*, Johannesburg, Penguin.

Davis, S.M. 1987, *Apartheid's Rebels: Inside South Africa's Hidden War*, New Haven, Yale University Press.

De Klerk, F.W. 1998, *The Last Trek – A New Beginning*, London, Macmillan.

Feit, E. 1971, *Urban Revolt in South Africa*, Evanston, Northwestern University Press.

Gordon, D. 2006, *Transformation and Trouble: Crime, Justice and Participation in Democratic South Africa*, Ann Arbor, The University of Michigan Press.

Harmel, M. 1959, "Revolutions are not Abnormal," *Africa South* (Cape Town), 2 (2), January.

Karis, T., G. Carter and G. Gerhart 1977, *From Protest to Challenge: A Documentary History of African Politics in South Africa*, vol. 3, Stanford, Hoover Institution Press.

Magubane, B., P. Bonner, J. Sithole, J. Cherry, P. Gibbs, and T. April, 2004, "The Turn to Armed Struggle," in South African Democracy Education Trust, *The Road to Democracy in South Africa, Volume I: 1960–1970*, Cape Town, Zebra Press.

Mandela, N. 1976, unpublished autobiographical manuscripts, Department of Correctional Services Files, Nelson Mandela A5, National Archives of South Africa.

Mandela, N. 1993, *Nelson Mandela Speaks: Forging a Democratic, Nonracial South Africa*, New York, Pathfinder.

Mandela, N. 1994, *Long Walk to Freedom*, Randburg, MacDonald Purnell.

Mashinini, A. 1988, "People's War and Negotiations: Are they Fire and Water?," *Sechaba*, August.

Meer, F. 1971, "African Nationalism – Some Inhibiting Factors," in Heribert Adam (ed.) *South Africa: Sociological Perspectives*, Oxford, Oxford University Press.

Phillips, I. 1988 "Negotiation and Armed Struggle in Contemporary South Africa," *Transformation*, 6, 1988.

Pillay, G. 1993, *Voices of Liberation: Albert Lutuli*, Pretoria, HSRC Publishers.

Pogrund, B. 2000, *War of Words: Memoirs of a South African Journalist*, New York, Seven Stories Press.

Seekings, J. 1993, *Heroes and Villains? Youth Politics in the 1980s*, Johannesburg, Ravan Press.

Suttner, R. and J. Cronin (eds.) 1986, *30 Years of the Freedom Charter*, Johannesburg, Ravan Press.

Suzman, H. 1993, *Memoirs: In No Uncertain Terms*, London: Sinclair Stevenson.

Waldmeir, P. 1998, *Anatomy of a Miracle*, Piscataway, NJ: Rutgers University Press.

12 The Nepali Maoists[1]

Successful transformation or compliance with a strategic plan?

Thania Paffenholz

Introduction

Armed conflict in Nepal began in 1996 with the declaration of a People's War by the Communist Party of Nepal-Maoists (CPN (Maoist)). It should be noted that there are different Communist and Maoist parties in Nepal (for an overview see graphic in Thapa 2003: 44). Until 2000, the armed conflict was waged with low-intensity specifically in the rural areas of Western Nepal between the CPN (Maoist) and the police. Then, from 2001 onwards, the Royal National Army was sent out to fight against the CPN (Maoist) following the onset of a countrywide destructive war that was now also affecting the cities. The armed conflict lasted for a decade, causing tremendous human suffering including the deaths of more than 15,000 people. In April 2006, mass demonstrations around the country led to a peaceful transfer of power from the King to the democratic parties and the CPN (Maoist), which was followed by the signing of a comprehensive peace agreement at the end of the same year. This agreement officially ended armed conflict in the country and re-integrated the CPN (Maoist) into the political arena.

Today, the CPN (Maoist) can be seen as the most successful left-wing communist–Maoist movement since the Chinese Revolution. No other movement of this kind has been able to enter the mainstream political agenda as well as achieve most of its demands. At the heart of these demands had always been the drafting of a new constitution as a means of achieving major political and socio-economic changes. This became the make or break issue during the different rounds of negotiations. From 2001 onwards, the CPN (Maoist) demanded a Constituent Assembly (CA) to be held as a vehicle for this change.

With the signing of the 2006 peace agreement, the CPN (Maoist) joined an interim government and subsequently took part in the CA elections held in April 2008. At this time, they became the largest party within the CA winning 29 percent of the votes. By virtue of commanding over one third of the CA, they can block any decision but are still in need of alliances with other parties to achieve major constitutional changes (for an analysis of the CA elections see International Crisis Group (ICG) 2008a).

In the first meeting of the CA in June 2008, the monarchy was abolished and Nepal was declared a democratic republic following the dignified exit of the King. However, major political, security and socioeconomic challenges continue to exist in the country (see outlook in the conclusion).

Though it is still too early to conclude that the transformation of the CPN (Maoist) into a solely political actor was a success, it is interesting to analyze the current conditions of the transformation process and the likelihood of its sustainability. My main hypothesis is that the CPN (Maoist) is *not* an interesting case of the successful transformation of an armed group into a political actor, since they (i.e. their predecessor parties) have mainly been political actors (see Thapa 2004: 44). Rather, it is a highly relevant and interesting case for study because the leadership of the CPN (Maoist) incorporated the use of violence during a certain period of time as a means to achieve their political goals. Therefore, they were not faced with significant difficulties when reintegrating into the political arena. Indeed, they were extremely successful in steering the mainstream political discourse in the direction of their demands. After ten years of a People's War and two years of political maneuvering, the monarchy has been abolished and the CPN (Maoist) has developed from a tiny guerrilla group armed with only two rifles in 1996 into the main political force in the country.

The objective of this chapter is to provide an analysis of the CPN (Maoist) as a political and military actor in order to understand why the leadership started, continued and ended the armed conflict. This analysis will provide a better understanding of the sustainability and future orientation of their involvement into current mainstream Nepali politics.

As such, this chapter presents first an overview of the Nepali context followed by an analysis of the armed conflict and the peace process. The main body of the text applies the analytical framework for this project, i.e. an examination of the factors that: (*a*) led to the People's War; (*b*) contributed to its ten year duration; and (*c*) helped to transform the CPN (Maoist) into a solely political actor. The concluding section sums up the findings and analyzes factors that might cause a recurrence into violence or a maintenance of the peace process.

Historical, political, socio-economic context

For more than 200 years, the Himalayan Kingdom of Nepal has been an independent state led by royal families. Nepal was never colonized and remained closed to foreigners until 1959.

Nepal is a multiethnic society, but the traditional caste system and the privileged position of Hinduism as the state religion has led to harsh inequalities that divided the society into advantaged and disadvantaged groups. The disadvantaged groups such as women, lower castes and certain ethnic groups had traditionally been under-represented politically, making their access to resources, education and political decision-making extremely limited. Women are in general underprivileged in Nepal, however, women from ethnic and caste discriminated groups are of course much more disadvantaged than women from higher castes. The inclusive composition of the new Constituent Assembly (see below) is therefore an encouraging sign, given that one third of its members are women, with ethnic groups and lower castes also having a fair representation.

Economically, Nepal is one of the poorest countries in Asia. Development assistance, tourism, and exports of carpets and garments play an important role in the Nepali economy, especially as a source of foreign currency. For the last ten years, the remittances of millions of Nepali working abroad have been crucial to the achievement of poverty reduction. The poverty rate for some disadvantaged ethnic groups, lower castes and women is almost double the national average.

Under a constitution promulgated in 1962, the King established a "panchayat" (assembly) system. Members of this assembly served only at the king's behest (Joshi and Rose 1966). A coalition of the two major political forces in the country provided the vanguard for widespread political protests that began in early 1990, and is commonly known as the "People's Movement" (Thapa 2004: 30–32). With growing domestic and international pressure, the King announced an end to the "panchayat" system and agreed to the restoration of multiparty parliamentary democracy. In November 1990, a new democratic constitution was established and Nepal became a constitutional monarchy. Parliamentary elections were held in 1991, and local elections supporting a decentralized system of governance were held a year later.

Despite these changes, the political landscape continued to be shaped by frequent government changes, inter-party conflicts, widespread corruption, slow implementation of important political changes (like further decentralization) and the manifestation of armed conflict during the following years.

In 1996 the CPN (Maoist) started a People's War that would last ten years (for the origins of the People's War see Thapa 2004).

In 2001, the country was hit by the shock of the "Royal Massacre" when almost the entire royal family, including the reigning monarch, King Birendra, was killed. Officially the King's son was held responsible for the killings, and subsequently killed himself. Nevertheless, many rumors spread that it was in fact the new King Gyanendra, the brother of the late King and also the only survivor of the massacre, that was actually behind the killings. These rumors, combined with the known criminal record of the new king's son and the king's mounting autocratic behavior, supported the gradual deconstruction of the monarchy as an institution (see information in ICG 2005b; 2005c and 2005d).

The political landscape in the following years was characterized by changing political alliances, instability as well as escalation and de-escalation of armed conflict. Two rounds of peace negotiations were held in 2001 and 2003, both ending in failure.

On 1 February 2005, King Gyanendra discharged the government and assumed absolute power (ICG 2005c and 2005d). As a result, the political parties aligned with the CPN (Maoists) and were supported by Indian mediation (ICG 2007b).

This joint political struggle culminated in a victory over the King in April 2006, by means of countrywide, peaceful mass demonstrations. The King gave up absolute power, the parliament was reinstalled and the army was put under parliamentary control. The political parties and the CPN (Maoist) agreed to set up a CA to write a new constitution, and in November 2006 a comprehensive peace agreement was signed. The CPN (Maoist) joined an interim government with the other parties, leaving briefly in 2007 and then rejoining in early 2008 after an agreement was reached involving major concessions to be made by the mainstream political parties. It was also agreed that the monarchy was to be abolished and Nepal would become a republic.

The implementation of the peace agreement(s) however was slow and characterized by the mounting power aspirations of regional actors who felt left out of the general peace deal. As a consequence, different opposition movements started violent upheavals in the southern Terrai region until they were accommodated in the political deal (ICG 2007a).

Elections to the CA took place in April 2008 the CPN (Maoist) became the largest party with the regional Madehsi parties from the Terrai region also doing well in the elections. The two main mainstream parties, now in opposition, have shown little willingness to recognize their defeat and are in danger of becoming major spoilers for the peace process (ICG 2008a and b).

India is the most important actor in economic and political terms. The Indian government has close and influential ties to the Nepali polity and the Nepali economy is heavily dependent on India. The US, the European Union countries and increasingly Japan, are also important political and economic actors for Nepal. Less visible in its relations to Nepal, China, is also a key actor (ICG 2008b: 14–15). Other actors like Norway, Switzerland and some non-government organizations have also played supportive facilitation roles in the peace process.

The armed conflict: 1996–2006

The devolution of armed conflict in Nepal occurred in three main phases. During the early phase, 1996 to 2001, the armed conflict was characterized by low-intensity guerrilla warfare that started in the rural areas of Western Nepal. In the early years, the CPN (Maoist) gained a lot of support throughout the country and established "People's Governments" and "People's Courts" in several districts. The main reason for this support for was that the political demands of the CPN (Maoist) related directly to the grievances of the Nepali poor and underprivileged (Thapa 2004: 51–81; Lecomte-Tilouine 2004: 16–17). For this reason, many women were also supportive. During this early phase, the government saw the Maoist low-intensity guerrilla warfare as a security problem to be addressed by the police. Thus, many human rights violations were committed by the police against the CPN (Maoist) and suspected followers.

The second phase of armed conflict, 2001 to 2003, began with the CPN (Maoist) withdrawal from negotiations in November 2001. Thereafter the government declared a state of emergency for the entire country, and the King authorized the Royal National Army (RNA) to fight the CPN (Maoist), who were declared terrorists by the government. Next to India, the US and British government began to support the Nepali government with military aid as part of the international anti-terror campaign started after 9/11. This led to increased tension all over the country with increased human rights violations. However, the human rights record of the RNA was always much poorer than that of the CPN (Maoist) (see various Amnesty International reports).

The political situation, too, became tenser. In October 2002, the King dismissed the then Prime Minister Deuba, dissolved the cabinet and post-poned parliamentary elections for an indefinite period. Many people's hopes were raised that the monarch would support stability and peace with this move. However, there were also many protests and demonstrations by student groups that were sometimes supported by the political parties.

The third phase of armed conflict, 2003 to 2006, started with the break-down of the second series of negotiations at the end of August 2003. The CPN (Maoist) enlarged their range of operations from rural areas mainly in the mid-west, to also include the Terrai, eastern parts of the country and the cities.

There are different interpretations of the causes of armed conflict in Nepal. The mainstream line of interpretation argues that injustice and inequality brought about by a society divided by caste, class, ethnicity, regional differences, religion and gender (Bray *et al.* 2003) led to the poverty and discrimination of large parts of the Nepali population. All the major international actors, especially donor governments and agencies shared this interpretation. A second line of argument supports the inter-pretation that the principle root cause of the conflict is of a political nature, i.e. political pressure for a change from a traditional feudalistic, authoritarian system of governance to a "modern" form of governance (Bleie 2002 in Simkhada and Oliva 2004). A third line of argument con-siders the ideology of the CPN (Maoist)'s People's War as the single most important cause of conflict (Muni 2003 and Pahari 2003 in Simkhada and

Oliva 2004). Finally, in my view the most valuable interpretation is a fourth line of argument that presents a variation of the cause–effects interpretation, i.e. inequality and poverty as a breeding ground for mobilization and revolt, which has been exploited by the CPN (Maoist) (for the most in-depth analysis see Thapa 2003: 51–81).

The peace process: 2001–2006

The peace process started in 2001 with the statement of the newly elected Prime Minister Deuba in favor of negotiations (Phillipson 2002). When the CPN (Maoist) responded positively, a ceasefire was ordered and three rounds of negotiations took place in August, September and November of 2001.

Each party had its own negotiation team and the talks were facilitated by two independent, highly respected Nepali civil society facilitators. Prior to the talks, the Prime Minister held all-party meetings and received a broad-based mandate for the dialogue (Phillipson 2002).

The CPN (Maoist) started negotiations with two main demands: a new constitution and an end to the monarchy. For the third round, the CPN (Maoist) were ready to compromise on the issue of the immediate abolition of the monarchy and demanded the installation of an interim government and elections for a Constituent Assembly that should decide on the constitution (Dahal 2003: 9).

During the third round of the negotiations a deadlock occurred on the above-mentioned issues, leading to the end of talks. The CPN (Maoist) walked out of the negotiations and armed conflict flared up once again.

After the breakdown of negotiations there were different attempts to prepare for renewed negotiations. In March 2002, the Maoist leader, Prachanda, offered a ceasefire to resume peace talks. However, the then Prime Minister Deuba ruled out peace talks until the CPN (Maoist) surrendered their arms. Moreover, the political situation escalated toward the end of 2002 when the King dismissed Deuba, dissolved the cabinet and postponed parliamentary elections for an indefinite period.

However, a few local groups independently conducted dialogue with the conflicting parties. Some of them were supported by international governmental and non-governmental organizations in one way or another. The UN, as well as individual governments, also tried to support peacebuilding in different ways. However, both parties declined external mediation.

At the end of January 2003, following secret pre-negotiations, a ceasefire was reached between the conflict parties. Three rounds of negotiations followed in April, May, and August 2003. Each party had a negotiation team and the talks were again facilitated by respected Nepali facilitators, two of them had already been facilitators during the first round of negotiations in 2001. The four facilitators were seen as close to the negotiation teams – two were appointed by the government, two by the CPN (Maoist). However, they were only allowed the limited role of providing Good Offices during and between the negotiations (interview by the author with the facilitators in 2004).

Despite the fact that the talks took place in a cordial atmosphere, the situation remained difficult for several reasons. The government changed during the negotiation period and only presented a negotiable proposal in the third round. However, by then, the position of the CPN (Maoist) on the issue of the Constituent Assembly had already become a "make-or-break" issue, a situation comparable to the end of negotiations in November 2001 (interviews by the author with the facilitators in September 2003 in Kathmandu).

When the RNA killed a number of unarmed CPN (Maoist) members with their hands tied behind their backs (there were 19 people killed, it was never 100 percent clarified whether two were non-Maoists) – an act that the National Human Rights Commission later confirmed as a war crime – the CPN (Maoist) ended negotiations and war recommenced at the end of August 2003.

The immediate cause of the breakdown of the 2003 and 2001 talks (occurring in the third round during both negotiations), was a fundamental disagreement with regard to major political issues. While the CPN (Maoist) insisted that a Constituent Assembly should be held that would leave the option open for a fundamental change of the constitution, the government wanted to only go as far as amending the current constitution. There were also a number of more proximate causes to the failure of the two negotiations including: a problem with ripeness as the hardliners on both sides believed in the possibility of a respective military victory; a lack of representation; the existence of only one negotiation channel; weak public support to the process; the insufficient legitimacy of the government; and an inconsistent role of the international community, which was divided into two main positions as to how peacebuilding should be supported in the country (see more detailed analysis in Paffenholz 2003).

In September 2003 different attempts through both military and/or peaceful means started to bring the parties back to the negotiation table, without success. The countrywide mass demonstrations of April 2006 then paved the way to the end of the armed conflict and the signature of the peace agreement in November 2006.

What factors influenced the CPN (Maoist)'s turn to violence?

In the literature the turn to violence is mainly explained by the CPN (Maoist) dissatisfaction with the slow pace of the democratization process during the early 1990s, and the autocracy of the monarchy. However, in analyzing the development of the communist movement in Nepal, it seems that the use of violence as a means to reach the stated political objectives was imminent from its inception.

The rise of the communist movement in Nepal was strongly influenced by the Indian independence movement and the success of the Chinese revolution. The rise of the different communist–Maoist movements from small urban, elite-based or scattered rural groups in the 1950s to a countrywide political force can also be explained by the failure of the Nepali democratization process (Khadka 1995).

As Nepal's first communist party, the Communist Party of Nepal (CPN) was founded in 1949 in India by a group of young Nepali aiming to establish a communist regime in their country (Khadka 1995: 56; Thapa 2004: 20). In the early 1950s, the main objective of the party – as stated in a policy statement from 1951 – was to transform Nepal into a republic through means of an armed revolt (Khadka 1995: 57). In the following years, the party suffered from leadership fights (Thapa 2004: 22) and eventually split over its ideological orientation between a more pro-Moscow/Leninist and more pro-Beijing/Maoist faction. As a consequence, different communist–Maoist parties and movements were founded, many of which still exist to date (Khadka 1995; Thapa 2003: 20–50 and graphic in Thapa 2003: 44). The groups with a Leninist urban-centered orientation talked about a multiparty people's democracy that could be achieved by taking part in mainstream political discourse and parliamentary elections. These latter groups were divided by different understandings of the concept of democracy. The CPN – Unified Marxist–Leninist Party of Nepal (UML) founded in 1991 became the largest party among them (Khadka 1995: 57).

The more radical groups wanted to establish "new democracy" through revolution. This concept was inherited from Mao Zedong, who had in turn adopted it from the views of Lenin, Trotsky and Stalin. The basic idea behind the concept is a transition from a capitalist bourgeois hegemony ("old democracy" or "old system") to a proletarian hegemony ("new democracy") (ICG 2005a: 3). In 1990, three of the Maoist parties merged to form the Communist Party of Nepal (Unity Centre)–United People's Front Nepal with Puspa Kamal Dahal (nickname Prachanda) as General Secretary. The party congress accepted Mao Zedong's thoughts and adopted a resolution to initiate a People's War (Phillipson 2002: 9; Thapa 2004: 43). The party was later joined by a break-away faction from another communist–Maoist party (CPN-Masal) led by Baburam Bhattarai (Thapa 2004: 37 and 44). In 1994, the party split over the question of the ripeness for the People's War to start. As a consequence, two parties were founded with one led by Prachanda, and the other by Nirmal Lama. In the 1994 elections, the election commission only recognized the party of Lama. The Prachanda-led CPN-UC was thus excluded from participating, and Baburam Bhattarai subsequently called for a boycott of the elections. Many interpreted this move as a face-saving exercise. However, the denial of participation in the elections could have expedited the decision to start the People's War (Thapa 2004: 45). The moderate CPN-ULM became the largest party and formed a minority government that lasted only ten months.

Still in 1994, the CPN-UC of Prachanda and Bhattarai put forward 38 demands to the CPN-ULM government and a few weeks later issued another 40 demands to the successor NC government along with an ultimatum of a few weeks. During the party congresses in 1995, the party had a series of critical discussions as to when would be the right time for the start of the armed conflict. Supported by the Indian Communist Movement, the Maoists declared their readiness to start a People's War in Nepal during the party congress of the Indian Communist Party in July 1995 (Dahal 2003: 2). Also in 1995, the decision was made to rename the party as the CPN (Maoist) (Thapa 2004: 45). Baburam Bhattarai explained the name change with an attempt to strengthen the radical nature of the party (Ogura 2008: 11). The famous 40 demands came with a response deadline of 13 February after which a People's War would be initiated. However, the armed attack on police posts in Rukum, Rolpa and Sinduhle districts in western Nepal had already started three days before the expiring of the ultimatum (Dahal 2003: 2–3). This indicates that the decision to launch the People's War had already been made, regardless of the government's response.

In fact, it seems that ideological, organizational and political preparation for the People's War had previously started in 1993 among the radical communist movements in Nepal and their Indian allies. Liz Phillipson (2002: 9–10) conducted a series of interviews with influential CPN (Maoist) cadres in western Nepal in 2002 and wrote:

> Ideological and organizational preparation commenced earliest and was deepest in the mid-west among the Kham Magar, who have a history of communist armed revolt. They began recruitment among disillusioned communist party cadres in the East, a historical stronghold of the CPN-ULM, using bases in India.

Moreover, "alliances with ethnic groups" were made. "The CPN (Maoist) were extremely effective and their cadres, members and supporters expanded rapidly." This is confirmed by Deepak Thapa's analysis (2004: 78–79).

In sum, and referring to the analytical framework for this chapter (see the analytical categories in Kriesberg and Millar in this volume), it can be concluded that the decision to wage the struggle in a violent way was made out of ideological reasons contextualized to the socio-political landscape and using structural inequalities as a main mobilizing factor.

People's War was the essence of the Chinese communist's military doctrine, and mainly advocated by Mao Zedong (1938). As the CPN (Maoist) followed this ideological path, one can therefore argue that the question was not in fact what factors influenced the turn into violence, but rather what factors influenced the CPN (Maoist)'s assessment of the ripeness of the timing for the People's War in the mid-1990s.

The decision to launch the People's War slowly built up in the early 1990s. The split in the party in 1994 and the denial of participation in the 1994 elections probably accelerated this decision. CPN-ULM became the strongest party in the parliament and formed an unsuccessful minority government that lasted only ten months. This additionally confirmed to the CPN-UC, as analyzed by Prachanda (The Worker 1997: 5 cit. in ICG 2005: 5), that "the parliamentary road to socialism" had been undermined by the constitution and the limited "politics" being adopted by what were evidently no more than fractions of the political elite. It also confirmed to the CPN-UC that acceptance of the doctrine of economic liberalization, and collaboration in parliamentary politics would put the party's revolutionary goals at risk.

What perpetuated the state of violence?

The continuation of the armed conflict for a certain duration was a logical consequence of the ideology embedded within the concept of the People's War and Prachanda's Path. According to Mao, a revolution is not born in only a few years but rather takes time until the political goals can be considered achieved and the military campaign results in success (Mao 1938). Bhattarai emphasized in June 2008 after the CA election victory: "We wouldn't be here without the armed struggle. It is the fusion of bullet and ballot" (cit. in ICG 2008b: 5 footnote 26).

The main political program of the CPN (Maoist) was to establish "new democracy" in line with the main radical Maoist groups in Nepal. The CPN (Maoist) contextualized the concept over the years to the situation in Nepal. In their analysis, the Nepali society is a feudal-agrarian society of workers and peasants with a small middle class and a king in control of politics and the army. As a consequence, the various stages of getting to a "new democracy" were not equally relevant for the Nepali context. During their central committee party meeting in September 1995, they decided that the aim of their struggle was the "completing of the new democratic revolution after the destruction of feudalism and imperialisms, then immediately move to socialism" (cit. in ICG 2005: 3). The CPN (Maoist) chief ideologist Baburam Bhattarai stated that

> The decision to create a "New Democratic System" by smashing the old system through the protracted People's War has been made when all attempts to carry out reform within the old semi-feudal and semi-colonial system, long ridden with crisis, had failed.
>
> (cit. in Seddon 2002: 14)

In an interview from 1990, Baburam Bhattarai explained that in "parliamentary democracy you do not redistribute property, you just advocate free competition. Free competition among unequals is naturally in favor of the powerful ones" (cit. in ICG 2005: 3–4). CPN (Maoist) thinking shifted between these radical and more moderate understandings. During times of negotiations, the party line was more open to a compromise on the idea of a competitive multiparty democracy and, after their re-entry into mainstream politics, they seem now to have accepted the idea as a stage on the way to a people's republic. This was confirmed by a statement in June 2006 by Bhattarai and further supported by Prachanda in an interview with the *Hindu* (ICG: 6 footnote 45).

The strategy of the CPN (Maoist) was a mix of political and military tactics, whereby the military part was always under political control. The CPN (Maoist) is organized like most communist parties, more or less strictly following the Chinese model of a threefold revolutionary organization of party, army and united front (ICG 2005a: 7–12). Prachanda, the party's chairman, holds the most powerful position.

The concept of the United Front is to establish an alliance of forces that can be united for the common cause of revolution. In practice, this meant the establishment of broad alliances on all levels. The CPN (Maoist) have established a range of fraternal organizations in order to win support in the rural and urban areas aimed at student and peasant organizations as well as trade unions.

In their People's War, the CPN (Maoist) followed many of the original concepts of the Chinese revolutionary Mao Zedong (Mao 1938). The Maoist strategy for revolution has three distinct phases mirroring the history of the Chinese Civil War. The revolutionaries start as a weak and vulnerable group, but by the end of the conflict, they have become a strong political and military force. In the first phase, the revolutionaries are building what Lenin called "the organizational weapon": the political, military, logistics, intelligence, and command infrastructure. Phase II is a combination of a military and political battle. During phase III, the revolutionaries carry out a final assault against the mortally wounded regime. This is the final revolutionary offensive leading to the establishment of a people's republic.

In 2001, the strict adherence to Maoism was abundant. Out of a mix of Maoism and Leninism both adapted to the Nepali context, "Prachanda Path" was born. This new line was proposed by Prachanda to the party in 2001 (ICG 2005a: 23 ref. 164). The need to change was justified by the argument that no single established model of proletarian revolution could still be appropriate given changing global conditions (CPN press statement 25 February 2001). Doubts that a slow build up of the People's War limited to the rural areas could lead to a successful revolution created the impetus for a merger of Maoist and Leninist tactics, i.e. the People's War in the rural areas would be completed by a push for "people's rebellion" in towns and cities (ICG 2005a: 23).

In 2001, the CPN (Maoist) already controlled 60 out of 75 districts in Nepal. They started to bring the war to the towns and cities after 2001 with targeted military operations such as small attacks or bombings and systematic political mobilization. The CPN (Maoist) thereby systematically enlarged the United Front.

The international linkages of the CPN (Maoist) have always been, and still are, very important. There are two main affiliations: the Revolutionary International Maoist Movement (RIM) and the Coordination Committee of Maoist Parties and Organizations in South Asia (CCOMPOSA). RIM was established in 1994 in London and sees itself as the guardian of Marxist–Leninist and Maoist principles. Given its success, the CPN (Maoist) has become the shining model for RIM (ICG 2007b: 8). According to Prachanda, RIM provided consistent support in the final stage of planning of the People's War and facilitated the exchange of experiences and strategies with other Maoist groups such as with Sendero Luminoso in Peru (Phillipson 2002: 19; ICG 2007b: 8). The CPN (Maoist) was a driving force behind the foundation of the CCOMPOSA in an attempt to form a regional Maoist network. CCOMPOSA is also believed to have assisted in military training and strategic advice. Next to the general communist–Maoist ideology, the other main uniting factor of the movements was always the Indian government as the common enemy.

CPN (Maoist) main source of finance was bank robberies, donations and extortions from within Nepal as well as some international support. Weaponry was mainly stolen from the army or brought in from India through the political links within CCOMPOSA. Military training was also received via the international and regional networks (ICG 2005a: 17–20).

There are also analyses that say that the responses of the King and the government(s) additionally served to prolong the armed conflict. When the government realized that the People's War was a national security threat and not just a minor issue in some rural areas, the decision was made to send the army to fight the CPN (Maoist). The army was then strengthened through military training and aid from the governments of the US and Great Britain as part of the war on terror after 9/11. Although it is evident that this intensifying of the armed conflict brought tremendous suffering to the Nepali people, it is less clear whether it was more influential to the prolonging or ending of the armed conflict.

In sum, and referring to the analytical framework for this project, it can be posited that the CPN (Maoist) had a strong ideological commitment to violence and successfully applied mobilization strategies (on their mobilization strategies see Eck 2008) to win broad-based support. Contrary to many assumptions in peace research, the armed conflict did not create self-perpetuating dynamics (see Kriesberg and Millar this volume, Chapter 2) but followed a well-organized strategic plan. Viewing it from this perspective, the ten-year duration for a Maoist revolution is not very long.

The path from war to peace

Prachanda explained in a press statement shortly after the peace agreement in November 2006 that "our experiences have shown we could not achieve our goals through armed revolution, so we have chosen the path of negotiations and formed an alliance with the political parties" (Washington Post 19 December 2006 cit. in ICG 2007).

At first glance this statement sounds like a defeat. However in Maoist/ Leninist logic, the question is not what paved the way from war to peace, but what paves the way from the "old" to the "new" democracy. The main reason behind the decision of the CPN (Maoist) leadership to end the People's War, was a situational assessment that the time was ripe for the final stage of the revolution to be achieved. The political establishment was deemed weakened in such a way that it was ready to make major concessions, thus allowing the CPN (Maoist) leadership to make this shift and achieve their remaining goals by political means (see the analysis in ICG 2007b: 4–7).

A number of factors have influenced the CPN (Maoist) leadership in their decision to give up the armed struggle. First, after the royal massacre in 2001, the CPN (Maoist) leadership initially thought that the time was ripe for the final phase of the war with mass mobilization against the weakened monarchy. However, this was determined to be a false analysis of the situation and in consequence, the CPN (Maoist) realized throughout the negotiations that the time had not come to achieve its objective with only political means. Nevertheless, the royal massacre did greatly contribute to the dissatisfaction of the Nepali people with the monarchy, making the main demands of the CPN (Maoist) easier to sell to the political establishment in the years to come (interviews of the author in Nepal in 2002).

The development of the armed conflict was also an important factor: the military road was a decisive element to achieve the political goals. For the CPN (Maoist), it was important that they had achieved a certain military stalemate in order to show the "old system" the impossibility of winning the war. At the same time, they also had to build up their political strategy through influencing the mainstream political discourse with their objectives. Only with the establishment of the CA and the end of the king's absolute power becoming evident, were they ready to stop fighting, which in turn led to the ceasefire and peace agreement in 2006.

However, King Gyanendra's behavior did play a key expediting role for the end of the People's War. His will to stay in power and his objection against taking up a more representative role culminating in his taking of absolute power in early 2005, initiated the final phase of the People's War. Not only did this bring the political parties and the CPN (Maoist) closer together, but it also took away almost all public and international support from the monarchy.

There were also important external factors that additionally influenced the situation, the most significant being the role of India. Some analysts (ICG 2007b) say that the CPN (Maoist) had underestimated the importance of the Indian government to influence the situation in favor of the government. The CPN (Maoist) was also weakened by the hard-line position of the Indian government through the arrests of key Maoist cadres in India and the political and military support of the US and Indian government to the Nepali government, King and army. The autocratic shift of the King in 2005 led to a more moderate position of the Indian and US government toward the CPN (Maoist) culminating in the Indian mediation between the different political/military parties.

Another supporting factor was the establishment of a UN human rights monitoring mission that helped to put pressure on the army and the king due to growing human rights violations.

Thus, referring to the analytical framework for this chapter, it can be argued that the main reason for the turn away from violence was the CPN (Maoist) leadership's assessment of the ripeness for the final stage of the revolution. The decision was supported by a number of factors including the action of the state (i.e. the King), that in turn changed the behavior of the main third party involved (i.e. India) (see chapters by Dayton and by Kriesberg and Millar in this volume). Moreover, the UN monitoring mission is a good example of how local grass roots action for human rights monitoring combined with international NGO support can culminate in pressure for change (see chapters by Atashi and by Golan and Gal in this volume).

Conclusion

The Communist Party of Nepal (Maoist) is the most successful movement of its kind since the Chinese revolution. After ten years of People's War and two years of political maneuvering they have won the majority of seats in the newly established CA and can conceivably shape the future of Nepal, if they manage to obtain the support of other political parties.

The use of violence was embedded in the ideology of the communist movement in Nepal from its inception in the 1950s. The starting and ending of the People's War was thus a consequent application of a Maoist ideology. The CPN (Maoist) has always been a political actor in control of its army that could end the armed conflict when it became clear that the set objectives could be better achieved by political means.

Besides the obvious gains of the CPN (Maoist) so far, from their ideological perspective there is still a long road to go until their vision of "new democracy" in Nepal comes true, whatever shape this will take, and major socio-economic and political change will be achieved.

The CPN (Maoist) is now part of the political system, thereby running the risk of becoming embedded in the "old" system and thus weakening its ability to successful influence change. This puts them under permanent ideological pressure both from within and among the regional and international "comrades."

The successful incorporation of the Maoists into the political system is therefore still in question. The further development of the process depends on the behavior of the major national and international actors. So far, the defeated mainstream parties show little willingness to accept a CPN (Maoist) led government and risk becoming spoilers in the peace process (see Kriesberg and Millar this volume, Chapter 2). They need to cooperate with the Maoists and accept the will of the Nepali people for change. Additionally, the security sector needs to be reformed, the issue of land reform tackled and the status of impunity ended. The main international actors, and in particular India, must be supportive to this process.

In the case that the implementation of the peace process and the mandate for change given by the Nepali people in the elections becomes blocked for a significant time period, there is a likelihood that the CPN (Maoist) will resort back to violence. Their army is still in place, fully equipped and well trained.

Note

1 The author would like to thank Rhoderick Chambers, Günther Bächler, Dev Raj Dahal and the editors for comments as well as Daniel Paffenholz and Meghan Pritchard for their assistance.

References

Amnesty International (no date) online, available at: www.amnesty.org/en/library.

Bray, J., Lunde, L. and Murshed, M. (2003) "Nepal: Economic Drivers of the Maoist Insurgency," in: Ballentine, K. and Sherman, J. (eds.) *The Political Economy of Armed Conflict: Beyond Greed and Grievance*, Boulder: Lynne Rienner, 107-132.

Dahal, D.R. (2003) *Maoist Problem in Nepal: Its Genesis, Growth and Resolution*, Kathmandu: Friedrich Ebert Foundation Conference Paper.

Eck, Kristine (2008) *Indoctrination in Rebel Recruitment: A Mechanism for Mass Mobilization*, paper presented at the 49th Annual International Studies Association Convention, San Francisco 26–30 March 2008.

International Crisis Group (2005a) *Nepal's CPN (Maoist): Their Aims, Structure and Strategy*, Asia Report 104, 27 October 2005.

International Crisis Group (2005b) *Nepal: Beyond Royal Rule*, Asia Briefing 41, 15 September 2005.

International Crisis Group (2005c) *Nepal: Responding to the Royal Coup*, Asia Briefing 36, 24 February 2005.

International Crisis Group (2005d) *Nepal's Royal Coup: Making a Bad Situation Worse*, Asia Report 91, 9 February 2005.

International Crisis Group (2007a) *Nepal's Troubled Tarai Region*, Asia Report 136, 9 July 2007.

International Crisis Group (2007b) *Nepal's Maoists: Purists or Pragmatists?* Asia Report 132, 18 May 2007.

International Crisis Group (2008a) *Nepal's Elections: A Peaceful Revolution?* Asia Report 155, 3 July 2008.

International Crisis Group (2008b) *Nepal's New Political Landscape*, Asia Report 156, 3 July 2008.

Joshi, B.L. and Rose, L.E. (1966) *Democratic Innovations in Nepal*, Berkeley: University of California Press.

Kadka, N. (1995) "Factionalism in the Communist Movement in Nepal," *Pacific Affairs*, 68 (1): 55–76.

Lecomte-Tilouine, M. (2004) "Regicide and Maoist Revolutionary Warfare in Nepal: Modern Incarnations of a Warrior Kingdom," *Anthropology Today*, 20 (1): 13–19.

Lichbach, M.I. (1989) "An Evaluation of 'Does Economic Inequality Breed Political Conflict?'" *World Politics*, 41 (4): 431–470.

Mao Zedong (1938) "On Protracted War," reprinted in *Selected Works of Mao-Tse-tung*, vol. II, (1967) Peking: Foreign Language Press, 113–194.

Murshed, M.S. and Gates, S. (2005) "Spatial-Horizontal Inequality and the Maoist Insurgency in Nepal," *Review of Development Economics*, 9 (1): 121–134.

Ogura, Kiyoko (2008) "Seeking State Power – The Communist Party of Nepal (Maoist)," Berghof Transitions no. 3, Berlin: Berghof Research Center for Constructive Conflict Management. Online, available at: www.berghof-center.org/uploads/download/transitions_cpnm.pdf

Paffenholz, T. (2002) *Peacebuilding in Nepal: The Role of the UNDP "Peace and Development Trust Fund*," report commissioned by and presented to the Donor Peace Support Group in Nepal and UNDP.

Paffenholz, T. (2003) "Getting Back to the Table: Why Two Negotiation Processes have Failed: Recommendations towards Democratic Peacebuilding in Nepal," report as an annex to *Peacebuilding in Nepal – The Role the German Development Cooperation (GTZ) and Other German Actors*, Nepal: GTZ.

Phillipson, L. (2002) "Conflict in Nepal: Perspectives on the Maoist Movement," unpublished paper, submitted to DFID.

Seddon, D. (2002) *The Maoist Insurgency in Nepal: Revolutionary Theory and Practise*, paper presented to the Symposium on South Asia – Conflict in South Asia, organized by the Research Group on South Asia in the School of Development Studies, University of East Anglia, 18 June 2002.

Sen, A. (1973/1997) *On Economic Inequality*, Oxford: Clarendon Press.

Simkhada, S. and Oliva, F. (2004) *The Maoist Conflict in Nepal: A Comprehensive Annotated Bibliography*, Geneva and Kathmandu: Graduate Institute of International Studies, Programme for the Study of International Organizations.

Thapa, D. and Sijapati, B. (2003) *A Kingdom under Siege: Nepal's Maoist Insurgency, 1996 – 2004*, London and New York: Zed Books.

Additional information used:

Interviews conducted by the author in 2002, 2003, 2004 and 2008 in Nepal.
Press statements by the CPN (Maoist) on the web.

13 Opportunity lost

The Guatemalan National Revolutionary Unit (URNG)

Michael Allison

Introduction

In 1982, four guerrilla groups that traced their roots back to the 1960s and 1970s merged to form the Guatemalan National Revolutionary Unit (URNG). For the next 15 years, the URNG struggled against a Guatemalan military that launched a genocidal campaign against the country's indigenous people in order to separate the rebels from their base. After a decade-long peace process, the URNG and the government of Alvaro Arzú of the National Advancement Party (PAN) officially ended the war with the signing of the Firm and Lasting Agreement in December 1996. From 1960–1996, Guatemala had suffered through one of the longest and bloodiest civil wars in Latin American history where an estimated 200,000 were killed or disappeared and another two million internally displaced or forced into exile.

As would be expected after three decades of war, the Guatemalan peace process was a complex one. The URNG was comprised of four organizations that, for the most part, had little interest or success in coordinating a common front against the military regime. For much of the war they operated in different areas of the country and had varying levels of political and military capabilities and strategies. The war began during the early years of the Cold War when the country was ruled by a military government, while the peace process spanned the administrations of five civilian presidents both during and after the end of the Cold War. Dozens of civil society groups provided input on the different components of the peace accords. Over ten states from the Americas and Europe provided some form of assistance. Finally, intergovernmental organizations such as the United Nations, the Organization of American States and the World Bank encouraged the warring parties to negotiate and helped to create a postwar environment that would minimize the likelihood that any of the actors would revert to violence.

The outcome of the peace process has been mixed. On the one hand, the peace accords definitively marked the end of the war. There has been no outbreak of large-scale political violence since 1996. The demobilization of the guerrillas and the acceptance of social and political actors on the left have contributed to the further democratization of the country. Finally, civil society no longer operates under the intense repression of earlier decades. On the other hand, most of the accords signed during the peace process have not been implemented. Many were defeated in a 1999 referendum or failed simply because of the lack of political will. Criminal violence has reached the same fatality levels as the average yearly death rate that occurred during the war. Civil society groups continue to suffer from harassment and assassinations. Finally, as several guerrillas have lamented, the conditions that led to the war persist to this day.

In this case study, I provide an overview of the Guatemalan conflict and then discuss what led the URNG to wage its violent struggle against the state, the factors that sustained the violence for over three decades, the factors that produced a negotiated settlement after ten years of negotiations, and, finally, those factors that have sustained the peace process ever since.

Thirty-six years of war

In July 1944, mass-based protests overthrew the repressive Jorge Ubico Castañeda regime. A college professor, Dr Juan José Arévalo, returned from voluntary exile in Argentina and won the presidency in December. Many Guatemalans were optimistic that their social, economic, and political conditions would improve with the incoming government. In March 1945, a new constitution inspired by the New Deal policies of Franklin D. Roosevelt in the US was adopted. In 1950, a second consecutive democratic election brought Captain Jacobo Arbenz to the presidency. Following a census that outlined the depths of the unequal ownership of the country's most productive land, Arbenz pushed for the Agrarian Reform Law in 1952. However, the land redistribution came at a serious cost, as the reform threatened the interests of the country's largest landowners: the US-owned United Fruit Company, the Guatemalan landed-elites, and the Catholic Church. While the reform threatened the commercial interests of these groups, they were also concerned about what they saw as the communist influence behind the reforms. In July 1954, a CIA-orchestrated military invasion deposed the Arbenz government. The new US-installed government quickly gained control, banned political parties, rolled back the reforms of the previous ten years, set out to return nationalized properties, and arrested or executed those deemed subversives. Within months, over 12,000 Guatemalans were arrested and 2,000 labor leaders and politicians were exiled (Recovery of Historical Memory Project (REMHI) 1999: 189).

The first violent threat to the regime occurred in 1960 when several military officers revolted against what they considered to be the government's excessive corruption and its complicity in allowing the US to train

Cuban exiles for the CIA invasion of Cuba in 1961, more famously known as the Bay of Pigs. The rebellion was quickly put down and most of the survivors fled into Honduras. Over the next two years, these rebels failed a few more times at spurring a successful uprising before joining forces with the Guatemalan Workers' Party (PGT). The PGT worked underground with mass-based organizations through non-violent activity while those who supported violent confrontation against the regime joined the Rebel Armed Forces (FAR). This alliance would last until June 1968 (Sichar 1999: 38).

Initially, the FAR was active primarily in the eastern, non-indigenous, regions of Guatemala. After limited success, the FAR was overwhelmed and nearly annihilated for several reasons. The organization had difficulties developing any significant relationship with the rural indigenous population, as most of the leaders and initial recruits were urban, ladino (non-indigenous), and spoke a foreign language (Spanish). Several key military leaders were also killed as US training transformed the army into a superior force. Exact numbers are difficult to come by, but 6,000–20,000 civilians are thought to have died in the late 1960s as part of the government's effort to wipe out the guerrillas (REMHI 1999: 200). At the time, the guerrillas numbered less than 500 (Dunkerley 1988: 453). Two new organizations then joined the struggle.

The Organization of the People in Arms (ORPA) initially operated in relative secrecy, not announcing its presence until almost ten years after its founding. ORPA cultivated relationships with the country's indigenous community and urban labor movements and it also "emphasized the need to make broad alliances with progressive middle-class intellectuals and professionals" (Jonas 1991: 138). Like ORPA, the Guerrilla Army of the Poor (EGP) focused on the needs of the indigenous, and successfully built a social base amongst these groups. In part, the EGP accomplished this by arguing that the war was no more than the poor against the rich (REMHI 1999: 222–223). Both ORPA and the EGP were able to capitalize on the "radicalization" of the indigenous that had taken place during the 1960s and 1970s (Jonas 2000; Manz 2004).

The guerrillas retook the offensive in the late 1970s by launching attacks throughout the country. Some estimate that the guerrillas counted on the support of one-quarter million supporters in the early 1980s (REMHI 1999: 222), perhaps even as many as one-half million (Jonas 2000: 23), at a time when the country's population was estimated at 7.5 million. Non-violent mass-based protests also intensified. The military responded viciously to this renewed challenge by launching an offensive against urban and rural social movements, opposition political parties, the guerrillas, and the guerrillas' real and imagined civilian support base. Between 1978 and 1980, the popular movements were the primary victims of state terror as they were operating unarmed and out in the open. The violence then moved to the indigenous highlands from 1980 until 1983.

During this period, over 400 villages were destroyed as part of the military's scorched earth program. In the midst of the onslaught, the FAR, ORPA, EGP, and PGT formed the Guatemalan National Revolutionary Unit on 8 February 1982. By this time, however, the guerrillas were in a relatively weak position.

Having "defeated" the guerrillas through a "successful" scorched earth campaign, the military took steps toward liberalizing the political system. In 1983, General Efraín Ríos Montt, one of the men most responsible for the genocidal campaign, was removed by a coup. A Constituent Assembly met to write a new constitution and paved the way for the election of Marco Vinicio Cerezo Arévalo of the Christian Democratic Party (PDC) as president. Beginning during Cerezo's second year in office, the URNG and the government engaged in several rounds of negotiations. However, the conflict would continue for another decade through the administrations of Jorge Antonio Serrano Elías (1991–1993) of the Solidarity Action Movement (MAS) and Ramiro de León Carpio (1993–1996) of the Union of the National Center (UCN). Finally, after years of on and off again negotiations, the URNG and the government of Alvaro Arzú of the PAN signed the Firm and Lasting Agreement in December 1996. These accords successfully ended the civil war and paved the way for the URNG's transition to political party. Since the end of the war, the URNG has competed in three national elections and remains a marginal player in Guatemalan politics.

The violent struggle

Why did the Guatemalan conflict become violent in the first place? As mentioned earlier, the initial failed rebellion came from military officers that were disgusted with excessive corruption and the government's assistance to the US for its invasion of Cuba. For the next 20 years, those who joined the armed rebellion did so primarily because of the "political exclusion, ethnic discrimination, and social injustice that permeates the state structures" (REMHI 1999: xxxii). While some were inspired by dreams of implementing a socialist political and economic system, most seem to have joined because the guerrillas were fighting against a repressive military and the unjust structures that it was protecting. They were not so much concerned or knowledgeable about any socialist political and economic project of the guerrilla leadership.

Economically speaking, Guatemala was, and remains, one of the poorest countries in the western hemisphere. Poor economic conditions, including access to land or the uncertainty surrounding the minimal land that they did possess, are frequently cited as factors for taking up arms (Comisión para el Esclarecimiento Histórico (CEH) 1999; Manz 2004: 106–108; Herrera and Molina 2005). Even though the economy grew throughout the 1960s and into the early 1970s, income inequality and inflation worsened, real wages declined, and unemployment increased (Booth 1991). Land "scarcity" also contributed to the growing discontent. In the 1960s, 2 percent of the population owned 67 percent of the land (Jonas 2000: 19). The most fertile land was taken away from individual and communal indigenous properties by ladinos (Booth 1991) and, eventually, by those with connections to the military (Manz 2004) in order to exploit the export opportunities. By 1979, Guatemala had become the most unequal country in terms of land ownership in Central America (Booth 1991).

Guerrillas also cited political exclusion as a cause for taking up violence. Like many countries, Guatemala had been ruled by governments that served the interests of a small group of elites. Historically, repeated administrations passed legislation that favored the agro-export domestic and international elites at the expense of small individual and communal landholders. Expectations rose during the Arévalo and Arbenz administrations. However, when the traditional power structures in the country came under attack, elites, the military, and the US put an end to these reforms. A new military government more in tune with Washington's desires was installed and anyone who openly questioned the authority of the military was deemed a subversive or a terrorist. The closing of political spaces led many to conclude that non-violent change through the ballot box or through social protest was impossible. The coup against Arbenz, the assassinations of social leaders following the coup, and another coup that prevented Arévalo from winning the presidency in 1963 seemed to bear this out. It is quite possible that civil war would never have occurred in the first place if the democratically-elected Arbenz had been allowed to complete his term.

Religion was also a cause for Guatemalans to take up the struggle. Beginning in the 1960s, many Latin Americans began to find a more progressive reading of the Bible as a source of inspiration that called them to struggle against injustice here on earth rather than a focus on otherworldly pursuits (Sichar 1999: 41; Manz 2004: 107–108). While the Bible and the Catholic Church did not call on people to take up arms against their oppressors, their call to struggle against injustice eventually led many people down this road. In addition, the actual repression unleashed by the military against the Catholic Church and other Christian-based organizations, led hundreds to join the guerrillas (REMHI 1999: 225).

Given that the Guatemalan Civil War lasted over three decades, it is not surprising that the motivations for new recruits evolved over time. While those that joined in the 1980s and 1990s maintained some concern with justice issues, several URNG militants lamented that there was a noticeable difference among these later recruits. They argued that many of them joined primarily because of the military repression that had affected them personally. A family member or friend had been "disappeared" or killed and he or she joined the guerrillas to seek revenge, to avoid being the next victim, or a combination of both. Unlike those that had joined earlier on, these individuals did not necessarily join because of a deep commitment to social justice or in support of a specific social or political project (Recinos 2004; Montes 2007). Finally, several joined through "social networks and peer pressure" (Manz 2004: 106–108; see also Dunkerley 1988; Herrera and Molina 2005). Given how long the civil war lasted, it is interesting to find several sons and daughters following their parents into the guerrillas over a decade later.

International factors were also important in explaining why opposition was of a violent nature. The US organized the 1954 coup primarily out of Cold War fears and for the next 30-plus years provided financial and military support in order to defeat the communist threat. The US identified most, if not all, agitators in the western hemisphere as Soviet inspired. The US would protect the region from Soviet interference, while the Latin American militaries would be responsible for threats emanating from within their borders. These "agents" came to be anyone who attempted to challenge the status quo. As a result, the victims of the counterinsurgency included insurgents as well as many students, union organizers, priests and nuns, pro-democracy politicians and civilians, and over 100,000 unarmed indigenous peoples. While Manz (2004) does not find that individual combatants alluded to "issues related to the US, the cold war, or redefining a political or economic global system," as motivations for joining the guerrillas, the US and the Guatemalan military certainly viewed their participation in these terms. The guerrillas received "political, logistical, instructional, and training support" from Cuba (CEH 1999: 4). The Cubans were also partly responsible for encouraging the four guerrilla groups to form a united front in 1982. Select militants traveled to Cuba, Nicaragua, Eastern Europe, Vietnam, and the Soviet Union to train. They also received aid from sympathetic governments in Western Europe. The URNG leadership often operated clandestinely from across the border in Mexico.

While the preceding paragraphs help to explain why the conflict in Guatemala became violent, it sheds minimal light on why the violence took the form that it did. The conflict rarely reflected the traditional conception of a civil war – an armed confrontation between a rebel group and a military force fighting on behalf of the government. In fact, the majority of the violence associated with the conflict occurred outside of pitched battles or skirmishes between these organized entities. The military and other security forces carried out the most brutal and inhumane violence against the guerrillas and their supporters. Since most of the guerrilla support came from the country's indigenous population, the military viewed the entire indigenous population as potential subversives. The destruction brought about by the conflict and the responsibility of the actors involved has been extensively detailed in two postwar reports. In 1998, the Catholic Church found that the military and its related security forces were responsible for 85 percent of all the human rights violations committed during the conflict. One year later, the Historical Clarification

Commission (CEH) again attributed 93 percent of the abuses to the state's formal and informal agents of repression. The guerrillas were blamed for 10 percent and 3 percent of the violations in the respective reports.

The Guatemalan soldiers were encouraged to be as violent as possible. Soldiers were promoted and praised based upon "the ability to kill, to take initiative during massacres, and to demonstrate cruelty in the course of operations" (REMHI 1999: 129). The army educated its recruits to believe that the guerrillas were the cause of the country's problems, that the army was the "victim," and that "the act of serving in the army was in itself a direct asset for the good of the country" (REMHI 1999: 128). This mindset was used to justify horrendous atrocities. They engaged in wide-scale murder, torture, rape, forced disappearances, collective punishment, and forced recruitment of soldiers (including minors) in order to control society and to break the social fabric of communities (REMHI 1999). The military turned communities and families against each other by forcing them to take part in torture and killings. At one point, roughly one million citizens participated in Civilian Self-Defense Patrols (PACS) which the military relied upon to search for guerrilla units and to keep the rest of the civilian population under control. No one was safe from the violence as "soldiers or patrollers frequently refer to the killing of children as a way of eliminating the possibility of rebuilding the community and of circumventing the victims' efforts to attain justice" (REMHI 1999: 31). According to REMHI (1999: 134), the state and its agents were responsible for over 400 massacres which involved "collective murders associated with community destruction."

The guerrillas, on the other hand, were more selective and humane in their use of violence. They sometimes killed, with or without substantial evidence, those that they suspected of cooperating with the military. They killed several within their own ranks for disobeying orders and for putting the lives of the other rebels in danger. The guerrillas put communities in danger even after it was well-known how the military would respond and were not prepared or willing to defend those that they had put in the army's crosshairs (Montes 2007). The rebels were also found responsible for having committed at least 16 massacres (REMHI 1999: 140). Unlike the state, however,

> Techniques such as the use of informers, congregating the people in one place, separating them into groups, and orgies were not reported in massacres attributed to guerrilla forces. There are, moreover, no cases of obligatory participation, rapes, repeated massacres, or razed hamlets.
>
> (REMHI 1999: 14)

None of these killings, by the government's security forces or the guerrillas, were traditional in the sense of having been committed in the midst of battle. Human rights violations attributed to the guerrillas must be condemned, but it would be a mistake to put them on par with those for which the state was responsible.

Sustaining the violence

Why did the Guatemalan Civil War last so unbearably long? To put it quite simply, many of the factors that contributed to the outbreak of violence in the early 1960s persisted. For the most part, the political system remained closed. The military continued to rule, showing little patience for dissent. Labor leaders, students, religious activists, and pro-democracy politicians continued to disappear. While there were periods of relaxed repression that allowed for non-violent political pressure, they were always brief and resulted in a return to repression. As a result, people who might have channeled their demands through the democratic political process felt that they had little choice but to take up the cause of armed resistance (Azpuru 1999; Manz 2004; Brockett 2005).

Economic hardship continued to be a motivational factor. The economy worsened following the oil crisis of the late 1970s. Unemployment, inflation and poverty rates climbed. By the end of the 1980s, the UN estimated that 90 percent of all Guatemalans were living in poverty (Jonas 1995: 30). These economic conditions pushed many into the streets in protest, north in search of economic opportunities, and into the ranks of the guerrillas.

The determination of the guerrillas and the military also played an important role in prolonging the conflict. For the guerrillas, it appears that they were simply resilient in the face of extreme odds. They were nearly destroyed on three separate occasions. However, they continued to believe in the prospect of victory and they kept telling their supporters and militants that success was just around the corner (Manz 2004). Even after the scorched earth policy of 1981–1983, the URNG managed to regroup and began to make inroads into new areas of the country. Other guerrillas had concluded that it was going to be impossible for them to take power militarily, but that continued military pressure might make success at the negotiation table possible. Rolando Moran continued to maintain this position after the war's end by claiming that the peace process was only possible because of the continuing armed threat of the URNG (Ibarra and Puig 2007: 51). The military continued to fight for several reasons. First, they argued that they were protecting the country from a communist threat and that they would continue to fight until they had their unconditional surrender. On the other hand, the CEH argued that the military kept up the fighting even when it knew that the guerrillas were no longer a threat (CEH 1999: 5). The military had full knowledge of the limited power that the guerrillas possessed, yet they continued to play up the guerrilla threat in order to "justify numerous and serious crimes."

In the international realm, the Cold War between the US and the Soviet Union continued. President Jimmy Carter had cut off aid to the Guatemalan government because of its egregious record of human rights abuses. This had little effect. Instead of improving its performance with respect to human rights in order to have US aid reinstituted, the military sought weapons and assistance from other states that were unconcerned with Guatemala's record on human rights; namely, Israel, Argentina, and Taiwan. In neighboring countries, the US was arming a counter-revolutionary force in Honduras to bring down the Sandinistas in Nicaragua and was supporting the Salvadoran government against the Farabundo Martí Front for National Liberation (FMLN). President Ronald Reagan was disinclined to negotiate with the insurgents and instead lent moral support to the Guatemalan regime by praising one of the two men most responsible for the genocide unleashed in the Guatemalan highlands, Ríos Montt, saying that he had been given a "bum rap."

Peace in sight

How, after three decades of war, did the warring parties successfully resolve the fighting without even a hint of the return to violence once the accords were signed? Changes in the military balance of forces and within the warring coalitions, as well as political, economic, and international factors all contributed to the turn away from violence. For the military and the elite, the guerrillas had been isolated, if not defeated, and were of little threat. Following the "successful" scorched earth campaign, some argued that in order to achieve long-term political and economic stability, Guatemala needed to repair its image in the international community. This was to be accomplished by allowing civilians to compete for the presidency and congress. However, these changes were primarily meant to be cosmetic (Azpuru 1999; Peceny and Stanley 2001: 170–171; Stanley and Holiday 2002: 426–427).

The weakened condition of the guerrillas also led to a de-escalation of violence. The early 1980 killings of their real and potential support base, as well as numerous rural and urban URNG militants and sympathizers, forced the guerrillas into a defensive position. The overwhelming repression convinced many insurgents that revolutionary success was unlikely, if not impossible. A faction of the EGP broke away from the URNG in 1984, with members either fleeing to Mexico or returning to participate in a revitalized civil society. They argued that the URNG failed to adequately respond to the repression and to the political liberalization of the 1980s (Vinegrad 1998: 217). At the same time, the URNG actually seemed to have changed its approach. It put more effort into its political organizing by "broadening its social and political alliances ... slowly beginning to recognize the role of popular and indigenous sectors acting autonomously," and believing in the "importance of an ideological pluralism that would allow the popular movements to follow their own organizational dynamic" (Jonas 2000: 30). The URNG also proposed to enter into a dialogue with the new civilian government.

The initial process of democratization of the country's political system began in 1984 with the holding of a Constituent Assembly and continued with the 1985 election of President Cerezo (PDC). However, leftist parties were still prohibited from participating. In 1986, the URNG proposed "a "grace period" to avoid distracting the government from fulfilling its campaign promises" and "presented a comprehensive proposal for purging and reorganizing the security forces" (REMHI 1999: 247–248). According to the government, the military agreed to a dialogue, but the guerrillas were unconvinced of its sincerity.

President Cerezo and the other Central American heads of state signed the Esquipulas II Agreement in August 1987. In the peace plan, the leaders committed themselves to furthering the democratization of their respective countries and taking steps to end the ongoing wars in their countries through negotiations. They also pledged not to support the rebels operating within each other's border. Months later, the Guatemalan government declared a general amnesty and formed a National Reconciliation Commission (CNR). The CNR, headed by Monsignor Rodolfo Quezada Toruño, sponsored a National Dialogue which made evident society's interest in a political settlement to the conflict while the URNG "reiterated its proposals for a cease-fire, the creation of demilitarized zones, and a political dialogue with the government" (REMHI 1999: 255). Government representatives met with the URNG for the first time in face to face talks in Spain in October. According to Azpuru (1999: 104), "the meeting was not successful, due in large measure to the contrary positions of the parties, particularly the government's requirement that the URNG lay down its weapons as a precondition for dialogue." Negotiations continued, however, and the CNR and the guerrillas eventually reached an agreement in Oslo, Norway in 1990. In the agreement, the URNG accepted the 1985 Constitution and the Esquipulas II Accords as a framework for negotiations. This agreement laid the groundwork for subsequent meetings held throughout Latin America and Europe involving representatives from the URNG, government, opposition political parties, business, unions, churches, and universities. Negotiations proceeded slowly because the military and the government continued to be more interested in the URNG's surrender than they were in any fundamental changes to the country's political and economic structures.

In April 1991, President Jorge Serrano Elías (MAS) opened direct negotiations with the guerrillas. Serrano introduced the military's Comprehensive Peace Plan that "proposed a cease-fire and the immediate surrender of the guerrillas, to be followed by negotiations over the nature of their political reinsertion" (REMHI 1999: 265). During these talks, the

Organization of American States (OAS) and the United Nations acted as observers to the process. Negotiations continued after the government and the military opened up to the possibility that substantive negotiations could occur prior to a ceasefire. Talks remained exceedingly difficult, however, because both the URNG and the military launched attacks meant to improve their standing in the negotiations. Talks were further interrupted when Serrano dissolved Congress and suspended the constitution. The May 1993 coup was defeated when most domestic and international audiences condemned Serrano's move. While the attempted coup illustrated the fragility of the new democracy, some argue that the mobilization of civil society, the media, the business community and the military in condemning the illegal coup signaled to the URNG that the democratization process initiated in 1984 was more than cosmetic (Peceny and Stanley 2001). The coup also led to the replacement of several officers who sought the unconditional surrender of the URNG with those who were more open to facilitating a negotiated settlement.

In January 1994, the URNG and Ramiro de León Carpio's (UCN) new administration signed the "Framework Accord." The accord developed an agenda and timetable for further discussion of human rights violations, the repatriation of refugees, and socioeconomic reforms, formalized the role of the "Group of Friends," and brought the United Nations more directly into the negotiations as moderator between the two parties. Previously, both the URNG and the government had envisioned that the UN would "verify but not mediate the peace" (Jonas 2000: 42). It was hoped that greater UN involvement would "induce both parties to negotiate more seriously and make it less likely that the parties would use the talks for tactical purposes" (Stanley and Holiday 2002: 433).

One of the unique aspects of the Framework Accord was that it brought almost all sectors of civil society into the peace process as part of the Assembly of Civil Society (ASC). The ASC was comprised of women's, indigenous, labor, and religious organizations. UN mediator Jean Arnault (Spence 2004: 43–44) and the URNG (REMHI 1999: 278) hoped that the ASC would lend greater support and credibility to any accords reached between the insurgents and the government by proposing solutions and commenting on the issues under consideration in the negotiations, even though its input would be in an advisory role. By March 1995, the parties had signed agreements on human rights, including the establishment of a Truth Commission, the resettlement of displaced persons, and indigenous rights.

In 1995, Alvaro Arzú (PAN) was elected president. These elections were important to the continuation of the peace process for at least three reasons. First, the URNG called on all Guatemalans to vote. The URNG had previously denounced all elections as farcical. Second, the leftist New Guatemala Democratic Front (FDNG) became the third largest political party in the congress. The FDNG was comprised of many social movements closely related to the URNG and already participating in the ASC. Finally, of the two presidential candidates that advanced to a runoff, Arzú was the one more likely to continue the peace process if elected. The party led by Ríos Montt, an individual responsible for the scorched earth policy of the 1980s, finished in second place. Fortunately for the peace process, the URNG and the FDNG were satisfied with the elections and Arzú won.

Arzú and the URNG would meet prior to his inauguration, demonstrating each party's commitment to following through on the negotiations that had been conducted by previous presidents. Arzú appointed proponents of the peace process to government positions, including a former guerrilla to the new Peace Commission, and worked to remove corrupt military officers (Jonas 2000: 50–51). The URNG declared a ceasefire in March 1996 and the two sides agreed on social, economic, and land issues in May. In September, the government and the URNG signed accords that began to dismantle the military's counterinsurgency structures including a reduction in forces, a reorientation toward external threats, and the dissolution of PACs. Arzú and the URNG commanders ended the war three months later.

Several international actors and external events contributed to the civil war's resolution. Between 1983 and 1987, a number of Latin American states worked to bring about an end to the conflicts in Guatemala, and Central America more generally, through the Contadora Peace Process. While the OAS and the UN were observers to the peace process in the early years, the UN became more involved in 1994 and was instrumental in mediating between the URNG and the government. Even prior to the formal signing of an accord, the UN hosted a human rights verification mission (MINUGUA) beginning in November 1994. In terms of external events, regional peace efforts had already helped to end the civil wars in Nicaragua and El Salvador. The end of the Cold War allowed the US to play a more constructive role in the peace process. Finally, the involvement of the Consultative Group of Donor Countries applied pressure to the government and the military so that "major funding for Guatemala would be withheld until a final peace accord was signed and until tax reforms in Guatemala guaranteed internal financing" (Jonas 2000: 46). This pressure helped speed the peace process along.

What sustains the transformation or undercuts it?

Following the signing of the peace accords, there are few indications that there was ever any serious threat of a renewed outbreak of war. The URNG was isolated and, while it had demobilized roughly 3,000 combatants, it only counted on an estimated 500 full-time combatants (Peceny and Stanley 2001; Stanley and Holiday 2002). The URNG had also been losing civilian support for the last few years. Supporters were outraged at the URNG's acceptance of a weakened Truth Commission that, in their opinion, held no one accountable for the crimes committed since 1954. Other supporters were frustrated with the URNG's acquiescence of last minute changes in the Socioeconomic Agreement of the accords and argued that they did not go far enough in reforming the economic structures that had produced unacceptable levels of poverty. Many civil society groups also became disillusioned with the URNG's vanguard mentality and argued that they were not going to take orders from the URNG. However, at no point did any URNG members seek to undermine the peace process by playing the role of spoiler.

The military gradually came to accept the inevitability of the peace process. After several failed coup attempts, most of its leadership had been replaced by soldiers more accepting of the peace process. Military and guerrilla leaders also met clandestinely in the last few years of the conflict in order to develop a level of trust that would be critical to a smooth transition. While the military did receive some bad press with the postwar reports on human rights violations that it had committed, none were held accountable through trials or with prison sentences. The limits of what the military would accept was brutally illustrated with the murder of Bishop Juan Gerardi, two days after he presented the REMHI report documenting the military's role in the abuse of thousands of civilians during the conflict.

Conclusion

While there has not been a return to political violence by any of the warring parties, the goals of the peace process have not entirely been fulfilled. The peace process called for more than simply an end to the war. The URNG, the government, civil society and the international community spent ten years designing a lasting agreement that some hoped would radically transform Guatemala's political, social, and economic systems. At best, progress on these goals has been mixed.

No doubt, the peace process contributed to the further democratization of Guatemala, a process that had begun ten years earlier. The period of the peace process witnessed the successful mobilization of historically marginalized groups. Since then, however, these groups have lost much of their ability to influence the country's political structures (García 2004). The URNG also has competed in three elections (1999, 2003, and 2007) since its reinsertion into the formal political system. However, after finishing a distant third in 1999, it is now on the verge of irrelevancy as it only captured 3 percent of the vote in the most recent election and former combatants occupy positions in no less than three other political parties.

One of the primary factors that contributed to the outbreak of war in the first place was the country's dire economic situation. Today, Guatemala remains one of the poorest countries in the region. According to the World Bank, 56 percent of the population lived in poverty in 2006. As of 2004, 80 percent of those living in the countryside and 76 percent of the indigenous people lived in poverty. As part of the peace accords, the government promised to significantly increase tax revenues and health and education expenditures. While these commitments were less than many had hoped for, the government has not even attained these modest goals.

Finally, the parties reached agreements on human rights that led to investigations by the UN (and the Catholic Church) into wartime abuses. These reports remain a critical contribution to the historical record. However, the investigations failed to hold anyone accountable for crimes committed during the war. This impunity most likely has contributed to today's crisis where violence has reached wartime levels. If one takes the number of deaths attributed during the 36 year war, an estimated 4,167 to 6,944 people were killed each year. Today, roughly 5,000 Guatemalans are murdered yearly. This makes Guatemala one of the most dangerous countries in the Western Hemisphere. While much of the violence is related to organized crime, drug trafficking, street crime, and violence against women, the victims also frequently include human rights workers, labor leaders, judges and lawyers. The failure to resolve any of the historical structures that led to the war, except perhaps political exclusion, is one of the greatest failures of the peace process.

Why have the results of the peace agreement been so disappointing? First, the two parties that signed the final agreements were relatively weak. The URNG demobilized roughly 500 combatants and had much less popular support than years earlier. Alvaro Arzú's governing PAN party had a relatively minor presence in the congress. The ASC, while it had an advisory role in the peace process, did not have a definitive say in any agreements. Several agreements were signed without its support which led to some animosity, especially with the URNG. The weakness of these three actors was critically important as several agreements required constitutional amendments, Congressional approval, and support from a national referendum. Sadly enough, some complain that the organized group most vocal in its support for approving the reforms was the international community which had staked a great deal of its reputation and resources on the peace process.

What lessons can one take from the example of the URNG? First, it is critical to understand the ratification process of any agreements signed. As ORPA commander Rodrigo Asturias told me, it is a mistake to count on the government and other political actors to expend political capital to push through reforms without outside pressure. Second, the guerrilla group needs to focus greater attention upon the process through which it can transform itself into a competitive political party in the postwar period. This is necessary so that it has the clout to pressure for the implementation of the agreements. While the URNG did receive some educational scholarships and reinsertion stipends for former combatants, it woefully neglected the building of a vehicle to carry out its political program once the accords were signed. As a result, those who struggled with the URNG for over three decades continue to suffer the consequences.

References

Azpuru, D. (1999) "Peace and Democratization in Guatemala: Two Parallel Processes," in Arnson, C.J. (ed.) *Comparative Peace Processes in Latin America*, Washington, DC: Woodrow Wilson Center Press, 97–125.

Booth, J.A. (1991) "Socioeconomic and Political Roots of National Revolts in Central America," *Latin American Research Review*, 26 (1): 33–73.

Brockett, C.D. (2005) *Political Movements and Violence in Central America*, New York: Cambridge University Press.

Comisión para el Esclarecimiento Histórico (1999) *Informe de la Comisión para el Esclarecimiento Histórico*, Guatemala: UNOPS.

Dunkerley, J. (1988) *Power in the Isthmus*, New York: Verso.

García, J.F. (2004) Interview with the author on 14 April 2004, Guatemala.

Herrera, R.L. and Molina, F.R. (2005) *Desandar los Caminos de la Guerra*, Guatemala: Unknown.

Ibarra, C.F. and Puig, S.M. (2007) "Guatemala: From the Guerrilla Struggle to a Divided Left," in Deonandan, K., Close, D. and Prevost, G. (eds.) *From Revolutionary Movements to Political Parties*, New York: Palgrave MacMillan, 43–65.

Jonas, S. (1991) *The Battle for Guatemala: Rebels, Death Squads, and U.S. Power*, Boulder, CO: Westview Press.

—— (1995) "Electoral Problems and the Democratic Project in Guatemala," in Seligson, M. and Booth, J. (eds.) *Elections and Democracy in Central America Revisited*, Chapel Hill, NC: The University of North Carolina Press, 25–44.

—— (2000) *Of Centaurs and Doves*, Boulder, CO: Westview Press.

Manz, B. (2004) *Paradise in Ashes*, Berkeley, CA: University of California Press.

Montes, C. (2007) Interview with the author on 28 June 2007, Guatemala City.

Peceny, M. and Stanley, W. (2001) "Liberal Social Reconstruction and the Resolution of Civil Wars in Central America," *International Organization* 55 (1): 149–182.

Recinos, A. (2004) Interview with the author on 6 April 2004, Quetzaltenango.

Recovery of Historical Memory Project (1999) *Guatemala Never Again!*, Official Report of the Human Rights Office, Archdiocese of Guatemala, New York: Orbis Books.

Sichar, G. (1999) *Historia de los Partidos Políticos Guatemaltecos: Distintas Siglas de (casi) una Misma Ideología*, 2a edn., Guatemala: Editorial Nojib'sa.

Spence, J. (2004) *War and Peace in Central America: Comparing Transitions Toward Democracy and Social Equity in Guatemala, El Salvador, and Nicaragua*, Brookline, MA: Hemisphere Initiatives Reports.

Spence, J., Dye, D., Worby, P., de Leon-Escribano, C.R., Vickers, G. and Lanchin, M. (1998) *Promise and Reality: Implementation of the Guatemalan Peace Accords*, Brookline, MA: Hemisphere Initiatives Reports.

Stanley, W. and Holiday, D. (2002) "Broad Participation, Diffuse Responsibility: Peace Implementation in Guatemala," in Stedman, S.J., Rothchild, D. and

Cousens, E.M. (eds.) *Ending Civil Wars: The Implementation of Peace Agreements*, Boulder, CO: Lynne Rienner, 421–462.

Vinegrad, A. (1998) "From Guerrillas to Politicians: The Transition of the Guatemalan Revolutionary Movement in Historical and Comparative Perspective," in Sieder, R. (ed.) *Guatemala After the Peace Accords*, UK: University of London; Institute of Latin American Studies, 207–227.

14 Mainstreaming the revolutionaries[1]

National Liberating Action and the shift from resistance to democracy in Brazil, 1964–present

Kenneth P. Serbin[2]

The resistance to military dictatorship (1964–1985) and the prolonged transition to democracy in Brazil provide an instructive case study of the assimilation of guerrillas into a peaceful political process. Brazil suffered only a small fraction of the violence experienced in Chile, Argentina, El Salvador, and Guatemala during the Cold War, and although thousands of people supported its guerrilla movement, the actual combatants numbered only about 800 (Gaspari 2002). But Brazil's immensity, booming economy, and geopolitical significance made it a leader in the region and an example for people on both the left and right. The US-backed coup of 1964 inaugurated a new wave of authoritarianism in Latin America, and the struggle between the security forces and the guerrillas became a defining characteristic of the period, mainly because the military institutionalized torture and therefore made repression a major political issue. During and after the democratic transition former guerrillas and their followers collaborated with the Roman Catholic Church in radical but non-violent pastoral programs in favor of minorities, the landless, and the poor; participated in one of the world's largest and most diverse grass roots movements; helped found the Workers' Party (Partido dos Trabalhadores, or PT); and worked in PT leader Luiz Inácio Lula da Silva's five presidential campaigns and two administrations (2003–2011). Since 1985 Brazil's elections have been free, void of fraud, and highly competitive. As of mid-2008 Lula's two chiefs of staff had belonged to guerrilla organizations, and a considerable number of political appointees had been political prisoners, exiles, members of guerrilla or other clandestine organizations, and/or persecuted by the military regime. Of 28 initial cabinet members, 18 had opposed the military regime, 14 belonged to clandestine organizations, seven were political prisoners, and seven were exiles (D'Araujo 2007). Former guerrillas have thus played an important part in the consolidation of Brazilian democracy, although the country's stark inequalities, violence, and other difficulties lead many to question the nature and quality of that democracy. Brazil's revolutionaries attained this role by mainstreaming into the political system.

This chapter focuses on Ação Libertadora Nacional (ALN, or National Liberating Action), the largest and most important of the revolutionary organizations that resisted the dictatorship. It analyzes the broad socioeconomic and political conditions that caused ALN members to participate in the return to a peaceful democracy. The transition consisted not merely of the restoration of civilian rule, regular elections, and parliamentary and political freedoms, although these were fundamental: It also sprung from the efforts of a generation of revolutionaries struggling to overcome the authoritarian legacies and violence of both the right and the left and to build a more just society. The chapter combines reflection on constructive transformations with the on-the-ground approach of social history. It presents the history of the regime and the ALN, the left's move toward the center, and specific ways of mainstreaming. Whereas much analysis focuses on world hot spots and on the successes and failures of peacemaking in the short term, this chapter considers the legacies of dictatorship and revolutionary warfare in a low-intensity conflict.

A brief history of the regime and National Liberating Action

Brazil's dictatorship began when army conspirators, backed by the US, anti-communist politicians, and large segments of the populace, overthrew the democratically elected leftist populist João Goulart on 31 March 1964. The overthrow ended a period of difficult but lively and creative democratic rule that had begun in 1945. US leaders welcomed the coup as the prevention of another, much larger version of the Cuban Revolution and immediately recognized the government of the military dictator, the first of five. While the Brazilian Communist Party (Partido Comunista Brasileiro, or PCB) had substantial influence, the evidence does not support the rightist contention that Goulart was planning a left-wing coup. The PCB, in fact, had adopted the Moscow line of peaceful coexistence with capitalism. Nobody died during the coup, although the military arrested tens of thousands of people, suspended the civil liberties of numerous politicians, and employed torture. The left remained overwhelmingly on the sidelines during the early years of the dictatorship.

As the regime hardened, the democratic, student-led opposition protested in the streets. In 1968 tensions reached fever pitch. As Kriesberg and Millar observe (this volume, Chapter 2), conflict erupts when either side believes the other will only respond to force. As the military cracked down further, more people turned to the idea of armed revolution. Meanwhile, the PCB split into two camps – one favoring the Moscow line and another advocating violent resistance and socialism. The revolutionaries exited the PCB to form their own organizations. By the early 1970s more than 40 underground groups had sprouted, typifying the fragmentation of the left seen elsewhere in Latin America and in the Palestine Liberation Organization. About 20 practiced armed resistance (Ridenti 2007).

The ALN was founded in 1968 by the charismatic, popular, and valiant Carlos Marighella, a lifelong communist. Marighella had been jailed and tortured during the dictatorship that ruled Brazil between 1937 and 1945 and subsequently rose into the party's upper echelons. He sharply criticized the inaction following the coup. In 1967 he broke with the PCB and traveled to Cuba, where he announced plans for a violent revolution in Brazil.

The ALN's initials synthesized Marighella's revolutionary strategy: "National" and "Liberating" referring to the ALN's struggle against the dictatorship and the organization's anti-imperialist, anti-American streak; revolutionary "Action" sharply contrasting with the PCB's non-confrontational policy. The term "a ação faz a vanguarda" (action creates the vanguard) meant armed revolution first, and reflection and theorization afterwards. Like revolutionaries across Latin America, the ALN found inspiration in Che Guevara's *foco* model, although Marighella recorded many reflections specific to the Brazilian case. The ALN rejected the centralized hierarchy of the PCB and armed groups such as the Partido Comunista do Brasil (the PC do B, an offshoot of the PCB) and stimulated the formation of small, independent cells of militants encouraged to act spontaneously. Borrowing a phrase from the Cuban Revolution, Marighella declared: "Nobody needs to ask permission to carry out revolutionary acts" (Ridenti 2007). He himself was unaware of the plans for the most spectacular guerrilla operation of all: the ALN's kidnapping of US ambassador Charles Burke Elbrick.

The existence of a US-backed dictatorship inspired the ALN, but so did the desire for a more egalitarian society. The left of the 1950s and 1960s believed Brazil stood on the verge of a nationalistic, non-violent revolution. The ALN aimed to establish a socialist state, probably with Cuba as the model. But Marighella welcomed people of all persuasions, including democrats, business people, and even clergymen. But the ALN had no specific blueprint for taking over the government. Had it achieved victory, a struggle for power would likely have ensued and perhaps included execution of opponents, as occurred in Cuba.

The ALN carried out numerous bank hold-ups, a train robbery, and the takeover of a radio station in order to transmit a message from Marighella to Brazilians. In alliance with another group the ALN abducted Ambassador Elbrick on 4 September 1969 and held him for several days. In exchange for Elbrick's freedom the guerrillas obtained the release of 15 leading political prisoners, flown to Mexico, and the dissemination of a revolutionary manifesto in the media. The ALN employed the tactics of revolutionary terror – Marighella himself employed the term – but its combatants scrupulously tried to avoid harming civilians and rejected the regime's label of "terrorists" (interview with Manoel Cyrillo de Oliveira Netto, Rio de Janeiro 19 June 2006). The mounting guerrilla threat provoked a counterattack by the military, police, and other security agencies, which had received greater powers after the generals declared a full-blown dictatorship on 13 December 1968. On that date the government had issued Institutional Act No. 5, suspending habeas corpus for political crimes and giving the security forces carte blanche against subversion. The military shut down the National Congress and censored the press. In the hunt for Marighella after the Elbrick operation, the political police arrested and tortured numerous individuals, including Catholic Dominican friars who belonged to the ALN and revealed information about his whereabouts. On 4 November 1969, he died in an ambush. The regime arrested and tortured thousands of others in the effort to defeat the guerrillas. By late 1973 most of the ALN guerrillas and their key supporters among the populace had been killed, *desaparecido* (literally, "disappeared"), imprisoned, exiled, or neutralized in some other fashion. The ALN did not dissolve itself or transform itself into another kind of organization such as a political party. Without pronouncement it simply ceased to act. By early 1975 Brazil's last guerrilla operation, an attempt by the PC do B to open a rural front in the Amazon jungle, ended in defeat.

The decision to employ violence was fraught with complexities generally unappreciated by the literature, films, journalistic coverage, and other cultural production about the revolutionaries. Then and now members of the ALN and other armed groups claimed that military repression, censorship, and violence – especially after 1968 – legitimized their own violence. Yet planning for violence preceded 1968, and in some cases even the coup of 1964 (Ridenti 2007). The armed groups competed with one another ideologically, although they frequently joined forces for operations. Other organizations concentrated on peaceful resistance but still suffered repression. Among the armed groups disagreement emerged over strategies of violence. Within the ALN tensions developed between the extreme "militarist" element and guerrillas who emphasized the need for political work, especially in the university student movement, the main source of recruits (Leite 1997; author's interview with Paulo de Tarso Vannuchi, São Paulo 16 July 2001). Militarism gained importance as the regime heightened the repression. It produced a tragic cycle in which guerrillas fought increasingly for mere survival and to honor dead comrades rather than for broader political purposes. In contrast with revolutionary successes in Cuba and Nicaragua, the mainly middle-class Brazilian guerrillas became isolated from the rest of society and thus failed to spark the intended popular rebellion.

The military regime dealt efficiently with the guerrilla threat. Its use of torture and violence caused indignation but did not deeply affect the poor classes, who were accustomed to everyday police abuses. In line with Atashi's concepts of zones of direct and indirect conflict (see this volume,

Chapter 4), the Brazilian masses can be viewed as having occupied the latter. Whether the regime met their daily needs carried much greater weight than the guerrillas' ideological outlook. With economic growth rates topping 10 percent, between 1968 and 1974 the regime garnered considerable support from the populace. It burnished its domestic image with a smart public relations campaign, helped by Brazil's victory in the 1970 soccer World Cup.

The hermetic, often elitist character of the guerrillas resonated with Brazil's social inequalities and the conciliatory nature of politics. The revolutionary organizations often receive greater attention from the government and the media than do other sectors of society. The state, for instance, has paid over a billion dollars in compensation to the victims of the military regime in what trenchant journalists have called the "bolsa terrorismo" (terrorism scholarship) and the "bolsa ditadura" (dictatorship scholarship) (Veja 2007; Gaspari 2007). Meanwhile, the state has lagged terribly in the defense of the common individual's human rights. Not surprisingly, however, the campaign for compensation – as well as other key demands such as the opening up of military archives containing data on the repression – has resonated little with the masses. Whereas Chile and Argentina had many large protests for human rights and punished the repressors, most Brazilians seem apathetic. The regime's torturers will probably never be charged with crimes. This apathy has its roots in an implicit pact of silence about the atrocities embraced by the governing elites of both the opposition and the right beginning with the amnesty law of the late 1970s (discussed below).

Significantly, the Brazilian military stopped far short of annihilating the left. The repression brought a pall of fear upon the middle class and the political world, but it killed or "disappeared" only 475 members of the opposition (Secretaria Especial dos Direitos Humanos da Presidência da República 2007). The dictatorship in the much smaller country of Chile eliminated 3,000 people, the Argentine generals at least 15,000. Beginning in 1974, Brazilian president Ernesto Geisel (1974–1979), an active participant in the 1964 coup, began to rein in the torturers and ultimately fired his Minister of the Army, Sylvio Frota, a hardliner who wanted to succeed Geisel and increase repression. Geisel understood the corrosive effect of the torture centers on military discipline and unity and moved to eliminate them for practical, if not moral, reasons. He belonged to a "soft-line" faction that wanted to combine Western, anti-communist democracy with elements of Brazilian authoritarianism. Geisel initiated a "slow, gradual, and secure" political liberalization ultimately known as the *abertura* (political "opening"). The *abertura* can be classified as a de-escalation of conflict and demilitarization of politics. Geisel and his advisors manipulated it to assure the predominance of the pro-regime political right in the Congress and the executive. His successor as president was yet another general, João Baptista Figueiredo (1979–1985), and the civilian who replaced Figueiredo was chosen by a carefully controlled electoral college. This process maintained the military's power, including cabinet posts for the heads of the three service branches.

During the liberalization, guerrillas began seeking political alternatives. Upon release from prison some wanted to resume fighting, but they quickly discovered that the conditions for guerrilla warfare no longer existed. They started to work quietly in other kinds of political organization. The work of non-violent, grass roots militants especially provided a convincing demonstration effect. These groups served the role of "interim institutions" for ex-combatants, a concept discussed by Lyons (this volume, Chapter 7). Expanding rapidly in the 1970s, the grass roots Catholic groups known as Comunidades Eclesiais de Base (CEBS, or Grass Roots Church Communities) served as both an alternative model of political activism and a protective political umbrella for people persecuted by the regime. The Catholic Church established innovative programs advocating land reform, defending poor urban and rural squatters and oppressed indigenous peoples, and assisting local groups to pressure the state on socioeconomic issues. Liberation theology, which flourished in the 1970s, attracted former ALN members with its demands for social justice and roots in the Christian-Marxist dialogue begun by the Church in the 1960s. Many former guerrillas found common cause with the Church because it helped galvanize the human rights movement, including the defense of political prisoners and the denunciation of torture. Brazilian activists referred to the panoply of grass roots initiatives as the movimento popular, best translated as "power to the people."

Many other groups of the center-left provided a demonstration effect of democracy. Because of its pre-coup experience with democracy and the military's belief that it was defending democracy, Brazil operated within a democratic mindset. In the 1970s the Ordem dos Advogados do Brasil (Brazil's bar association), the Associação Brasileira de Imprensa (the national press club), the many exiles who had lived in European democracies, and politicians of the Movimento Democrático Brasileiro (MDB, the Brazilian Democratic Movement, the official opposition party) all contributed significantly to liberalization. Many business leaders and conservative politicians also jumped onto the democratic bandwagon. As a result of these pressures, a complex dialectic between state and opposition shaped redemocratization (Alves 1984). The democratic mindset received crucial reinforcement from the non-violent PCB. The PCB had profound influence within the MDB, and even some ALN members returned to the PCB in the 1970s and 1980s (Segatto and Santos 2007). The revolutionaries had starkly rejected this ostensible accommodation in the 1960s but embraced it ever more strongly after the return to civilian rule.

Some of the ALN's members took part in building the independent, anti-government union movement (as opposed to traditional unions formally tied to the state). They sought to influence proletarians by teaching classes, and to assist by offering input, political experience, and support during key strikes in 1978, 1979 and 1980. As Lech Walesa contested the Soviet Empire in Poland with the Pope's backing, the Church's support of striking laborers and Lula was crucial. The ALN militants witnessed the rise of Lula to power in São Paulo's heavily unionized industrial suburbs and in some cases became his advisors, as in the case of former ALN member and Dominican friar Frei Betto. The unions became a major pole of opposition to the regime.

By its very nature the *abertura* included the left. In 1978 Geisel removed a key instrument of repression by abolishing Institutional Act No. 5. In 1979 the Congress passed the Lei de Anistia (Amnesty Law) under President Figueiredo. The amnesty permitted the return of some 10,000 political exiles and the release of practically all remaining political prisoners. Scores of former guerrillas and thousands who sympathized with them could once again participate freely in politics.

Passage of the amnesty law was fraught with political tensions. As in many countries, amnesty was a tradition. It stretched back to colonial rule under the Portuguese and was decreed after revolts and political crises in the nineteenth and twentieth centuries. Shortly after the coup of 1964 people began advocating amnesty. Several proposals arose in Congress and received support from both opposition and pro-government politicians. Amnesty finally became viable during the *abertura*. Imprisoned ALN members and other guerrillas wanted a complete amnesty and also the punishment of abusers of human rights. The guerrillas, the democratic opposition, and thousands of leftists protested in the streets and at the Congress in favor of the full amnesty. However, the military-controlled Congress denied amnesty to some of the remaining political prisoners. Significantly, the law included vague language granting protection to violators of human rights (Mezarobba 2003).

Since the inception of the amnesty pro-regime forces have insisted forcefully against revising the law. Leftist leaders have also hesitated to reignite debate. The judiciary has refused to intervene; Brazil's Supreme Court, for example, has made no pronouncements about repeated assertions by government officials and others that torture was covered under the amnesty. The political compromises of the time, a strong tradition of elite conciliation, the desire to forget the past and political expediencies in the present have all combined to produce a pact of silence, which stands in stark contrast to the clamorous efforts to remember the authoritarian era in Chile and Argentina (Wilde 1999; Jelin 2002; Feld 2002; Serbin 2006). Vivian states that particular presentations of memory can contribute to or damage conciliation (this volume, Chapter 6). In Brazil forgetting has favored conciliation. Although military political influence and share of the budget have declined, the armed forces are still a central institution whose feathers Lula has avoided ruffling. His status as a leftist, albeit greatly deemphasized, makes it difficult for him to focus on past abuses. He has refused to open military and government archives that likely contain sensitive information about repression. In sum, it has been easier for everybody to keep quiet. As critics have pointed out, this attitude harms the consolidation of democracy and respect for human rights. The former guerrillas in Lula's government have also kept silent or, if seeking change, have achieved very little (Mezarobba 2003; Reis Filho 1997; Leitão 2008; Magnoli and Piovesan 2008).

The *abertura* included a reform of the party system that created new political opportunities for former combatants. The regime abolished the two official parties it had created in 1965 and permitted several new opposition parties to form. The regime baldly used this divide-and-conquer strategy to bolster the political right, but in so doing it accelerated the return to electoral democracy and discredited hard-line ambitions for prolonged dictatorship. The ensuing elections promoted peaceful democratic politics, but they also upheld the social status quo.

In 1980, Lula, other union leaders, Catholic progressives, former guerrillas, leaders of the movimento popular, and a mixture of other radical leftist groups formed the socialist Workers' Party (PT). In comparison with the inept, ethnically tainted transition of Guatemalan guerrillas from fighters to politicians as described by Allison (this volume, Chapter 13), the PT formed quickly and professionally and was immediately ready to take part in elections. The PT cast itself as a radical opposition party, demanding full democracy and transformation of socioeconomic structures. Whereas the Church had been the glue holding together the left in the traumatic 1970s, the PT took on that role in the less repressive, more democratic 1980s. Throughout the decade the PT, the alternative union movement, and the movimento popular pushed Brazilian society to the left. The Church's Pastoral Land Commission (CPT) gave rise to the Movimento dos Trabalhadores Rurais Sem Terra (MST, Rural Landless Workers' Movement), the largest and most radical of Latin America's social movements of the past quarter century. Other groups fought to bring environmental protection, women's rights, and gay rights onto the political stage.

Despite its harsh critique of the Brazilian system, the PT participated fully in the military's electoral scheme. In the hotly contested presidential election of 1989 Lula became a frontrunner. He finished second but strengthened his and the PT's electoral appeal. By carefully opening the electoral system to the left the military provided a disincentive for more radical political action by the opposition. Once in the electoral game, the left – including former guerrillas – found it hard to exit.

The left seeks the center

Lula and the PT dominated the left and stood as the main opposition to the central government between 1989 and 2002. Lula ran for the presidency again in 1994 and 1998, losing both times to a center-right coalition headed by Fernando Henrique Cardoso, an internationally renowned sociologist and himself a staunch opponent, and victim, of the military regime. Cardoso belonged to the center-left Partido da Social Democracia Brasilieira (PSDB, Brazilian Social Democratic Party) but recognized that he could not win election or garner sufficient support for his measures in Congress without the support of the traditional right-wing politicians whose power resulted in part from the past manipulations of the military regime. Coalitions have been necessary in Brazil because of a multi-party system in which no party gains a majority in the Congress. The PT harshly criticized the Cardoso government and sought to block practically all of its initiatives, including the privatization of state-owned companies and other neo-liberal strategies.

But the PT also began to moderate. The fall of communism undermined its radicalism, and its increasing presence in municipal and state government and in the Congress helped to institutionalize the party and draw it toward the center. This shift reflected the general tendency of the political leadership. Contrasting itself with most other parties, the PT took pride in stressing clean, efficient government. This strongly identified the PT more with democracy and less with revolution. In the mid-1990s evidence began to emerge of corruption within the PT, and the party sought to achieve electoral victories at the expense of radicalism. For the 2002 election Lula and the party leadership decided to make an all-out effort. Adopting the same strategy used by Cardoso, the PT struck alliances with former right-wing enemies. By now the PT had abandoned socialism in favor of social democracy. (A parallel can be drawn with the Frelimo party in Mozambique, which abandoned Marxism–Leninism and became democratic socialist, as Lyons illustrates in this volume, Chapter 7.) Lula strongly affirmed respect for private property and contracts and the country's agreement with the International Monetary Fund, loathed by the party's grass roots and leftist thinkers. The PT hired one of Brazil's most skillful political marketers to reshape Lula's image. Lula handily won the election and proceeded to conduct a fiscally conservative government. Significantly, Lula avoided the kind of strident anti-Americanism and strongman rule of Fidel Castro's Cuba or Hugo Chávez's Venezuela. He oversaw an increasingly stable democracy with vigorous press freedoms and generally good ties with the US. On social policy Lula showed little innovation, mainly consolidating and extending welfare programs already in place. He distanced himself from progressive Catholics and the "power to the people" movement, relying for support on poor, politically unorganized voters who had benefited from his welfare programs.

In 2005 and 2006, Lula and the PT relinquished the final remnant of the party's image: its claim to clean politics and government. The press, congressional investigators, and other authorities uncovered a massive scheme of alleged vote-buying in the Congress. Lula's chief of staff, the former ALN underground member José Dirceu, resigned. So did PT president José Genoino, a former guerrilla of the PC do B. Other PT officials and congressmen left their posts. The public now perceived the PT as acting just like any other political party. As one Brazilian observed, there were no longer any good alternatives at election time. With the PT brought down to earth, the Brazilian tradition of seeing presidential candidates as messiahs was perhaps coming to an end (Hunter 2008; Amaral *et al.* 2008).

Finding a place in the system

While dreams of revolution faded after the 1970s, political activism did not. Many former guerrillas not only found a place in the Brazilian system, but rose to high positions in government. One of the kidnappers of Ambassador Elbrick, Fernando Gabeira, later wrote a best-selling book (Gabeira 1996) and received more than 100,000 votes as an independent in the 1989 presidential contest. Barred from entering the US, Gabeira is today a respected congressman with the Green Party. Dirceu was a political prisoner freed during the Elbrick operation. Taking his place in Lula's government was another ex-guerrilla, Dilma Rousseff. In 2007 and 2008 she emerged as a possible candidate for the presidency in 2010. As stated above, Lula took numerous other former guerrillas and regime opponents into his cabinet. Explicitly or implicitly these former comrades in arms embraced peaceful, Western-style democracy and accommodated to or even fully supported capitalism.

An analysis of the lives of 22 former ALN militants sheds light on social and political mainstreaming. The first variable is the transition from violence to non-violence. Mesmerized by Marighella and Che and moved by a profound desire for social justice, they had rushed into the revolution as youths in their early twenties (one was only a teenager) with no military experience and little time to digest the events and ideas of the turbulent late 1960s. Kriesberg and Millar's observation about the romanticizing and glorifying of violence certainly applied to many youths in the Brazilian case (see this volume, Chapter 1). But the ALN militants did not make their choice for violence easily. They rejected the PCB's notion of a pacific, united, and democratic front, although some clearly viewed their fight against the dictatorship as defending democratic liberties and not necessarily as an effort to make Brazil communist. Such was the case of Manoel Cyrillo de Oliveira Netto, one of the ALN guerrillas who kidnapped Ambassador Elbrick (interview with Manoel Cyrillo de Oliveira Netto, Rio de Janeiro 21 June 2006). The ALN guerrillas viewed violence as a legitimate means of resisting a regime that had cut off those liberties, allied with the imperialist US, and oppressed the common man and woman. Later they had to come to terms with military defeat, and in the process they reflected on the use of violence, strategies and tactics, and ideology.

Over the years most continued to defend the choice for violence, but many admitted that the strategies of guerrilla warfare, and, for some, even the very decision to engage in it, were mistaken. A common theme in many of the interviews conducted with the 22 militants was the political isolation noted above. While the ALN saw violence as the only solution, subsequent lessons brought the combatants to appreciate the necessity and efficacy of peaceful politics. In the words of former guerrilla Paulo Vannuchi:

> A dictatorship can be toppled by other kinds of pressure or even dissolved.... What happened was a political process – a controlled transition in which they [the military] won the confrontation against the left by liquidating us and, paradoxically, we were victorious historically.
> (Interview with Paulo de Tarso Vannuchi, São Paulo, 3 July 2003).

Other experiences schooled the militants in the practice of non-violent, democratic politics – first as defenders of the *abertura* and then as participants in the post-dictatorial system. The revolutionary left that first viewed democracy and civil liberties as mere instruments of the bourgeoisie conveniently rewrote their collective political biography to portray themselves as staunch defenders of democracy once the transition became clear and they joined the system (Ridenti 2007). In the 1990s the left shifted away from the notion of class oppression and toward the idea of *cidadania* (citizenship). Practically all of the interviewees remained active in politics at least in some phase of the post-ALN period, and those continually active assumed positions of greater importance over time. They both strengthened and benefited from the democratic system.

The militants' political activities included a good deal of ideological compromise. Paulo Vannuchi worked in the liberation theology movement, became a close advisor to Lula, and, starting in late 2005, served as Secretary for Human Rights. In that cabinet-level post Vannuchi had to balance his fellow ex-guerrillas' demands for justice for victims of the dictatorship and their families with the political realities of a government with many powerful, competing interests, including the military. Through his political experience and study Vannuchi gained an appreciation for liberalism (Vannuchi 2001). Hamilton Pereira da Silva worked for many years with the Church's Pastoral Land Commission, led the PT's radical wing against the more centrist Lula wing, and then headed up the party's independent think tank. Having dedicated his life to the grass roots, in 2007 he took on a high-level post in the federal Ministry of the Environment, his first position in government. Thus the critical revolutionary outsider became an insider. In the 1980s former ALN militant Ruy de Góes Leite de Barros helped start the Brazilian branch of Greenpeace, the radical environmental organization. Greenpeace was highly critical of the Brazilian government. With Lula's election as president, Ruy moved to the Ministry of the Environment, where he learned a far slower, more institutionalized, more nuanced, at times frustrating but perhaps more balanced approach to environmental questions. After imprisonment ALN campus organizer Adriano Diogo became involved with Catholic grass roots groups. As Councilwoman Luiza Erundina's aide in the early 1980s he took part in contentious squatting actions with the urban homeless. By the time he became Secretary of the Environment for the city of São Paulo in 2003 and 2004, Diogo had moderated considerably, working with large private corporations to bring in funding for city projects. Under Lula former ALN guerrilla and exile Enzo Luís Nico Júnior earned the praise of businessmen for rooting out corruption while serving as the director of the National Department of Mineral Production office in the state of São Paulo.

Amparo Araújo lost a brother and two husbands to the military repression and took part in the condemnation of an alleged traitor, who was executed. Throughout the 1970s she remained in the underground. In the 1980s she founded the Tortura Nunca Mais (Torture Never Again) movement in the state of Pernambuco. It is the largest, most institutionalized of the Tortura Nunca Mais sections in Brazil, with numerous programs, a substantial budget, and funding from overseas. Amparo held positions in the Pernambuco government and was recently appointed as the police ombudsman in the capital, Recife. Jessie Jane Vieira de Souza spent a decade in jail for an attempted hijacking that resulted in the death of an ALN comrade. After her release Jessie worked with CEBS. She obtained a PhD in history, ran the archives of the state of Rio de Janeiro, and is today a professor at the Federal University of Rio de Janeiro. Manoel Cyrillo de Oliveira Netto, who wounded Ambassador Elbrick during the 1969 kidnapping, became a highly successful public relations specialist and under Lula landed a good job in a semi-public company. Upon his release from prison in 1973 Márcio Lacerda resumed a career in telecommunications and started his own firm. He worked with military officers trained in engineering or telecommunications and sharing his nationalistic vision of economic development. Lacerda experienced internal conflict between revolutionary ideals and the demands of business. His success made him a multimillionaire, and in 2003 he joined the Lula administration as the second-in-command at the Ministry of the Interior.

Some former militants outright shifted their ideals. After living in exile, Ricardo Apgaua became a real estate agent and embraced Cardoso's neoliberalism. Aloysio Nunes Ferreira, who helped Marighella stage a major train robbery, served in two cabinet jobs in the Cardoso government. Itoby Alves Corrêa, the ALN's main Cuban connection, worked as a cultural affairs officer in the administration of a right-wing mayor who had staunchly supported the military regime.

The former militants' party membership confirmed mainstreaming. Of the 22 interviewees, 11 are affiliated with the PT or in some manner have supported it consistently or voted for PT candidates, three have ties to Cardoso's PSDB, two have important standing in the Brazilian Socialist Party, which often allies with the PT but maintains its independence. The remaining six can be classified as independent leftists. Four of these are harshly critical of Brazil's political system and its parties. Of the 22, four can also be described as continuing with revolutionary ideas or desiring some form of revolutionary change. The sample illustrates the importance of ex-ALN members in the PT and the PT's leadership of the Brazilian left. But it also underscores the heterogeneity of former ALN members' political paths and a willingness to seek political alternatives outside the left. Many interviewees, even those strongly associated with the PT, are critical of that party. Taken as a whole, the sample reflects the convergence of political ideology in Brazil since the return to civilian rule in 1985 (Power 2008). Isolation from the system and politics, for whatever reason, has produced skepticism. But militants who participated in the system gained a greater appreciation for democracy and more easily left behind revolutionary dogmas. The system's investment in these people paid off. Had the military barred them from politics, they might have continued to work for destabilization of the system.

Conclusion

The case of Brazil's revolutionaries suggests a holistic approach for understanding constructive transformations. Such an approach accounts for the many variables involved in peacebuilding, including historical, religious, and cultural factors.

The Brazilian case cautions against examining only traditional, highly violent kinds of conflict and ignoring the long-term effects of other kinds of violence. Brazil did not have a large-scale civil war or ethnic conflict or formal peace negotiations, but a long dictatorship and long transition to democracy involving a dialectical relationship between the regime and the opposition. It was strictly a domestic phenomenon. Geisel began the *abertura* by bringing the security forces firmly under military control but did not create any public accountability. Torturers avoided punishment and became ensconced in the police and military bureaucracy, and the police remained immune from reform. Brazilians, especially the poor masses, today face an immense problem of public insecurity and police corruption and abuse. Their plight is often comparable to that of people in war-torn countries. Drug traffickers and organized criminals wield political power in local communities and intimidate the general populace and even the state. In her chapter in this volume Atashi has similarly observed how political violence ceased in South Africa while other violence increased. The Brazilian "street" is still awaiting effective action from the governing authorities. While on the surface Brazil's low levels of traditional political violence and the assimilation of former guerrillas might be interpreted as a success story, the long-term social benefits of the process for the average citizen are murky.

One major benefit, however, was clear: Brazil achieved political stability thanks in part to its mainstreaming of the armed opposition. The military seized power hoping to purge the system of communists and other leftists. Not only did it not achieve this: it reopened politics to everybody on the left. In return it received immunity for abuses committed. In contrast with other post-conflict situations, Brazil's tradition of forgetting the past blocked the establishment of a truth commission and the prosecution of dictators and torturers.

Military defeat led members of the ALN and Brazil's numerous other guerrilla organizations to seek alternative, non-violent forms of political action. The rise of liberationist Catholicism and the "power to the people" movement afforded revolutionaries new ways of seeking social justice and influencing society. No longer able to dream of a mass revolutionary move- ment, they worked in political parties, governmental institutions, human rights organizations, universities, think tanks, labor unions, environmental movements, schools, non-governmental organizations, religious move- ments, and an array of other initiatives that aimed to improve Brazilian society. In the process they remade themselves as both individuals and col- lective actors. The revolutionaries moved toward the center and, in the process, learned to deemphasize ideological purity and confront daily struggles in a pluralistic world where capitalism, at least for the time being, was the dominant system.

Of paramount importance for mainstreaming was Brazil's brief though highly significant pre-conflict experience with a vigorous procedural democracy. The regime and many of the revolutionaries embraced author- itarianism. But the regime maintained some democratic institutions, including regular elections for all offices except the presidency. Elections legitimized the regime and were manipulated by it, but they also allowed the voters and the opposition to express disagreement. Brazilians lived through the dictatorship hoping for a return to democracy. Even the dic- tators stated that such was their aim. Some revolutionaries believed that they had won the larger political battle against the military by fostering the return to democracy (interview with Aloysio Nunes Ferreira 20 July 2003). Less optimistic revolutionaries believed that the military won because it imposed the conditions of the transition and thus blocked social transfor- mation (interviews with Manoel Cyrillo de Oliveira Netto in 2006 and 2007; and with Guiomar Silva Lopes in 2006). Regardless, by the late 2000s Brazil had arguably the strongest democracy in Latin America. The Brazil- ian case suggests that analysts might gauge prospects for peacemaking by examining a society's preexisting level of democratic culture. A high level would provide motivation to seek peace and democracy, whereas a low level would indicate a rockier path to peace and political stability. The rev- olutionary left at first eschewed elections, but as the *abertura* proceeded, militants joined in and sought to influence the system and gain power. The PT and allied parties such as the PC do B, which had absorbed many of the former guerrillas, gradually became a recognizable part of the political landscape to the point where Lula ran a close second in 1989, became a fixture of the 1990s, and rose to the status of highly popular – and centrist – president of a capitalist giant in the 2000s.

The challenge for Brazil's former revolutionaries – and all of Brazilian society – continued to be the need to reduce the vast social inequalities that breed violence and could lead to larger conflicts in the future.

Note

1 Support for this research came from the National Endowment for the Humanities Summer Stipends, the Fulbright-Hays Faculty Research Abroad program, the American Council of Learned Societies, and the University of San Diego.
2 The author wishes to thank the following individuals for their comments on oral presentations and previous versions of this chapter: Bruce Dayton, Louis Kriesberg, Marcelo Ridenti, and the faculty and student participants at a seminar at the Latin American Centre at Oxford University on 20 November 2007 and at the Seminário Internacional "1968 – 40 Anos Depois: História e Memória," Universidade Federal do Rio de Janeiro, Rio de Janeiro, Brazil, May 6–9, 2008. Any shortcomings are exclusively the author's responsibility.

References

Alves, M. H. M. (1984) *Estado e Oposição no Brasil (1964–1984)*, Petrópolis, Rio de Janeiro, Vozes.

Amaral, A. D., Kingstone, P. and Krieckhaus, J. (2008) The Limits of Economic Reform in Brazil. In Kingstone, P. and Power, T. J. (eds.) *Democratic Brazil Revisited*, Pittsburgh, University of Pittsburgh Press.

D'Araujo, M. C. (2007) *Governo Lula: Contornos Sociais e Políticos da Elite do Poder*, Rio de Janeiro, Centro de Pesquisa e Documentação de História Contemporânea do Brasil/Fundação Getúlio Vargas.

Feld, C. (2002) *Del Estrado a la Pantalla: Las Imágenes del Juicio a los ex Comandantes en Argentina*, Madrid and New York, Siglo Veitiuno de España Editores and Social Science Research Council.

Gabeira, F. (1996) *O que é isso, Companheiro?*, São Paulo, Companhia das Letras.

Gaspari, E. (2002) *As Ilusões Armadas: A Ditadura Envergonada*, São Paulo, Companhia das Letras.

Gaspari, E. (2007) Bolsa Ditadura. *Folha de S. Paulo*.

Hunter, W. (2008) The "Partido dos Trabalhadores": Still a Left Party?, in Kingstone, P. and Power, T. J. (eds.) *Democratic Brazil Revisited*, Pittsburgh, University of Pittsburgh Press.

Jelin, E. (2002) *Los Trabajos de la Memoria*, Madrid and New York, Siglo Veitiuno de España Editores and Social Science Research Council.

Leitão, M. (2008) Conluio do Silêncio, *O Globo*, Rio de Janeiro.

Leite, P. M. (1997) O que foi Aquilo, Companheiro, in Reis Filho, D. A. and

Ridenti, M. (eds.) *Versões e Ficções: O Seqüestro da História*, São Paulo, Editora Fundação Perseu Abramo.

Magnoli, D. and Piovesan, F. (2008) A Exeção Brasileira, *O Estado de S. Paulo*, São Paulo.

Mezarobba, G. (2003) Um Acerto de Contas com o Futuro: A Anistia e suas Conseqüências – um Estudo do Caso Brasileiro, *Departamento de História*, São Paulo, Universidade de São Paulo.

Power, T. J. (2008) Centering Democracy? Ideological Cleavages and Convergence in the Brazilian Political Class, in Kingstone, P. and Power, T. J. (eds.) *Democratic Brazil*, Pittsburgh, University of Pittsburgh Press.

Reis Filho, D. A. (1997) Um Passado Imprevisível: A Construção da Memória da Esquerda nos Anos 60, in Reis Filho, D. A. and Ridenti, M. (eds.) *Versões e Ficções: O Seqüestro da História*, São Paulo, Editora Fundação Perseu Abramo.

Ridenti, M. (2007) Esquerdas Armadas Urbanas, 1964–1974, in Ridenti, M. and Reis, D. A. (eds.) *História do Marxismo no Brasil: Partidos e Movimentos após os Anos 1960*, Campinas, São Paulo, Editora da Unicamp.

Secretaria Especial dos Direitos Humanos da Presidência da República (2007). *Direito à Memória e à Verdade: Comissão Especial sobre Mortos e Desaparecidos Políticos*, Brasília, Secretaria Especial dos Direitos Humanos da Presidência da República.

Segatto, J. A. and Santos, R. (2007) A Valorização da Política na Trajetória Pecebista: Dos Anos 1950 a 1991, in Ridenti, M. and Reis, D. A. (eds.) *História do Marxismo no Brasil: Partidos e Movimentos após 1960*, Campinas, São Paulo, Editora da Unicamp.

Serbin, K. P. (2006) Memory and Method in the Emerging Historiography of Latin America's Authoritarian Era, *Latin American Politics and Society*, 48, 185–198.

Vannuchi, P. (2001) Democracia, Liberalismo, Socialismo e a Contribuição de Norberto Bobbio, Departamento de Ciência Política da Faculdade de Filosofia, Letras e Ciências Humanas, Universidade de São Paulo.

Veja (2007) Bolsa Terrorismo, *Veja*.

Wilde, A. (1999) Irruptions of Memory: Expressive Politics in Chile's Transition to Democracy, *Journal of Latin American Studies*, 31, 473–500.

15 Factors helping to overcome the use of violence for political purposes in the Basque Country

Juan Gutierrez

This chapter begins with a brief presentation of the human geography of the Basque Country. The Basque Country, or Euskadi, straddles the western Pyrenees and is situated on Europe's Atlantic shore along the Bay of Biscay. According to radical Basque nationalists, it includes lands along the French and Spanish slopes of the western Pyrenees and the eastern portion of the Bay of Biscay. According to the Spanish Constitution, only one-third of this area, its western region (Biskaia, Gipuzkoa and Araba) forms the "Autonomous Basque Community." Biskaia, Gipuzkoa and Araba have more than two million inhabitants. The south-eastern Basque area, the former Kingdom of Navarra with 610,000 inhabitants, is part of Spain. The north-eastern Basque area, with 260,000 inhabitants, is French territory. Everyone speaks Spanish in Biskaia, Gipuzkoa, Araba and Navarra. A large minority also speak the Basque language, Euskera, a non Indo–European tongue that is grammatically different from all other known languages.

Violence as "the Basque exception" in the Spanish context

From 1936 until 1939, the whole of Spain was deeply affected by a cruel civil war that was provoked by a military uprising against a democratically elected republican government. According to conservative estimates, the Spanish Civil War caused more than 500,000 deaths and forced more than 200,000 people into exile. Thanks in part to his close alliance with Hitler and Mussolini, General Francisco Franco was victorious and imposed a fascist regime that lasted for more than 40 years. Franco's dictatorship exerted pervasive terror in the war's aftermath, holding 280,000 prisoners and executing more than 50,000 – and possibly more than 100,000 people.

The defeated forces that sided with the republic were made illegal but continued their resistance as an underground movement. In the early 1960s, this resistance grew and became a democratic movement, which gradually developed into a mainstream movement throughout Spain. In the early 1970s, the resistance movement destabilized Franco's totalitarian regime and acted as the main force for its removal and eventual replacement by a democratic system of government. With few exceptions, the resistance practiced non-violence as it confronted the ideological, structural and direct violence of the totalitarian regime.

The Basque Country, however, is an exception to this general record of non-violent resistance in Spain. Historically, violence within the Basque Country has taken many forms; it has occurred in different places and at different levels and has been exerted by different institutions and persons. From the 1960s onwards, the violence that affected the Basque Country, the rest of Spain and, to a lesser extent, France, has revolved around the extreme Basque nationalist movement known as Euskadi 'ta Askatasuna (ETA) or Basque Homeland and Liberty. ETA has split into related groups: ETA-Militar, ETA-Politico-Militar and other autonomous groups. The movement as a whole has continued to carry out violence, ranging from low-intensity organized street fighting, carried out by groups of young ETA supporters, to kidnappings, assassinations and bombings. Violence has also been perpetrated by anti-ETA terrorist groups, sometimes sponsored by Spanish security forces and the Spanish government.

The Basque nationalist conflict has been waged violently, while anti-Franco resistance in other areas of Spain was largely non-violent. Differences between the structural and direct violence that oppressed the Basque Country, as compared to the rest of Spain, are not deep enough to explain this difference. Indeed, wealth and prosperity in the Basque Country is high and inequality low in comparison with the rest of Spain. Equally interesting, the Basque "exception" takes place in an area that has achieved advanced self-rule within the Spanish state. This makes it difficult to argue that terrorist violence is caused by the structural – and even the direct – political violence exerted by the Spanish state. Nevertheless, ETA continues to act through deadly violence. Practically all policymakers and public officials and figures in Spain – with the exception of Basque nationalists – feel forced to surround themselves by bodyguards as they move around the country.

Up to the present, no single factor or set of factors – economic, political or social – has dissuaded ETA's members from further acts of violence. Nevertheless, the scourge of deadly violence has currently diminished and the long-term process of overcoming it is well advanced and possibly even close to a successful end. On the other hand, Spanish society continues to be torn by a virulent controversy among public opinion leaders, politicians and researchers about what strategies will be most decisive in resolving the conflict.

Under these circumstances, it would be unrealistic to pretend that "scientific" evidence could prove what factors would guarantee the overcoming of violence in the Basque Conflict. What can be done is to take stock of the present stage in this process of overcoming violence, by taking these steps:

- Survey the historical transformation process of the Basque Conflict since the first appearance of insurgent violence 40 years ago until today, assessing the escalating/de-escalating effects caused by the conjunction of operating, structural and cultural factors that led to its emergence and development.
- Focus on terrorist violence, not just as the isolated actions of individual persons, but as particular acts in a collective strategy of a group of persons connected to a constituency, influenced by it and acting in its name.
- Identify two cultural and ideological factors – Spanish "crusader" nationalism and ETA's view of the Basque "historical identity" – both of which are mythical and fundamentalist in nature and assess their influence on the use of coercive action as a means of "solving" the conflict.
- Propose a succession of dialogue, negotiation/mediation and prosecution/punishment steps which, after a critical evaluation, reasonably permit one to expect they would contribute decisively to overcoming armed violence.

Origin and initial context for ETA's violence

ETA was founded in 1959 and held its first assembly in 1962, when it decided to use violence in the nationalist struggle for the liberation of the Basque Country from Spanish rule. ETA wanted to integrate Navarra within Euskadi's boundaries, establish a socialist regime and recover the Basque identity from the military occupation by the Spanish State. Just nine years after its foundation, ETA executed its first deadly blow in the summer of 1968.

At that time, most of the Spanish and Basque people opposed Franco's regime and participated in a vigorous movement to bring about its overthrow and to establish a democratic system Although the mainstream of this movement rejected the use of violence, a great majority not only in the region but also in Spain regarded ETA's violence as a gallant response of freedom fighters to the dreadful and systematic violence of General Francisco Franco. The Catholic Church in Spain, which had sided with Franco during the civil war, had justified the systematic violence exercised by the dictatorship. By the late 1950s, however, it allowed some of its members join the democratic movement, with some serving as "worker priests." The Church's Basque parishes even offered ETA assemblies a protected space to operate within a number of churches, abbeys or monasteries.

In the early 1960s, many in the region and everywhere in Spain as a whole considered the use of violence by insurgents to be morally justified, courageous, and an efficient and unavoidable way to overthrow colonial rule in occupied countries. In the Basque Country at that time, most intellectuals and seminarians were tempted to join ETA. The great majority of Basque people celebrated ETA's activities. Although some people expressed mixed feelings, Spanish society also generally accepted ETA and rejected the treatment its members suffered through military courts, within police stations and prisons. In December 1970, when six ETA members were condemned to death by a military court in Burgos, a widespread protest throughout the country involving the Catholic Church, artists, factory workers and members of the universities successfully pressed for an amnesty. This was an important victory that established ETA as a moral authority for the democratic movement.

By the late 1960s and early 1970s, the increasing vulnerability of Franco's regime and its lack of any capacity to respond to the emerging democratic movement were obvious. In 1964 the *comisiones obreras* were established, constituting a new form of union within the workers movement. Nationalist forces were increasing their opposition to Franco's regime, students and intellectuals were increasing their resistance, and more and more Catholic forces were supporting the democratic opposition. The works and ideas of Marx, Sartre, Franz Fanon, Che Guevara and Mao exerted a dominant influence in the democratic movement, causing it to shift toward a more revolutionary attitude. ETA's attacks, such as the shooting in August 1968 of Melitón Manzanas, a police officer and notorious torturer who was serving in the police station in San Sebastián, and the December 1973 killing of Franco's Prime Minister Carrero Blanco, were celebrated everywhere in Spain and interpreted as major contributions to the democratic movement. In this sense, ETA had a number of reasons for seeing its armed action as legitimate, courageous, and effective.

During this period, both the victims among those defeated in the civil war, as well as the victims of ETA's violence, were ignored everywhere in Spain. In Basque society, ETA's victims were even regarded with suspicion. The bereaved families found themselves isolated from their neighborhoods. There was no space in the Basque Country for ETA victims to mourn, to express grief or anger or to demand any form of restitution for their loses. From 1968 until 1978, such victims were as silent and invisible as were the Basque and Spanish victims of Franco. Consequently, ETA viewed its victims as politically inconsequential.

The ideology behind the ETA

From its very beginning, ETA followed the beliefs of Sabino Arana, the founder of Basque Nationalism and of its first political party PNV (Basque Nationalist Party). Foremost among these was the belief that the Spaniards and the Basques exclude each other by virtue of their antagonistic relationship (Conversi 1997: 53–54). Arana's beliefs also espoused that while Basques are handsome, pure, truthful, hard-working, clean, religious, honest and clever, Spaniards are ugly, mischievous, lying, dirty, frivolous, and lazy. In the past and even in prehistory, the Basques formed a nation with its own language, customs and culture, which successfully fought and defeated all invaders. During the eighteenth century, the Basques had accepted a "tit for tat" deal with the King of Castille, swearing loyalty to the monarch who, in turn, swore to respect traditional Basque self-rule. During the nineteenth century, however, the Spanish crown, on a step-by-step basis, deprived the Basques of their self-rule. After 1870, waves of immigrant workers came to the Basque region from other parts of Spain, thus eroding its language and identity and exacerbating this political loss.

This underlying ideology – obviously an "inflammatory invocation of memory" in Vivian's terms (this volume, Chapter 6) – was based to great extent on mythical assumptions. For centuries, the Basques *had*, in fact, considered themselves Spaniards and perceived no antagonism between Spain and their own country. The Castilian crown ruled the Basque Country, including Navarra. The historical record suggests that around 1530 the Castilian crown declared that all Basques belonged to a "universal nobility." This declaration was made because of their contribution to the fight against the Muslim regime ruling in southern Spain (known historically as *La Reconquista*) and because of the perception that Basque blood was "uncontaminated" by Jewish or Moorish blood. From that time to around 1870, the Basques held themselves to be "the best" Spaniards. This feeling was reinforced by the fact that while in other Spanish regions many people were still illiterate, Basques were largely a literate people and, therefore, could occupy key posts in the Spanish state and have great influence throughout the Spanish empire. Hence, many secretaries to the kings in Madrid and not a few Spanish *conquistadores* in Latin America were Basque (Baroja 1984: 26–31; Aranzadi 2005: 155–158). For centuries, most Spaniards shared the feeling that Basques were "good Spaniards This friendly, person-to-person relationship between Basque and non-Basque Spaniards still marks daily life in Spain. Indeed, people who regard themselves as "Basques" frequently intermarry with persons who identify themselves as "Spaniards."

However, as noted above, during the second half of the nineteenth century, many immigrants came from other Spanish regions to the Basque Country to escape life in poverty. Often they accepted work under extreme conditions in the flourishing iron mines and industries around Bilbao. As this happened, the descendents of old and established Basque families – including peasants, middle and upper classes – saw themselves as confronted with another kind of Spaniard, speaking the Spanish language but being workers of humble condition, with different habits, traditions and ways of life. Many Basques perceived this as a threat to their identity and responded by joining PNV, embracing the Basque traditional identity based on the "ancient laws." This further shifted emphasis from Spanish to the Basque language which, paradoxically until that time, had been considered to be the "low" language of uneducated people. For many decades this shift was more symbolic than real, with Basque nationalists cherishing Euskera as "their own" language, but in reality merely mixing a few Euskera sentences in with their normal Spanish.

For centuries, the Basque Country and other Spanish regions lived with a loose dependence with the Spanish crown, which allowed much autonomy. In the nineteenth century this changed somewhat, as the expanding market economy opened new commercial routes though Europe. In northern and eastern Spain – and particularly in the Basque Country – this took the form of a conflict between the ancient regime, which existed prior to the French Revolution, and the new regime that followed it. The three so-called "Carlist Wars," which took place between 1836 and 1870, ended with both the defeat of the old feudal order and the partial abolition of the self-rule of the Basques. This remembrance fosters the view of the "repressive Spanish state" and confirmed Sabino Arana's thesis that everything Spanish was detrimental to the Basques.

Franco's troops had conquered and militarily occupied the Basque Country "in the name of Spain," abolishing all traces of autonomy, prohibiting the use of Euskera in public spaces, churches and in school, and forcing people to change their Basque family names into Spanish. Schools taught the imperial history of Spain exclusively. To a great extent, posts in the government, administration, police, the Church and politics were occupied by non Basque-speaking people coming from other Spanish regions. This consolidated a biased perception of the civil war as Spain's war against the Basque Country and of Franco's regime as representing "the Spanish State." Such attitudes still mould ETA's perceptions today. Accordingly, ideas of freedom through separation from the Spanish state are central to Basque radical ideology – and not by means of dialogue or negotiation, but by means of fighting. The goal is to build up a Basque-speaking society in an independent Basque state. Furthermore, embedded as it was in the revolutionary segment of the democratic movement, ETA defines this fight for independence additionally as struggle for a socialist and democratic state.

The democratic transition of the 1970s

By Franco's death in 1975, his regime had lost its legitimacy. It was rejected at home and abroad, and was rapidly losing its capacity to govern under the challenge of the democratic movement. Many social forces that had sided with Franco – big money, the Church hierarchy, and high-ranking military elites – were cautiously building alliances with the forces that had conducted the resistance for decades. This inevitably broadened the democratic front and counterbalanced its revolutionary tendency. On the one hand, a broad consensus existed about ending the fascist regime. On the other, a disagreement between alternative ways of overcoming Franco's rule; either (*a*) the demolition of the old regime and building up of a new democracy (*rotura democrática*); or (*b*) a transition from the old fascist to a new democratic regime (*transición democrática*). The democratic transition received strong social and institutional support and ultimately prevailed. It offered the country a peaceful transition process, integration into Western Europe, sharing its economic prosperity, and entry into the United Nations.

The democratic transition took place between October 1975 and December 1978. In October 1976, the old non-democratic parliament issued a "law for political reform" and in June 1977, elections took place for a two-chambered democratic parliament, which negotiated and passed a democratic constitution, later approved by a referendum. A statute of the constitution called "Estatuto de Gernika" was subsequently drafted to establish the Basque Country as an autonomous region within the Spanish state. After its approval by the Spanish parliament, it was also approved in a referendum held in October 1979.

However, the supporters of Basque nationalism only reluctantly accepted the democratic transition. The PNV decided to abstain from the original referendum that approved the Spanish Constitution, but asked for a "Yes" vote in the referendum about statutes that dealt with the Basque Country. The party has participated in all subsequent elections and for the last 27 years has placed one of its members as President of the Basque Country and – with few exceptions – has governed regionally by building coalitions with other forces in the country and each of its three provinces. It is generally acknowledged that these Basque governments, headed by the PNV, have greatly contributed to the welfare and self-rule the Basque Country is presently enjoying (Arregi 2000).

ETA's violence, however, did not recede during this period. From an average of eight killings per year between 1968 and 1978, the death toll rose from 65 in 1978, to 78 in 1979 and to 96 in 1980, its highest yearly number (See Aranzadi 2005)

The democratic opportunity revisited after 28 years

The post-Franco democratic system reframed the Basque region. According to the new constitution, the Basque Country would continue being part of Spain as an autonomous region with its own government with Basque as the second official language, after Spanish, which was declared compulsory. Political parties were granted the freedom to speak and organize, even those with the explicit aim of independence from Spain, as long as they acted according to constitutional laws. According to the "Estatuto de Gernika," a government would be elected in the Basque Country with important decision-making powers in the fields of health care, education, taxes, mass media, and promotion of the Basque language and culture; Navarra could join the Basque autonomous region should it decide to do so by a majority vote.

For over 28 years, the Basque conflict has been a "conflict resolution laboratory." Numerous conflict-solving procedures, measures, expertise and conflict resolution "tools" have been employed at all levels to try to resolve the continuing conflict. Political, legal, cultural, and social approaches have been tried alone or in combination. Some have proved to be highly effective and achieved important results. Thanks to these activities, ETA is much diminished today, rejected by a majority of Basque nationalists in the Basque Country, as well as throughout Spain as a whole and abroad. For these 28 years, people have hoped that the constitutional spaces opened for negotiation would eventually overcome the violence. This hope grew and, following four years without bloodshed, ETA declared a "permanent" ceasefire in May 2005. Then, tragically, on 30 December 2006, to everyone's consternation, ETA members placed a bomb in a parked car at Madrid airport, killing two foreign workers, and officially breaking the "permanent" ceasefire.

The tension between fighting and negotiating

Factors that hinder today's efforts to overcome the use of violence by insurgents can be compared to the factors that first promoted the use of violence 40 years ago. The flexibility the new Spanish Constitution opened for self-rule achieved an important result, as a strong minority in ETA was moved to accept the constitution as a framework for its struggle toward self-determination. With the help of some nationalist lawyers, this minority built a legal political party – Euskadiko Eskerra – and abandoned the armed struggle. The Spanish Minister of the Interior accepted negotiations with a leading member of the party and agreed to a gradual return to Spain and a degree of amnesty for all members of this ETA faction living abroad. This agreement affected more than 200 exiled or imprisoned former ETA members (Clark 1990). This process took place between 1981 and 1984, but it has remained an isolated achievement. Instead, coercive force has been the dominant feature, determining events time and again and hindering the introduction of any non-coercive dynamic. Step-by-step, coercive forces have closed or even eliminated almost all spaces needed to achieve a substantial breakthrough in peacemaking. They have become what Stephen Stedman (1997) has characterized as "total spoilers" and John Darby has labeled "zealots" (2001).

Furthermore, the "democratic" use of coercive countermeasures has become problematic; a strong civic rejection has taken place, not only in the Basque Country, but everywhere in Spain. In the Basque Country, the nationalist constituency reacts with street actions and protests each time the security forces are accused of mistreating or torturing ETA members. After 14 years in government in Madrid, the Spanish Socialist Workers Party (Partido Socialista Obrero Español – PSOE) lost the 1996 Spanish general elections. To a great extent, this loss was attributed to the Supreme

Court's finding that from 1983 to 1987 the Ministry of the Interior was closely connected to groups of "ETA hunters" and the "antiterrorist liberation group." Moreover, the "Guardia Civil" –the Spanish military and civilian police force – had targeted ETA members, killing 28 of them, mostly living in France. This "dirty war against terrorism" resulted in a political disaster and, not surprisingly, proved to be counterproductive for any solution of the conflict.

Other talks took place during this period. In 1987 a negotiation was conducted among Basque political forces not siding with ETA, including conservatives, socialists and Basque nationalists. They reached an historic agreement in January 1988 known as the Ajuria Enea Pact. According to this agreement, a terrorist group such as ETA would be totally excluded from any future negotiation process. However, if it declared "a firm willingness to abandon arms," it would be allowed to negotiate directly with the Spanish government on how it and its members would be treated in courts and prison. In parallel, it called for the establishment of a negotiating table with participation of all political forces represented in the Basque parliament, including those embracing ETA's political program and goals, to discuss and agree upon a political solution to the Basque conflict.

The Ajuria Enea Pact initially confronted ETA with a united front of relevant political forces, but not for long. Instead of opening a road for negotiation and agreement, this fragile unity broke. In February 1989, the PSOE government in Madrid unilaterally responded to a ceasefire by ETA and engaged in official talks with ETA in Algeria keeping PP and PNV on the sidelines.

One week after having reached an initial agreement about the political character of the dialogue, this process collapsed as the Basque nationalists of PNV and the conservatives of PP signaled to the chief Spanish negotiators they would not endorse this agreement reached at the negotiating table, thus forcing them to back away from the initial agreement and in turn provoking an ultimatum from ETA. A breakdown of the negotiations and the ceasefire followed (Egãna and Giacopuzzi 1992).

Since then, the Spanish government has tried negotiating with ETA time and again without success. Often a ceasefire is declared by ETA in order to facilitate the negotiation process. However, such ceasefires, without exception have collapsed, very early in a "pre-negotiation phase." I have firsthand experience with this. In the fall of 1993, John Paul Lederach, Christopher Mitchell and I engaged in one and a half months of intensive and informal, preparatory talks for a negotiating table in Paris which collapsed as soon as the question of if Basque self determination would be part of an agreement was raised (*El Mundo* 16 January 1994).

In 1998, five years later, ETA again held conversations with the three major Basque nationalist parties and Basque trade unions in an arrangement entitled the Pact of Lizarra. They even, apparently, reached a formal political agreement. One week after the pact's signing, ETA declared a "definitive truce." When it came to the actual implementation of the agreement, however, it became clear that the different parties had profoundly misunderstood each other.

The purpose of the agreement for ETA was to start a process of complete, step-by-step separation. The objective for the main-stream nationalist parties was to construct a unified social, trade-unionist and political majority to force negotiations for self-determination. After 14 months, ETA announced that it had been betrayed by the cowardly nationalist forces, declared the "unlimited" truce broken, and resumed its terrorist activity.

A more promising non-coercive initiative took place in 2006 once the PSOE had returned to political power in Madrid. In May 2005, the Spanish parliament allowed the government to hold talks with ETA, exclusively about ETA's disarmament and the treatment of ETA members in prison, not about "political issues." PP was the only political force opposing this; it accused the PSOE-majority government of yielding to terrorism and sacrificing the unity of the country, thus managing to mobilize people by the millions to march through the streets against anything that could be interpreted as "negotiation with terrorists."

In March 2006, ETA announced an unlimited ceasefire. The Spanish government responded to this by holding some talks while contacts were also made among the political parties in the Basque Country to discuss "political issues" at a second table. This process likewise dragged on slowly and seemed unable to achieve any progress. On 30 December 2006, after repeated warnings, ETA exploded a bomb in a car parked at the Madrid airport. This was a major terrorist strike, which was probably intended to avoid bloodshed while also demonstrating an undiminished capacity for violence in order to break the deadlock and restart the negotiation process. However, the blast had unexpected collateral effects, killing two foreign workers who were sleeping in the car park. Its results were devastating, breaking the negotiation process itself rather than the deadlock. For some time, ETA did not accept this and insisted that the talks had not been affected, but after five months, it announced the continuation of the armed struggle. However, quite apart from ETA's huge tactical error, it again seems clear that there were serious misunderstandings about this peace process, which jeopardized it from its beginning. The ETA conceived this initiative as a process that would allow the Basques to decide unilaterally about their key political issues, including independence. The Spanish government declared that the process would never trespass on constitutional boundaries, which explicitly guarantee Spain's continuing unity and excludes the Basques to any right to self-determination.

The "crusader" ideology

For centuries, Spaniards – with Basques among the political elite – were educated with a fundamentalist Christian "crusader" mentality. This partly involved perceiving any conflict as a battle between good and evil, where "the crusader" holds the cross to justify action and uses the sword to execute violence for the victory of "the good over the evil." This unhindered use of violence of the cross and the sword as means and method of solving conflicts seems to be confirmed by the official – if mythical – history of Spain, in which violence pays dividends. It was successful during La Reconquista and laid the foundations of the Spanish empire. It also paid during the conquest (*la conquista*) of America. Last, but not least, it paid during the Spanish Civil War, also declared by the Vatican under Pius XII to be "a crusade."

Although one has to be cautious, there is clear evidence that this "crusader mentality" was deeply anchored in the mentality of all Spaniards and is still pervasive. For instance, the leader of the PP, Jose Maria Aznar, is pressing the Vatican to canonize Queen Isabella, who established the Inquisition in Spain in 1478 and in 1492 expelled Jews and Muslims from the country, as a holy person.

For the last 30 years, this crusader ideology has been continuously eroded to the point where today its influence on daily life in Spain is largely gone. However, the escalation of terrorism internationally still prompts the "crusader" response in Spain. Spanish people in despair over what they perceive as ETA's fundamentalist stubbornness are apt to seize upon this Crusader mindset. This has also been reinforced by President George Bush's rhetoric in the immediate aftermath of the Al-Qaeda attacks in September 2001.

But the crusader ideology has led its Spanish followers into making devastating mistakes. For example, the official insistence that ETA was the perpetrator of the terrorist attack on the trains in Madrid in 2004, resulted in the PP's massive defeat in the general elections three days later. In fact, a sentence of the Spanish Supreme Court established that the bombings were directed by an Al-Qaeda inspired terrorist cell.

The process of erosion of the crusader ideology seems to be irreversible and can be fostered by education in tolerance, civility and conviviality among communities guided by sets of shared values. Tolerance for different attributes can be pursued as an antidote to fundamentalism, which can be the source of terrorism. Over time in both Spain and the Basque Country, this can lead to a widespread social consensus.

The changing influence of "victims"

The many victims of the violence throughout the conflict also contribute to the continued promotion of an exclusive strategy of coercive action.

Franco's dictatorship imposed a public cult that its followers were "the victims" in the civil war. Each town was forced to build a memorial for "the heroes and martyrs who gave their lives for Spain." Many churches preserved their names in the façade and their relatives became public persons following guidelines set by those in power. Today, the Catholic Church continues canonizing them by the thousands. Although ETA's victims were also listed as "fallen for Spain," they were actually ignored by the state institutions. For decades they were avoided and regarded with suspicion and mistrust by other Basques.

In the Franco era, human suffering on an individual level was utterly disregarded. As late as 1980, the first democratically elected Minister of the Interior, Martin Villa, went so far as to say on television: "Yesterday we won the match against ETA two to one. One member of the *guardia civil* has been killed, but we managed to kill two ETA terrorists" (recollection of author). Currently, such a cynical statement is unthinkable.

To a great extent, this transformation is due to the work of NGOs such as Gesto por la Paz. For more than ten years, members of this NGO have commemorated each death caused by violence committed by ETA or by Spanish security forces, police or anti ETA groups. They gather in silence for half an hour in central public spaces in nearly every town in the Basque Country the day after each incident. This continual, silent presence has gradually altered the public image of ETA from that of "freedom fighter" to the killers of innocent children who have been victims of bomb attacks.

A first step to overcome the isolation of ETA victims was the 1981 creation of the Association of Victims of Terrorism (AVT), which soon developed to a pressure group campaigning with more than one million collected signatures for new laws imposing harder sentences and longer imprisonments of ETA prisoners. This made AVT the rallying point for fundamentalist strategies of the war against terrorism. In 1997, Jaime Mayor Oreja, at that time Minister of the Interior in the Partido Popular government in Madrid, declared "victims are always right," demonstrating a lasting alliance between the PP and the Association. This alliance is backed by the Bishops Conference, which just before general elections in March 2008 asked people not to vote for any party that might negotiate with ETA.

Currently the support for fundamentalist strategies seems to be gradually shifting to more democratic alternatives. Only a small group of victims associations maintain hard-line attitudes, and AVT, the most important among them, has lost a number of its regional chapters (for example in Catalunya, Andalucia and Valencia). At the same time, new victims associations rejecting fundamentalist approaches have been created. The Asociacion 11-M Afectados de Terrorismo, in gathering together over 1,000 severely affected persons, became a major influence on public opinion, contrasting its concern for peace and democratic justice against the fundamentalist approaches used by ETA victims' groups. This shift in the victim's response to violence is accompanied and empowered by a widespread sympathy and compassion toward all victims of terrorist violence. This has even moved mainstream Basque nationalist forces to make public statements of regret for having turned their backs to them for a long time.

The issue of ETA prisoners

The victims of ETA are not the only ones influencing the Basque conflict. Apart from the state-sponsored terrorism mentioned earlier, a systematic dispersal of ETA prisoners has occurred since 1989, which contradicts Spanish laws and bylaws. Today, more than 450 ETA prisoners are held in more than 50 prisons all over Spain. Many are held between 500 and 1,000 km from their homes. This results in severe collateral punishment inflicted on family members and friends, who are forced to travel under severe conditions to visit the prisoners, often for less than an hour. Furthermore, France also holds about 160 ETA prisoners, dispersed in around 30 jails (see *Guardian Unlimited* 21 April 2001).

A substantial grass roots movement has arisen in the Basque Country for the reversal of this dispersal policy, demanding "Basque prisoners back to the Basque Country." There is little doubt that this reversal alone – by no means an amnesty – would greatly alleviate the suffering and anxiety among family members, calm the anger and feeling of repression among friends and generate hope of a near peace in the country. Moreover, this prelude to peace contributes to the restoration of respect for legality and would not imply the slightest political concession to ETA. It is difficult to understand why no Spanish government has responded to the various ceasefires from ETA with anything more than minor moves, utterly insufficient to reverse this dispersal policy. Such a move would have an immense effect on ETA's constituency, which is in favor of giving up its essential support for the use of violence.

A new approach: coercive force versus mutual understanding

After 28 years, it is clear that an exclusive strategy of coercion has prevailed in the Basque conflict, over a strategy of dialogue or negotiation. A broad social consensus has emerged in favor of fighting ETA and excluding any kind of dialogue or negotiation. This is largely because each negotiation process initiated in the past stagnated at its beginning, resulting in its own, somewhat harmful stalemate and collapse. As a consequence, coercive strategies have been adopted by previous promoters of dialogue.

This victory of the hardliner approach has, however, had a paradoxical effect. Its political promoter, PP, has not had electoral victories. It seems that ordinary citizens are willing to reject dialogue and negotiation only after it has been tried and proven unsuccessful.

The logic of fight, victory, capture and punishment, when conducted in accordance with the democratic system of law, has proved able to weaken and almost defeat ETA and is, therefore, accepted by all major political forces. Today, the struggle between them is over the way to avoid violence after the end of ETA. So far, the PP insists that after this end only coercive force should be employed, while PSOE and the Basque nationalist parties would seek to open a space for negotiation. In light of these changes, the end of ETA would open the way for its former followers and present constituency to look calmly for an agreement that would somehow safeguard the insurgents' dignity and consolidate their abandonment of arms. The Spanish civil society, finding itself free from armed confrontation, would most probably agree to reopen a space for negotiation among political forces. Without interference from terrorist attacks or threats, this could be a way for a deeper agreement that could resolve the conflict between Basque and Spanish identities, create a "sense of normalcy," and avoid the pitfalls of an "uneven peace" (see Atashi this volume, Chapter 4).

Steps to overcome violence in the Basque conflict

This analysis suggests that an exclusive strategy of coercion and counter-violence is unlikely to succeed, while an exclusive strategy of dialogue and negotiation is unlikely to be supported by all relevant parties in either Spain or the Basque Country and is, thus, also unlikely to succeed. What is needed is a combination of *both* strategies, whereby support for ETA's disappearance is tempered by recognition that the aspirations of Basque citizens concerning their identity as represented by their democratic parties must be taken seriously. A space for dialogue is needed in which mutually acceptable and durable solutions can be sought. The ideas suggested below try to outline such a "mixed" strategy. They include the following steps:

1   To fight against the violence of the armed insurgents with all instruments of a democratic state operating within its own system of law, as a measure that is necessary but not sufficient to overcome that violence.
2   To apply the penal law to *all* perpetrators of violence, but to modify punishment, especially in regard to prisoners and family members, to the extent permitted by the law.
3   To try to agree on a political framework, which cannot be vetoed by opposing political forces, as the first step for a negotiation process, in order to avoid false expectations about its foreseeable outcome.
4   To acknowledge and restore the previously denied dignity of all victims of political violence, to take into consideration their proposals for overcoming violence, and to refrain from selective and one-sided anger directed toward one group of perpetrators.
5   To question existing taboos and to demystify history as it is currently presented in the Basque and Spanish school systems, focusing more

on the commonalities and positive dynamics between the Basque and Spanish throughout history and deconstructing the official history of Spain as a crusader nation and founder of an empire.

6   To continue promoting peace education as means to encourage all people – including immigrants – to live together as co-citizens in diversity.

7   To encourage cultural support for a shift of Basque identity from one of fighters striving for separation from Spain to key contributors to its democratic transformation into a multi-cultural, federal state of equal nations, made up of equal citizens.

8   To protect the diminishing agreement spaces and to wait for the opportunity to enlarge them once the negotiation process reaches an agreement.

References

Aranzadi, J. (2005). Good-Bye ETA, San Sebastián, Hiria Liburuak.

Arregi, J. (2000). La Nación Vasca Posible, Barcelona, Critica.

Baroja, J. Caro (1984). El Laberinto Vasco, San Sebastián, Txertoa.

Clark, R.P. (1990). Negotiating with ETA, Reno, University of Nevada Press.

Conversi, D. (1997). The Basques, the Catalans and Spain, London, Hurst.

Darby, J. (2001). The Effects of Violence on Peace Processes, Washington, United States Institute of Peace Press.

Egaña, I. and Giacopuzzi, G. (1992). Los Días de Argel, Tafalla, Txalaparta.

El Mundo (1998). Una Asociación Vasca Intentó Mediar entre Interior y el Entorno de ETA, 16 January.

Guardian Unlimited (2001). Bloody Bequest: ETA: The New Generation, 21 April. Online, available at: www.guardian.co.uk

Mitchell, C.R. (1996). Evitando Daños: Reflexiones sobre la "Situación de Madurez" en un Conflicto, Guernica, Gernika Gogoratuz.

Stedman, S.J. (1997). Spoiler Problems in Peace Processes, in International Security 22 (2), Cambridge MA, Harvard University.

16 The Palestine Liberation Organization and the Oslo process
Incorporation without accommodation

Nigel Parsons

This chapter explores the Palestinian journey up to and through the Oslo process (1993–2000), wherein the state of Israel incorporated the Palestine Liberation Organization (PLO) into restructured governance arrangements for the indigenous population of the Occupied Palestinian Territories (OPT). The terms of the Oslo framework, and the course of diplomacy conducted within it, are said to have signally failed to accommodate the PLO's mandate. Institutional transformation has been sustained up to a point: the Palestinian Authority (PA) has remained technically, and at least in part physically, extant. Financial pledges following the 2007 Annapolis summit underlined international society's readiness to sustain the project. However, accelerated Zionist colonization greatly hampered economic, social and political development, contributing to a failure to develop adequate foundations for stable incorporation. Proximate events in 2000 brought to crisis the dislocation between political form and colonial reality. Driven by conviction and a need to restore political capital, the al-Aqsa intifada marked a return to the field by nationalists nominally subject to PLO leadership, most prominently the Fatah *tanzim*, alongside non-PLO Islamists. The electoral triumph of Hamas in January 2006, and the subsequent division of the OPT into the West Bank under Fatah and Gaza Strip under Hamas, are logical, if not inevitable, consequences of a failure to accommodate the minimal requirements of the PLO's secular-nationalist agenda.

The genesis of armed struggle

On 3 February 1969, Yasir Arafat became the third chairman of the PLO executive committee, the culmination of a short campaign by guerrilla groups to take over the organization. The PLO charter was amended to reflect an emphasis on armed struggle, the leitmotif of Palestinian agency for the next two decades. The socio-political landscape against which the guerrilla ascendancy unfolded would be forged of a refugee population born with the state of Israel. For Yezid Sayigh, armed struggle was not inevitable but contingent: first, on the failure of non-violent alternatives; second, on the availability of receptive constituents (both of which echo the LTTE experience addressed by Camilla Orjuela); and third, on the post-1967 Arab systemic crisis (Sayigh 2000: 219). In these circumstances Fatah came to lead the PLO, and the struggle with Israel began to assume the four generic criteria for sustained conflict put forward by Louis Kriesberg: collective identity, an articulated sense of grievance, an agenda for restitution, and hope in the outcome (Kriesberg 2007: 53–87).

British Mandate Palestine drew to a close on 14 May 1948. In light of colonial withdrawal, and informed by the principle of partition put forward in United Nations General Assembly (UNGA) Resolution 181, the Zionist leadership announced the independence of the Jewish state. Indigenous resistance drew support from Arab armies, but Zionist forces triumphed. Palestinian society endured *al-Nakba*, the catastrophe, transformed extensively into a refugee population. By 1950, the United Nations Relief and Works Agency for Palestine Refugees in the Near East (UNRWA) counted 914,221 persons registered for assistance. The first wave from late 1947 included urbanites with mobile capital. But by March 1948 the rural population was in flight, the majority peasants for whom loss of land meant destitution. They would form the bulk of the camp population in Gaza, the West Bank, Jordan, Syria and Lebanon, UNRWA's five areas of operation. In a nation-states system, they endured what Peter Nyers identifies as a "two-fold *lack* with respect to the privileged resolutions to questions of political identity (citizenship) and community (nation-state)" (Nyers 1999: 21). In radically altered environments, identities would evolve to redress that. Dispersed geographically but focused in camps, increasingly literate and ripe for mobilization, within a generation refugees would power the organized Palestinian resistance.

Failure to achieve statehood, coupled with structural inequalities in the Zionist new order, attest to the veracity of Nyers' observation that "the space of politics is not just *there* in some timeless fashion. Rather, political space is created and sustained by ongoing human activity, some of which is of a very violent character" (Nyers 1999: 9). Post-war to 1952, the Knesset passed a sequence of legislation determining the ethnocentric character of the state. In December 1948, Israel's Custodian of Absentee Property undertook the disposal of assets belonging to Palestinians, the remit extending to residents (Peretz 1958: 151–152). Such powers, deployed in conjunction with those of the Jewish Agency, were used to cope with massive immigration, encouraged from July 1950 by the Law of Return granting Jews worldwide the right to citizenship (Smith 2004: 219–222). The Palestinian remnant was subject to harsh restrictions on residence, property rights and movement until 1966.

For Palestinians inside and outside Israel, UNGA 194 of 11 December 1948 looked to provide redress, establishing what has since become known as the right of return. Israel rejected culpability, any possibility of substantial return, and in turn the concepts of Palestinian identity, self-determination and statehood. Resettlement in neighboring Arab countries, with some sort of compensation, was proffered instead. Palestinians for their part hoped for the dissolution of the Zionist state. But two decades would pass before they seriously took up the cudgels.

The PLO was established in 1964 by the League of Arab States on the initiative of Egyptian president Gamal Abdel Nasser. It was not intended as a vehicle for social mobilization, let alone militant armed struggle. The PLO developed a conventional military, the Palestine Liberation Army (PLA), but for the most part the organization was a tame, state-sponsored forum for venting frustration, in the words of Patrick Seale "a sort of corral in which Palestinians could charge about harmlessly letting off steam" (Seale 1988: 121). But outside this forum, two main strands of independent Palestinian activism were emerging. From southern Palestine to Gaza, via Cairo to the Gulf, Arafat and colleagues were coalescing into Fatah. From northern Palestine to Lebanon, Christian Palestinians George Habash and Wadi Haddad, with Arab and Muslim colleagues, were building the Arab Nationalists Movement (ANM). It would develop, bifurcate and present the principal leftwing opposition to Fatah within the PLO: the Popular Front for the Liberation of Palestine (PFLP), and Nayif Hawatma's Popular Democratic Front for the Liberation of Palestine (PDFLP, later the DFLP). Both strands were committed to armed struggle, but whereas Fatah held an essentially non-doctrinaire nationalism, the Left adopted Marxist–Leninist platforms and an avowed hostility to the socio-political status quo (Sayigh 1997: 71–80). Fatah launched its armed struggle on 31 December 1964 under the name of *al-Asifa* (the Storm); the operation was no great success, and the movement remained marginal, but 1 January 1965 would henceforth be commemorated as the birth of the Palestinian revolution.

Labeled in a moment of understatement *al-Naksa* (the setback), the 1967 war transformed the political field, discrediting Arab regimes and the associated PLO leadership. Incumbent PLO chairman Ahmad Shuqayri was removed in favor of pro-guerrilla caretaker Yahya Hammuda. Then in March 1968 came a battle of seismic political significance. A large Israel Defense Forces (IDF) column crossed to the East bank of the Jordan, heading for al-Karama; they met stiff resistance, and suffered significant casualties, mostly at the hands of well-equipped Jordanian troops. The guerrilla contribution, whilst brave, was marginal. But this was beside the point: the myth of al-Karama spread, not primarily due to guerrilla propaganda, but rather, "because it met critical human needs amongst the Palestinians" (Terrill 2001: 91). Karama restored self-respect and propelled guerrillas to the forefront of Arab popular consciousness. Recruits and patrons multiplied, and confident guerrillas entered the PLO at the fourth PNC in July 1968 (Terrill 2001: 102). By the close of the fifth PNC, Fatah constituted the major bloc and guerrillas of lower-middle class origin were advancing amidst an established bourgeoisie to lead a refugee people of peasant origin (Sayigh 1997: 220). PLO assets now included a bureaucracy, the PLA, guerrillas in the Popular Liberation Forces, diplomatic representation and finance (Sharabi 1970: 32–33).

Political violence proved central to a reworking of Palestinian identity. Experience of armed struggle, and an extending roll of martyrs, reinforced the trend: as Allen and Eade note, "once the mythologized constructions of ethnic identity are sealed in bloodshed, to all intents and purposes they become objective social phenomena" (Allen and Eade 2000: 493). The celebration of martyrdom echoes again the Tamil experience discussed in the chapter by Orjuela, the Hindu and Christian symbolism contrasting with Palestine's essentially Islamic vocabulary. The popularity of armed struggle drew too on global anti-colonialism and especially the local example of Algerian triumph over France. Independence in 1962 saw the Front de Libération Nationale (FLN) return Palestinian admiration with encouragement, training, political introductions and ideas (Sayigh 1997: 102). Decades later, serious Fatah cadres could still cite Frantz Fanon, the social psychologist with experience of Algeria, and advocate of the purgative, restorative power of anti-colonial violence (Fanon 2001: 74). Fanon points further to the emotional dimensions of armed struggle, alluded to by Jean Genet during his time with guerrillas in Jordan: "It wasn't impossible" wrote Genet, "that, deep down, every Palestinian blamed Palestine for lying down and submitting too easily to a strong and cunning enemy" (Genet 2003: 84). In this respect, it has been argued that shame in the face of "errors, failures, and rejection" may be experienced by nations in defeat (Scheff 1994: 39). Thomas J. Scheff's treatment of France between 1871 and 1918 and Germany between two world wars recalls the Palestinian condition: a people "humiliated and vengeful," endlessly "reminded of their shame" in confrontation with a "living wound" (Scheff 1994: 121). Equipped with armed struggle, Palestinians aspired to do better, and Karama seemed to expedite the Fanonesque transformation in practice. Fatah literature was emphatic: proactive political violence would remedy "the worst diseases of dependency, division, and defeatism … and restore our people's self-confidence and capabilities, and restore the world's confidence in us and respect for us" (Sayigh 2000: 219).

The change in spirit took institutional form through amendments to the PLO charter at the fourth PNC: of 33 articles, seven made some reference to "arms," "armed struggle," "armed Palestinian revolution" or "armed popular revolution" (Hartley 2006: 383–387). This resembles the Prachanda Path doctrine of Nepali Maoists, examined in the chapter by Thania Paffenholz. Political violence was now pivotal in the Palestinian idea of self, institutions and agenda. On Nyers' terms, this refugee people were asserting their political subjectivity, claiming an agency and identity that was more than "the negative, empty, temporary, and helpless counter-part to the positive, present, permanent, authoritative citizen" (Nyers 1999: 26). To recall Kriesberg, Palestinians informed by a cohering sense of identity and articulating a profound sense of grievance, set out to secure redress through armed struggle with considerable optimism (Kriesberg 2007: 86). In theory and practice, in Fanon and al-Karama, the prospect of individual and collective restoration through violence did seem momentarily axiomatic.

Political violence in the search for self-determination

But faith was quickly tested. Immediate post-occupation attempts to foment rebellion in the OPT failed. Moreover, under threat and affronted by spectacular hijackings unfolding in Jordanian territory, the Hashemite regime engaged in bloody repression of its own between September 1970 and July 1971. Short of a bridgehead in the West Bank or Gaza, PLO forces were now routed from their East Bank stronghold. The Palestinians, it was said, had "been "dangerous for a thousandth of a second" (Genet 2003: 275). But the mobile revolution adjusted and decamped to Lebanon where it established a second haven of sorts for the next decade. Like Jordan before it, Lebanon's combination of weak state apparatus and receptive constituency, much of it in camps, afforded institutional space and social depth. The 1969 Cairo Accords guaranteed PLO autonomy over camps and operational freedom. The camp-bound diaspora from Israel-proper, towns such as Lydda, Ramla and Haifa, reinforced attachment to maximal goals. However, the debacle in Jordan and the gravitational pull of the OPT pointed to a case for reappraisal. The limited goals of the 1973 Arab–Israeli war and pragmatic advice from the USSR further counseled diplomatic initiative. Fractious debate ensued.

Guerrilla takeover rendered the PLO a complex organization, an umbrella for competing factions with contrasting views, while ferment in the Arab-states system encouraged interference. Besides the nationalist mainstream and leftist opposition were other players tied closely to Arab regimes: al-Saiqa answered to the Syrian Bath Party, the Arab Liberation Front (ALF) to its erstwhile Iraqi counterpart. The PFLP-General Command (PFLP-GC), the Palestinian Popular Struggle Front (PPSF), and the Palestine Liberation Front (PLF) also jostled for elbow-room. Driven by ideology, self-interest and sponsorship, relations could be tense. Fatah resolved to drop terrorism as a tactic outside of Palestine as early as 1973. However, determination to keep all forces in orbit of a sole reference point reinforced an indulgence for militancy that did not always seem to accord with the organization's best interests. For Sayigh, "This seeming paradox was in fact a logical consequence of the premium placed by the international community on sovereignty, since it prompted the PLO to work ceaselessly to demonstrate its effective political control, at least, over its own population" (Sayigh 1997: xii). The cost of an extra-organizational schism outweighed the cost of external vilification.

The radical idea of resolution through an interim "national authority" was first aired by the PDFLP in 1972, with Fatah's discreet blessing. Israel behind its 1948 borders was said to constitute a colonial presence that would be difficult to overturn. But Israel in the OPT was an occupying presence that lacked either demographic heft or popular attachment to the land (Gresh 1988: 124). Institutional changes reinforced the trend: the OPT-based and communist-led Palestine National Front announced allegiance to the PLO in 1973 and secured incorporation at the executive committee level. PDFLP head Hawatma's defense of the national authority concept spoke directly of cohering national identity:

> Yes, we are Arabs; but we are, at the same time, Palestinians. Just as every Arab people has a full right to an independent national existence, so the Palestinian people too has a full right to an independent national existence.
>
> (Gresh 1988: 140)

The twelfth PNC in June 1974 then produced the ten-point "Phased Political Program," with wording sufficiently vague for internal consumption, potentially enticing for would-be interlocutors, and reflective of Soviet counsel toward specificity. Following Alain Gresh, the significance was threefold: a modest intermediate goal in the "national authority"; a territorial target in the OPT, and a particular state instead of Arab Nationalist romance. The consequences were quickly felt. In September 1974 the USSR invited the PLO to establish an official mission in Moscow. The following month the Arab Summit in Rabat accorded the PLO the status of "sole legitimate representative" of the Palestinian people. In November, Arafat was invited to address the UN General Assembly, during which he made use of the "freedom-fighter's gun" and "olive branch" motifs to denote the search for procedural means. UNGA Resolution 3236 granted the PLO observer status at sessions of the General Assembly. Stimulating a huge leap in legitimacy, resources and bureaucratic staff, the twelfth PNC constituted a watershed comparable to the fifth PNC five years earlier.

The debate over means and goals has parallels in the Brazilian case discussed by Ken Serbin. But whereas the PCB split, the PLO largely held together. Important factions opposed to the new direction, including the PFLP, established the Rejection Front and suspended participation at the executive committee level, but remained within the organization. The non-PLO Fatah-Revolutionary Council of Sabri al-Banna (Abu Nidal), and later Fatah Intifada of Said Musa Maragha, were essentially marginal. Nor did the initiative make much difference: it was sharply out of sync with OPT opinion, which applauded Arafat at the UN and voted for pro-PLO candidates in municipal elections (Gresh 1988: 186). Perhaps more importantly, PLO diplomacy gained no real traction on Israel. Indeed, the organization's legitimization only rendered it a greater threat. This peaked when Fatah expedited an almost year-long cross-factional ceasefire on Israel's northern border from July 1981. Brokered by the US, it was understood as a serious operational achievement, and consequently abhorred by Israel's right-wing Likud government. The Iraqi-sponsored Abu Nidal group broke the impasse with an attempted assassination of Israel's ambassador to London, and three days later on 6 July 1982 Israel launched Operation Peace for Galilee to demolish the PLO and facilitate imposition of the client Village Leagues on the OPT. The semantic reduction of PLO personnel to "terrorists" helped dehumanize the living and the dead.

Internationalization through the escalation phase had mixed results. The People's Republic of China helped equip the nascent guerrillas, but Soviet courtship tempered Chinese enthusiasm. Eastern bloc sponsorship sustained conventional armed forces but took a dim view of terrorism and drew the organization toward diplomacy. Caught up in Cold War calculations, US engagement proved elusive. In 1975, US secretary of state Henry Kissinger precluded the possibility of negotiation with the PLO until it accepted UNSC Resolutions 242 and 338 and Israel's right to exist. These conditions would later cohere and extend to a rejection of terrorism. The 1978 Camp David accords, which addressed both Israel–Egypt and Israel–Palestinian relations, conceived of no role for the PLO. The invasion of Lebanon, intended to preclude the need for Israeli engagement on any terms, might have been hoped to have a similar effect in Washington.

De-escalation: negotiation in Oslo, incorporation in the OPT

De-escalation unfolded unevenly. Evacuated from Beirut in 1982, Arafat was expelled from Lebanon a second time in late 1983, this time from Tripoli. En route to Yemen via the Suez Canal, the PLO chairman held an impromptu meeting with Hosni Mubarak, head of then pariah-state Egypt on account of the separate Camp David accords with Israel (Sayigh 1997: 573). It was a controversial initiative, more so in the context of the post-Beirut tumult gripping the organization; disillusioned, highly critical and encouraged by Syria, dissidents in Fatah and beyond contested Arafat's leadership. He prevailed, and tilted westwards via Egypt and Jordan in search of US engagement. The seventeenth PNC in 1984 convened in formerly hostile Amman, with a view to securing a joint PLO–Jordanian negotiating team; the agreement ran aground on familiar obstacles: acceptance of UNGA Resolution 242, official renunciation of terrorism and recognition of the state of Israel (Golan 1992: 34).

The manifest nationalism of the first intifada prompted Jordan to concede its claim on the West Bank in mid-1988. Resolutions of the nineteenth PNC in November then sought to fill the vacuum: an independent Palestinian state in the West Bank and Gaza was declared, with Jerusalem as its capital, consistent with UNGA Resolution 181. Denied a visa for the US, Arafat addressed a special meeting of the General Assembly in Geneva. He eventually foreswore recourse to political violence (specifically terrorism), and accepted, subject to PLO interpretation, UNSC Resolutions 242 and 338. The PLO charter was declared "*caduc*," and Israel implicitly acknowledged, meeting in principle Kriesberg's de-escalation provision for minimal mutual security or "safety from physical injury by the other side" (Kriesberg 2002: 552–553). Israel declined to officially reciprocate, but perceptions were shifting; hard-line defense minister Yitzhak Rabin was heard to opine: "As a soldier I feel that these people have fought with a courage that deserves respect. They deserve to have an entity. Not the PLO, not a state, but a separate entity" (Heikal 1996: 384). Interruption accompanied the first Gulf War, but conceptual foundations were laid. The defunct charter would be officially revised a decade later by the twenty-second PNC meeting in Gaza, rendering it fully consistent with the terms of the Oslo framework.

Narrower PLO decision-making helped expedite de-escalation in practice. For Fatah, upheaval in Lebanon and exile in far away Tunis, battlefield losses, assassinations and the passage of time thinned out the historic leadership to Arafat's advantage. In the PLO, Fatah itself became ever more central. The fallout from Beirut eroded Syrian influence to leave the once powerful al-Saiqa utterly marginalized. The decline and fall of the USSR then permanently undermined the Palestinian Left. The secret Oslo channel amplified the trend: the Declaration of Principles (DoP) was negotiated by a select band of senior Fatah members and loyalists close to Arafat: the deal concluded, the executive committee and central council, with pro-Syrian, leftist or independent representatives, engaged with a fait accompli (Parsons 2005: 125–130; Groth 1995). The trend continued in the fledgling PA: Arafat took to convening joint sessions of the executive committee and PA cabinet to constrain the latter as an independent body (Shu'aybi 2000: 95). In a moment of post-Cold War US hegemony, PLO interlocutors were primarily western: Israel, the US and the EU, plus Arab states in the same camp, especially Egypt and Saudi Arabia.

From a socio-structural perspective, transformation in the OPT counseled a swift return to Palestine: an educated, erudite and confident local leadership were proving increasingly visible. Glenn E. Robinson identified the long-term factors at work. Traditional landed families were being undermined by land confiscation for Israeli settlement, loss of peasant labor to the Israeli job market and separation from patrons in Jordan. New elements were on the ascent, thanks in part to increased tertiary education coupled with access for lower socio-economic groups such as refugees, often on PLO scholarships. They would help organize the secular-nationalist Unified National Leadership of the Uprising, coordinating the essentially non-military first intifada from late 1987 (Robinson 1997: 14–37, 97–99), and were much more familiar with the occupier, its methods and agenda. Like guerrillas or *fida'i* before them, OPT cadres underwent a transformation through violence, punishment and prison forging another particular identity. Julie Peteet captured the dynamics:

> The meaning of the beating is central to new conceptions of manhood and ultimately access to leadership positions ... it is constitutive of a resistant subjectivity that signals heroism, manhood, and access to leadership and authority. Practices that intimately situate Israelis and Palestinians are construed by Palestinians as transformative and agential.
>
> (Peteet 1994: 45)

Absent the official PLO, cadres such as these would inform the Palestinian delegation to post-Gulf War negotiations in Madrid and Washington. In Tunis, fears of an alternative leadership were compounded by an ascendant Hamas.

Concurrent with the PLO's domestic travails, regional and international standing had also reached a low-ebb in exclusion from Madrid and Washington. An ambivalent if misrepresented stance on the Iraqi invasion of Kuwait played well with domestic constituents but alienated Gulf patrons. The post-liberation destruction of the tax-paying Palestinian community in Kuwait added to financial turmoil, to the extent that salaries could not be paid to portions of the PLA (now the Palestinian National Liberation Army, PNLA). Policy revisions in Moscow eroded Soviet commitment, embodied in institutional relations: "perestroika reduced the involvement of the [Soviet Communist] party in foreign affairs, shifting treatment of the PLO from the sympathetic care of the International Department of the Central Committee to the more formal, business-like treatment of the Foreign Ministry" (Golan 1992: 39). Steadily warming relations with Israel saw Soviet–Israeli diplomatic relations resumed in full by October 1991. Rewarded for co-operation in the Gulf, the USSR secured full co-sponsor status at the Madrid conference, but by that point it constituted "a virtually neutral great power, acting in concert with the US and the Western democracies to achieve some stability in the region" (Golan 1992: 73). Then it collapsed.

Thus it was that the state of Israel chose a good moment to come to preliminary terms with Palestinian nationalism. In June 1992 the Labor Party edged electoral success. Responding to popular sentiment, party-leader Rabin undertook to negotiate the Palestine issue but revealed no intention of talking to the PLO. Indeed, to do so was illegal until a small faction under the dovish Yossi Beilin prompted repeal of legislation prohibiting private (but not official) contacts with the old enemy (Makovsky 1996: 19–20). Rabin was predisposed to consider dialogue on multiple grounds. First, the former chief-of-staff and long-standing defense minister feared deterioration in IDF combat efficacy, remarking in 1988: "You cannot saddle the IDF with a mission that is outside its proper function. The unrest in the areas reflects a problem that can only have a political solution" (Sucharov 2005: 125). Second, Labor's pragmatist carried none of the ideological baggage of Likud. Third, negotiations in Washington pointed up Tunis as the key to diplomatic movement. Fourth, as prospects for a deal with Syria receded, the attractions of a settlement with the Palestinians increased. Fifth, diplomatic progress would undoubtedly be welcome in Washington (Makovsky 1996: 114–116; 121). So it was that the secret Oslo channel (only one of many), introduced via Beilin and long-time Labor rival Shimon Peres, was deemed worthy of pursuit.

The adopted Norwegian initiative provided formal mediation, one of five intermediary functions delineated in this volume by Bruce Dayton, and aspired to a second; the transformation of Palestinian–Israeli relations through dialogue. Just as important, the Scandinavians could not claim any of the other three: they were in no position to stop the violence, or address structural issues such as occupation and colonization, and short of the constrained Temporary International Presence in Hebron, made no provision for post-DoP monitoring or implementation. The advantages bestowed on the state-party to the agreement were considerable, centering on asymmetrical recognition coupled with Israeli security. The PLO gained recognition as the legitimate representative of the Palestinian people, conditional on an end to armed resistance. Israel gained recognition as a state and retained an extensive role for its armed forces in the OPT.

With political violence now officially conceded, the PLO could be deployed to police the agreement. In Foucauldian terms, the arrangements would reduce "the return effects of punishment on the punishing authority" (Foucault 1991: 91). Collectively, the Oslo canon:

> Formed the framework for transition from PLO to PA, defined the essential characteristics of the PLO's national project, and allowed the diaspora-based elite to re-establish their authoritative leadership. In so doing, Oslo facilitated the transformation of the PLO's bureaucracy and armed forces into the civil and military institutions of autonomy, the subordination of indigenous forces to the returnee elite, and the establishment of a new governing coalition in Palestine.
>
> (Parsons 2005: 83)

The new institutional array opened multiple avenues for incorporation funded through the EU, the US, the International Monetary Fund and the World Bank. For Christopher Parker, the Oslo framework allowed the PLO to tap into the reorientation of "international patronage networks occurring in the post-cold war international environment generally" (Parker 1999: x). They did so in big way: $6 billion or so pumped into the OPT over a decade was reckoned to amount to "the highest sustained rate of per capita disbursement to any aid recipient anywhere since the Second World War" (Bruderlein 2005: 79). The immediate gains seemed impressive, but long-term viability, even with this level of financial support, required PA institutions to settle properly in Palestinian society.

Palestine's unstable transformation: incorporation without accommodation

Through the Oslo process the state of Israel incorporated the PLO into restructured governance arrangements for the OPT. But it did so through a formula that suspended engagement on key issues from the Palestinian nationalist agenda, principally sovereignty, borders, settlements, Jerusalem and refugees. Thereafter, through seven years of attritional negotiations and a crowning all-or-nothing summit at Camp David, the parties failed to reach agreement on final status arrangements capable of accommodating the organization's much-pared down mandate (Parsons 2005: 253–260). Moreover, the unfolding of Zionist colonization, intrinsically linked to restrictions on population movement, did much to undermine indigenous development indices that might otherwise have underpinned incorporation. The elite continued to enjoy some benefits, including salaries, sinecures and mobility. More broadly, economic development did occur, albeit unevenly. But the unmet demands of national accommodation, experienced in the context of accelerated colonization, dislocated senior echelons from organizational grass roots and constituencies. Popular alienation from the Oslo framework, the process, and the PA left the OPT prone to combustion. The provocative assertion of Israeli sovereignty over East Jerusalem by Likud politician Ariel Sharon in September 2000 provided a spark.

The dynamics of institutional incorporation are reflected in PA staff composition: the bulk of personnel were drawn from PLO returnees, administrators from the IDF's OPT bureaucracy (the Civil Administration), and technocrats from NGOs and the private sector. Cadres from Fatah's two senior echelons, the central committee (CC) and revolutionary council (RC), held command positions at sites of executive, bureaucratic, parastatal, coercive and legislative power. In the first decade or so of cabinets, CC members held as many as six and an average of four ministerial portfolios; inclusive of CC colleagues, RC members accounted for between six and 14 cabinet seats. Only pressure for reform and electoral defeat at the hands of Hamas reversed the trend. These cadres were similarly well-represented in the second and third tiers of bureaucracy as deputy and assistant deputy ministers. The fourth tier, director general, incorporated many local intifada leaders with prison records. Roughly one half of the OPT governorates were led by RC members. Parastatals ranging from the petroleum monopoly and Gaza airport to the Olympic committee offered further incorporation opportunities. In the security apparatus, all six main

branches were at one time or another commanded by RC members. Legislative Council elections in January 1996 returned an 88 member parliament, exemplary of the 1990s trend for post-conflict elections discussed in
the chapter by Terrence Lyons. Of 51 seats in the West Bank, the CC held
four, the RC a further 13; of 37 seats in Gaza, the CC held two, the RC a
further seven (Parsons 2005: 142–207). In total, official Fatah legislators
held 50 seats for 57 percent representation, of which 26 accrued to the RC
for 30 percent of the body. They were correspondingly influential in parliamentary committees. This legislative hegemony persisted until the post-
Arafat electoral earthquake that shook the PA a decade later. By then, in
common with the URNG in Guatemala examined here by Michael Allison,
a decade of plodding negotiation, separation from constituencies and
electoral fragmentation had helped undermine the movement.

Preceded by IDF redeployment from the major West Bank urban
centers, the 1996 elections lent Oslo a brief sense of momentum. The
result met the form, but not the substance, of Elham Atashi's condition of
a post-agreement platform for the articulation and realization of popular
expectations. In a culture shaped by resistance and unencumbered by a
proper state-apparatus for decades, aspirations were readily aired. But
incorporation on the terms of the Oslo framework did not provide for substantive Israeli–Palestinian power-sharing or the creation of an effectively
integrated socio-economic system. On the contrary, the PA was conceived
as an administrative means of separating Israelis from Palestinians, but
without empowering the latter. Limited scope for planning between non-
contiguous enclaves and a remit to police indigenous resistance left the
PA little more than a quasi-colonial modification of Israeli rule. The
opportunities for expediting an effective response to articulated demands
were few. Failure colored perceptions of Fatah, perceptions already
blurred by political and functional ambiguity: recalling Lyons, the movement set out to assemble the institutions of government but found itself in
limbo: between occupation and independence, semi-autonomy and statehood, resistance and party, security apparatus and militia. The dangers of
political transition pre-accommodation were understood by Fatah and are
illustrated here in Orjuela's account of the LTTE: state reprisal post-truce
would cost the lives of many newly visible cadres. Ambiguity was evident
again in demobilization: the PNLA morphed into the PA security apparatus, absorbed local activists and undertook to uphold the new order. But
hemorrhaging political capital and confronted with the state's colonial
agenda, cadres were drawn back to the field in numbers. Oslo imploded.
The psychological dimension considered by Avram Bornstein returns us to
shame: "While the level of violence by the PA against Palestinians is
dwarfed by the practices of the IDF, it is far more bitter because the experience is mixed with feelings of betrayal by their own people." The intifada
presented an opportunity to make amends: Fatah's real enough history of
leadership notwithstanding, Bornstein observed that "Fatah's decentral-

ized pursuit of the new uprising by their rank and file has grown from their fantasies of vanguardism and the attempt to repair and obfuscate their role as victimizers" (Bornstein 2001: 564–568).

Further insight into the social-psychological aspects of the uprising can be gleaned from Ted Gurr's concept of relative deprivation: socialized into awareness of their rights under international law and thwarted in their efforts to attain them, Palestinians confronted a profound "discrepancy between their value expectations and their environment's apparent value capabilities" (Gurr 1972: 37–38). Informed by a particularistic national identity forged through resistance and sacrifice, Palestinians retained both an infrastructure and outlook that permitted them to resume the fight, albeit on very asymmetrical terms. Bringing precision to the dynamics, Atashi's notion of "zones of incorporation" disaggregates post-agreement political geography into direct and indirect zones of conflict. Direct zones experience the full impact of conflict; indirect zones do not. But in peace, direct zones are typically bypassed by development, whereas indirect zones, enjoying the presence of political elites and international agencies, draw attention and investment. Subjective evaluations weigh heavily: is perceived suffering commensurate with perceived reward? In the small spaces of the OPT – universally but not uniformly impacted by occupation and colonization – calculations varied. Development gravitated toward Jerusalem, Ramallah and Nablus (World Bank 2001: 6), but poverty was always near at hand, emphasized by the wide distribution of refugee camps (19 in the West Bank and eight in Gaza). Locally, relative wealth in Jerusalem adjoined the Shufat refugee camp. In Ramallah, the Balu suburb accommodated the main Fatah offices, a growing number of villas, and new cars. It was not far from the camp at al-Amari. In Nablus, Rafidiyya stood in contrast to Balata, al-Askr, Camp no. 1, and nearby al-Fara. Even in Gaza, well-heeled Rimal adjoined the battered camp at Shati (not coincidentally home to Hamas PM Ismail Haniyya). Elites embedded in governing structures might manage qualified optimism, if only through cognitive dissonance. Suffering might just about seem commensurate with empirical circumstance, given the hoped-for political settlement. It echoes Lyons' observation that given the right sort of incentive, "actors may become trapped in a politics of moderation whereby [as] the attractiveness of maintaining peace rise[s], the rewards for returning to war shrink." This calculation did not apply to the bulk of villagers, the urban poor, camp residents and many former-prisoners: uneven incorporation delivered little material benefit, and negotiations pointed to precious little hope of political accommodation on the terms of the nationalist agenda.

The zones of incorporation concept might be usefully extended to include the entirety of former-mandate Palestine, with the OPT constituting a direct zone and Israel behind the Green Line an indirect zone. The contrast in empirical circumstance, conflict-specific suffering and perceived reward, suggests an explanation for popular Israeli surprise at the onset and ferocity of the second uprising. Physically and psychologically, mainstream Israeli society inhabited a very different space to ordinary Palestinians in the OPT.

Patterns in the violence illustrate the alienation, anti-colonial and Islamist character of the al-Aqsa intifada. Fatah grass roots in the form of the *tanzim* took a prominent role from the outset. Tensions and organizational space between senior returnees and local leaders meant that resistance was often sporadic and decentralized, but the fact of Fatah's involvement *in any capacity* highlighted the failings of incorporation and accommodation. The geography of the fighting explained the alienation. Clashes were focused at IDF checkpoints on junctions in the bypass-road network connecting the dynamic settlement enterprise. From 1996, Likud PM Netanyahu had been vocal in his support for colonization, but his actual building record varied little from Labor leaders Rabin, Peres and Barak. Palestinian military operations overwhelmingly targeted colonial structures in the OPT, exemplified by early exchanges around the settlements of Gilo and Har Homa neighboring Jerusalem and Bethlehem. The innovation of the al-Aqsa Martyrs' Brigades, and a subsequent resort to suicide bombing across the Green Line, were an internal response to the popularity of Hamas. The Israeli military response reflected dislocation within Fatah: CC and RC headquarters were untouched and members left almost entirely free; in contrast, *tanzim*-affiliated offices across town were gutted, the cadre base hunted down, killed or imprisoned. The destruction and immobility of the security apparatus only encouraged reliance on local militia such as the Popular Resistance Committees in southern Gaza. Collapse in the provision of public services widened the space for Islamist welfare, as well as opportunities for smuggling that would come to characterize Rafah.

Gaza under siege returns us to post-Annapolis diplomacy, third party mediation and aid. In Oslo's rough division of labor, the original breakthrough was brokered by Norway, the process managed by the US, incorporation funded extensively by the EU, and a modicum of aid, particularly starting with the second intifada, delivered by the League of Arab States. In combination, third parties combined to make a massive investment in Oslo's incorporation project. But to what end? The post-Oslo revival mechanism of the Roadmap offered little cause for celebration. It has been argued that given occupation, colonization and the paralysis of movement, aid may actually be counterproductive, the triage of humanitarian relief facilitating a cheap occupation that spares Israel the consequences of its actions; furthermore, around 40 percent of aid to the PA flows over the Green Line into the Israeli economy (Le More 2005: 27–29; Shearer and Meyer 2005: 175). Third parties have seemed willing to sustain a minimal form of incorporation, much less willing to press the state on the terms of accommodation. Palestine, like Sri Lanka, has been a chastening experience. Both cases recall Dayton's observation that: "There is nothing inherently positive about intermediary activity."

Conclusion

Coming to terms with *al-Nakba*, the diaspora-led armed struggle provided for the restoration of individual and collective Palestinian identities in conflict with Israel. Through time, refugees became subjects aspiring to citizenship in a nation-state order. Diplomatic gains to that end were resisted by the state party to effect conflict prolongation, until indigenous resistance to colonization prompted a search for alternatives that became manifest in electoral change. For the non-state party, institutional imperatives on multiple levels rendered key agents amenable to incorporation on the DoP's terms. Thereafter, third party financial support sustained institutional incorporation and construction of a ruling coalition in the territories. However, accelerated Zionist colonization undermined development indices and the basis for national incorporation. Refugee camps and other marginal areas gleaned little material benefit. Lack of accommodation on the right of return and other issues offered equally bleak prospects for psychological compensation. Institutional incorporation was a necessary but not sufficient condition for sustained conflict resolution. In light of the privileges afforded the most favored of all US-client states, the prospects for extending inclusion or reaching accommodation in Palestine seem remote. In a conflict more likely to be managed than solved, and with international collusion, the PA might continue to incorporate governing agents in the West Bank under Fatah. But Palestine's enduring lack of inclusive incorporation or national accommodation suggests that it could be resistance and siege and Gaza under Hamas that better speaks to the future.

References

Allen, T. and Eade, J. (2000) "The New Politics of Identity," in T. Allen and A. Thomas (eds.) *Poverty and Development into the 21st Century*, Oxford: Oxford University Press.

Bornstein, A. (2001) "Ethnography and the Politics of Palestinian Prisoners in Palestine–Israel," *Journal of Contemporary Ethnography* 30: 546–574.

Bruderlein, C. (2005) "Human Security Challenges in the Occupied Palestinian Territory," in M. Keating, A. Le More and R. Lowe (eds.) *Aid, Diplomacy and Facts on the Ground: The Case of Palestine*, London: Royal Institute of International Affairs (RIIA).

Fanon, F (2001) *The Wretched of the Earth*, London: Penguin.

Foucault, M. (1991) *Discipline and Punish: The Birth of the Prison*, trans. A. Sheridan, London: Penguin.

Genet, J. (2003) *Prisoner of Love*, New York: New York Review of Books.

Golan, G. (1992) *Moscow and the Middle East: New Thinking on Regional Conflict*, London: RIIA.

Gresh, A. (1988) *The PLO: The Struggle Within*, new edn., London and New Jersey: Zed.

Groth, A. (1995) *The PLO's Road to Peace: Processes of Decision-Making*, London: Royal United Services Institute for Defence Studies.

Gurr, T.R. (1972) "Psychological Factors in Civil Violence," in T.R. Gurr, I.K. Feieraband and R.L. Feieraband (eds.), *Anger, Violence and Politics: Theories and Research*, Englewood Cliffs, NJ: Prentice Hall.

Hartley, C. (ed.), (2006) *A Survey of Arab–Israeli Relations*, 3rd edn., London: Routledge.

Heikal, M. (1996) *Secret Channels: The Inside Story of Arab-Israeli Peace Negotiations*, London: HarperCollins.

Kriesberg, L. (2002) "The Relevance of Reconciliation Actions in the Breakdown of Israeli–Palestinian Negotiations, 2000," *Peace and Change* 27: 546–571.

—— (2007) *Constructive Conflicts: From Escalation to Resolution*, 3rd edn., Lanham, Maryland: Rowman & Littlefield.

Le More, A. (2005) "Are 'Realities on the Ground' Compatible with the International State-Building and Development Agenda?," in M. Keating, A. Le More and R. Lowe (eds.) *Aid, Diplomacy and Facts on the Ground: The Case of Palestine*, London: Royal Institute of International Affairs (RIIA).

Makovsky, D. (1996) *Making Peace with the PLO: The Rabin Government's Road to the Oslo Accord*, Boulder, CO: Westview Press.

Nyers, P. (1999) "Emergency or Emerging Identities? Refugees and Transformations in World Order," *Millennium: Journal of International Studies* 28: 1–26.

Parker, C. (1999) *Resignation or Revolt: Socio-Political Development and the Challenges of Peace in Palestine*, London: I.B. Tauris.

Parsons, N. (2005) *The Politics of the Palestinian Authority: From Oslo to al-Aqsa*, London and New York: Routledge.

Peretz, D. (1958) *Israel and the Palestine Arabs*, Washington, DC: The Middle East Institute.

Peteet, J. (1994) "Male Gender and Rituals of Resistance in the Palestinian Intifada: A Cultural Politics of Violence," *American Ethnologist* 21: 31–49.

Robinson, G.E. (1997) *Building a Palestinian State: The Incomplete Revolution*, Indiana: Indiana University Press.

Sayigh, Y. (1997) *Armed Struggle and the Search for State: The Palestinian National Movement 1949–1993*, Oxford: Oxford University Press.

—— (2000) "War as Leveler, War as Midwife: Palestinian Political Institutions, Nationalism and Society since 1948," in Steven Heydemann (ed.) *War, Institutions, and Social Change in the Middle East*, Berkley and Los Angeles: University of California Press.

Scheff, T.J. (1994) *Bloody Revenge: Emotions, Nationalism, and War*, Boulder, CO: Westview.

Seale, P. (1988) *Asad of Syria: The Struggle for the Middle East*, London: I.B. Tauris.

Sharabi, H. (1970) *Palestine Guerrillas: Their Credibility and Effectiveness*, Beirut: Institute for Palestine Studies, 32–33.

Shearer, D. and Meyer, A. (2005) "The Dilemma of Aid under Occupation," in M. Keating, A. Le More and R. Lowe (eds.) *Aid, Diplomacy and Facts on the Ground: The Case of Palestine*, London: Royal Institute of International Affairs (RIIA).

Shu'aybi, A. (2000) "A Window on the Workings of the PA: An inside View," IPS Forum, *Journal of Palestine Studies* 30: 88–97.

Smith, C.D. (2004) *Palestine and the Arab–Israeli Conflict*, 5th edn., Boston, MA: Bedford/St. Martin's.

Sucharov, M.M. (2005) *The International Self: Psychoanalysis and the Search for Israeli–Palestinian Peace*, New York: State University of New York Press.

Terrill, W.A. (2001) "The Political Mythology of the Battle of Karameh," *Middle East Journal* 55: 91–111.

World Bank (2001) *Poverty in the West Bank and Gaza*, World Bank. Online, available at: http://lnweb18.worldbank.org/mna/mena.nsf/Attachments/Poverty+Report+WBG/$File/poverty+report.pdf accessed 30 June 2008.

17 Domesticating Tigers

The LTTE and peacemaking in Sri Lanka

Camilla Orjuela

When the leader of the Liberation Tigers of Tamil Eelam (LTTE) met the world press in northern Sri Lanka in April 2002, the focus was not only on what he was saying, but also on what he was wearing. The visiting journalists noted that Vellupilai Prabhakaran had replaced his customary military outfit with a (some commentators thought) smart, gray safari suit. It was a time of peace hopes. The guerrilla leader had just signed a ceasefire agreement with the Prime Minister of Sri Lanka, the population experienced a welcome respite from war-time hardships, and the two principal warring parties were entering into a peace process which could potentially end their 20-year old civil war. Prabhakaran's choice of clothing was by optimistic analysts interpreted as an illustration of the willingness of the LTTE to transform from the highly efficient military organization they were and instead enter the political scene.

The man in the safari suit was hailed by his supporters as a freedom fighter that, with his military might, had stood up for the Tamil people against discrimination and repression by the Sri Lankan state and the Sinhalese ethnic majority. Others saw Prabhakaran as a ruthless terrorist who did not hesitate to sacrifice innocent lives in his unyielding pursuit of a separate Tamil state (Tamil Eelam). With its hallmark suicide bombings and dedicated young cadres dying to become martyrs for the Tamil cause, the LTTE was one of the world's most vigorous rebel groups, known to be "at the cutting edge of terrorist technology" (Gunaratna 2001: 13). Prabhakaran and his Tigers had killed an Indian Prime Minister, a Sri Lankan president, scores of soldiers from the Sri Lankan and Indian armies, Tamils that were seen as "traitors" to the Tamil cause, and numerous ordinary civilians. However, the Tigers were in no way the only ones with many lives on their conscience. The Sri Lankan government forces and state-supported paramilitary groups had killed not only Tiger rebels but also countless Tamil civilians in their quest to wipe out the insurgents.

During 20 years of warfare, however, the Sri Lankan government had not succeeded to subdue the Tamil separatists, nor had the Tigers won their separate state. The 2002 peace process brought, with Norwegian facilitation, the LTTE and the Sri Lankan government to the negotiation table. Most analysts agreed that any sustainable peace in Sri Lanka needed the blessings of the Tiger leader. The underlying assumption of those engaged in or supporting the peace process was that the LTTE would be willing to transform, and to swap weapons for political power.

Since Prabhakaran formed the Liberation Tigers in 1976, the organization had indeed gone through a process of transformation. In the 1970s it was merely a group of youth carrying out sporadic violent attacks to protest what they saw as the anti-Tamil politics of the Sri Lankan state. In the 1980s the LTTE had become a mushrooming guerrilla movement with Indian support, and in the 1990s it had gained control over and ran a virtual Tamil state covering a considerable area in northern Sri Lanka.

As the peace process took off in 2002, opinions in Sri Lanka were deeply divided about whether Prabhakaran would be willing to permanently get out of his military gear and accept a political solution. In retrospect, with the ceasefire agreement formally ended in 2008, the attempt at making peace and at "domesticating" the Tigers was a failure. Nevertheless, the window of opportunity for transformation which had opened up may teach us important lessons about military-to-political change and about the implications of failed attempts at "taming" rebel groups. The fact that this chapter focuses on the transformation of the LTTE may create a false impression that the LTTE is the only party to the armed conflict in Sri Lanka that needs to transform for peace to come true. This is certainly not the case. To fully understand peacemaking it is absolutely essential to also analyze the role of the Sri Lankan state, as well as that of international structures and actors. Nonetheless, since the transformation of the LTTE will be one of the key challenges for peacemaking, and since it is worth noting the steps taken by the rebel organization toward the political arena, a special focus on the LTTE is justified.

War can be described as the breakdown of "normal" politics. Ending wars hence entails a shift back from violence to non-violent politics, and a demilitarization of politics (see Lyons in this volume; Söderberg-Kovacs 2007). To understand what it takes for armed groups to demilitarize, we need to understand the structural and historical factors that led to the militarization of politics and the incentives that make rebels continue their armed struggle – or go for peace. The first part of this chapter analyses the breakdown of "normal" politics in Sri Lanka, the escalation and perpetuation of violence, and the attempt at peacemaking in 2002. The second part of the chapter looks more closely at the steps taken toward a transformation of the Tigers, and the obstacles encountered. The aspects discussed are: (*a*) the building of state structures; (*b*) LTTE's organization and internal dynamics; (*c*) LTTE's engagement in mainstream politics; (*d*) LTTE's popular support; and (*e*) the international legitimacy granted to the LTTE. Apart from secondary sources, the chapter draws on qualitative interviews and observations carried out in Sri Lanka, including in LTTE-controlled areas, in connection with different research projects during the period 1995–2007.

Militarization, perpetuation and de-escalation of conflict

Conflict roots and the militarization of politics

The seeds of the breakdown of "normal" politics in Sri Lanka were sown at the beginning of modern politics, during British colonial rule. Colonialism meant the suppression and marginalization of indigenous languages, religions and culture, the institutionalization of ethnic difference through censuses and in political structures, and the overrepresentation of Tamils in the administration and higher education. Sinhalese nationalist mobilization after independence was largely a reaction to this colonial heritage. The Sri Lankan state went through a process in which Sinhalese (being 74 percent of the population) consolidated their power over the state. The result was a "Sinhalesation" of the state, which was institutionalized through government policies such as those that made Sinhala the sole official language in 1956, restricted access to higher education for students from certain geographical areas, launched settlement programs for Sinhalese in traditional Tamil areas, and granted special privileges to Buddhism, the religion of the Sinhalese majority. The minorities' sense of being second-class citizens laid the ground for Tamil political mobilization.

It was soon apparent that efforts to advance Tamil rights within a political system where the Tamil political representatives were a small minority were futile. Tamil leaders signed pacts with the Sinhalese Prime Ministers in 1957 and 1965 on Tamil language rights and regional autonomy. However, both agreements were abandoned after protests led by the Sinhalese opposition. Outside the political system, Tamil politicians and civil society leaders organized non-violent protests. Many of these peaceful sit-ins, marches, demonstrations and strikes were met with violence. In 1961, for example, a civil disobedience campaign paralyzed the civil administration in north-eastern Sri Lanka for several months. The campaign ended when the Prime Minister ordered the police to use violence against the protesters (Swamy 1996: 16).

The inability of the Tamils to instigate change either from inside the parliament or through non-violent struggle prompted the shift toward violence. In the 1970s, a number of militant groups were formed, all in northern Sri Lanka. They were made up by Tamil youth frustrated with the difficulties to access university education and employment. For them, revolutionary politics seemed a desirable alternative to the inefficient conservative politics of Tamil upper-class, upper-caste politicians.

The turn toward increased violent strategies should also be understood in the context of an increasingly harsh interethnic climate in Sri Lanka. Sinhalese politicians and religious leaders pictured the Tamils as a privileged group, which threatened the power, wellbeing and security of the Sinhalese. This provided the rationale for several outbursts of anti-Tamil violence between the 1950s and 1980s. Although the violence against Tamils in 1983 has been described as a spontaneous Sinhalese reaction to the killing of 13 government soldiers by the LTTE, a closer look suggests that the bloodbath was politically sanctioned and well-organized (Tambiah 1996: 96ff). Its brutality and scale shocked both the Tamils and the international community, and increased the support for a Tamil military struggle. India's support of the Tamil militants further encouraged the militarization of politics in Sri Lanka. Strong cultural and historical links and popular pressure, as well as Cold War politics motivated India to provide training and weapons to the LTTE and several other Tamil rebel groups during the 1980s.

As the conflict deepened, the goal of the Tamil struggle shifted – from a focus on individual and minority rights within the Sri Lankan political system, to a struggle for territorially-based self-determination. In the parliamentary elections in 1977, the main Tamil political party, Tamil United Liberation Front (TULF), gained massive support for their demand for a separate state. The conflict increasingly came to be framed as an ethnic conflict between a Sinhalese-dominated government and Tamil separatists. The polarization between these two sides has hidden the importance of the Muslim minority (7 percent of the population), caught in-between conflict lines, as well as the many conflicting interests (along class, caste, geographical and party political lines) within the Sinhalese and Tamil communities respectively.

LTTE and the continued struggle for Tamil Eelam

The LTTE's struggle for Tamil Eelam has been sustained for over a quarter of a century because of: a strong base of popular support, solidified by a common sense of discrimination; a strong nationalist ideology; powerful leadership, and discipline within the LTTE; and a steady supply of resources, provided first by India and later increasingly by the Tamil diaspora.

The popular support for Tamil nationalism, separatism and the LTTE is intimately linked to the centralized and ethnicized nature of the Sri Lankan state, and, maybe more importantly, the extent to which Tamil civilians have been affected by the violence used by the state in its attempts to wipe out the LTTE. Tamil nationalism has provided an ideology in which the governance problems in Sri Lanka are framed as ethnic discrimination, and which is built on the conviction that the Tamils have the right to self-determination within their homeland in north-eastern Sri Lanka. This ideology assumes Tamil unity against a monolithically described enemy – the Sri Lankan state and, by extension, the Sinhalese who dominate and are favored by it.

To this, the LTTE has added its own rituals and traditions which honor the sacrifice of life for the Tamil cause. Those who have died in the struggle are paid tribute to, their portraits are displayed in public places and their family members venerated. Poetry and other cultural expressions picture the struggle as a necessary and honorable surrender of the individual self to protect and liberate the ethnically defined community. The martyr is a metaphoric seed "out of which new life sprouts both literally and spiritually": the death of one person strengthens the motivation of others to continue the struggle (Hellmann-Rajanayagam 2005: 151).

The Tiger leader Prabhakaran is celebrated as the national leader and holds an almost godly status. Strict discipline and loyalty to the leader – traditional Tamil virtues – have been reinvented by the LTTE. LTTE's first constitution declared a death penalty for those who quit and formed rival groups (Swamy 2003: 38). In the early days, the LTTE was only one of many rebel groups in northern Sri Lanka. In 1986, Prabhakaran launched a major offensive against Tamil Eelam Liberation Organization, accusing it of being submissive to Indian interests. By the late 1980s, the LTTE had emerged as the all-dominant Tamil rebel group.

Central to the LTTE's political cosmology is not only the "hero," but also its antonym, the "traitor" (Sumathy 2001). The LTTE defends its lack of tolerance for internal criticism by referring to the need for unity when facing the enemy. A large number of dissidents from within LTTE ranks, from other rebel groups, from Tamil political parties, and from the Muslim community have been branded "traitors" and killed. Such killings are seen by the LTTE and its followers as necessary to maintain the unity and discipline required to fight a much crueler enemy (the Sri Lankan state). Paradoxically, hence, what started as a resistance movement against state oppression has turned into a movement that uses internal oppression to achieve political and military interests.

The resources to build-up and sustain an efficient rebel movement came initially from India. However, Prabhakaran soon set up his own networks to procure weapons in order to decrease his dependency on this patron. When India's support ceased after a few years, the LTTE looked to the rest of the world for support. As in many other armed conflicts, the diaspora became a key player (see Golan and Gal this volume, Chapter 9). The Tamil diaspora, estimated to be between half a million and a million people in North America, Europe and Australia, became the most important financier of the Tamil militant struggle. The LTTE had opened its first office abroad in London in 1978 and then gradually developed its fundraising, propaganda and weapons procurements networks. By the early 2000s the LTTE operated in at least 40 countries (see Gunaratna 2001: 3). The Tigers have been highly efficient in keeping track of the diaspora Tamils and convincing them – sometimes by threats – to contribute money to the struggle (see Human Rights Watch 2006). A number of front organizations and businesses have also raised money. The extent to which the Tamil diaspora can influence the strategies of the LTTE is debated. While Christine Fair argues that the diaspora was instrumental in making the LTTE enter into the peace process in 2002 (Fair 2007), other accounts point to the limitations of diaspora influence over Prabhakaran (see Orjuela 2008a).

Peace attempts

Several attempts have been made to end the war in Sri Lanka through negotiations and political reform. In 1987 the Sri Lankan and Indian governments signed an accord which was to solve the conflict by devolving power to the provinces, including a merged North-East Province covering large parts of what the Tamils saw as their homeland. Tamil militants and political parties were not directly involved in the talks, and the LTTE only hesitantly agreed not to sabotage what they saw as an insufficient accord. "The transformation from gun to politics is not easy," the Tiger leader is reported to have said after a meeting with Indian representatives in 1987 (Swamy 2003: 160). During this time the LTTE symbolically handed over some weapons, but soon took to arms against the Indian Peace Keeping Forces that were to monitor the implementation of the agreement. The Indians, along with armed Tamil militants supportive of the accord, fought back. Paradoxically, opposition to the accord in the south led the Sri Lanka government to oppose the deal and briefly to support the LTTE against the Indian troops (see Rupesinghe 1998; Balasingham 2004).

The peace process that took off in late 2001 was the first that involved direct negotiations between the Sri Lankan government and the LTTE mediated by a third party, Norway. In February 2002, the LTTE and the Sri Lankan government signed a ceasefire agreement, which froze the current boundaries between LTTE- and government-controlled areas, hence implicitly recognizing LTTE's control of substantial parts of north-eastern Sri Lanka. The ceasefire was monitored by a Nordic mission, which was to record and investigate violations, but which lacked enforcement powers. Between September 2002 and March 2003 six rounds of talks were held between representatives of the LTTE and the Sri Lankan government. The talks focused on implementing the ceasefire agreement, reconstructing the war zone, and (briefly) on exploring the possibility of self-determination for Tamil areas within a united Sri Lanka.

A number of factors made this peace attempt possible. Both the Sri Lankan government and the LTTE were war-weary, and an outright victory appeared unachievable. LTTE had made substantial military gains, and hoped that these could be translated into political gains at the negotiation table. At the same time, the international community was pushing for a negotiated solution to the conflict. The war against terrorism after 11

September 2001 had increased the pressure on the LTTE to prove that it was not a terrorist group, but a liberation movement willing to talk peace. For the government, generous promises of foreign aid and the prospect of reviving the weakened economy were important incentives for peace. Equally important was the willingness of the Sri Lankan government and the international community not to challenge the LTTE's claim to be "the sole representative of the Tamil people." Finally, trust and mutual respect had developed between key persons from the respective negotiation teams (see Rupesinghe 2006; Balasingham 2004; Gooneratne 2007).

However, although initially promising the peace process gradually collapsed. The LTTE withdrew from talks in April 2003, accusing the government of not fulfilling its promises of "normalization" in the north-east, excluding the LTTE from an important donor meeting, and canvassing international support against the rebels. Meanwhile, the criticism against the peace process was vociferous in the south, where the political opposition, Sinhala nationalist civil society groups and Buddhist clergy staged protests. The many violations of the ceasefire agreement by the LTTE (including child recruitment and killings of political opponents), and the inability of the Nordic monitors and other international actors to stop them, further strengthened the opposition against the peace process. Public disapproval of the peace process eventually brought the opposition to power in the parliamentary elections of 2004. By 2005 both the Sri Lankan government and the LTTE questioned the other's willingness to respect the ceasefire agreement or make any substantial concessions. After repeated LTTE attacks on military targets in the north-east, the government responded in mid-2006 with a full-scale offensive against the Tigers, and in January 2008 officially abrogated the long defunct ceasefire agreement.

Transforming the Tigers?

A rebel group's internal dynamics, the possibilities for it to act through mainstream politics, and the legitimacy it has among the population and internationally can facilitate or hinder military-to-political transformations (see Lyons this volume, Chapter 7; Söderberg-Kovacs 2007). This section analyzes the LTTE's attempts at forming its own state, its organization and internal dynamics, the LTTE's experiences of engaging with Sri Lanka's political system, and its popular support and international legitimacy.

Building a Tamil state

At the press conference referred to at the beginning of this chapter, the LTTE's chief ideologue introduced Prabhakaran to the world media as "the President and Prime Minister of Tamil Eelam." While Tamil Eelam – a separate Tamil state – has been the ultimate goal of the Tigers' struggle, it has also for years been, at least partially, a reality. According to an estimation published in 2007 (before the Sri Lankan government captured large areas from the Tigers), the LTTE controlled 44 percent of the Northern and Eastern Provinces, inhabited by half a million people (Sarvananthan 2007: 1186). The LTTE-run "state" originated in the mid-1980s, when the LTTE gained control over large parts of northernmost Sri Lanka. The LTTE collected money from traders, imposed taxes on household goods, and ran a television station. After the Indian peacekeepers left in 1990, the LTTE put its own police force and judicial system in place, and made its tax regime more effective. The Tigers also established a visa system to monitor and regulate the flow of people to and from LTTE areas (Swamy 2003: 140ff., 216).

Sri Lankan government departments, for instance those responsible for agriculture, education and health, have been allowed to operate in parallel with the LTTE administration, under the conditions that they follow LTTE instructions. However, the north-east has generally been underserviced, and is estimated to have the highest prevalence of poverty in Sri Lanka (Sarvananthan 2006). The LTTE accepts the government presence because it frees them from having to use their own resources to service the population. For the government, a continued presence in rebel-held areas is an important message that they do not recognize Tamil Eelam. The LTTE has set up shadow institutions, for instance a Department for Education, which has engaged in advocacy against the government neglect of Tamil areas. However, these institutions do not provide services to the general public and play only a symbolic role (giving visiting foreigners an impression of a functioning Tamil state) (Sarvananthan 2007). Non-governmental organizations (NGOs) and the Tamil diaspora have played a crucial role in catering to the needs of civilians in guerrilla controlled areas as well (Stokke 2006).

After 2002, the LTTE administration expanded with a number of new "state" institutions. A Planning and Development Secretariat was established to conduct development planning, needs assessments, and the coordination of assistance from NGOs and the diaspora. The LTTE also created a Northeast Secretariat for Human Rights, which claimed to function as a neutral body where people could report human rights abuses. Moreover, a so-called Peace Secretariat was established, with the purpose of coordinating activities related to the peace process. The Peace Secretariat's Director described it as an embryonic Tamil Eelam Ministry of Foreign Affairs, in charge of diplomatic relations (interview 2006).

The ceasefire agreement allowed unarmed LTTE cadres to enter government-controlled areas to carry out political work. A number of LTTE political offices came up in non-LTTE areas, enabling Tamils in these areas to approach the LTTE for assistance to resolve disputes or to make complaints about government abuses. The LTTE's police and judiciary system reached into government-controlled areas and was used by Tamils who considered it more efficient and trustworthy than that of the Sri Lankan state. According to Muttukrishna Sarvananthan the most important LTTE activities in government-controlled areas during this period were: recruitment of cadres, collection of taxes, commemoration of martyrs and harassment of political opponents (Sarvananthan 2003: 13). The ceasefire made it possible for the LTTE to collect taxes more systematically in government areas. The opening of the main road through LTTE-controlled area increased the incomes of the LTTE through taxation of goods passing through. Taxes were also collected on income, business revenue, and property transactions. The LTTE's tax regime has served not only to raise funds, but also to exercise control over the population. Taxes have been unevenly collected, and some (e.g. traders and NGOs) could get away with lighter taxes, while poor people or those refusing to cooperate with the Tigers would be subject to harsher taxation (Nesiah 2004).

The LTTE did take steps toward developing the non-military parts of its organization. For instance, it built up embryonic political institutions and received some recognition for its effective relief and rehabilitation work after the disastrous 2004 tsunami. But the LTTE's "state" was never fully functioning. The LTTE did not, for instance, use its tax money for services to the population, and freedom of speech and organization remained curtailed (Sarvananthan 2007).

Organization and internal dynamics

During the ceasefire and peace talks, the political wing of the LTTE took on a more prominent role. But its *raison d'être* had always been to assist the LTTE's military efforts: "unlike political parties that develop military wings, the LTTE is predominantly a military organization that has developed a political wing. It is confident and totally reliant of its military capability rather than on its political capabilities" (Gunaratna 2001: 4). The dominance of military priorities over political considerations has been evident in the LTTE's child recruitment and attacks on civilians, which have continued despite massive international condemnation. While the LTTE leader has been described as an all-dominant hard-liner (see Swamy 2003), others within the organization have been more inclined toward a political solution. LTTE's ideologue, Anton Balasingham, with his good rapport with the peace mediators and government negotiators, played an important role convincing Prabhakaran to try the peace path and stay on it. However, the Tiger leadership continued to be most concerned with the security threats posed by the Sri Lankan Forces, which were still heavily present in north-eastern Sri Lanka, and neither the demobilization of the Tiger guerrillas nor the decommissioning of weapons was ever on the agenda during the 2002 peace process. The deaths of Balasingham in 2006 and of Tamilchelvam, the head of LTTE's political wing, in 2007 further weakened the political capacity of the LTTE. That the government forces had purposely targeted and killed Tamilchelvam signaled their unwillingness to seek a negotiated end to the war.

Any permanent solution to the conflict is also complicated by Prabhakaran's legal status. India has requested Sri Lanka to extradite Prabhakaran for his involvement in the killing of Rajiv Gandhi, and in Sri Lanka he has been sentenced to 200 years of imprisonment. Peace attempts may hence threaten Prabhakaran's position. This is also true from the perspective of internal LTTE politics. While in the past, Prabhakaran has managed to eliminate anyone who challenged him, he was in 2004 unable to prevent his senior-most commander in the east, known as Colonel Karuna, from instigating a split in the movement. The non-war situation removed the sense of emergency that kept the LTTE together, and opened up space for dissent. The contacts between the government and the LTTE during peace talks (which Karuna attended) may also have facilitated the defection. The loss of a large number of cadres and the government's subsequent support of Karuna's faction against the LTTE seriously weakened the Tigers. In 2007 Karuna's faction formed a political party and entered the political mainstream. It has retained its arms and functions simultaneously as a government-supported paramilitary group.

LTTE and mainstream politics

> We are not politicians. We are revolutionaries.
>
> (Pirapakaran 2007: 258)

The LTTE had from the start an ambivalent, and increasingly hostile, relation to moderate Tamil political parties. A number of Tamil politicians have been killed by the Tigers. By 1983 the LTTE wanted recognition as the only voice of the Tamils, and asked people not to vote in local elections (Swamy 2003: 76). The Tigers despised the Tamil politicians:

> They [TULF] never had any sincere intentions to liberate our oppressed people.... The flame of revolution is fast spreading all over Tamil Eelam. But the TULF leaders are trying their best to smother the fire. In this sense you can term the TULF leaders as betrayers.
>
> (Prabhakaran, quoted in Swamy 2003: 103)

In the late 1980s, the LTTE set up its own political party to demonstrate the LTTE's intentions to enter the political mainstream. However, the party was soon dissolved (Swamy 2003; Balasingham 2001). During the 2002 peace process, the LTTE made no attempts at forming a political party, but an alliance of established Tamil parties emerged as the LTTE's arm in mainstream politics. The Tamil National Alliance (TNA), as it was called, was openly supported by the LTTE and recognized the LTTE as the sole representative of the Tamil people. The TNA can best be understood as a political voice of the LTTE, but not necessarily as a demonstration of the LTTE's wish to enter the Sri Lankan political system. Since the re-escalation of conflict in 2005, threats and killings of TNA politicians, believed to be carried out or supported by the government, have further limited the space for LTTE supporters to engage in politics. In 2005, interestingly, the LTTE determined the outcome of the presidential elections; not by participating in them, but by calling for an election boycott which enabled the more hard-line candidate to come to power.

The LTTE argues that entering mainstream politics would be both inefficient and serve to legitimize an unjust system (Nadarajah and Vimalarajah 2008). As an alternative, the LTTE has proposed new political structures. A proposal from 2003 suggested an interim administration for the north-east, dominated by the LTTE. This was rejected by the government. Attempts during the peace process to create structures where the government and the LTTE could cooperate around humanitarian issues in the north-east were never implemented, and hence could not serve as test-cases for power-sharing or facilitate confidence building between the LTTE and the government.

During the 2002 peace process, the LTTE and pro-LTTE groups engaged in political work at the grass roots level. A number of popular protests were held in north-eastern Sri Lanka, as it became possible to openly criticize the Sri Lankan government. There were *hartals* (during which shops close down in protest), marches, protests outside of army camps and large manifestations. So-called Pongu Tamil (Tamil uprising) events mobilized people in thousands in north-eastern Sri Lanka, as well as in the diaspora. Pongu Tamil expressed the Tamil demand for self-determination, while displaying LTTE symbols (pictures of Prabhakaran, Tiger flags, Tamil Eelam maps). In some cases participants did not come voluntarily but out of fear of the LTTE (UTHR-J 2002: 29). This LTTE-sanctioned popular mobilization indicated an attempt by the Tigers to use – or encourage people's use of – non-violent protests against the government during times where the violent struggle was put on hold.

The LTTE-supported political engagement was endorsed by some international actors who saw this as a way for the LTTE to transform, and organizations behind the Pongu Tamil received some donor funding. However, the political involvement turned out to have severe consequences for many participants. The demonstrations and other events had been reported and filmed by media and the government forces. As the war restarted, persons who had been even vaguely politically associated with the LTTE were identified and became the targets for abductions and extra judicial killings (*Asiantribune* 2007; Human Rights Watch 2008). It is hence important to note that a failed process of transformation of rebel groups may have grave consequences for the security of participants in political activities.

The LTTE and the people

> We have a love and hate relationship to the LTTE, it is said. We love them when they die for us, and hate them when they take money from us.
>
> (Academic interviewed in northern Sri Lanka 2002)

The level of popular support for a rebel group and, most importantly, its ability to sustain that support, will be decisive for any attempt to demilitarize (Söderberg-Kovacs 2007). Measuring popular support for the Tigers is complicated due the lack of alternative Tamil voices against government repression, as well as the lack of freedom of speech in north-eastern Sri Lanka. Opinion polls carried out during the peace process pointed to strong popular support for the LTTE and its leader (*Peace Confidence Index* 2002; UTHR-J 2003). However, the result of such surveys may tell more about the climate of fear than of the actual support. People's support of the LTTE is often relative and dependent on context. While people may not endorse the LTTE's violent methods and harsh rule, many see them as the only viable protector of the Tamils against state atrocities:

> So many people question LTTE. They might raise their hands with the crowds. But inside their house, they tell about so many problems. But experience tells them to keep quiet. When threatened by Sinhalese people, the LTTE is their strength, their protector. .. when the government is shelling, people support the LTTE.
>
> (Interview with civil society leader, northern Sri Lanka 2002)

Although there are some examples of individuals or groups who have challenged the LTTE, the integration of the LTTE in Tamil society contributes to making dissent unthinkable. Most families in north-eastern Sri Lanka have family members in "the movement," while mandatory military training for civilians in many areas has contributed to blurring the distinction between cadres and civilians (Gunaratna 2001: 14). Moreover, house-to-house campaigns, LTTE-controlled media and education, cultural events and propaganda (e.g. DVDs from the latest battles) have ensured that the Tamil population is well aware of the rationale behind the struggle and the malevolence of the enemy. While peace awareness programs and pro-peace media reporting were common in southern Sri Lanka at the start of the 2002 peace process, LTTE-controlled media continued to cast the government as the enemy, and civil society peace awareness programs were discouraged (Orjuela 2008b).

After the start of the peace process in 2002, people were, according to some accounts, less willing to accept the LTTE's harsh rules and taxation, and the space to challenge LTTE decisions widened somewhat (see UTHR-J 2002: 42). The conversion of the Sri Lankan government from an obvious suppressor and aggressor to a peacemaker promising to develop Tamil areas had a negative effect on the Tamil support for the LTTE. The willingness of the diaspora to contribute money is also believed to have declined during the peace process. The LTTE's official discourse focused on the shortcomings of the government, and attempted to keep people alert, and to foster unity and submissiveness. The defection of the LTTE's eastern commander made visible the cleavage between Tamils in the east (who supplied recruits and funds) and the north. It is likely that an end to warfare would expose the divisions among Tamils, along class, caste and regional lines. In times of emergency, Tamils unite behind the LTTE and accept the leadership of predominantly northern Tamils of Karava (fisher) caste, which is relatively lower class compared to the upper-caste Tamil leadership of the past. Times of peace risk opening up divides and conflicts within the Tamil "nation," and hence weakening the Tamils as a group, as well as the LTTE.

Terrorists or freedom fighters? LTTE's international legitimacy

Along with the military struggle on the ground, the LTTE and the Sri Lankan government wage a war over international legitimacy. At the heart of this struggle is the labeling of the LTTE as "freedom fighters" or "terrorists" (see Nadarajah and Sriskandarajah 2005). The terrorist label has been used by the government, media and LTTE-critical groups to justify a military strategy (including the killing of civilians), particularly since the beginning of the US-led global "war on terror." The LTTE's international legitimacy and support has been relatively low, with the support from the Tamil diaspora as one significant exception. The killing of Rajiv Gandhi (1991) and of Sri Lanka's Foreign Minister (during the ceasefire in 2005) brought massive international criticism, as has the continued recruitment of children. No country has recognized the LTTE's de facto state, and the LTTE has only received direct military support from one government (India, during the 1980s). In 2006 the European Union listed the LTTE as a terrorist organization. LTTE is banned also in the US, Canada and India.

During the peace process, the LTTE's participation in negotiations and signing of the ceasefire agreement increased its international legitimacy. LTTE representatives were invited on trips abroad to study constitutional arrangements for power sharing, and were welcomed to ministries of foreign affairs. In the enthusiasm over the seemingly successful peacemaking effort in Sri Lanka, international players chose to overlook ceasefire violations, including the LTTE's systematic killing of Tamils from rivaling groups. When international players at long last realized that the peace process was about to collapse, the LTTE – with its higher number of ceasefire violations and its provocative attacks against government forces – stood out as the party that was most to blame. The terror listing by the European Union followed a logic that assumed that if the LTTE was sufficiently reprimanded and pressured by the international community, it would return to the negotiation table. But, as one LTTE sympathizer expressed it, "when a tiger is cornered, it attacks" (interview 2006). Accordingly, the EU ban did not increase the LTTE's willingness to reengage in peace talks, but served to weaken it by affecting its ability to raise funds abroad and further distanced it from the peace-process.

Norway was, at least in the beginning of the peace process, seen by the LTTE as an ally. This may explain the success of bringing the LTTE into the peace process, but it was not enough to entice the Tigers to transform themselves from military to political actor. A strengthening of military cooperation between the Sri Lankan and US governments during the peace process also had a negative effect on the peace process by threatening the military balance between the LTTE and the government which had been a prerequisite for constructive engagement. LTTE saw the lack of international support to its development of political structures as an obstacle for transformation, while from the point of view of donors, the LTTE's lack of transformation prevented their support (Nadarajah and Vimalarajah 2008).

Conclusion

"You can take the tiger out of the jungle, but you can't take the jungle out of the tiger" Calvin says in the comic Calvin and Hobbes (Watterson 2004: 98). In the case of the Liberation Tigers in Sri Lanka and the peace process of 2002, the Tigers never properly left the jungle, and never really had a chance to prove their ability to transform. The discussions in Sri Lanka regarding the possibilities to transform the LTTE from a military to a political organization have polarized around two main arguments. One viewpoint, lodged by a broad range of LTTE-critics and analysts, is that the LTTE has developed its own self-sustaining dynamics, and that the resolution of the ethnic conflict has become secondary for the leadership (see Gunaratna 2001). This argument gains support from the LTTE's unwillingness to discuss a political solution and the rebels' lack of consideration for the wellbeing of the Tamil civilians who suffer the government's retaliation for Tiger violence. The lack of incentives for the LTTE leadership to lay down arms, when it risks prosecution, is also pointed to.

On the other hand, analysts more sympathetic to the LTTE argue that the problem lies with the reluctance of the centralized, majoritarian Sri Lankan state to transform. The government's long-standing lack of investment for development in the north-east, repeated failures to respond to humanitarian needs of Tamils affected by war and natural disaster, and indiscriminate targeting of civilians in the war against the LTTE provide evidence that the Sri Lankan government is unwilling to take Tamil demands seriously. Staying in or gaining power is a primary driving force for Sri Lankan politicians. The conflict between the two main (Sinhalese-led) political parties dominates Sri Lankan politics, and makes sincere attempts at addressing minority concerns a secondary issue. The strong influence of Sinhalese nationalist groups – political parties, civil society organizations and Buddhist clergy – further cripples the political will to find non-military solutions. It is not only the political leaders that are behind the reform resistance of the state, but also the bureaucracy, which lacks incentives to give up the benefits of a centralized structure. LTTE sympathizers further argue that if the threat by the Sri Lankan Forces against the LTTE is removed, the Tigers would be able and willing to both demilitarize and democratize (see Stokke 2006: 1035).

Both of these arguments appear to have merit, and together they point to a vicious circle: the LTTE will not transform until the Sri Lankan state transforms, and the Sri Lankan state will not transform until the LTTE transforms. The peace process initiated in 2002 can be seen as a relatively modest attempt to reverse this vicious circle and provide space for transformation.

In hindsight, it is easy to dismiss the peace process as mere window dressing. Nevertheless, it is worth noting that during the ceasefire the LTTE expanded its state-like structures and increased its ambitions to be a civilian actor. The continued military threats and lack of a solution to the conflict make it difficult to judge whether these were real steps toward a transformation, or merely a military-driven strategy. Meanwhile, the Sri Lankan government did little to show that it was serious about power-sharing; its centralized nature and reluctance to share power with the LTTE was evident, for instance, in its approach to post-war and post-tsunami reconstruction.

When analyzing the prospect for military-to-politics transformation in the case of the LTTE, the question "transformation to what?" is crucial. While the LTTE sees a transformation in terms of state building (which would not necessarily entail giving up arms), the government and the international community has expected transformation to include demobilization, decommissioning of weapons, and participation in a reformed Sri Lankan political system. That the LTTE has had autonomy rather than incorporation as its driving goal sets a higher threshold for peaceful transformation. What type of transformation is possible will depend on the parties' international legitimacy. While the entrance into the peace process increased LTTE's international standing, the continued international disapproval of the Tigers, visible in the terror listing, continued economic and military support to the Sri Lankan government and the reluctance to support LTTE structures, alienated the Tigers from the international community. It is also important to note the asymmetric power relations between the LTTE and the government. The Sri Lankan government, being an internationally recognized state which can legitimately arm itself against insurgency, has a stronger interest in avoiding conflict resolution and maintaining status quo. The LTTE, as the weaker and internationally illegitimate party, has advocated for international involvement in the conflict (e.g. Norwegian mediation), but been reluctant to accept solutions which do not guarantee substantial self-determination and continued LTTE-dominance over the Tamils.

When it comes to LTTE's legitimacy among the population, it is important to note that peace engagement weakened the LTTE by temporarily removing the threats to the Tamil people posed by the Sri Lankan government. This most likely diminished the ability of the Tigers to control the Tamil population, and allowed intra-Tamil conflicts to surface. The attempt at ending the war in Sri Lanka also teaches us important lessons about the consequences of failed transformations. The acceptance of the LTTE as the "sole representative of the Tamil people" was a prerequisite for getting the LTTE to engage in the peace process. At the same time, this acceptance institutionalized the marginalization of other Tamil voices, and turned a blind eye to the fate of Tamil political parties and paramilitaries which were attacked by the LTTE. Moreover, the political work carried out by the LTTE and their supporters – endorsed by some international actors as a step toward transformation – had grave consequences for those involved when the war restarted and persons even vaguely associated with the LTTE became targets.

References

Asiantribune (2007) "Mano Ganeshan, Member of Parliament, says abductions are both political and economic." Online, available at: www.asiantribune.com 4 July.

Balasingham, A. (2001) *A Will to Freedom: An Inside View of Tamil Resistance*, Mitcham: Fairmax Publishing.

—— (2004) *War and Peace: Armed Struggle and Peace Efforts of Liberation Tigers*, Mitcham: Fairmax Publishing.

Fair, C. (2007) "The Sri Lankan Tamil Diaspora: Sustaining Conflict and Pushing for Peace," in H. Smith and P. Stares (eds.) *Diasporas in Conflict: Peace-Makers or Peace-Wreckers?*, Tokyo, New York and Paris: United Nations University Press.

Gooneratne, J. (2007) *Negotiating with the Tigers (LTTE): A View from the Second Row*, Sri Lanka: Stamford Lake.

Gunaratna, R. (2001) *International Dimension of the Sri Lankan Conflict. Threat and Response*, Marga Monography Series on Ethnic Reconciliation, Colombo: Marga Institute.

Hellmann-Rajanayagam, D. (2005) "And Heroes Die: Poetry of the Tamil Liberation Movement in Northern Sri Lanka," *South Asia: Journal of South Asian Studies*, 28 (1): 112–153.

Human Rights Watch (2006) *Funding the "Final War" LTTE Intimidation and Extortion in the Tamil Diaspora*, 18 (1).

—— (2008) *Recurring Nightmare: State Responsibility for "Disappearances" and Abductions in Sri Lanka*, 20 (2).

Nadarajah, S. and Sriskandarajah, D. (2005) "Liberation Struggle or Terrorism? The Politics of Naming the LTTE," *Third World Quarterly*, 26 (1), 87–100.

Nadarajah, S. and Vimalarajah, L. (2008) *The Politics of Transformation: The LTTE and the 2002–2006 Peace Process in Sri Lanka*, Berghof Transitions Series no. 4, Berlin: Berghof Research Center for Constructive Conflict Management.

Nesiah, V. (2004) "Taxation Without Representation, or Talking to the Taxman about Poetry," *Lines* 2 (4). Online, available at: www.lines-magazine.org/Art_Feb04/Editorial_Vasuki.htm.

Orjuela, C. (2008a) "Distant Warriors, Distant Peace Workers? Multiple Diaspora Roles in Sri Lanka's Violent Conflict," *Global Networks: A Journal of Transnational Affairs*, 8 (4) (forthcoming).

—— (2008b) *The Identity Politics of Peacebuilding: Civil Society in War-torn Sri Lanka*, New Delhi: Sage (forthcoming).

Peace Confidence Index (2002) "Top-Line Results, September 2002, Social Indicator," Colombo: Centre for Policy Alternatives. Online, available at: www.cpalanka.org.

Pirapakaran, V. (2007) *Tamil Source in English Translation: Reflections of the Leader. Quotes by Veluppillai Pirapakaran*, trans. by Peter Schalk and Alvappillai Veluppillai, Sweden: Uppsala University.

Rupesinghe, K. (ed.) (1998) *Negotiating Peace in Sri Lanka: Efforts, Failures and Lessons*, vol. 1, London: International Alert.

—— (2006) *Negotiating Peace in Sri Lanka: Efforts, Failures and Lessons*, vol. 2, Colombo: Foundation for Co-Existence.

Sarvananthan, M. (2003) *What Impedes Economic Revival in the North & East Province in Sri Lanka?*, working paper no. 2, Point Pedro, Sri Lanka: Point Pedro Institute of Development.

—— (2006) *Poverty in the Conflict Affected Region of Sri Lanka: An Assessment*, working paper no. 5, Point Pedro, Sri Lanka: Point Pedro Institute of Development.

—— (2007) "In Pursuit of a Mythical State of Tamil Eelam: A Rejoinder to Kristian Stokke," *Third World Quarterly*, 28 (6): 1185–1195.

Söderberg-Kovacs, M. (2007) *From Rebellion to Politics: The Transformation of Rebel Groups to Political Parties in Civil War Peace Processes*, report no. 77, Sweden: Department of Peace and Conflict Research, Uppsala University.

Stokke, K. (2006) "Building the Tamil Eelam State: Emerging State Institutions and Forms of Governance in LTTE-controlled Areas in Sri Lanka," *Third World Quarterly*, 27 (6): 1021–1040.

Sumathy, S. (2001) *Militants, Militarism and the Crisis of (Tamil) Nationalism*, Colombo: Marga Institute.

Swamy, M. R. N. (1996) *Tigers of Lanka: From Boys to Guerrillas*, 2nd edn., Colombo: Vijitha Yapa bookshop.

—— (2003) *Inside an Elusive Mind: Prabhakaran. The First Profile of the World's Most Ruthless Guerrilla Leader*, Colombo: Vijitha Yapa Publications.

Tambiah, S. (1996) *Levelling Crowds: Ethnonationalist Conflicts and Collective Violence in South Asia*, New Delhi: Vistaar Publications.

UTHR-J (2002) *The Plight of Child Conscripts, Social Degradation and Anti-Muslim Frenzy*, special report no. 14, Colombo: UTHR-J.

—— (2003) *Rituals of Words without Substance*, Information Bulletin no. 33, Colombo: UTHR -J. Online, available at: www.uthr.org/bulletins/PDF/Bul33.pdf.

Watterson, B. (2004) *The Indispensable Calvin and Hobbes*, New Jersey: Andrews McMeel Publishing.

Index

Printed in the USA/Agawam, MA
January 2, 2014

583733.224